From Adolescent to Adult

From Adolescent to Adult

By PERCIVAL M. SYMONDS

With Arthur R. Jensen

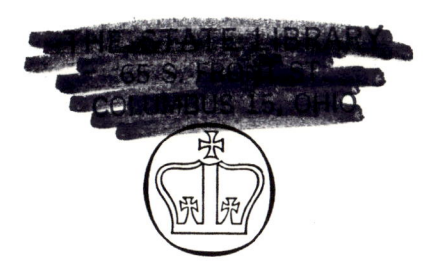

Columbia University Press · New York · *1961*

Copyright © 1961 Columbia University Press, New York
Published in Great Britain, India, and Pakistan
by the Oxford University Press
London, Bombay, and Karachi
Library of Congress Catalog Card Number: 61-5468
Manufactured in the United States of America

Preface

In the winter of 1940–41 the writer, ably assisted by Dr. Sylvia Silverman and Dr. Milton Wexler, was privileged to study forty adolescent boys and girls by means of a variant of the thematic apperception method, using a special set of pictures designed to tap adolescent fantasy.[1] This early study, published under the title *Adolescent Fantasy* (New York, Columbia University Press, 1949), threw light on the nature of adolescence from data based on fantasy that had not previously been used in studying adolescents. It also provided information concerning the thematic apperception method, and helped orient clinical psychologists toward more correct ways of thinking about this important clinical test. Even at the time of the study there was speculation as to the predictive value of the Picture-Story Test. How would an adolescent who told wild stories of adventure, mystery, excitement, and crime turn out in later life? What would be the career of a boy or girl who told stories with themes of ambition, striving, conflict, or dependency? Would differences be noted in later life between boys and girls who told short, repressed stories or long, expansive stories, stories with distinct plots as contrasted with stories that were merely descriptive, stories that were highly realistic as contrasted with stories that were bizarre and fantastic?

Eventually, with the passage of time, the value of a follow-up study of these cases became apparent, since a later study would throw light on the real significance of fantasy in the determination of human affairs. Is fantasy merely a whim or caprice unrelated to the events of life, or

---

[1] A selection of twenty of these pictures, known as the Symonds Picture-Story Test, is published by the Bureau of Publications, Teachers College, Columbia University.

is fantasy something that eventually finds expression in the actual conduct of life? If the former, then fantasy can be dismissed as one of the interesting by-plays of the mind without any practical significance. If the latter, then it would be important to know how fantasy is related to behavior and personality. If a fantasy is related to the actual affairs of life, then it would have predictive significance and from fantasy one might be able to predict the development of personality during the later course of events in a person's life.

It would be of value to know whether the later personality can be predicted more surely on the basis of a continuation of overt trends which are expressed in living or on the basis of fantasy which contains impulses and wishes of the individual which may develop into more overt behavior in later years.

Suggestions for such a follow-up study came with increasing urgency from the Council for Research in the Social Sciences of Columbia University, and with gentle prodding from the Council, plans for such a follow-up study were drawn up in 1951.

This follow-up study has been supported by three grants from the Council. The first grant made it possible in 1953–54 to locate twenty-eight subjects of the study and to carry out the program of testing and interviewing which furnished data that enabled us to make comparisons with studies of the same subjects made thirteen years earlier, in 1940–41. I was fortunate in securing the services of Dr. Arthur R. Jensen as assistant in this project, and it was his zeal, thoroughness, and competence that led to the location of the twenty-eight subjects and the securing of the excellent records on them.

A second grant by the Council made it possible in 1954–55 to have Dr. Jensen's services for the major processing of the data. He arranged to have all the stories from the Symonds Picture-Story Test typed and he made competent abstracts of the recorded interviews. Dr. Jensen analyzed the fantasy material and compared it with corresponding material collected in 1940–41. He also made theme counts from the fantasy material and rated the subjects on forty graphic rating scales from his impressions gained during the testing and interview sessions.

For the analysis and interpretation of the Rorschachs collected as part of the data in the follow-up study I was fortunate in securing the services of Mrs. Stephanie Dudek, a highly competent Rorschach analyst who had studied under Dr. Zygmunt Piotrowski.

Preface

One small additional grant by the Council made possible certain statistical computations which were carried out by the Service Bureau Corporation, a subsidiary of the International Business Machines Corporation.

Matchings of sets of stories gathered in 1953 with those gathered in 1940 were made by Dr. Robert Drummond, Mrs. Kit Lee Wong, and Mrs. Stephanie Dudek.

Even with all this assistance much remained to be done in the detailed analysis of the material which was necessary in order to make the comparisons which constitute this report.

Many readers will question the wisdom of such an elaborate analysis of data on only twenty-eight subjects. There is a belief in some psychological quarters that reliable conclusions can be reached only when based on samples many times the size of that in this study. Some of the conclusions with respect to the shifts in thematic content of the stories have been tested with approved statistical tests of the reliability of differences in small samples, and the differences reported have successfully met these criteria. It must be admitted that many of the other conclusions have not been put to rigorous statistical tests, and they must be looked at as only tentative conclusions or fruitful hypotheses.

The data from the interviews, stories, and the Rorschachs were not quite detailed enough to permit ratings to be made of the degree to which subjects displayed characteristics by which these data were analyzed. The writer used a method that consisted of inspecting anecdotal material of individuals at each end of a distribution in order to determine roughly whether differences existed. It must be admitted that this method lacks statistical refinement, but it has the merit of pointing to possible relationships.

Also, the question will certainly be raised as to how much one can generalize concerning growing out of adolescence into adulthood from twenty-eight subjects who came from one locality and were seen in the course of one year. One chapter, devoted to a description of the sociological background of these subjects, provides data which will permit the reader to decide how representative they are of people in general, if such a concept has any meaning. In general, they fall into the range of lower middle-class society, and from the statistical comparisons they do not differ from people in this category in any important respect.

It is believed that the results of this follow-up study justify the efforts that have been expended on it. It has demonstrated the remarkable persistence of personality over a thirteen-year interval and, in particular, the fact that it is possible to estimate personality adjustment in later years from facts gathered about a person when he is adolescent. It has shown that fantasy, instead of being a frothy epiphenomenon, is really a highly important part of personality, and the study has given justification to the conviction that overt personality and behavior is in large measure a precipitate of and a working out and resolution of fantasy.

PERCIVAL M. SYMONDS

Morningside Heights
New York

The untimely death, on August 6, 1960, of Percival M. Symonds deprived him of the opportunity of reading more than a few galley proofs of *From Adolescent to Adult*. In his absence it became the responsibility of his wife, who was not fully competent to complete the task but who had assisted him in many similar undertakings, to work in collaboration with members of the staff of Columbia University Press in carrying out the editorial work. The sympathetic interest and skilled efforts of the Press staff, especially of Mrs. Elizabeth M. Evanson, have resulted in a rare service which the author undoubtedly would have acknowledged with gratitude. One may be sure that he would also have been charitable, as most readers probably will be, toward any instances—if such exist—in which his purpose may not have been fully realized in the present publication.

JOHNNIE P. SYMONDS

October, 1960

Contents

1. Introduction — 1
2. The Community and the Population — 14
3. Comparison of Adolescent with Adult Fantasy — 27
4. Correspondence between Adolescent Fantasy and Subsequent Experience and Personality — 50
5. Change in Fantasy Related to Experience — 74
6. Relationship between Adolescent and Adult Personality — 95
7. Analysis of the Rorschach — 119
8. Summary of Comparisons between the Rorschach Reports, Interview Material, and Fantasies — 170
9. Prediction of Mental Health — 176
10. The Significance of Fantasy — 188
11. Growing out of Adolescence into Adulthood — 194
12. Summary and Conclusions — 208

Appendix
A. Resumé of the Subjects of the Study — 213
    WALLACE, SUBJECT 1 — 214
    RALPH, SUBJECT 2 — 215
    ROY, SUBJECT 6 — 220
    JEROME, SUBJECT 7 — 221
    ROGER, SUBJECT 8 — 222
    SAM, SUBJECT 9 — 226
    KARL, SUBJECT 11 — 227

CATHERINE, SUBJECT *12*	*233*
LAURA, SUBJECT *13*	*240*
VIOLA, SUBJECT *14*	*244*
EDITH, SUBJECT *17*	*252*
ISABEL, SUBJECT *18*	*257*
STELLA, SUBJECT *19*	*258*
BARBARA, SUBJECT *20*	*264*
NATALIE, SUBJECT *21*	*271*
MABEL, SUBJECT *22*	*276*
MARGARET, SUBJECT *24*	*280*
JULIA, SUBJECT *25*	*281*
OLIVE, SUBJECT *27*	*282*
CELIA, SUBJECT *28*	*287*
PANSY, SUBJECT *29*	*293*
DOROTHY, SUBJECT *30*	*299*
NANCY, SUBJECT *31*	*305*
EDWIN, SUBJECT *33*	*310*
SEYMOUR, SUBJECT *36*	*311*
JIMMY, SUBJECT *37*	*317*
JOHN, SUBJECT *39*	*328*
ALBERT, SUBJECT *40*	*335*
B. *The Case of Jack*	*342*
Index	*403*

Tables

1. Distribution of Subjects by Age — 16
2. Distribution of Subjects by I.Q. — 16
3. Distribution of Subjects by Residential Areas in 1940, Corresponding Roughly to Socio-Economic Levels — 17
4. Education of Subjects — 18
5. Number of Jobs Held by Subjects — 20
6. Residence of Subjects in the 1953 Study — 21
7. Age of Subjects at Marriage — 22
8. Number of Subjects' Children per Family — 23
9. Age of Subjects' Children — 23
10. Strength of Religious Interest on the Part of Subjects — 24
11. Number of Subjects and Total Number of Stories Presenting Themes in 1940 and 1953 — 28
12. Difference in Number of Occurrences of Theme of Depression, 1940 and 1953 — 30
13. Mean of the Distribution of Differences between the Occurrence of Themes in 1940 and 1953, the t Value of these Means, and the Probability of Chance Occurrence of Differences — 31
14. Totals of Differences in Occurrence of Themes from 1940 to 1953, by Subjects — 43
15. Average Frequency of Rorschach Signs in the Present Study and in Five Other Studies Presenting Normative Data — 122
16. Intercorrelations of Rankings on Adjustment — 177
17. Special Sets of Intercorrelations of Rankings on Adjustment, Taken from Table 16 — 183

From Adolescent to Adult

1. Introduction

This follow-up study of the forty subjects seen as adolescents in 1940–41 had as its primary purpose the determination of the predictive value of the tests, autobiographies, interviews, and other data collected on these subjects. In discussing plans for the follow-up study, the question was frequently raised as to whether predictions would first be made of certain outcomes to be expected from the adolescent data and then such predictions checked against the facts gathered in 1953–54, thirteen years later. Frankly, I did not know enough to make such predictions.

In one small discussion group in which the writer presented the case of Jimmy,[1] he expressed the point of view that Jimmy would turn out to be a well-adjusted, normal, successful man. This prophecy was based on the fact that Jimmy at the time was making a good adjustment at school and at home. He was well liked by teachers and fellow classmates and had leadership qualities. His home life was all that could be desired. To be sure, he was shy with girls, but it was believed that this was normal and should not be taken too seriously. Dr. Erich Fromm, however, on the basis of the fantasy material, predicted that this boy was headed for trouble, that he had an unstable element in his personality and he would have difficulty in making a satisfactory heterosexual adjustment. His stories showed strong Oedipal themes—contempt and hatred toward father figures and strong love (mingled with contempt) toward mother figures. Guilt and death were outcomes of incestuous wishes in his stories. Which of these predictions was right?

Or take the case of Jack, also reported in *Adolescent Fantasy*.[2] He

[1] See P. M. Symonds, *Adolescent Fantasy* (New York, Columbia University Press, 1949), pp. 272–319.
[2] *Ibid.*, pp. 227–71.

was a boy with poor home background. His father was dead, and his mother was unable to keep the family of five children together. An older brother was apparently shiftless and unstable and an older sister had been in a reformatory on a morals charge. Jack himself was living in a foster home as a state ward. Jack was a disciplinary problem in school and had been suspended on several occasions. Yet his stories contained themes of ambition and striving and the recognition that comes from success. Jack's stories indicated that he was struggling in a conflict between his ideals and his aggressive needs. In real life he had potentialities for becoming a good citizen or a ne'er-do-well. Which way would he go? As this case was discussed in the writer's classes there were increasingly insistent demands to know the facts about Jack's later career.

A more modest aim than direct prediction has guided this study in comparing the 1940 fantasy material and the personality descriptions with the corresponding data gathered in 1953. Hindsight in human affairs is always easier than foresight. It was hoped that if correspondences were found over the thirteen-year interval these would serve others in the future for purposes of prediction.

An equally important aim in the study was to gather information concerning the process of emerging from adolescence into adulthood. This phase of human development has been neglected. Much attention has been devoted to infancy, childhood, and the transition from childhood into puberty and adolescence. This study provided an opportunity for looking at some of the steps by which adolescents emerge from immaturity and dependency to assume their roles as responsible adults, a change that involves separation from their parental home and in many instances establishing families of their own, the completion of their formal education and their induction into the world of work. In this particular era most of the subjects also experienced military service.

Before discussing the plans for this follow-up study, a brief review of the original study is in order. It has already been stated that the intention was to study adolescence by means of a specially prepared set of pictures to be used as a thematic apperception test. Through the cooperation of the public schools in a metropolitan community neighboring New York, arrangements were made to study boys and girls in the junior and senior high schools. Eventually forty cases were included in the study, twenty boys and twenty girls—twenty-three being

Introduction 3

in the junior high school, eight in the high school for girls, and nine in the high school for boys. It was our intention to study normal boys and girls, pupils who would volunteer to take part in the study but who otherwise would not be selected as being bright or dull or presenting particular problems. These forty adolescents ranged in age from 12 to 18, twenty-seven being 14, 15, or 16 years old. Stories from the forty-two pictures which comprised the set prepared for use in the study by Lynd Ward were secured from all of the subjects. In addition, as many data as could be obtained about each case were secured by a variety of methods including (1) a general interview with the pupil, (2) an interview with a parent, (3) interviews with all of the pupils' teachers, (4) an autobiography, (5) the Sheviakov-Friedberg Questionnaire on Interests and Attitudes, (6) pupil rating by teachers, (7) data provided by the school records, and (8) ranking on degree of adjustment, made by the investigators.

A detailed analysis of the themes contained in the stories resulted in an inventory of themes, which was one of the principal outcomes of the study, making it possible to draw up one of the first sets of norms of thematic material using the thematic apperception method. In this initial study one of the main objectives was to determine the relation between fantasy and character. It was found that the relationship is by no means obvious; indeed, the correlations between fantasy based on the results of the theme count and ratings of adjustment are in the neighborhood of .00. The following quotation from the original report indicates the conclusions which were reached regarding the relation between fantasy and character:

> This summary shows certain obvious correspondences and also opposites. In general, the correspondences are best with the best-adjusted individuals. Normal, happy individuals told realistic stories free from exaggeration or distortion. They were also freer in relating stories which recognized the erotic interests of life and personal relationships. But less well-adjusted individuals told stories which failed to correspond to their characters. In many instances the dynamics at work were clearly discernible.
>
> In many cases the stories revealed unacceptable trends, wishes, desires, or goals; the individual's character was an armor, a protection against admitting the reality of these trends. Individuals who told hostile stories were docile and sissy; those whose stories were depressed were actually cheerful and gay. One whose stories bordered on the vulgar was sweet and demure. Those whose stories were passive and masochistic were ambitious and strove to excel, while those whose stories showed high ambition were constantly

backsliding. Those whose stories were anxious were cheerful and popular. In a large number of cases it was clear that the trends which children attributed to characters in their stories had been repressed in themselves, and their characters which show opposite trends could be thought of as a kind of defensive armament against these trends. To discover the correspondence or discrepancy between stories and life character should tell something important about the structure of personality of the individual and should indicate the top level of resistance in the defensive armor to be attacked and dispelled in character analysis.[3]

Although the thematic apperception method could not be used with any assurance to describe the overt character, personality, or behavior of a person, there was evidence that it did reveal underlying latent personality trends indicated by wishes, hopes, and fears. It would point unfailingly to erotic and aggressive impulses, to the active or passive, the giving or receiving orientation to these trends, to anxieties, guilts, and needs for punishment that they aroused and the defenses raised against them. Even though the thematic apperception method cannot be used to describe overt personality and behavior, it does have value because it throws light on the dynamic forces underlying behavior and personality.

Plans for the Follow-up Study

A preliminary survey indicated that between twenty and twenty-five of the individual cases still lived in or in the neighborhood of the city in which the original study was conducted. This seemed promising enough to warrant undertaking a follow-up study.

The first step in the study was to locate the subjects. After an interval of thirteen years one might expect that many of the subjects would have moved away so that they could not be reached or would not be located at all. Actually, of the original forty, thirty-four were located and contact was made with them.

The following letter was sent to all those who were located and for whom we had found an address:

While you were a student in ——— High School, back in 1941, you participated in a study which we were conducting here at Teachers College at that time. Perhaps you still remember that you made up some imaginative stories to a set of pictures as part of the study. It may have all seemed very

[3] *Ibid.*, pp. 110, 111.

Introduction

strange to you, but we were trying to find out whether there was any value in that "picture-story" method of understanding people better. This method has proved to be so important and significant that those who sponsored the study wish to evaluate it further.

We are now planning to get in touch with the same persons who participated in the original study in order to find out whether the results obtained at the time could have been useful in predicting their subsequent careers. In order to do this we are asking those same students to help us in what we are calling a "follow-up" study.

We would like very much to have your cooperation again. We should like to see you and learn directly from you about your subsequent school, work or other experiences. Without your help we cannot make the follow-up, but with your cooperation we feel sure the results will be fully as valuable as the original study.

It would be greatly appreciated if you would fill out and return the enclosed form to bring us up to date. Then either I, or Mr. Arthur R. Jensen, assistant in the study, will get in touch with you. Please fill out the enclosed form, printing clearly your name, your present address and your telephone number, and put it in the mail today.

Of these, twenty-eight participated in the study (twenty-seven took both of the tests and fulfilled the interview schedule; one was unwilling to continue after the first contact so that for this person all that is available is ten stories and an interview). Two individuals were unwilling to participate in the study, and two lived too far away (Florida and Oklahoma) to make the necessary arrangements for giving the tests and conducting the interviews. A year later an additional subject was located, but he was unable to arrange to take the tests and participate in the interviewing. Still later, Jack (subject 4) was located and the complete set of tests and interviews was obtained from him, but too late to be included in the main sample of the study. Altogether the population of the present follow-up study is twenty-eight; this is 70 percent of the original forty, which is a satisfactory sample.

After the subjects had agreed to participate in the follow-up study, contact was made with them, usually by telephone, an explanation was made of what we would expect of them in general terms, and an appointment was made for the first meeting.

It was planned to attempt to see each subject twice, and this was accomplished with all but one of the subjects with whom contact was made. One subject who elaborated his experiences at considerable length was seen five times. First in importance was the repetition of the

Picture-Story Test. This time, instead of using all forty-two of the pictures included in the original study, it was believed that it would be sufficient to use the twenty pictures now included in the Symonds Picture-Story Test.[4] Since each subject was to be seen twice, it was planned to secure stories from series A on the first sitting and series B in the second sitting. This time the stories were mechanically recorded on a Gray Audograph and the stories were later transcribed to typescript from these discs. This, of course, gave a more faithful reproduction of the stories than when they were recorded in handwriting in 1940. Those taking down the stories in the 1940 study did their best to produce a verbatim report of the stories, but frequently, when the storyteller was fluent, about the best that could be done was to record the ideas expressed so as to preserve the sequence of the story without necessarily getting every word. The typescript from the mechanically recorded stories came closer to being a complete reproduction, and consequently comparisons of the stories in terms of their word length would not be meaningful.

It was planned also to secure Rorschachs on the subjects, as the Rorschach would fill out the personality picture of the individual. In retrospect one could have wished that Rorschachs were included in the original study, as the comparisons with the current materials would have been so much the more valuable, but of course such regrets at this stage are quite futile.

Finally, interviews were held with each subject. This had the twofold purpose of securing a record of the experiences over the inter-

[4] Published by the Bureau of Publications, Teachers College, Columbia University, 1948. For those who have access to the pictures which are included in the original report, the old and new numbers of the pictures are given below.

Symonds Picture-Story Test, Series A	Corresponding Number of Picture Used in Original Study	Symonds Picture-Story Test, Series B	Corresponding Number of Picture Used in Original Study
A1	18	B1	23
A2	25	B2	29
A3	3	B3	19
A4	20	B4	41
A5	28	B5	38
A6	26	B6	22
A7	17	B7	39
A8	33	B8	31
A9	32	B9	9
A10	8	B10	42

Introduction

vening thirteen years and also serving as the basis for a direct personality study.

When the subject was willing, the sessions were held in rooms in a YMCA. Nineteen subjects were seen in this way. Seven chose to be seen at their homes. Two subjects were seen both at the YMCA and at their homes. Naturally, conditions at the YMCA were much more satisfactory as they offered greater privacy and freedom from interruption.

Throughout a session, the subject and interviewer were seated facing each other across a conference table. Beside the examiner, on a low table (actually a piano bench) out of sight of the subject, was the recording equipment. It was explained to the subject that a recording of the projective tests and the interview was desirable, and in all cases the subject's express permission for recording the session was obtained. This procedure obviated note-taking and the interviewer was able to give the subject undivided attention. None of the subjects objected to the recording. A small, lightweight microphone was clipped to the subject's clothing, usually on the lapel or breast pocket. A few subjects were at first self-conscious about being recorded but soon seemed at ease and apparently the fact that what they said was recorded had little influence on their production. The table top between the subject and interviewer was kept clear of everything except an ashtray. Many of the subjects smoked during the session. Test materials, etc., were kept on a chair beside the interviewer.

A typical session at the Y began with the interviewer, Dr. Jensen, meeting the subject in the lobby. After introducing himself, Dr. Jensen took the subject to the conference room. Dr. Jensen spent the first few minutes reviewing the earlier study and asked if the subjects could recall Dr. Symonds, Dr. Wexler, or Dr. Silverman, the interviewers in the first study. After the subject had warmed up to the situation, the recording apparatus was explained, the subject's consent obtained, and the microphone was attached to the subject's clothing.

The Picture-Story Test was introduced and the standard instructions given to the subject for making up stories. Only the ten pictures of series A were presented in the first session. Subjects were asked if they could recall any of the pictures after fourteen years. Only one subject (Albert, subject 40) was able to describe one of the pictures, a picture which Symonds did not include in the Picture-Story Test used in the follow-up study, of a nude boy and girl standing face to face, with a stern mother-figure in the background. None of the other subjects reported having any clear recollection of the pictures or of the stories they had told to them thirteen years earlier.

The PST was followed by the Rorschach, administered in the standard manner. Whatever time remained after this was devoted to the personal-history interview. Rarely did the session last more than two hours. The second session with the subject, conducted in the same setting in all but two cases, consisted of series B of the PST and the completion of the personal interview.

In the case of some of the first subjects seen, the Rorschach was put off until the second session and a major part of the interviewing was done in the first session. But it was felt that in some cases so much material of a confessional nature had been revealed during this first session that it aroused certain resistances in the second session. So after the first few subjects the interview during the first session was kept on a factual level with the result that there was much greater freedom and less resistance in the second interviewing session.

It is difficult to know to what extent the subject's knowledge that his every word was being recorded might have had an inhibiting effect. There were very few overt signs of any such inhibition. Dr. Jensen has similarly tested and interviewed many subjects in his clinical work without the benefit of electrical recording, and has noticed no consistent differences in their behavior and that of the subjects in the present study as far as the presence or absence of a recording machine was concerned. One subject (Karl, 11) preferred that one part of the interview not be recorded. The machine was turned off and Dr. Jensen took notes. Another subject (Dorothy, 30) did not mention her marital difficulties until the machine was turned off and the formal part of the interview was terminated for that session. In the second session, however, she consented to being recorded and was able to discuss her marriage problems at great length.

Several subjects, at the conclusion of their session, offered to drive Dr. Jensen to the train station. Dr. Jensen also received, but declined, invitations to dinner and to a party.

Dr. Jensen visited nine of the subjects in their homes, usually because they lived too far away to be asked to come to the YMCA. Reaching some subjects might take more than half a day's train journey. In general, the home visits were more difficult and less satisfactory than the sessions at the YMCA. A mother, for instance, might be interrupted by young children, by having to answer the telephone, or by tradesmen calling at the door.

In general, the home sessions took more time, for subjects generally were inclined to be hospitable. If they had a new house, they wanted to show Dr. Jensen around. Some of them mixed Dr. Jensen a highball. On some occasions Dr. Jensen was introduced to other members of the family, who later retired to another part of the house. However, once these preliminaries were over and the recording apparatus set up, there was little difference in the behavior of the subjects at home from that of the subjects seen at the YMCA. But the conditions were such that the subject was sensitive to the fact that members of his household were in the vicinity and while there is no evidence as to this, it stands to reason that a subject seen at home must have been somewhat constrained in both his tests and his interviews.

Probably the most inhibiting or restricting influence on the interview was the presence of a third adult. Certain areas in the personal interview were not fully explored under these circumstances. For example, the subject would not be inclined to bring up the topic of relations with members of the opposite sex or to mention marital troubles or other highly personal matters. But in only one case (Roger, 8) was another adult (subject's wife) present in the same room during part of both sessions. The husband of another subject (Nancy, 31) was in the kitchen while the interview was conducted in the living room. From time to time during the Rorschach testing he interjected what were intended as witty remarks. Fortunately he was away from home during the second visit, so the personal interview suffered no distractions.

More often children were in the room during part or all of the testing and interviewing. The children, all below the age of three or four, may have caused momentary distractions, but Dr. Jensen was never aware that they had any significant influence on the projective tests or interviews. One subject had a maid to look after the children. Other subjects had to take a minute out now and then to attend to their children.

At the conclusion of each meeting, as soon as the subject had left Dr. Jensen wrote a brief description of the subject and the conditions of the session, along with notations of any significant material that had not been recorded. Later, detailed notes were taken during the playback of the recorded interview; these notes were assembled into an orderly personal-interview summary. A typist transcribed verbatim the PST and Rorschach directly from the recordings.

The following list of headings served as a rough guide to the sort of things that the interview could be expected to cover. It was not intended that this outline should be followed in any slavish fashion. Dr. Jensen, who conducted all of the interviews, was instructed first of all to size up the person in a general way from his first impression and from subsequent relationships during the interview. Subjects were told in general that we wanted to know about their experiences after junior or senior high school. They were then given freedom to tell their stories in whatever way they wished with occasional promptings in order to fill gaps in the account at appropriate pauses in the subject's report. In the interviews it was our purpose to secure not only the objective facts but also to note the subject's feelings, particularly with reference to the persons who had crossed his path.

Following the outline itself are a number of specific suggestions which were intended to guide the conduct of the interviews.

Interview Schedule

A. General description of the person
  1. Physique
  2. Clothing
  3. Energy level
  4. Outgoingness
  5. Voice
  6. Mannerisms
  7. Posture
  8. Gestures
  9. Assertiveness
  10. Vivacity
  11. Fluency in talking

B. Work experiences—including full-time employment and also part-time
  1. Relation to superiors in work
  2. Relation to associates

C. School experiences
  1. High school
  2. College
  3. Other specialized education and training

D. Members of family
  It is not necessary to secure impressions of the subject of father, mother, brothers or sisters or other members of the family going back to early childhood, but be sure to note any feelings and reactions to members of the family as they are related to the subject.

E. Friendships—relationships with others both of same and opposite sex

F. Marriage
  1. Attitude toward marriage
  2. Attitude toward members of the opposite sex
  3. Attitude toward dating and other heterosexual experiences
  4. Sex experiences and attitudes
G. Hobbies and activities
H. Recreations
I. Sports
  1. Interest in
  2. Participation in
J. Clubs and organizations
  1. Membership in
  2. Participation in
K. Illnesses, accidents, injuries (health)
L. Religion
M. Specific habits, such as drinking, smoking, gambling
N. Fears
O. Anxieties and worries
  1. Complaints
P. Depression—the "blues"
Q. Obsessive or compulsive tendencies—excessive neatness, cleanliness, orderliness, repetitiousness
R. Tendencies toward perfectionism
S. Aspirations, goals, and ambitions
T. Attitude toward self
  1. Self-esteem
  2. Self-depreciation, feelings of inferiority
U. Attitude toward sex role—being a man or a woman
V. Attitude toward aggression
  Note if subject is able to tolerate own aggression or whether he avoids getting into competitive situations or situations where he is forced to assert himself.
W. Prejudices
  1. Racial
  2. Religious
X. Tendencies toward liberalism or conservatism (politics)
Y. Attitudes
  1. Courage
  2. Generosity
  3. Resentment
  4. Responsibility
  5. Friendliness
  6. Enthusiasm
  7. Feelings of futility
  8. Discouragement
  9. Dependency
  10. Resignation
  11. Selfishness
  12. Sensitiveness
  13. Affection
  14. Restlessness
  15. Kindness
  16. Gentleness
  17. Self-pity

Following are some suggestions with regard to the conduct of the interviews:

1. Do not feel that it is necessary to cover all of the above topics in order. In general give the other person the lead and do not try to be systematic or thorough. After the person has spoken freely concerning those matters which he wishes to tell you, it may be appropriate to have him respond to topics which he may have omitted.
2. Do not pump.
3. Use open-ended questions such as, "Tell me about your hobbies and interests." In general avoid questions that ask for specific information or that can be answered by yes or no.
4. Follow leads wherever they may go. In general let a person talk as long as he wishes to on any topic although one has to be sensitive to the tendency that some people may have of talking interminably on some topics in order to avoid approaching other topics.
5. Do not interrupt a person while he is talking to ask questions which may divert his train of thought.
6. If the person seems embarrassed or ill at ease, it would be appropriate to comment on it and to encourage him to tell how he feels. This is true not only with regard to the topics about which a person may talk but also about his participation in the project itself.
7. If necessary, reassure about the confidential nature of the project and of the records. Assure the person that what he tells will be used only by the members of the staff of the study and that anything that he may tell will not be revealed to family, friends, employers, or other individuals.
8. Do not talk about yourself.
9. Give any information that is asked for concerning the nature of the study.
10. Note resistances as they may appear—excuses, evasions, digressions, failure to follow through on topics, and recognize the feelings back of them.
11. Deal with the topic of sex only if it is brought up first by the subject. It would probably be wiser to omit any reference to sex in the interview rather than to run the danger of alienating the subject because of his sensitivity to this topic. Subjects may not reveal their feelings at the moment, but in many cases an approach to sexual matters would arouse strong emotion and create antagonism to the whole study and defeat our purposes. Consequently it would be prudent to avoid this topic unless you feel that it is something that the subject wishes to bring in.

This interview study may be compared with the much more extensive and detailed plans for interviewing in the Authoritarian Personality Study,[5] which was principally the responsibility of Frenkl-

[5] T. W. Adorno and others, *The Authoritarian Personality* (New York, Harper, 1950).

Introduction

Brunswik; however, the conditions of the two studies were somewhat different. In the Authoritarian Personality Study, the problem was somewhat simpler in that they were concerned with contrasting personalities and life background of two groups—those who were and were not prejudiced. In the present study, however, no such sharp contrast can be made and the problem here is rather one of making general comparisons over the thirteen-year period. Consequently, it was not possible to pinpoint the aims in the interviewing as carefully as was done in the Authoritarian Personality Study and it was necessary to use more of a shotgun approach.

Instead of transcribing the complete interviews, Dr. Jensen listened to each Audograph record, took full notes, and then dictated a summary which could be used for analysis. This summary organized the materials under the following headings:

A. General Description
B. Education
C. Work Experience
D. Members of Family
E. Friendships
F. Marriage
G. Hobbies and Activities
H. Recreations
I. Sports
J. Clubs and Organizations
K. Illnesses, Accidents, Injuries (Health)
L. Religion
M. Specific Habits, such as Drinking, Smoking, Gambling
N. Fears
O. Anxieties and Worries
P. Depression—the "blues"
Q. Obsessive or Compulsive Tendencies
R. Tendencies toward Perfectionism
S. Aspirations, Goals and Ambitions
T. Attitude toward Self
U. Attitude toward Sex Role
V. Attitude toward Aggression
W. Prejudices
X. Tendencies toward Liberalism or Conservatism (Politics)

2. The Community and the Population

Although the population of this study is not large, it was originally selected as being an unbiased sample of adolescents from a suburban city and it should be of some interest to see how representative it is of young adults at the present time.

The original data were gathered in the fall of 1940 and the spring of 1941. The community in which the original study was conducted was a city, suburban to New York, standing near the top in size in cities of the United States, according to the 1950 census. It is predominantly a manufacturing city with only 4 other cities in the state having a higher percentage of manufacturing, and it was exceeded in density of population by 15 of the 28 cities in the state. Its population tended to be on the young side, being exceeded in the percentage of those 65 years or older and in median age by 15 other cities in the state. It tended to have a better than average educational level, being exceeded in median school years completed by only 10 other cities in the state. The average annual salary paid to teachers was exceeded by 15 of the other cities, but only 4 other cities spent more, on the average, per pupil. As for individual income, it was average. However, one would say that its citizens live modestly, as the percentage of dwellings with hot running water, private toilet, and bath and not in dilapidated condition was exceeded by 15 other cities, and the percent of those owning their own homes was exceeded by 15 of the other cities.[1]

Of the forty individuals in the original study—twenty boys and

[1] The data for this statistical description were taken from Table 4 (pp. 396–403) of U.S. Bureau of the Census, *County and City Data Book, 1956* (*A Statistical Abstract Supplement*) (U.S. Government Printing Office, Washington, D.C.), and is based on 1950 census data.

The Community and the Population

twenty girls—twenty-three were pupils in a junior high school, eight were from a girls' high school and nine from a boys' high school. Following is a description of the students as it appeared in the original study.

In planning the study in the three schools it was emphasized that it was our wish to study normal or typical and unselected boys and girls. That is, we did not wish to select predominantly bright pupils, or predominantly dull pupils, nor were they to be selected because the school considered them problem children and wished the assistance which our test battery might yield for understanding them. It was decided to select the boys and girls on a volunteer basis. This would, of course, introduce a selective factor, but at the same time it was a desirable one, inasmuch as the co-operation of the subjects was important.

The method by which the subjects were selected in the junior high school can best be described by quoting from a letter from the Guidance Director.

"Volunteers were asked for in classes of varying achievement and interests. The eighth grades were contacted on two levels—those who were accelerated and those of average ability. In the ninth grade we asked for volunteers from the college preparatory, commercial, and general arts groups. The commercial students are generally not as advanced as the college group. The general arts pupils are the slow-moving, over-age, retarded, maladjusted, and less than average ones.

"The girls were selected in the same way. There were only twelve in the general arts section. We tried to give you a cross-section of the school."

One boy in the junior high school, the last to be selected, was chosen because he was a problem and the school wished help from our study in understanding him. The fact that he was maladjusted was evidenced in that he was at the bottom of the list in the ratings of adjustment.

When the ratings of adjustment are studied, it will be noted that a larger proportion of the poorly adjusted were found in the junior high school than might be expected by chance. Is it possible that younger adolescents show greater signs of conflict and restlessness than the older adolescents? This study would incline toward that belief.

In the High School for Girls, girls were selected by asking for volunteers from the four lowest classes in the commercial department. Since students from lower intellectual levels tend to gravitate into the commercial department in high schools, it is probable that these older girls tend to be placed slightly lower on the scale of intelligence than an unselected group from the school would be.

The High School for Boys was busy and crowded, and the overworked counselor was slow to select cases for use in this study. Wexler solved this problem ingeniously by approaching boys in study halls, explaining the nature of the study, and asking them if they would care to participate. It is believed that this resulted in a very representative and unselected group of older boys for the study. By and large it can be truthfully said that these are forty normal boys and girls taken at random from the secondary schools of an American city.[2]

Of the 28 individuals included in the present (1953) study, 12 were men and 16 were women. Sixteen of the original 23 junior high school pupils and 12 of the original 17 high school pupils took part in 1953.

Ages and I.Q.s are given in Tables 1 and 2.

TABLE 1. DISTRIBUTION OF SUBJECTS BY AGE

Age in 1940	Number in 1940 study	Number in 1953 study	Age in 1953 [a]	Number in 1953 study	Number from 1940 study not included in 1953 study
18	1	1	31	1	0
17	4	4	30	5	0
16	8	4	29	4	4
15	7	3	28	5	4
14	12	10	27	9	2
13	7	6	26	4	1
12	1	0	25	0	1
	40	28		28	12

[a] The base for computing ages was taken a little later in the year in 1953 than in 1940.

TABLE 2. DISTRIBUTION OF SUBJECTS BY I.Q.

I.Q. in 1940	Number in 1940 study	Number in 1953 study	Number from 1940 study not included in 1953 study
140	1	1	0
135	2	2	0
130	2	1	1
125	0	0	0
120	4	3	1
115	5	4	1
110	10	6	4
105	4	3	1
100	4	1	3
95	3	2	1
90	2	2	0
85	3	3	0
	40	28	12

[2] P. M. Symonds, *Adolescent Fantasy* (New York, Columbia University Press, 1949), pp. 54–55.

The Community and the Population

The twelve who were not included in the present (1953) study tended to be slightly younger than those included, but intelligence was not a selective factor. Klausner [3] for his doctoral study divided the city in which the initial study was conducted into residential areas which he called "prestige areas." These areas correspond roughly to the socio-economic level of the district, but in the case of two of the areas ethnic factors were also a consideration. Klausner drew this map from conversations with several citizens of the community for whose judgment he had respect because of their thorough acquaintance with the areas with which they were familiar. Several of these individuals were teachers or principals in the public schools.

Table 3 gives the distribution by residential district, Area 1 representing the district at the top of the prestige ladder and Area 7 that at the bottom.

TABLE 3. DISTRIBUTION OF SUBJECTS BY RESIDENTIAL AREAS IN *1940* CORRESPONDING ROUGHLY TO SOCIO-ECONOMIC LEVELS

Area where subject lived in 1940	Number of subjects in 1953 study	Subjects not included in 1953 number
1	0	0
2	2	1
3	20	10
4	2	0
5	0	0
6	1	0
7	3	1
	28	12

It will be noted that the large majority of the subjects came from Area 3, which may be roughly defined as middle class. The junior high school which twenty-three of the original subjects attended was located in Area 3 and naturally its pupils came largely from this area. Only four of the original study came from lower-class areas in the city. One of these was a junior high school pupil, two came from the girls' high school and one from the boys' high school. Socio-economic factors apparently exercised no pronounced selective influence in the follow-up study, although only one of the four from lower-class districts did not participate in 1953.

It has already been stated in Chapter One that of the twelve sub-

[3] S. Z. Klausner, "The Relation between Certain Socio-Economic Factors and Self-Concept," Doctor of Education Report, Teachers College, Columbia University (typewritten), 1954.

jects who did not participate in the study, one actually was located, took the tests, and was interviewed, but too late to be included in the tabulations; five others were located, of whom three did not care to participate in the study and two lived too far away. This leaves six who could not be located. So far as is known all forty of the original subjects are still alive.

Education

Table 4 shows the educational experience of the 28 subjects.

TABLE 4. EDUCATION OF SUBJECTS

Level	Number of subjects
Did not finish high school [a]	3
Did not go beyond high school	8
Attended college, but did not graduate	2
College, B. A. or B. S.	
Liberal Arts	4
Engineering	3
Business	1
RN (Registered Nurse)	2
Other schools	
Dental technician (2 years)	1
Dental technician (1 year)	1
Business school (2 years)	1
Vocational school (6 months)	1
Modeling (2 months)	1
Beautician (6 months)	1
Photography school (2 months)	1
	30

[a] Of two who did not finish high school, one attended a photography school and one a dental technician school; they were therefore counted twice.

The population statistics of the United States show that 81.8 percent of persons in the 25–29 age bracket had no more than a high school education, 10.2 percent had one to three years of college, while only 7.7 percent graduated from college.[4] It is evident that the twenty-eight subjects in this study exceed the national average in their education.

The three who did not finish high school were boys; but the eight

[4] U.S. Bureau of the Census, *Statistical Abstract of the United States, 1955* (76th ed.; Washington, D.C., 1955), Table 129, p. 112.

who finished high school yet went no further were girls. Six of the eight who graduated from college and two who started college were boys. Of the ten who took some form of vocational education, not college, after graduating from high school, six were girls. From this small sample it is not possible to generalize. But if these trends were generalized they would produce certain conclusions: (1) high school is the terminal point in academic education for girls at this socio-economic level, although some girls go on for specialized vocational training; (2) boys either drop out before they finish their high school course (this was true also of Jack, who was not included in the tabulations) or they tend to go on to college in larger proportions than the girls. Two of the junior high school boys who went on to college were far from successful academically, but persisted with considerable struggle until they received a degree. The three boys from the senior high school who completed a college education did so in the face of great economic difficulties by attending night courses and working to support themselves.

Vocation

Of the twelve men in the study, four were salesmen and the others were distributed among a variety of vocations, including auto repair mechanic, engineer, electrical contractor, mail carrier, factory foreman, advertising manager, deliverer of automobiles; one is a student. The six who had a college degree included the engineer, electrical contractor, factory foreman, advertising manager, and inside salesman. One who in Table 4 was counted as having a degree in engineering expected to receive the degree in June, 1954, but for purposes of vocational classification was considered a student.

Of the sixteen girls in the study all except three were married and could be counted as housewives; but of these thirteen, three were still working, two as secretaries, one in editorial work. One had never worked. Nine of the married women had worked before marriage, two as nurses, two as secretaries, one each as typist, bookkeeper, mail clerk, beauty operator, and in advertising. Of the unmarried, two were secretaries and one was a purchasing agent. It will be noted that all except three of these women who were working or who had worked held office jobs. Two of the three were nurses and one a beautician. Since the seven from the girls' high school had been in the commercial curriculum, it would be natural to expect that they would find office jobs, but actually three of them did not (beauty operator, nurse, and no occupation); while of the nine junior high girls, eight later found work of a clerical nature.

Again, to make tentative generalizations from this very small sample, there is an almost universal tendency for girls today to work before marriage and for some to continue working after marriage. By far the larger number of these women went into work of a clerical nature or into office positions.

TABLE 5. NUMBER OF JOBS HELD BY SUBJECTS

Number of jobs	Number of men	Number of women
10	1	0
9	0	0
8	0	0
7	0	0
6	1	0
5	1	0
4	1	2
3	3	3
2	1	6
1	4	4
0	0	1
	12	16

An interesting bit of data tabulated from the records concerns the number of different jobs or positions held. It will be seen that typically a man or woman has held more than one job. Apparently there is a trial period at the beginning of one's work experience when he (or she) is trying out different kinds of work (and employers). As discussed elsewhere, Albert (subject 40) found holding a job one of his special problems.

Military Service

Ten of the twelve men saw military service during World War II —four in the Army, four in the Navy, and two in the Air Force. Of the two who did not serve, one had a physical handicap, and while no reason is given on the record as to why the other did not serve, one

The Community and the Population

may assume it was because he was in an essential industry. Only one of the women reported serving in any of the armed services—as a Wave.

Residence of Subjects

TABLE 6. RESIDENCE OF THE SUBJECTS IN THE *1953* STUDY

Place	Number of men	Number of women
Original city	3	7
Nearby community, same state	7	7
Adjoining state	2	2
	12	16

Of the 28 subjects in the study only ten in 1953 resided in the city in which the study was originally conducted. Five of the seven unmarried subjects still lived in this city and one unmarried subject was away at school but returned to his parental home in this city at vacation times.

Fourteen lived in nearby suburban communities. Many of those communities were real-estate developments and the subjects of the study in several instances had purchased new houses in the new communities where they were making their homes. Most of these homes had a new look with modern labor-saving equipment and new furniture.

Four of the subjects lived farther away in adjoining states, but near enough that they could be reached for the tests and interviews.

Of the six subjects from the 1940 study who were located but not included in the 1953 study, two lived in the city in which the study was conducted, two lived in suburban areas and two lived in far-away states. Contact was not made with six subjects.

Of the married subjects all but one lived in their own homes (including six in apartments). The one exception, with her husband, lived with her mother, a widow. But all seven of the unmarried subjects still lived in the parental home. One subject had a living-in maid.

Marital Status

Of the twelve men in the study eight were married and four were single. For one of the married men this was his second marriage; he had divorced his first wife at age 20.

The Community and the Population

Of the sixteen women, thirteen were married and three were single. For one of the married women also this was a second marriage, following a divorce at age 26.

The U.S. Statistical Abstract of 1955 shows the following figures on marital status in 1954 for the age group 25–29 (figures are percentages).[5]

	Male	Female
Single	17.0	9.8
Married	80.8	86.7
Widowed	0.4	1.1
Divorced	1.8	2.3
	100.0	99.9

The number of those unmarried in the present study for both men and women is greater than in these national figures. There were neither men nor women in this study, who, having been divorced, were still single.

Table 7 shows age at which the subjects married.

TABLE 7. AGE OF SUBJECTS AT MARRIAGE

Age	Number of men	Number of women
27	1	0
26	1	2
25	1	1
24	1	2
23	2	1
22	1	5
21	0	1
20	0	1
19	1	0
Median age	24.0	22.9

The median age for first marriage for men in a neighboring state in 1954 was 24.1 years and for women 21.3 years, as given by the U.S. Census figures.[6] The women in the present study seem to have married somewhat later than the average by about a year and a half, the median age being 22.9.

[5] *Statistical Abstract of the United States, 1955* (U. S. Government Printing Office, Washington, D.C.), Table 46, p. 49.
[6] *Statistical Abstract of the United States, 1958* (U.S. Government Printing Office, Washington, D.C.), Table 80, p. 73.

Children

From the twenty-one marriages of the individuals in this study twenty-five children were reported, ten from the eight marriages of the men and fifteen from the thirteen marriages of the women. Nine of the children were boys and sixteen were girls.

The number of children per family is given in Table 8; ages of the children are given in Table 9.

TABLE 8. NUMBER OF SUBJECTS' CHILDREN PER FAMILY

Number of children	Number of families, male subjects	Number of families, female subjects	Total
0	1	5	6
1	4	2	6
2	3	5	8
3	0	1	1
	8	13	21

TABLE 9. AGE OF SUBJECTS' CHILDREN

Age	Number of boys	Number of girls
4	3	3
3	1	0
2	2	4
1	0	3
0 (less than one year)	3	6
	9	16

Five children were also reported on the way, four by the women in the study, one by a man. It is difficult to assess the size of the family since obviously the families were still growing.

Religion

The group was very evenly divided between the three religious groupings—ten were Protestant, nine Catholic, and eight Jewish, while one mentioned no religious affiliation. According to data presented in the 1958 *Statistical Abstract of the United States* the number of Jewish persuasion in this study is considerably above expectancy, while the number of Protestants less than expectancy.[7] Of the Protestants

---
[7] *Statistical Abstract of the United States, 1958*, Table 53, p. 51.

four were Presbyterian, two Episcopalian, one Methodist, one Lutheran, and two not stated. Of the seven unmarried, three were Catholics, two Jewish, and one Protestant. Four of the marriages (all involving women subjects) crossed religious lines. One Presbyterian and one Baptist had married Catholic men and a Catholic had married a Presbyterian. In one case a Presbyterian had married a man who was a Methodist.

In only three instances had a person shifted his religion from that of his childhood. In one instance both a man and his wife, originally Catholics, became Episcopalian. One of the women who was originally a Baptist and who married a man who was Catholic joined the Catholic Church at the time of her marriage. One subject shifted from Episcopalian to Presbyterian, but no reasons were given. In all other instances subjects remained loyal to the religious affiliation of their childhood family.

The impression was gained that in many instances where a religious connection was mentioned the interest was superficial, so a rough tally was made, the results of which are shown in Table 10.

TABLE 10. STRENGTH OF RELIGIOUS INTEREST ON THE PART OF SUBJECTS

	Protestant	Catholic	Jewish	Total
Mild	7	1	7	15
Moderate	2	2	1	5
Devoted	1	6	0	7
	10	9	8	27

The original impression was verified by the tally. Over half of the subjects had only a mild interest in or devotion to their religion. Those of the Catholic persuasion showed the greatest devotion; Protestants and Jews tended to be desultory in church attendance and religion was remote in their interests. The impression was gained that even though some of the Jews may have given little attention to formal rituals and attendance at synagogue, there was a substratum of deeper loyalty to their religious background.

Politics

Dr. Jensen pressed his own interest in the authoritarian personality by discussing political attitudes and attitudes toward authority with the subjects at some length. Sixteen stated that they were Republican and ten Democrat, but one of the latter voted for Eisenhower. Two showed little interest in politics and could not be persuaded to state an affiliation. It must be remembered that this study was conducted following the 1952 national elections when Eisenhower's popularity was high and there was strong protest against the long, unbroken years of Democratic sway.

An attempt was made to learn the trends in political thinking with a little greater detail, but this was hard to do as many different shades of opinion were expressed. Only one was an enthusiastic Republican; four could be counted as loyal and emotionally involved Democrats. Six leaned toward and voted Republican but without definite conviction; they were following the current trend. Two stated that they voted Republican, but had always been Democratic before. Two were counted as Democrats, but had no great conviction. Three announced themselves conservatives, five were liberal in sentiment, while three could be counted as middle of the road. Several showed very little interest in politics and expressed opinions only when pressed by questions. In the majority of instances when it was mentioned, political affiliation followed the family tradition, but in two instances subjects called themselves Republican yet stated that their parents had been Democrats; one subject was a Democrat but his parents had been Republican.

Racial Background

All the subjects in the study were born in this country. Five of the subjects, however, were of foreign parentage—one Italian, two Polish, and two Czechoslovakian.

Miscellaneous

None of the subjects in the study had a criminal record, at least, by their own testimony. None of them had been in a mental hospital. One subject's parents had consulted a psychiatrist about him as a child, and another, not among the twenty-eight included in the statistical tabulations, had a record of having been discharged from a Veteran's Administration Hospital, but the nature of the disturbance was not stated.

Summary

In summary it may be stated that the twenty-eight subjects in this study constitute a fair sample of an urban population in the year 1953. Ranging in age from 26 to 31, they were somewhat above average in intelligence and education, coming predominantly from middle-class homes. The men in the study had entered a number of different occupations; and all but one of the women were working or had worked, the majority in occupations of a clerical nature. Ten of the twelve men and one woman saw military service in World War II. Twenty-one of the subjects were married, the women having married slightly later than is normal in the population at large. One man and one woman had been divorced, but both had remarried. In all a total of twenty-five children were reported for these twenty-one families, with five more on the way. Six families were as yet childless, while one family had three children. The group was evenly divided between the Protestant, Catholic, and Jewish religions, but religion was a remote concern for the majority of Protestant and Jewish subjects. So far as is known none of the subjects had a criminal record and none had been in a mental hospital.

3. Comparison of Adolescent with Adult Fantasy

The obvious first step in analyzing the data for the purpose of comparing the twenty stories told by each subject in 1940–41 with those told in 1953–54 was to make a count of the themes contained in the stories. In 1940 there was no prior experience which would serve as the basis for a check list of themes, so an effort was made at that time to carry through a complete theme count. One of the outcomes of the original study was a tabulation of the frequency with which themes occurred in the original stories. It was hoped that out of this earlier experience a check list could be prepared to serve as a guide for a theme count in the present follow-up study which would be much more satisfactory for research purposes than the shotgun method originally used.

When the tabulations in *Adolescent Fantasy* were inspected, however, they looked far from satisfactory. Much has transpired in thematic apperception testing theory over the thirteen intervening years and there is closer rapprochement between testing analysis and psychodynamic theory in general.

Quantitative Comparisons

A check list was finally constructed, based only in part on the results of the earlier tabulation in *Adolescent Fantasy*. Another helpful source was the so-called "Psychogram Scoring Sheet for Verbal Projective Techniques," prepared by Reuben Fine.[1] In addition to using these two sources, several sets of stories were analyzed using a preliminary

---

[1] Reuben Fine, "A Scoring Scheme for the TAT and other Projective Techniques," *Journal of Projective Techniques*, XIX (1955), 306-9; and "Manual for a Scoring Scheme for Verbal Projective Techniques," *ibid.*, pp. 310-16.

check list, and further modifications and additions were made. As a result the check list given in Table 11 was adopted for use in this study.

TABLE 11. NUMBER OF SUBJECTS AND TOTAL NUMBER OF STORIES PRESENTING THEMES IN 1940 AND 1953

	Themes	Number of subjects presenting themes 1940	1953	Total number of stories presenting themes 1940	1953
1.	Altruism	6	6	10	10
2.	Anger	12	13	20	19
3.	Anxiety	22	22	51	43
4.	Concealment	6	5	12	7
5.	Conflict	5	8	6	10
6.	Crime against person	9	7	19	8
7.	Crime against property	19	12	50	17
8.	Criminal death	15	6	28	6
9.	Accidental or natural death	20	10	48	15
10.	Depression	14	23	24	54
11.	Disobedience-rebellion	11	8	17	10
12.	Dominance-coercion	9	12	14	15
13.	Eroticism	21	24	44	54
14.	Escape	13	3	24	3
15.	Excitement	9	7	16	9
16.	Giving-receiving	15	12	26	14
17.	Guilt	8	14	13	22
18.	Hostility	26	15	55	27
19.	Masculine identification				
20.	Feminine identification				
21.	Confusion as to sex				
22.	Illness, accident	15	9	26	15
23.	Jealousy	16	7	22	23
24.	Morality	16	17	24	29
25.	Mystery, strangeness	12	2	20	2
26.	Orality	7	4	20	26
27.	Positive outcome	28	24	227	146
28.	Negative outcome	22	24	90	71
29.	Passivity, aggressed against	21	10	57	16
30.	Passivity, erotic yearning	13	17	21	30
31.	Pathological indicators	1	2	5	4
32.	Pleasure	13	10	23	15
33.	Punishment	25	23	71	46
34.	Reform, repentance	20	17	44	23
35.	Rejection	12	14	20	22
36.	Presence of self-confidence	13	13	17	17

TABLE 11. NUMBER OF SUBJECTS AND TOTAL NUMBER OF STORIES
PRESENTING THEMES IN 1940 AND 1953 (Cont.)

	Number of subjects presenting themes		Total number of stories presenting themes	
37. Lack of self-confidence	11	11	18	17
38. Sexuality	1	3	13	9
39. Separation	13	12	25	20
40. Striving, effort	19	19	49	43
41. Success	19	16	41	33
42. Thinking, planning	18	15	27	29
43. Trick, joke, plot	11	1	18	1
44. Wishful thinking	11	20	20	47
Number of ideas			9028	9871

In 1940 length of story was determined by counting number of words; but in 1953 number of ideas was used instead. One reason for this is that the method of recording the stories was different on the two occasions. In 1940 stories were taken down by the examiner in longhand; often it was impossible to get a verbatim record and frequently the account was too abbreviated to incorporate the main ideas. But in 1953 the stories were electrically recorded on a Gray Audograph and were typed verbatim from the records. Number of ideas expressed seemed not only to be a fairer method of comparison, but also to be a more meaningful measure of the length of the story.

It will be noted from Table 11 that in general there is a tendency for the total number of occurrences of a theme to remain the same over the thirteen-year interval. Only three themes—*depression, guilt,* and *wishful thinking*—appear to increase; while a larger number—*crime against property, criminal death, accidental death, escape, hostility, illness and accident, mystery, being aggressed against,* and *trick*—decrease. Whereas the total number of ideas appears to have increased, this is due to the influence of two subjects who told excessively long and detailed stories in 1953. Actually the number (14) of those who told stories with more ideas balances the number (13) of those with fewer ideas.

This comparison in terms of number of subjects telling stories with certain themes or in terms of total number of stories with a given theme is somewhat illusory because, even though the numbers may be alike, different subjects may have contributed to these totals. For instance, in Theme 1, *altruism,* there were six subjects in 1940 and six in 1953 who produced stories including this theme, but only two of the six were the same subject.

A more meaningful comparison is in terms of the shifts or changes in theme production over the thirteen-year interval. For instance, a tabulation of the differences, subject by subject, between 1940 and 1953 for Theme 10, *depression,* gives the distribution shown in Table 12.

TABLE 12. DIFFERENCE IN NUMBER OF OCCURRENCES OF
THEME OF DEPRESSION, 1940 AND 1953

Difference	Frequency
+4	3
+3	1
+2	6
+1	8
0	3
−1	3
−2	1
	25

Three individuals did not produce a story including the theme of depression either time, so the total number of differences in the table is 25 instead of 28.

Table 13 presents the results of this comparison, giving the mean of the distribution of differences, the *t* value of these means, and the probability that a mean could have been as large as it was by chance.

In connection with Table 13 the amount of change exceeds that which could be attributed to chance or the unreliability of the method. If the differences were due to unreliability and chance variability over the thirteen-year period, there could not be so many differences significant at better than the .01 level and the number of plus and minus changes would be about equal, which is not the case here. This seems to be convincing evidence that we have more than an artifact of unreliability and that the changes represent actual differences in fantasy content.

In general the same trends are present here that were found in the simpler tabulation of themes by individual occurrences and total themes. Of the sixteen themes that showed mean differences from zero with a probability less than .05, fourteen were in the negative direction and only two showed increased frequency, namely *depression* and *wishful thinking*.

The themes that showed a decrease are the ones that characterized the fantasies of early adolescence, and this tabulation makes still more clear the essential characteristics of adolescent fantasy. Among the themes that showed a decreased frequency are *crime against property, criminal death, accidental death, hostility, being aggressed against, punishment*, all dealing with violent aggression or punishment for aggression. Guilt over these fantasies during the adolescent period may be shown by the theme of *reform*. Early adolescence is a time when impulses are heightened and they break through the repressive forces that hold them in check in the latency period. These impulses find an outlet in fantasy, particularly in those instances where the adolescent is kept in close check by a dominating parent or parents.

TABLE 13. MEAN OF THE DISTRIBUTION OF DIFFERENCES BETWEEN THE OCCURRENCE OF THEMES IN 1940 AND 1953, THE t VALUE OF THESE MEANS, AND THE PROBABILITY OF CHANCE OCCURRENCE OF DIFFERENCES

Theme	Mean difference from zero	t Value of means	Probability that the mean difference occurred by chance
1. Altruism	0.00	0.00	
2. Anger	−0.06	−0.16	
3. Anxiety	−0.35	−0.72	
4. Concealment	−0.50	−0.71	
5. Conflict	+0.33	+0.89	
6. Crime against person	−0.79	−1.53	
7. Crime against property	−1.50	−3.41	.01
8. Criminal death	−1.38	−2.52	.05
9. Accidental or natural death	−1.52	−3.42	.01
10. Depression	+1.24	+3.80	.001
11. Disobedience-rebellion	−0.50	−1.73	
12. Dominance-coercion	+0.41	+1.13	
13. Eroticism	−0.15	−0.32	
14. Escape	−1.40	−4.58	.001
15. Excitement	−0.54	−1.20	
16. Giving-receiving	−0.67	−2.13	.05
17. Guilt	+0.60	+1.50	
18. Hostility	−1.00	−2.75	.02
19. Masculine identification	−0.71	−2.28	.05
20. Feminine identification	+0.32	+0.68	

TABLE *13.* MEAN OF THE DISTRIBUTION OF DIFFERENCES BETWEEN THE OCCURRENCE OF THEMES IN *1940* AND *1953*, THE *t* VALUE OF THESE MEANS, AND THE PROBABILITY OF CHANCE OCCURRENCE OF DIFFERENCES (*Cont.*)

Theme	Mean difference from zero	t Value of means	Probability that the mean difference occurred by chance
22. Illness, accident	−0.65	−1.51	
23. Jealousy	+0.04	+0.18	
24. Morality	+0.22	+0.66	
25. Mystery, strangeness	−1.58	−3.98	.01
26. Orality	−1.62	−2.03	.1
27. Positive outcome	−2.89	−7.91	.001
28. Negative outcome	−0.70	−1.12	
29. Passivity, aggressed against	−1.90	−3.42	.01
30. Passivity, erotic yearning	+0.43	+1.17	
32. Pleasure	−0.44	−1.03	
33. Punishment	−0.93	−1.98	.1
34. Reform	−0.98	−1.99	.1
35. Rejection	+0.12	+0.34	
36. Presence of self-confidence	0.00	0.00	
37. Lack of self-confidence	−0.10	−0.30	
38. Sexuality	+2.00	+2.00	
39. Separation	−0.25	−0.66	
40. Striving, effort	−0.04	−0.09	
41. Success	−0.16	−0.28	
42. Thinking, planning	+0.09	+0.29	
43. Trick, joke, plot	−1.55	−4.54	.001
44. Wishful thinking	+1.30	+3.08	.01

Another group of themes, including *mystery*, and *trick* or *magic*, also show decreases. It is probable that these are symbolic references to sexual fantasy. Still other themes which are connected with the adolescent's fantasies with reference to parental relationships and control are *escape, giving-receiving,* and *orality*.

It may be noted that there is a decrease in the number of stories with favorable or *happy endings*. In part this may be coupled with the increase in depression themes, and in part with the decrease in the adolescent's defense against guilt by magically turning catastrophe into a happy ending.

A less pronounced tendency toward a decrease in *masculine identification* with a corresponding nonsignificant increase toward feminine identification has no obvious explanation. It may represent a general decrease by both sexes of masculine striving. It may be part of the deepening of repression and protection against self-revelation on the part of the men. Or it may be a decrease of defense against homosexual fantasies on the part of the men in the study.

The increase in themes of *depression* was a marked characteristic in the 1953 stories. There were undisguised expressions of disappointment, discouragement, and dejection. Apparently adolescence is a time for vague but exaggerated hopeful fantasies. The adolescent fantasies for himself riches, prosperity, fame, success, a beautiful wife, a virile but sympathetic husband, a good education, a good position, friends, a home of his own. But life has not granted all of these easily, and thirteen years later disillusionment has set in.

Themes of depression also probably indicate aggression turned inward. In adolescence aggression is outgoing and the stories are full of violence and crime. Later the youth attempts to translate his aggressive fantasies into action by his striving in college and at work. But this striving has to be highly channelized in socially acceptable ways. So the young man or woman tends to convert some of his or her aggression into self-recrimination and feelings of inferiority, discouragement, and hopelessness.

These trends were evident in the original report, *Adolescent Fantasy*, in comparing the older and younger groups. In the original report it was said:

The only characteristic in which the young exceeded the old is in being *happy*. The older group, on the other hand, produced more themes of *discouragement* and *disappointment*, of *anxiety* and *worry*, of *fear, dread*, and *alarm*. This paints the picture of early adolescence as a carefree period, characterized by more violent expression and a minimum atmosphere of guilt. Adolescents over fifteen, on the other hand, face stronger conflicts with family, social standards, and the expectations of society. Stories given by the younger group express crude hopes and longings, set in a world of primitive passion—those given by the older group show some disillusionment, disappointment over the past and present, and anxiety concerning the future. These anxieties are evident in the greater number of themes relating to *job, work,* and *school.*[2]

Today one would modify this statement somewhat. Anxiety and guilt were present in the younger adolescent, but they were not necessarily expressed as such in so many words. But on the whole the present

[2] P. M. Symonds, *Adolescent Fantasy,* p. 92.

study substantiates these trends revealed in the original study and shows that they tend to become more pronounced as young men and women enter their twenties.

Comparisons of Individual Stories

The most convincing demonstration of the way in which there is similarity in fantasy over a period of years is to reproduce pairs of stories told by the same individual thirteen years apart. The stories themselves help to make more concrete and vivid the trends which are shown in the statistical tables. Following are the first three pairs of stories told by Albert (40).

Subject 40, Story B-1:1940

Boy just had fight with father. They live in factory district of town and he's like average boy—gets into a little mischief and while father is no prize package he's very strict and picks slightest occasion to beat son. Although boy is well able to defend himself it would never occur to him to defend self against father. Has severe argument with father, walks out in rage, father says never to come back and boy is determined not to. He soon cools off and comes back. Father more or less forgot argument. This keeps up, happens over and over again. Seems as if father and son can't get along. Boy finally gets job so he can shift for himself. Moves into place where he can live by self. He doesn't leave town. Still on fairly good terms with father but don't have much to do with each other but many times son regrets he left. Often thinks of going back but always changes his mind after thinking it all out.

Subject 40, Story B-1:1953

In this one I get the impression of a young boy with a very angry expression on his face. He seems to be scowling at the whole house. There must have been an argument. He must have had a fight with someone at home and the expression is one of intense anger, I think, especially since his hands are clenched. When I said home I meant his home, not visiting somebody or anything. Probably just a family affair. The first impression I got of a home, not just a house. What the argument is about I wouldn't guess. Whatever it was, it was something that was against his wishes, as if he wanted to do something very much that was forbidden. Apparently he lost out. He couldn't get away with it. Parental authority was final and in an angry, frustrated mood, he's running out of the house.

One will note the same anger, quarrel, argument with the father. In 1940 he said "father" quite openly in the story; in 1953 it is "a family

Adolescent and Adult Fantasy Compared

affair" and "parental authority." In both stories he is leaving home in anger.

Subject 40, Story A-6:1940

Boy has gone to party with mother's permission and is returning sort of late. Mother left light burning and something to eat in case he is hungry. She has gone to bed. But somehow she couldn't sleep and was just waiting to hear door open and came down as soon as she heard him coming. Boy didn't like the idea of her waiting up. Thought he was old enough to take care of himself and he didn't see his mother's point of view. Thought she was babying and watching over him. He grew very angry. Mother was deeply hurt by his actions. That's all.

Subject 40, Story A-6:1953

Number 6 seems to be the husband coming home at two o'clock in the morning with the night light on. Seems to be walking very stealthily so as not to wake anyone up. Looking at the apple on the table I imagine it is like a high school kid. His mother left an apple on the table to have before he went to bed but the hat I don't associate with young boys and the stealthy approach he seems to be taking is that he was out a little later than he should have been and didn't want to wake up the people in the house, either the wife or the mother, and is trying to come in as quietly as possible.

Here the theme is the same except that in 1940 he tries to creep in late past his mother and in 1953 it is a husband creeping in without disturbing his wife. He himself makes the association with a boy and his mother in 1953. In 1953 he does not express his anger or the mother's "feeling hurt."

Subject 40, Story B-5:1940

Girl just received news from mother that father was killed in an auto accident. Girl had never really loved her father because he wasn't a success in life. But when she heard news of death she realized how much she did care for him. It was a great shock to her and changed the entire course of her life. She was forced to leave school to seek employment and grew very bitter, for she felt she was being deprived of the pleasures of youth. She married rather young but really didn't love her husband. Did it to give up job and have home life. Life turned out rather uneventful. Got along with husband fairly well, but was always complaining.

Subject 40, Story B-5:1953

There are two women talking and one of them looks startled, aghast at the news that she has just heard. She looks unbelievingly at the horrible news that she has just heard. She just can't believe it. She holds her hand up and her mouth open and staring in disbelief. We're going to have a mother and daughter relationship because one's younger—her hairdo—and the other's a little bit older. It's probably a personal family problem and the idea of death of the father. That's what she's just been told by her mother. Something horrible has just happened to her father, something in the family. (Any idea what this could be?) Well, as I said, it's probably a death in the family. Some sad news of that nature anyway. First I thought there were two women of the same age talking, both married, but looking closer one takes on the appearance of a younger girl who is horrified and the other woman seems a little more mature, a little more solid in understanding. (Is it her mother?) Yeah, I would say it would be her mother. (To make the story complete, who died?) Well, I'm making it the father.

It is more than a coincidence that the death of the father is the theme in both stories, told thirteen years apart. Indeed, the picture itself does not even portray a male figure. The idea of the father is completely determined by Albert. In 1940 Albert makes it a death in an auto accident. In 1953 it is called "horrible news" without specifying the nature of the accident.

It will be noted that in each of these three illustrations Albert becomes less detailed and specific in 1953; he is unable to spell things out with the same concreteness.

Or take the case of Olive (27). In 1940 she told the following story to card B-6.

Subject 27, Story B-6:1940

It is quite a pity to see a young person like this. He probably lost something very dear to him. Sitting with his head bowed, hands in pockets, and nothing to do. Home in which he is sitting is not properly lighted. There is only a door through which the light is coming. It must be a poor person. Probably he lost his position which he was so much interested in. He liked it very well. He doesn't seem to have any enthusiasm about anything. If in real life I would see a person sitting like this alone I would certainly enquire what was the matter and see if I could help him in any way.

In 1953 the story told to this picture became:

Subject 27, Story B-6:1953

Could it be that John made up his mind that he is a failure in life? He is sitting and meditating over his past. He seems very dejected. He is not very old, presumably about 25. He's debating in his own mind, is it really worth living? He has a mediocre education and he is not satisfied with what he has done with his education to date. He would like to further his education but somehow he hasn't got the ambition. He thinks about it all the time but he does nothing. He is a shy type and he knows that if he doesn't make up his mind and get out and do something that no one will be of any help to him. He is picturing himself a lazy fisherman. That's exactly the way he's been living, just lolling around, getting up every morning and just taking his sweet time, but he's not very contented. "I must wake myself and get up and do something. Of course I really don't know what I want to do. I've done almost everything. I'm a jack of all trades but I'm master of none. Could it be that maybe some day I'll get the contented feeling that I can do a little bit of everything and a lot of nothing. Perhaps some day I'll really get out and do what I really want to. Right now I can't make up my mind of exactly what I want to do."

Both are stories of extreme depression. In 1940 the main character "does not seem to have any enthusiasm about anything." In 1953 he seems "very dejected." But in 1953 Olive is able to spell out with more detail the things about which the subject is discouraged—and there appears just a small ray of hope and a feeling of self-exertion "perhaps some day I'll really get out and do what I really want to do." But this sounds very much like fantasy.

Or take Celia (28), who in 1940 told the following story to picture A-4.

Subject 28, Story A-4:1940

A young boy and his father. Asked his father for a certain amount of money he needs. Clothes or something he needs for school. By expression he is reluctant to give it to him. While he is giving him the money he is telling him he will have to pay it back or earn it, or he will never give him money again. The boy is obedient and will do what his father wants him to.

In 1953 Celia told the following story to this same picture.

Subject 28, Story A-4:1953

Mr. John Smith is taking his best girl to a Virginia farm and he has got a somewhat Irish father, should I say, and he is asking him for enough money to show this girl a good time and his father very begrudgingly is handing him five dollars and saying that he will have to make that do because that's all he can afford and to be sure he is home by twelve o'clock and he is not to take the car because they were going to use it that evening and he would just have to make use of the five dollars because that is all he can afford now and anyway, a boy shouldn't be given too much money or he will not learn the value of money.

In both stories there is a severe and begrudging father who reluctantly gives money to a demanding son. In 1940 the story ends on the theme of the boy's obedience but the son's attitude is omitted in 1953.

In the case of Dorothy (30), the repetition of themes occurs, but in stories to *different* pictures. This is even more convincing evidence that there is a persistence of psychodynamic trends in an individual. In response to picture B-8, in 1940 Dorothy told the following story.

Subject 30, Story B-8:1940

Mary and father live alone because mother is dead. She is to be married in a week. Asks father if he will miss her. She says she hates to leave him, wants him to come to live with her. He says he will be all right. Cares only about her happiness. They talk a while about old times when she was a little girl and about her mother. Gets late. Goes to bed. Feels relieved because she was worried about father.

In 1953, she told the following story to card B-7.

Subject 30, Story B-7:1953

It's twenty-five after three and Mary Jane has just come home from school. Since her mother died, Mary Jane has taken care of the whole house and taken care of her father and kept everything nice for him and made his meal at night ever since she's been a young girl. After school most of her friends go out to the sweet shop and have sodas and refreshments and things but Mary Jane knows that her father works nights and he'll have to get to work so she will have to get home to make his dinner for him. She would like to go now with her friends too, but she has a sense of responsibility to her father. Right now she's entering her house and she's going up the stairs and it looks like the shadow of her father waiting for her to come home from school. She doesn't have any other brothers or sisters and her father is a very lonesome man. He sort of waits around all day even when he works nights. When he gets up he waits around for Mary Jane to come home so that they can talk a little while and he gets a great kick out of her. I think that Mary Jane will always be a very considerate, conscientious daughter and also when she grows up she will probably be a very conscientious wife. She thinks in her mind that if possible she will take her father in to live with her when she gets married and she'll take just as good care of him as she does now.

Here we have the theme of a girl whose mother is dead who feels that her father is lonesome. In both stories she plans to have her father come to live with her after she is married. This an excellent example of an Oedipal theme persisting over the thirteen-year interval.

Although the persistence of themes pervades the fantasy material in this follow-up study, it seems easier to provide illustrations of the *shift* in thematic content and emphasis.

Adolescent and Adult Fantasy Compared

Ralph (2) told the following story to picture B-6 in 1940.

Subject 2, Story B-6: 1940

Man is a train engineer. A bachelor. Drove train for twenty-five years. One day some crooks want to sell him insurance. Fifty percent of pay. He refuses. They press tracks together. Train falls over hill. He wasn't hurt but he is bleeding bad. The boss fires him. He tries to explain it was an accident. Boss says O.K., but if it happens once more you're fired. Crooks come again. Still no insurance. Next time they fix wheels. Smash, many people are killed. Lady is injured but train does not fall. Engineer sits here worried about his job. Tells boss what happened. Boss puts cops in coal car. Crooks threaten. Crooks try to wreck train. They are arrested. Man keeps job in peace.

In 1953 he told the following story to this same picture.

Subject 2, Story B-6: 1953

All of these pictures seem to have a sad outlook. I don't know. (They're gloomy?) They *are* gloomy. My gosh! This picture reminds me of a fellow who's had a setback. Things haven't been going his way and he's sort of sitting down and moping over it, trying to find out what went wrong, what happened. Maybe his girl friend's left him or one of his friends walked out on him or something like that. He's sitting there thinking about it and he'll probably go on like this for a while and then he'll . . . He looks rather young. He probably feels it pretty much and he'll probably walk around like this for a while and then he'll suddenly forget it and he'll be happy-go-lucky like he should be. But right now he looks pretty depressed.

This is a typical shift to depression. In 1940 this young thirteen-year-old boy told a story full of wild excitement with danger, threats, violence, accidents, but ending "man keeps job in peace." But in 1953 this twenty-six-year-old man is impressed with the gloominess of the picture at the very beginning and ends by saying "Right now he looks pretty depressed."

Or take the case of Sam (9). He, too, told wild stories of adventure, excitement, and aggression as an adolescent, but thirteen years later these same pictures evoke themes of discouragement and depression. In 1940 he told the following story in picture B-6.

Subject 9, Story B-6: 1940

Buggsy was lone bandit. Always robbing. One day he pulled a big job and got shot in the arm. Went to the doctor. Fixed up. Wasn't a bad guy. Driven to it by man who owned parents' land. Parents driven off. Wanted to get even with them and the whole world. Went to Mexico. Got a hut. Hired person to make meals. He was weak from loss of blood. Had time to think of crime. Killed one man. He wasn't bad. Conscience got him. Slowly going crazy. Decided to give up. Now really crazy. Put on the stand. Altogether out of his mind. Doctor said he was unable to testify. Dismissed. Sent to insane asylum.

In 1953, this same picture elicited the following story.

Subject 9, Story B-6: 1953

Dejected. Posture like mine. I should sit up straight. This young fellow just decided to go out in the world and get a job trying to gain experience. He has just returned from his first day's work. He worked as a helper on a large construction job and naturally wasn't accustomed to carrying heavy lumber and running around to get this and that. He's home now, a little discouraged by the fact that he's so tired and he's sitting in his chair, thinking over the events of the day. Happy in one thing, that he finished the day but a little discouraged that the work is so hard and hopes that he can continue to learn what he would like to.

The first story is one of revenge and murder. The excitement aroused by the hatred which his fantasies evoked leads to a feeling that his is going crazy. But in 1953 this same picture evokes themes of deep depression.

The story that Ralph told in 1940 illustrates a trend that shows a decreasing frequency—having the story end happily. This trend occurs much more frequently in 1940 than in 1953. Jerome (7), for instance, showed this trend in fifteen of his twenty stories in 1940 and in none of them in 1953. As an illustration consider story B-1 told in 1940.

Subject 7, Story B-1: 1940

Fellow lives in large old house. Maybe father did own it and lost it. Not paying taxes. Boy wants to go out for teams and all that in school. Finally realized he should help at home, too, as does older sister. "Sorry fellows, can't practice." Goes for job. Finally gets work. Through all working, regain house. Realizes place is in the home. He doesn't give up school. He will get afternoons off. Plays football on Saturday and Sunday. He is happier anyway knowing that he is helping support the family.

In 1953 he told the following story to the same picture:

Subject 7, Story B-1: 1953

Looks like a home itself where this fellow's coming out. It doesn't look like it's too wonderful an establishment. Doesn't look in too good condition. Looks like he has kind of got a worried look on his face. He is going to where the house is. Looks like it's poor section of town or something. Kind of discouraged. Might be going out to look for a job or something according to this place and according to the looks of his home.

In 1940 everything is shining at the end in spite of the fact that at the beginning the father lost his home because of tax delinquency. The story in 1953 is one of unrelieved depression.

A number of themes seem to belong to the pattern of early adolescence, including the use of tricks and mystery, as well as the presence of aggression and its aftereffects in terms of guilt and reparation. Some illustrations may help to highlight these trends. Ralph gave four stories which included the theme of trick or joke in 1940 but none in 1953. In 1940 picture B-9 yielded the following story.

Subject 2, Story B-9: 1940

What's that? A man? Looks funny. There was a young lawyer. Won his first three cases reading at home. Card from friend asking him to come to house. He went and was slugged with a blackjack. Unconscious. Woke and found himself in jail. Asked why. Told him he had killed a man. Shown fingerprints on gun. There was a trial and he was sentenced to die August 5, at midnight. It is now August 1. Here he is himself thinking he's going to die. Let's see, I've got to get him out of this mess. He's laying on the bunk. He sees soap. Carves it to look like gun. At meal time he got up. New man in there. He had new man take his place. Ran away. Guard stops him. Struck him with soap pistol. Got key. Saw garbage pail. Nailed cover on after getting in. Rolled it in the sea. Floated off. Picked up by schooner. He had no clothes but got some from captain. On land he saw a friend. Told him he'd throw him to the sharks if he didn't confess. Friend confesses. He is freed and friend is convicted.

In 1953 he told this story to picture B-9.

Subject 2, Story B-9: 1953

All right. This looks rather symbolic. Looks like a prisoner in jail who was rather sorry he did what he did and he's trying to repent and through the bars of the window he can see the church steeple very plainly and apparently this is what he's thinking of now. He's thinking of his past—what he's done, what he did to get here—and he's probably saying to himself why didn't he follow the way of the Lord. He's thinking it over and he looks very, very depressed, very unhappy because he is where he is and because of what he did to get there, and he's probably thinking of the better things in life and why he didn't follow in the path of righteousness. Well, it's a very symbolic picture, specially with the steeple here. It looks like he's trying to repent his sins, and possibly he will. From this, quietly sitting, I take it for a short time he will turn out to be a better man. He looks very sorry, very unhappy. Most of these pictures are unhappy. I don't know.

One sees here again the abandon and impulsiveness in 1940 which have disappeared in 1953 and in their place we find depression and guilt.

The first of the following pair of stories told by Ray (6), represents the typical adolescent's fantasies of mystery and spookiness which turn out to be a hoax.

Subject 6, Story A-6: 1940

Two men had committed suicide in a supposedly haunted house for some unknown reason, and the owner couldn't get anybody to rent it. A man who lived in another one of his buildings who owed him for three months rent was told that if he would stay in the house for a month to show people it wasn't haunted that he would give him a year's rent free. So he went to live there. One night in bed half asleep he heard weird, low music, so he got up to investigate. It seemed to come from upstairs in the attic. He climbed the stairs and when he got there the music stopped. He looked around and could find nothing. As he went down it started again. He listened for a moment and looked over to the corner. A bird had been caught in a spider's nest and had been living on insects. Every time he tried to get free he would brush up against this harp. From that day on there's never been thought of it's being a haunted house.

In 1953 this story becomes watered down to the following matter-of-fact story with its theme of responsibility and hopelessness. However, in this story there is also the theme of self-confidence, which is not present in the earlier story.

Subject 6, Story A-6: 1953

This is a small-town doctor being called on an early morning case to a man he knows is hopelessly ill and all he can offer him is some comfort before he finally does pass away. As he leaves he knows to himself that following days will only bring similar cases to which his power goes only so far.

There is a marked reduction after thirteen years in the number of stories showing overt aggression or even being aggressed against. Story B-9, told by Ralph and described above, illustrates this trend well. Additional illustrations are not needed here.

The foregoing analysis has been in terms of changes in themes over the thirteen-year interval. Perhaps a more important question concerns the tendency of subjects to retain their personality characteristics or to change them. This can be measured roughly by totaling the changes for each subject (without regard to algebraic sign) of the differences in each theme from 1940 to 1953. Table 14 gives the totals of these differences by subject. It will be noted that subject 2 has a total shift of theme count of 90 as compared with a total shift of 20 for subject 19, a ratio of 4.5 to 1. There appear to be great differences in the shift in number of themes among subjects.[3]

TABLE *14*. TOTALS OF DIFFERENCES IN OCCURRENCE OF THEMES FROM *1940* TO *1953*, BY SUBJECTS

Subject	Total change in theme	Subject	Total change in theme	Subject	Total change in theme
1	74	14	38	27	41
2	90	17	31	28	40
6	82	18	39	29	41
7	59	19	20	30	32
8	77	20	48	31	37
9	52	21	25	33	50
11	32	22	40	36	54
12	47	24	50	37	61
13	50	25	44	39	50
				40	37

Global Comparisons by Matching

This mathematical method of describing the stability or change in personality hardly tells one whether on the whole there is a marked or negligible shift in personality. One way of estimating stability of fantasy is to attempt to match the stories of subjects told thirteen years apart.

The 1940 and 1953 Series B stories of six subjects taken at random (subjects 1, 9, 17, 22, 31, 39) were given to assistants [4] to be matched.

[3] This rough measure of changes in individuals is in part an artifact. The measure (given in Table 14) correlates with total number of themes (1940–1953), .682, and with total number of ideas (1940–1953), .333 (the correlation between total number of themes and total number of ideas is .426). Hence it is not correct to say that the sum of differences for each individual represents the change in his personality, but only the change manifest from the changes in his stories. Naturally if a person told longer stories he had more room to change and if he told fewer stories there was less evidence on which to base an estimate of change although a change might actually have taken place.

[4] This matching was done by Dr. Robert Drummond, Mrs. Kit Lee Wong, and Mrs. Stephanie Dudek.

For each subject there were 10 stories (Series B) from the 1940 series stapled together, and the same 10 stories from the 1953 series. The six sets of 1940 stories were shuffled, as were the 1953 stories. Perfect matching was accomplished by one of the assistants and with only one shift in position by the other two assistants, indicating that the total personality as shown by the stories retained individual identity with remarkable fidelity.

The problem of matching individuals or of identifying an individual apparently has not received much attention from psychologists. One might ask how one recognizes a friend in a crowd or how one recognizes the burglar of the night before in the police lineup the next morning. This is done *most* surely by noting stigmata—unusual scars, blemishes, unusual features, and so forth—that could be possessed by one person in a million. It is not possible to identify an individual by those characteristics which everyone possesses—mouth, eyes, hair, chin, ears.

In the usual case we recognize our friends not by stigmata, although such distinguishing characteristics make the recognition most certain, but by patterns of characteristics that deviate perhaps only slightly from the normal. We recognize one friend because he has red hair, a broad forehead and a sharp chin. (That man is not the person whom we are seeking even though the hair is red and the forehead broad because the chin is not sharp.) Criminals know these facts and attempt to disguise themselves by shaving the mustache, growing a beard, dyeing the hair, or even undergoing plastic surgery.

One identifies a person, in addition to the foregoing methods, by a more detailed examination of any given characteristic. A man's complexion may be smooth or rough, his hair may have a slight wave in it. The mouth, which may be like the mouths of hundreds of other men in general, may wear a habitual expression of contempt or the trace of a smile. In identifying our friends we become sensitive to these very fine differences.

One matches the stories of one person with another not only by noting how they are similar to each other, but at the same time noting how a given story is unlike the stories told to the same picture by other individuals. To return to the problem of identifying a friend, one would eliminate one person after another who does not have the same pattern of characteristics of the friend we are looking for. (He is not my friend because his nose is too big, or he has sandy hair, or because he wears a bow tie or rimless glasses.) In other words, in comparing stories told to the same picture, one can frequently find characteristics in stories that are quite improbably those of the story with which one is trying to match.

Dr. Drummond noted the factors in the stories on which he based his matching. These factors broke up into two groups—the formal factors and the content or thematic factors. Actually the formal factors were more reliable indicators on which to base the matching. Apparently matters of style, language, special comments, fidelity to the picture, emotional tone, and the like are somewhat more prominent characteristics of an individual than are his fantasy themes.

This can be illustrated as follows. The 1940 and the 1953 stories of subject 1 often began sentences with verbs ("calls up friends") and there was a tendency to repeat ("this young girl is very happy," and "she's happy beyond words"). Subject 9 used the terms "young fellow" and "this fellow" in both sets. Subject 17 introduced many stories with "I think" or "I say." She was sensitive to the figures in the background ("girl in the background"). She made remarks about her stories ("I can't think of anything else"). Subject 22 first identified her characters ("man lives in the lowest part of town") and frequently used the word "this." Her characters tended to be impersonal (man, girl, husband) and her sentences tended to be short and choppy ("she made it all wrong. Sewed up the wrong parts").

Subject 31 tended to use proper names (Mary) and many names beginning with J (Jane, John Jones). The vocabulary tended to be limited. Many ideas were strung into one sentence ("He dressed slowly and carefully, went down for breakfast, and with great expectations walked out of the door.") Her stories showed an awareness of nature. Subject 39 went far beyond the picture in creating his stories. The last sentence in a story was frequently a summary sentence. He made an attempt to impress the examiner ("I'll make this one a little better than the others.").

These similarities are not so striking in the themes. To say that there is concern with moral values, a desire for independence, criminal themes, or a desire to be popular or successful hardly is an adequate basis for matching or personal identification because such themes are to be found in both the 1940 and the 1953 stories of so many individuals.

There are, however, also themes which are more or less peculiar to certain individuals. For instance, subject 1 showed unusual hostility to members of his family. In story B-5 the girls were jealous both times. Subject 9 showed strong feminine identification. Subject 17 expressed anxiety. Boy-girl relationships were desired. There was concern over failure or misfortune. Subject 22 showed concern over separation or rejection. Both sets of stories showed depression and there was frequent reference to death. Subject 31 showed a masculine identification. There were themes of concern over success and popularity. There was concern over problems of love and marriage. There was a strong sense of morality and signs of guilt if one deviated from accepted norms. Subject 39 showed great interest in erotic themes. He had a low opinion of women. Themes of concealment and crime appeared in both sets of stories.

As an illustration let us take one story, B-1, from the 1940 series and try to match it with one of six stories from the 1953 series.

Subject 22, Story B-1:1940

Man lives in the lowest part of town. Hasn't had a job in several months. Got an offer for job as chauffeur where his daughter has married into great riches. He leaves his house and on his way there he gets a heart attack and dies.

Subject A, Story B-1:1953

This could be a fella who just got his draft call, which is very common nowadays, takes it from the mail box there, types it out, and tries to enlist before he gets called into the Army as a foot soldier. So he goes down and he does this and he spends four happy years in the Navy or the Air Force, whatever it might be, and he comes back home and he's a single fella, young, probably groping around waiting for the call to come anyway. He gets back and everything works out all right.

Subject B, Story B-1:1953

This is a young fellow again and his teeth are gnashing, his fists are clenched and he's on his way out, dead set to do something. I don't know, seems like the weather outside is fairly nice. Someone has really told him [Trouble with recording and, when this was remedied, subject started new thought.] This fellow, to get back, is sixteen years old and he has gone up to his family and said, "I shall enlist." Very definitely, without any ifs, ands, or buts, and his parents have tried to talk to him, tried to rationalize that he's too young and shouldn't leave high school in the middle of his junior year and enlist. It's ridiculous and although he has his mind set on it, all his friends have gone in and he feels that he should do his part too. He's been definitely turned down and he is now leaving the house, dead set on doing it some way.

Subject C, Story B-1:1953

I'd say that this young man had just had some sort of, something to do with home. Whether it was an argument with his parents, something like that is causing him to leave. He looks like he might have a clenched fist or is a little bit angry or upset or something. He is going out. He looks determined like he's going to see someone and work something out about whatever he's quarreled about. That's what it looks like to me.

Subject D, Story B-1:1953

This is a man going off to work in the morning. He just had a fight with his wife—so it looks from his clenched fists and so on. He works in a factory. He is off for a day's work, he's a poor man, doesn't have too much money. Thinking that he never wants to come back to this house again. He will cool off at work and come home as he does every night and everything will turn out O.K.

Subject E, Story B-1:1953

The day dawned bright and cheery and everything had looked wonderful. This is the day Don was to meet his great adventure. He dressed slowly and carefully, went down for breakfast and, with great expectations, walked out of the door ready for the wonderful things that were to come his way that day.

Subject F, Story B-1:1953

It reminds me of a man going out of the house in the morning going to work. He's got about six kids and the youngest one kept him up all night and he's ready to lower the boom if anything comes up. He got downstairs. He must have fell asleep about six o'clock and his wife woke him up about seven. He decides he's going to sleep ten minutes more. He's going out the door now to go to work. He gets to work about ten minutes ahead of time with a chip on his shoulder to start with. The first thing, the guys are discussing the football game or the previous night's wrestling match and he right off the bat gets real grouchy and says "why don't you guys shut up and go to work." As soon as the guys hear this they really start to put the needle on him and they needle the guy and needle him. By the time noon time comes he's just shot as far as nerves go. He won't eat nothing for lunch. He goes to the cafeteria to be by himself. He gets a liverwurst sandwich and a cup of coffee. This guy drinks coffee—he's nervous. Then he goes home and the kids start in on him as soon as he gets in the house. He's got the same thing again. Then he stops and wonders, boy what a jerk he was to get married.

One can analyze the 1940 B-1 story as containing the following elements: (a) there is poverty, (b) a family relationship is mentioned, (c) a man is seeking work, (d) there is aggression ("he gets a heart attack and dies").

If we look at B-1, 1953, for subject A, we find a story of entering the service. For subject B there is a theme of defying his family in order to enlist. In subject C there is aggression with family, with feelings of anger. In subject D there is a theme of work, aggression with members of family, poverty. In subject E there is euphoria. In subject F the story is longer and more complicated; the main theme is disgust with family.

It is quite obvious that the original story is most similar to the later story of subject D and that happens to be the correct matching.

This identity may not always be as clear as in this instance, but usually there will be features in common in two comparable stories of a given individual that are not present with other individuals.

One must conclude that there is a remarkable persistence in both the formal and thematic factors over the thirteen-year interval so that it is possible to identify the person's stories at the later date from stories that he told at the earlier date. This is in contrast with the experimental evidence [5] showing that stories change their thematic emphasis whenever the individual has a new experience such as becoming hungry, afraid, or angry. Apparently these changes are made

---

[5] Sanford, R. N., "The Effects of Abstinence from Food upon Imaginal Processes: A Preliminary Experiment," *Journal of Psychology*, II (1936), 129-36.
Sanford, R. N., "The Effects of Abstinence from Food upon Imaginal Processes: A Further Experiment," *Journal of Psychology*, III (1937), 145-59.
Atkinson, J. W., and D. C. McClelland, "The Projective Expression of Needs: II. The Effect of Different Intensities of the Hunger Drive on Thematic Apperception," *Journal of Experimental Psychology*, XXXVIII (1948), 643-58.
Bellak, Leopold, "The Concept of Projection: An Experimental Investigation and Study of the Concept," *Psychiatry*, VII (1944), 353-70.
McClelland, D. C., R. A. Clark, T. B. Roby, and J. W. Atkinson, "The Projective Expression of Needs: IV. The Effect of Need for Achievement on Thematic Apperception," *Journal of Experimental Psychology*, XXXIX (1949), 242-55.
Rodnick, E. H., and S. G. Klebanoff, "Projective Reactions to Induced Frustration as a Measure of Social Adjustment," *Psychological Bulletin*, XXXIX (1942), 489.
Lindzey, Gardner, "An Experimental Examination of the Scapegoat Theory of Prejudice," *Journal of Abnormal and Social Psychology*, XXXXV (1950), 296-309.
Murray, H. A., "The Effect of Fear upon Estimates of the Maliciousness of Other Personalities," *Journal of Social Psychology*, IV (1933), 310-29.

within limits for a given individual and never stray very far from the individual's typical pattern. These findings ought to put to rest the popular notion that stories merely reflect some recent experience, such as the television program one witnessed the night before, or that the themes shift with every change of mood.

4. Correspondence between Adolescent Fantasy and Subsequent Experience and Personality

Each of the twenty-eight cases was carefully reviewed in search for possible correspondence between the fantasy themes in the 1940 stories and subsequent experiences or personality characteristics revealed in the 1953 interviews. Naturally a listing of such correspondence is subjective and depends in part on the sensitivity and attentiveness of the reviewer. Moreover, no restricted definition as to what was meant by a correspondence was set up. A correspondence might mean that an event in a story might have been lived out rather literally in actual life. For instance, Isabel (subject 18) told a story (A-1) in 1940 of a boy showing dependence upon and attachment to his home, and in 1953 she was still unmarried and living at home.

Or a correspondence might mean that an individual who included as a theme in one of the 1940 stories a certain relationship later on lived out a similar relationship in real life. For instance, Albert (subject 40) told stories (such as B-1) in 1940 about a boy who could not get along with his father. In actual life Albert has had ten different jobs, each of which he left because he could not get along with the boss.

Or the correspondence may not be so much a matter of conduct and performance as of personality. As an illustration, Pansy (29) told stories (such as A-4) [1] with masochistic implications. In real life Pansy became a nurse because she liked helping the sickest people, and she married beneath her status and lives in a poor neighborhood.

The correspondence may be one of feeling and attitude. Margaret

[1] The stories referred to in this chapter are those told by the subjects in 1940 when they were adolescent.

Adolescent Fantasy and Subsequent Experience

(24) told stories (such as B-8) with obvious Oedipal implications of hostility toward the mother and love for the father. She reported in her 1953 interview that before her marriage she was jealous of and hostile toward the mother of her future husband.

Or it is possible to see correspondences that require assumptions of a more tenuous character and that could be challenged as making too much out of what might be a mere coincidence. Unfortunately, with only the data at hand there is no way of proving that the correspondence has dynamic significance, and so some of the more speculative correspondences must be presented as very tentative.

Five types of themes that were observed to show correspondence between adolescent fantasy and later real life either in behavior, attitude, or personality are analyzed below. These are *dependency, eroticism, aggression, self-striving,* and *anxiety* with its defenses.

Dependency

Three groups of persons exhibiting dependency can be distinguished: (1) those who are still dependent—who still live in the parental home, or are devoted to wife, home, and family or other persons, who have yielded by giving up pleasure or by refusing to take responsibility; (2) those who have achieved independence or who are still struggling to break away; and (3) those who feel lonely and isolated, who have no close friends, who have difficulties with interpersonal relationships and who yearn for close relationships.

Two of the four subjects still living in the parental home told adolescent stories showing fear of being away from home and satisfaction at being home. Karl (11) showed his dependence by stories with themes of inordinate orality (such as B-6). Celia (28) told a story (B-10) of being afraid of being away from home alone. Isabel (18) told a story (A-4) of a boy who planned to visit another boy but whose mother was hurt by an automobile so he canceled the trip. Each of these three subjects still lives at home. One may speculate that Isabel lives at home in part because of guilt for deep hostile fantasies toward her parents.

In the case of Catherine (12), however, there is ambivalence. Whereas she told stories (such as A-1) of leaving home with considerable joyful anticipation ("he was looking forward to go to the school"), actually she lived at home with her mother when first married. This again may have been to assuage the guilt that she had for her great hostility and antagonism toward her mother as shown by the fact that following psychotherapy she was able to express these negative feelings openly. Later she left her parental home because, as was reported, she could not get along with her mother after she married, and she and her husband moved into an apartment. She says that she had feelings of guilt about her marriage after this, because of leaving her mother, whom she described as a very possessive and selfish woman.

Three of the subjects who have married show their dependence by their devotion to wife, home, and family. Jerome (7), who told a story (A-2) of being homesick when away from home and then found that his mother was dead when he returned home, speaks fondly of his wife and says he would like a dozen kids if he could afford it. Sam (9) told a story (A-7) of a boy who studied hard and became a great scientist to please his mother. Now he is reported to be quite fond of his wife, whom he describes as "an ideal wife." Seymour (36), who told a story (A-6) about an English boy whose house was bombed and who rushed into the wreckage to find his mother, "says he must never go out and leave her again." In real life Seymour leans heavily on his wife for guidance. "He lets his wife make most of the decisions. His wife usually gets her way and it is O.K. with him." Seymour is a man with little ambition and initiative, and he avoids taking responsibility.

Natalie (21) in one of her stories (B-3) showed the conflict between yielding to pleasure or observing the wishes of her parents. "Friend says he never thinks of what he wants to do, only what his mother wants him to do." In later life this is Natalie's own decision. She describes her life as "rather humdrum, drudging along the same old groove, day in and day out." It is interesting that she projects the reason for her restricted life on to her husband, who is described as a man with no cultural interests.

A second group consists of those who have broken away and achieved independence or who are striving to do so. This desire for independence is frequently coupled with hostility toward a parent. Pansy (29) showed her defiance of her parents and her desire to achieve independence of them by her marriage (see page 58). Celia (28) fantasied as an adolescent being independent of her parents (B-8) and as a mature unmarried woman living at home she still cherishes her

Adolescent Fantasy and Subsequent Experience 53

independence. Karl (11), described earlier as oral and dependent, fantasied leaving home as a boy (A-6), and while living at home in 1953 he still fantasies leaving home for bachelor's quarters. Jimmy (37), whose adolescent stories indicated a close tie with a mother, is still struggling to break away from these close ties in reality.

A third group exhibits a "burnt-child tendency." Having been disappointed in a relationship when a child they have become afraid of closeness as adults and as a result are lonely and isolated individuals.

Pansy (29), already referred to, told a story about losing friends (B-5). Now she complains that she has no close friends. This she projects by asserting that the people whom she knows are gossipy, but that she would be glad to help any of her neighbors if there were need.

Albert (40) in a significant story (A-2) projects his feelings of unworthiness onto a girl by asserting that "she doesn't enjoy his company" and so "he doesn't want to take advantage of her good nature." Even in 1953 Albert has difficulty in establishing a relation with a girl although there is a possibility that this may be modified through psychoanalysis, which he is now undergoing.

In three of the subjects there were fantasies of losing or being separated from a parent. Isabel (18) fantasied a story in which the mother was not at home (A-1). In actual life Isabel is afraid of any close relationships. Nancy (31) told stories of returning home (A-2, A-6, A-9). In real life, although married she yearns for a close relationship, which she is unable to achieve. She reports that "they do not go out much because they cannot afford it and they have to take care of the children. She feels lucky if she gets out to visit friends once a week. . . . Her husband's hobby is raising pigeons. . . . She said these pigeons are a pain in the neck to her, but her husband loves it." And Mabel (22) fantasied as an adolescent being left alone without a father (B-7). She married a man who travels and she actually had a miscarriage while her husband was away on one of his trips. Perhaps this is nothing more than a coincidence, but there is also a strong possibility that the fantasy was so strong that Mabel sought for an opportunity to work it out in reality.

Because of the complexity of personality it is difficult to summarize. In some instances adolescent fantasies have been lived out in reality. There is a presumption that in some of these cases this working out had a compulsive aspect. There is a displacement from parents to wife or husband or child. And in one instance the struggle has been idealized into the competition between family demands and pleasure. Ambivalence and conflict between being dependent and independent were noticed both in fantasy and in real life. In one instance the desire for independence, a fantasy in adolescence, is still a fantasy in later years. In one instance the adolescent struggle to achieve independence was still in process and had not been resolved. It appeared in some of the subjects that failure to achieve independence might have been due to guilt over hostile fantasies. Where dependence was recognized as undesirable the reason for it was projected on to another person.

Eroticism

Adolescent fantasy anticipates some of the characteristics of later love life. Three main tendencies can be recognized: (1) eager anticipation of sexual relationships, (2) fear of sex, and (3) homosexuality or cross-sexual identification.

Oedipal themes are common in adolescent fantasy and they have been clearly recognized in the stories of thirteen of the subjects (1, 8, 9, 12, 13, 14, 21, 24, 25, 30, 31, 36, 37). A superficial inspection would indicate that those who told stories with Oedipal themes were among the better adjusted and more stable of the subjects.[2] Usually when the Oedipal theme did not emerge in open expression, the subject had a need to work out themes of a more specialized sort.

In the 1940 stories of three of the subjects (19, 24, and 31) marriage was prominent and was held to be important. These three subjects were all women. It is significant that all three subjects did marry early and the marriages turned out to be stable and happy. Margaret (24) told stories (B-8, A-3) in which there was strong identification with father figures and hostility toward mother figures.

Dorothy (30) told stories in which a girl expressed strong feelings about living with and caring for her father. And, interestingly enough, in real life Dorothy has married an older man who is a father figure to

[2] This was checked statistically by comparing the rankings for adjustment of those who included Oedipal themes in their stories with the rankings of those who did not. Using the Kruskel-Wallis One-Way Analysis of Variance by Ranks the difference between these two groups was statistically significant at the .01 level of confidence. See W. H. Kruskel and W. A. Wallis, "Use of Ranks in One-Criterion Variance Analysis," *Journal of the American Statistical Association*, XXXXVII (1952), 583-621.

her. In her case the incest taboo is so strong that there is difficulty in sexual relations which Dorothy projects onto her husband, claiming that he is impotent. One can speculate that she may have deliberately chosen this kind of man as her mate.

In three cases there is clear-cut difficulty in sexual relationships that was foreshadowed in the stories. Karl (11), who is immature in many ways, told stories in which boy interest in girls is clearly missing. Karl had one romantic episode which he was unable to carry through and reports now that he has no love life.

John (39) seems to have very distorted sexual fantasies. At an early age he apparently associated sex with automobiles—both the excitement and the danger (A-5, A-8, B-8). Because of the danger in sex his relationships with women are distorted. He spends lavishly on models and actresses yet speaks very depreciatingly about women in general. He knows many "goddesses and beauties" but "is afraid to marry one of them because one of his friends married Miss Pennsylvania, a girl who won a state beauty contest, but they were divorced after a couple of months." John lived at home with his mother.

Isabel (18) told stories that indicate both a realistic (A-6) and symbolic and fantastic fear of sex (A-6). Isabel has never married and is a lonely, isolated individual.

In the case of the women, appearance is a very important aspect of being considered sexually desirable and wanted. So in the case of four of the subjects appearance occupies a prominent place in the adolescent stories and the reverberation of these fantasies is noticeable in later adult years. Barbara (20) told stories in which there was concern about appearance and now she is described as a "smart dresser." Celia (28), although attractive both as an adolescent girl and as a mature woman, in 1940 told stories (A-3) in which girl figures felt themselves to be unattractive. She now has the same feelings about herself and mentions that she scares men away and wonders if there is something about her that is repulsive. Celia has never married. Catherine (12) who is described as a healthy robust woman with a peaches and cream complexion told a story (B-2) about an ugly girl ("funniest looking girl in town") who went to New York and had her face lifted. In later life she states that she was frigid until she underwent psychotherapy. She was later found to be sterile and her physician told her that as a result of an earlier infection her Fallopian tubes were blocked off. After this condition was corrected by gynecological treatment she became pregnant. It is of course possible that this deformity of her sexual apparatus and her adolescent fantasies about appearance are similar only by coincidence. But it is also possible that concern about appearance and the need to have it corrected had symbolic reference to sexual adequacy even as early as adolescence.

Quite another outcome of adolescent concern about appearance is to be found in the case of Pansy (29). In adolescence her fantasies (B-5) revolved around the desire to make herself more attractive and opposition to this by a mother figure. In real life she was reported to be very shabby in her appearance with missing teeth conspicuous. In the case of Pansy there was apparently an introjection of the mother's point of view. Guilt because of certain oppositional tendencies on her part led to the adoption of a masochistic form of expression. From this we learn that it is untrustworthy and treacherous to attempt to predict from fantasy data. In every subject there are many concomitant forces operating and it is extremely difficult to tell which will have the determining influence.

The Picture-Story Test is admirably adapted to indicate sex identification because there are both male and female figures in the pictures. Sam (9) shows feminine identification in his stories. In later life there is evidence that he has identified with his mother in many ways, particularly striking in being nervous. During the war he was hospitalized for "battle fatigue" while his mother had a series of nervous breakdowns. Barbara (20) showed strong masculine identification in her stories and as an adult openly questions whether she is satisfied with her role as a woman.

Laura (13) showed strong hostility toward mother figures in her stories which had obvious Oedipal themes. In one story in which the mother was dead and the father went away on a trip the main character in the story stayed with a girl friend. Apparently a homosexual crush is a defense against the full impact of the Oedipal fantasies. Now Laura claims that she is very close to an older woman in the office in which she works.

In summary the stories told in adolescence anticipate some of the attitudes later to be revealed in real life toward sex and erotic relationships. Subjects who told stories in which themes of romance, love and marriage were prominent married early and in general these marriages were successful. But other subjects whose stories revealed either openly or symbolically that sex was dangerous or unimportant to them have not married or have had difficulty in establishing heterosexual relationships. Appearance is important to the woman as a sign of sexual desirability and effectiveness. Cross-sexual identification in the stories may indicate either strong identification tendencies with the opposite sex or homosexual tendencies. However, it is difficult to generalize because in each case the particular adjustment and attitude toward sex has its own particular form and since many trends are always present it is not possible to know which will turn out to be predominant.

Aggression

In *Adolescent Fantasy* it was reported that aggression was a universal characteristic of adolescence. It was also reported that in a number of cases the aggression that appeared in the stories did not have a counterpart in real life, and in a number of instances the subjects who told stories with the most aggression were themselves meek and mild individuals. It will be of interest, therefore, to find how the aggression as displayed in the stories revealed itself in later life.

In four of the subjects (2, 8, 9, 11, all male) who told stories with much aggression it appears that aggression is one of their characteristics in later life. Ralph (2) apparently directed his aggressiveness into hard work and the struggle to succeed. Roger (8) showed sibling rivalry and hostility toward mother figures (B-4 and B-6) in adolescent fantasy. Roger's aggressiveness in real life appears in sporadic outbursts. His hostile impulses get out of hand "especially at salesmen who try to be engineers and go over his head in making decisions." He has a severe temper, is highly competitive with other men, and has a fear of failure and a sense of inferiority. Sam (9) also transfers his adolescent aggressiveness into energetic ambition and determination to succeed in his work. Aggressiveness is a problem with which he has to contend. Most of the time he can keep himself under firm control but occasionally when he gets pushed too far he will "really blow his top." Karl (11), with less ego control, becomes angry much more easily under slight provocation.

In six of the subjects (12, 13, 14, 21, 24, and 29) the adolescent fantasy depicted strong hostility toward mother figures. It is undoubtedly more than a coincidence that these were all girls. In the case of three of the subjects (13, 14, and 29) marriage was undertaken over the vehement protest of the mother. Laura (13), although described as "sweet," overly polite, prim, and submissive, married a Catholic in spite of her mother's energetic protests. The mother will have nothing to do with Laura's husband and has all but disowned Laura herself. Laura claims that this was the first time she ever felt like defying her mother. Previously she had always done whatever her mother wanted and she seemed never to have any desires of her own. The mother said, "I will give you three days to decide whether you love me or [her future husband] more."

Viola (14) reacted in a similar fashion to a dominating mother. In her adolescent stories there are themes of rebellion against mother figures. In one story the heroine marries and the aunt that opposed the marriage dies, foreshadowing the actual events that later took place in Viola's life.

Pansy (29), reared a Protestant, has married twice—the first time a Catholic and the second time a Negro Catholic priest, who gave up the priesthood for factory work. As a result of these marriages her parents have completely disowned her and she is out of communication with them. Her adolescent stories depicted mother figures as scolding, domineering, and critical, and one story (A-10) fantasied her desire and intention to become independent of her parents. Although she tends to be masochistic as a person, her marriages express in dramatic fashion her desire to become independent of her parents and to hurt them in doing so.

In the case of the other three subjects (12, 21, and 24) mother hostility expresses itself differently. Catherine (12) as an adolescent girl was unable to express any hostility toward her parents—"They are the best parents in the world." It was not until she had undergone psychotherapy that she became able to criticize her mother and to say "There is not one thing I like her for." However this hostility was expressed in her adolescent stories when she depicted mother figures as bad and punitive. These themes in the adolescent stories were quite mystifying as they seemed to correspond to nothing in the girl herself. The meaning of the adolescent fantasy was not revealed until years later through psychotherapy.

Margaret (24) too, was unable to express hostility to her mother in

Adolescent Fantasy and Subsequent Experience

real life either as a girl or at present as a woman. However, her adolescent fantasies contained Oedipal themes with competition and struggle with a mother figure. In the case of Margaret this hostility has expressed itself openly in her attitude toward her mother-in-law. Everywhere the feelings are reversed projectively and she accuses her mother-in-law of being bitter about the marriage and causing her (Margaret) a great deal of heartache.

In the case of Natalie (21) the hostility clearly expressed in adolescent fantasy (see story B-4) is repressed and she impressed the interviewer as being dull and colorless.

This illustrates very well the point that any dynamic trend may have any of a number of vicissitudes. This makes it difficult if not impossible to predict from fantasy material alone. But these cases also seem to indicate that the direction of hostility adopted in adolescence persists into adult life. But in the case of the marriages there were instances where the instigation piled up and eventually hostility broke through into active expression which had not been possible before.

In two of the subjects dominance by the mother still persists. Celia (28) describes a dominating mother figure in her 1940 stories (B-1). Celia is still unmarried and lives at home apparently quite satisfied to continue the relationship in which her mother has a ruling hand.

Sam (9), who told stories including mother figures who were controlling and dominating, now describes his wife in these same terms "A very nice girl, very attractive and very strong willed."

In two of the cases the hostility is directed toward the father in fantasy, one a girl Mabel (22) and one a boy Albert (40). Mabel (22) told a story about a boy who becomes angry when he is told by his father that he cannot go out. In real life Mabel gets angry when her husband complains that she spent too much for a dress or a hat, or something similar. In other words the fantasied feelings of hostility toward father in adolescence are now directed toward husband in reality.

Albert (40) exemplifies hostility which was expressed in adolescence in fantasy toward father figures and is expressed toward bosses in later life. In all, Albert has had ten different jobs since leaving school, and in most of them he left after a few months following a quarrel or disagreement with the boss. Here father hostility was worked out in real life. Albert is now in psychoanalysis and there is an indication that his father hostility may be modified with a corresponding change in his attitude toward work. "He claims that he is always fighting with his analyst and always trying to bring the analyst down to the level of himself." Incidentally, Albert is critical of Eisenhower and MacArthur.

Aggression also shows itself in sibling rivalry. Sibling rivalry is prominent in the stories of Edith (subject 17, stories A-5 and A-8). In her case this rivalry showed itself in real life most clearly by the reaction formation of a feeling of altruism and responsibility for the members of her family. She spoke in the interviews affectionately and admiringly of her sisters and her mother and father. In her adolescence she fantasied death to a member of her family (B-5). Story B-6 was about a man who failed in something that he attempted to do and worried about what would become of his dependents. The death of her son when he was sixteen months old was the tragic event in her life. The child had a virus infection and, confident of her own ability to nurse it, she waited too long in getting medical help. It is highly speculative to attribute psychological significance to this event, and if unconsciously Edith did have a hand in the boy's death it certainly was overdetermined. There is a possibility that it was an acting-out of the old sibling hostility which was all but stifled in her relations to her own family. One may also speculate that there was guilt and self-punishment for her earlier hostile fantasies toward her siblings. In describing the episode Edith spoke of her failure in connection with it. Since she herself sees this as a failure on her part one may speculate that failure has been an obsession in her fantasy life which she had to work out in real life.

Stella (19) is another subject who reacted to sibling rivalry by reaction formation. Both in actual life and in fantasy as an adolescent Stella displayed sibling rivalry (story A-8). When a child, Stella associated with an older set and resented having her younger sister go places with her, but in later years she attended college with her sister and they had a double wedding, indicating that there was warm and positive feeling underlying the hostility and competition.

Celia (28) told a story (A-9) of a chambermaid who was envious and wished "she could meet someone she could marry who would give her the things she wants." Celia has two sisters, who have married. She stated in the interview that "she has always admired her sister greatly and wishes she could be more like her." But about her other sister she said, "after seeing what happened to her sister who became divorced, she claims that she is going to think twice before she marries." On the other hand, "she wonders at times if something is lacking in her that she isn't married since all of her girl friends are married."

To summarize this section on aggression, the expression of fantasy aggression has many vicissitudes. In the case of some of the boys, aggression in the stories obviously expressed itself in later life through hard work, striving, and effort to get ahead. It may appear in an aggressive personality, or it may be acted out only sporadically in an otherwise passive person.

There was mother hostility in six of the girls. In three of these the girl was described as quiet, demure, submissive, but rebellion showed itself in marriage against the mother's wishes. In other instances the girl still lives at home, unmarried, apparently never rebelling against a dominating mother.

There was also father hostility. In both instances aggressiveness is displaced, in the case of a woman onto her husband and in the case of a man onto his bosses.

Sibling rivalry is frequently expressed in fantasy and there is reaction formation against it in real life. Repressed hostility may arouse guilt, which finds expression in sundry ways.

Self-Striving

Adolescent fantasy abounds in themes of self-striving, of success and failure, of self-confidence and feelings of inferiority. The material was inspected to ascertain what relation there is between these fantasies and later experiences of success and failure.

Three of the subjects can be said to be successful in the popular sense of the term denoting social prestige. One of these, Sam (9), told an adolescent story with an Oedipal theme of the father dead and the boy responding to his mother's ambition so that he became "one of the greatest scientists ever and president of an experimental scientific concern." Sam now works very hard as an electrical contractor and has charge of the business now that his father has retired. But, as has been commented on elsewhere, Sam is a nervous individual and although he is energetic and masterful in his work he married a strong-willed woman like his mother.

John (39) also illustrates the story of a man who according to his own words is highly successful. In his adolescent stories there is a theme of mother ambition for a son (A-7), but also fear of failure and of not having enough to eat (B-6). By hard work and study John has risen to be foreman in an auto plant and he claims that he has consistently received promotions of greater responsibility and higher pay. But John lives at home with his mother and is obviously maladjusted in his relations with women.

Mabel (22), from a material point of view, is highly successful in that she has married a business man and lives in a four-bedroom house with two television sets and a full-time maid. In one of her stories (A-8) she tells of a girl who is a great success after she fixes herself up and has her hair dyed.

It is significant to note the extent to which these subjects identify education, and particularly a college education, with success. Jerome (7) told stories which indicate that he puts a high premium on education. In one story (A-5) he tells about a girl whose brother was putting her through college. She felt like quitting and then decided that education would help her get a better job so that she could repay her brother. "She gets education and a good job." But in real life Jerome is anything but a success—he is a salesman in a retail liquor store. He has studied to be a dental technician, was at one time a filer in a factory, and more recently has taken courses and read books on liquor because he would like to become a liquor salesman on the road, but no one has offered him this job.

Although Julia (25) told a story about a girl who liked to read and wanted to go to college if her family could afford it, this was pure fantasy. She did not go to college but married instead, and now states that she never wanted to go to college. But she married a graduate of Boston College and in the interview discussed the importance of having a college man for a husband. In spite of her ambitions Julia now lives in a very poor section of the city in the upstairs part of a two-family house.

In the case of Stella (19) her fantasies of going to college (B-6) worked themselves out in reality: she attended and graduated from Rutgers University. In her interview she makes it appear that she attended college largely to satisfy her father's wishes and ambitions, but it is also clear that she was motivated in part by rivalry with her sister, as described above in the section on aggression.

There were also stories with fantasies of greatness and wealth, but in the case of these subjects such fantasies did not eventuate in reality. For instance, Julia (25) mentioned above, told fanciful stories of high status and wealth. The girl in story B-8 went to live with her divorced father, who sent her to a very nice school because he was wealthy. Julia had an elaborate and expensive wedding and then went to live in very modest, ordinary circumstances. Julia apparently is satisfied with her life if she can have occasional showy but insubstantial indulgence. Even now she indulges in unrealistic fantasy without any evidence that it will be possible of fulfillment. She hopes to be able to move into a new home in a better neighborhood.

Edwin (33) fantasied greatness (story A-7). He told a story of a boy who was one of the school's best scholars and who was trying to be valedictorian of his class. But other stories showed feelings of inferiority. Edwin has failed in business and is now an unhappy salesman in a store.

Seymour (36) told the success story of a man who adopted a strange youth and willed him his estate and fortune. Seymour still fantasies greatness but after many different kinds of work he is now a letter carrier. To show the ethereal nature of his ambitions, he was emphatic in asserting that he did not wish to assume greater responsibilities.

In this regard Wallace (1) is in a class by himself. As a boy Wallace was cocky and smart-alecky and this same bumptiousness also characterized his stories. There were themes of grandiosity and omnipotence. He was sensitive to questions of status and superiority-inferiority. There was evident class consciousness and prejudice. He was overconcerned with a person's front and the impression he made. All these themes that were in his adolescent fantasy characterize him as a man. He is cocky and competitive. The impression that he makes on others is important to him. He is prejudiced and opinionated and is keenly aware of his status.

There were two subjects who told stories of failure and ineffectiveness. Ralph (2), for instance, told a story of a girl who was ineffectual. Due to an accident she could not walk, but she saw all the other boys and girls having fun walking by. Ralph was told in high school that he was not college material but in spite of this he attended Carnegie Institute of Technology. There he worked very hard for a C plus average and hopes he will graduate the coming year.

Roger (8), already mentioned, told the story of a boy who would not cooperate, never did anything, never went to dances or washed dishes, and who played hooky from school. This boy came to a bad end. Roger had difficulty in getting through college and has failed to rise in his present job.

Edith (17) has already been discussed. One of her stories told of a man who failed. Edith has failed as a mother in the death of her infant son. There is a suspicion that she may have had a compulsion to fail.

Feelings of inferiority and inadequacy were present in adolescent fantasy. Olive (27) related stories containing distinct themes of self-abasement; and today, as a mature woman, she still exhibits this depressed tone with feelings of unworthiness.

Edwin (33) told stories with themes of timidity and feelings of inferiority indicating great insecurity covered over by self-conceit. Toward attractive girls in his stories he took a "sour-grapes" attitude—they were silly and spoiled. Is it a coincidence that he married a girl with one leg missing—lost in an automobile accident?

There are plenteous illustrations among these subjects of the phallic woman, both from the men and the women. Four of the women in the study (subjects 12, 14, 20, and 28) fantasied men as weak and ineffective. Catherine (12), for instance, says in one of her stories that she could not marry a man shorter than she (story A-7). "When she finally got home and saw him she found he was three inches shorter than she was and she told him she would never marry a man shorter than she was and that she would never see him again. Tragic ending to a love story." Ironically, Catherine married a small, quiet, soft-spoken man.

Viola (14) told of a man (story B-1) who lost confidence in himself. He took up peddling as a last resort, and he became discouraged and despondent. Viola, too, married a man like that. She would have married during college but the man was too indecisive. Later they eloped and lived for a while in Louisiana. When she returned to the North "her mother came to their home only a few blocks away after they had been married two or three months just when Viola was arguing with her husband's aunt. Her mother thought that this was no environment for her daughter, so she packed her daughter's suitcases and took her home,

Adolescent Fantasy and Subsequent Experience 65

against which Viola made little resistance." So she was cut off from her husband. Her husband did not even come to see her although he lived just a few blocks away. But later they would meet on the sly and finally eloped a second time, this time to Chicago where her two children were born.

Celia (28), who has never married, told stories in which men are described as being like little boys because they need to be watched, scolded and supervised. Today Celia refers to her father as "my poor dad" and "my poor pop." She stated "poor pop has a back seat in our family," and she does not have a very high opinion of him.

Barbara (20) is a woman with an obvious masculine identification. In one story (A-10) a father was killed. A fortune teller said: "There will be a great misfortune in your life. I see a car driving along a highway at night. In this car there is a man hurrying home to his wife and child. It is raining and the highway is very wet. All of a sudden the car skids and goes off a steep embankment. This man is your father. He is killed instantly." The symbolic significance of this story need not be commented on. See John, in the section on anxiety, below.

Barbara's father in real life was pictured as fiery and quick-tempered, and she was identified closely with him. She stated that she would want a man to be something like a boss, someone who would put his foot down sometimes to keep her in line. She would not want a man who would give in to her too easily. But in another story she depicted men as weak. Actually, when her father died he left large debts and the family had to pitch in to straighten out his financial affairs. To Barbara, a relationship with a man was competitive. "She claims that she likes a good fight or a good argument once in a while regardless of what it is about. . . . She claims that she also gets in fights with fellows just to start things up . . . she has never wanted to be a man but she wants them to know that she is as good as they are."

On the other hand, two of the boys saw women as castrating. Ralph (2) depicted women in his stories as strong and masterful. There were obvious castration fantasies in his long and rambling stories. Ralph had delayed marriage and it is possible that his fear of the dominating, castrating woman was responsible for his delay in marrying the girl that he had been going with for two years.

The best illustration of this is to be found in John (39). John told stories involving speeding and crashing automobiles with obvious sexual symbolism indicating the danger in sexual relations. John is unmarried and lives with his mother, but goes out with models and actresses and boasts of his conquests of them, although he shunned marriage. He saw women as heartless, disinterested, and fickle.

In sum, the real life of subjects illustrates both success and failure, but the fantasy themes may find expression in real life in diverse ways. Education seems to be a common symbol of success. In some instances reference to education in the stories led to ambition and striving in real life; but in other instances it never got beyond fantasy and there were idle dreams even in adult life of how one would rise through education. In some instances, fantasies of easily acquired wealth and success did not find expression in anything tangible in actual life. Fantasies of grandeur and omnipotence were likely to find expression in the ebullient personality; whereas fantasies of feelings of inferiority led to lives of ineffectiveness and struggle to compensate for one's imagined deficiencies. The masculine phallic woman was represented in several subjects, both by women who tended to despise men and by men who were afraid of the masterful woman.

Anxiety, Depression, and Defenses against Anxiety

Finally, the stories included obvious references to anxiety and to several defenses that were raised against anxiety.

Roy (6) indicated much anxiety in his stories by introducing themes of mystery, of strangeness that would cause chills to run up the spine and then turn out to be Hallowe'en pranks. In real life Roy is stolid, placid, overcontrolled. But he is also tense and inhibited in speech and manner. This exterior covers up turmoil within. He states that he has high blood pressure under stress.

Depression not identical with, but related to anxiety, appeared in adolescent fantasy, and as the statistical analysis in Chapter Three shows, occurred with increasing frequency in real life.

Edith (17) is one individual who told stories with a depressed mood. In real life she has recently experienced a depressive episode. This is to be explained, perhaps too simply, as the result of mourning following the death of her infant son. But this is obviously too simple an explanation in this complicated case, for the seeds of depression were

Adolescent Fantasy and Subsequent Experience 67

present in adolescent fantasy. One speculative explanation is that the depression is a result of repressed sibling rivalry.

Olive (27), when seen as a high-school girl, was a sad, colorless individual and her inhibited stories corresponded to the impression she gave the examiner. As a mature woman she is still a drab, forlorn, poor person.

Two of the subjects complained of the dullness of life (subjects 21, 28). Natalie (21), in one of her adolescent stories, complained of the boredom in life, and today she reports that she finds life dull. There was much anxiety in her 1940 stories. This complaining attitude was one that she easily adopted in response to a dominating, pushing mother. While it is true that her husband is a dull, narrow, uninteresting man, it is obvious that Natalie has carried her complaining attitude down from childhood—and one may speculate that she was attracted to the man she married because he gave her an opportunity to continue into married life the kind of adjustment she had adopted in her earlier surroundings.

Celia (28) also told stories with a somewhat sombre cast. A-5 was about a "dejected high school boy." B-6 told of a "young high school girl—on way home from school. Perhaps she is tired. Looks pensive." Today Celia is not married but marriage is her goal. She is described as listless and depressed. She is bored and filled with ennui toward life. This attitude was also present thirteen years earlier.

Intellectualization is a favorite defense among adolescents today. Viola (14) told stories indicating intellectual and aesthetic interests. In real life she has taken part in amateur dramatics while in college and also later in Louisiana. During the interview she placed stress on intellectual ability. She was second in her high school graduating class and seemed proud of her intellectual ability. Viola, it will be remembered, is the one who eloped in order to marry against her mother's wishes. As a matter of fact, there is nothing in the record to indicate that Viola has unusual intellectual or scholarly interests. Actually, as she describes her husband, who majored in Business Administration in college, it appears that he had better abilities than she.

Olive (27), who has been described as very depressed, told stories showing intellectual yearnings and in the interview she tried to impress the interviewer with her intellectual interests. She believes that a good education is important and wants one for her child. She told the interviewer that she liked lectures and that she especially likes an eloquent speaker, no matter what he talks about. Although she stated that she liked good music, the interviewer gained the impression that she had been to very few concerts and hence knew very little about music. She makes it a point to read at least one book a year. Her favorite magazine is *Look*. She emphasized that her husband is not as intellectual as she.

Stella (19) as a girl told stories filled with high superego standards. Characters were polite, aggression was obviously repressed. In story A-4 a man tried to cheat a boy who delivered papers. "Boy decided to leave his job instead of causing any more trouble." As a girl Stella was quiet and conscientious and not overly aggressive. As a woman she is described as tense, anxious, worrying, and afraid of a nervous breakdown. This illustrates well the strain of the hypermoralistic attitude adopted in adolescence (and before), with the result (in this case, at least) of increasing tension and anxiety.

Pansy (29) illustrates the defense against anxiety by masochism. She told a story (A-4) in which a man was trying to teach his son right and wrong. He showed the boy two piles of money—one large, the other small—and asked his son which he would take. When the boy indicated the larger pile the father became angry and said, "You should learn to take smaller things and leave larger things for others." Pansy became a nurse and took the most difficult assignments. She was most interested in urogenital disorders and in cancer. It excited her to see patients come in desperately ill and then to see them make a recovery and to think that she had a hand in it. She especially liked the charity ward because the patients there seemed more grateful. She now lives in a very poor district and has three children—and will take as many children as the Lord gives her.

John (39), already mentioned several times, has made hard work part of his life philosophy. As an adolescent he told a story of a young fellow who became a salesman to distribute a national magazine. "He continued to climb until he became a manager of men. To all fellows who call on him for advice he tells them 'If you want to succeed you have to work hard.'" John has put his advice into practice himself. Of 79 persons from the local automobile assembly plant he was the only one to remain in, and graduate from, a training course given at the company's headquarters. He claims that he has consistently received promotions to positions of greater responsibility and higher pay. One has to view his earlier anxieties about fear of failure and actual fear of not having enough to eat to recognize this hard work and striving as a defense against anxiety.

Although Edith's (17) stories were very realistic, she speaks of herself as an idealistic person. She has a deep sense of obligation toward others. In one of her stories (B-9) the condemned man was not "sorry for himself but for someone who depends on him or her and what will happen to that person after he is dead or she is dead." And now in real life Edith has a feeling of responsibility toward the members of her family. This may be interpreted as a reaction formation to hide the sibling rivalry which was so prominent in her at one time.

Karl (11) had bizarre and childish references to food and eating in his stories. As a man he boasts of his prowess in drinking. He claims that he can drink a whole bottle of liquor in one evening and not get a hangover. He claims that he has never been extremely drunk, never to a point where he would lose his self-control and self-respect. The contradiction here is apparent. He shows his immaturity in his emphasis on drinking, but he also shows his need to deny his inferiority by boasting about his drinking.

Dorothy (30) is a person who has a great need to hide the truth about herself. This was true even as an adolescent. In one story (A-1) a boy who found himself lonesome in the big city decided "to write to mother saying that he likes it even though he doesn't." In another story (A-5) a girl refused an invitation from a boy to go to the prom —"said she didn't want to go but really did, but didn't have a gown." As an adult woman she tried to assure the interviewer that she was happily married—"She stated that they got along all right together" —but said this in a rather half-hearted way and the interviewer suspected that the marriage might not be wholly satisfactory. In a later session it was brought out that the husband was sexually impotent. One may surmise further that Dorothy in marrying an older man is still bound by the incest taboo and that the difficulty in establishing satisfactory sexual relations may be in part due to her own problems.

Jimmy (37) clearly portrays his struggle with anxiety in his "search for himself." In one of his stories (A-1) he told about a youth trying to find himself in the cold, heartless city. "He writes poems, short stories, novels about the great city. His work was not discovered and appreciated until after his death. He always knew while alive that the heart (of the city) was warm, but never realized that it was he that was part of that heart (in other words, searching for self, I guess)." Actually, Jimmy took up writing while in high school and when he returned home from war he set about writing a lengthy novel—in an effort to work through the problem of his separate identity from his mother.

Finally, pathology is clearly depicted in some of the stories. Sam (9) told of being "sick in the head" or crazy. As an adult he describes himself as a nervous person. The case of Karl (11) was somewhat puzzling. His stories were very bizarre and preoccupied with numbers and other precise details. Dr. Jensen described the 1940 stories as follows:

The stories have little continuity and jump from one idea to another much too readily and without any logic. The stories are mixed up, impulsive, and with signs of poorly developed secondary-process thinking. Incongruous ideas pop up and are put together in a story whether or not they make any logical sense. Often there appears to be no connection between thought, word, feeling, and action.

The bizarre character of the stories is also present in the 1953 interview—immature tone, illogical twists, sudden shifts in viewpoint, preoccupation with numbers. There apparently is an absence of delusional thinking, hence he cannot be called schizophrenic, but there is no doubt but that he is able to maintain his balance in part because he lives in the shelter of his parental home.

Ralph (2) told the story (A-3) of a girl who had an accident and an operation on her stomach. "Doctors had to cut piece of rock out of stomach and sew it." It is perhaps more than a coincidence that in later life he had stomach ulcers. In the inquiry following story A-3 when it was told in 1940 Ralph said: "My mother had an operation on her stomach and my father, he has ulcers of the stomach." The story undoubtedly revealed the fantasies that Ralph invented as a result of the happenings in his family and his own ulcers indicate identification with his father in methods of defense against anxiety.

Nancy's (31) stories showed a cyclical tendency. Most of the stories had a euphoric character (B-8), but some had a depressed tone. Nancy reported in her interview that she alternated between being very short-tempered and down in the dumps and grumpy to being very easy-going and happy.

In this section illustrations have been given to show that there is a marked parallel between the anxiety and defenses against anxiety in adolescent fantasy and in personality in later life. The correspondence is more marked here than in some of the previous sections. Apparently if a person is anxious in adolescence he will carry the pattern of anxiety down to later years, and the defenses that he adopts against anxiety—repression, projection, intellectualization, masochism, escape into work, responsibility for others—is the pattern repeated in later life. Examples are also given to indicate that psychosomatic or psychotic trends that appear in adult life may also be revealed in adolescent fantasy.

The foregoing comparison of adolescent fantasy and subsequent experience and personality makes an impressive story. But a critical reader might say, "You have merely pointed out correspondences—or rather, the coincidences—that are apparent between adolescent fantasy and material in the interviews thirteen years later. How do you know that there are not just as many themes in the adolescent stories that do not have any counterpart in the current interviews?" To be really convincing it is necessary to attempt to trace in later experience evidences of the working out of every theme in adolescent fantasy.

Naturally this is an impossible task. Not only do we not have the resources for such an elaborate analysis, but the interview material itself is by no means detailed enough to reveal all possible connections between fantasy and later behavior.

A token investigation was made by tracing vicissitudes in later life of the aggression which was revealed in adolescent fantasy. It may be remembered that aggression was found to be a theme in every one of the original forty subjects. However, in some cases the aggression was exceedingly mild and in others it was passive, directed against rather than by the subject.

First, let us review and summarize the discussion of aggression presented in the earlier pages of this chapter. Fifteen subjects referred to in the discussion all had showed obvious aggression in their stories. Two of them (subjects 2 and 9) who told typical adolescent stories of adventure and crime now have turned their aggression into hard work, energetic ambition, and struggle to succeed. Two of them (8 and 11), originally described as mild and even-tempered, as adults had sporadic outbursts of occasional anger under strong provocation. Six told stories of hostility toward mother figures. Three of these (13, 14, and 29) married against their parents' wishes as a sign of rebellion although as adolescents they were known to be docile and apparently cooperative. One (12) could express hostility toward her mother only after psychotherapy; one (24) could express hostility toward her mother-in-law but not toward her mother; and one (21) was depressed and bored, a pattern also shown in adolescence.

Two subjects told stories with themes of dominating mothers. One (28) still lives at home unmarried with her dominating mother; the other (9) had a dominating wife. Two told stories with themes of father hostility. One (22) gets angry at her husband; the other (40) gets angry at his bosses. Two (17 and 19) showed sibling rivalry in adolescent fantasy and in both instances there was strong reaction formation against sibling rivalry as adults.

What about the other thirteen subjects not mentioned in this discussion? Ten of these can be described as nonaggressive, mild persons. Roy (6), whose fantasy aggression tended to be of the sly, sneaky variety (spying, counterfeiting), is now a very overcontrolled man suffering from high blood pressure. Jerome (7), who had death wishes toward mother figures in fantasy followed by guilt and a desire to reform others, is described as not very forceful and anxious about his work. Isabel (18), who told stories with strict, punitive mother figures, today is most unaggressive and does not like to boss others. Julia (25), whose stories referred to punitive father figures, also is not aggressive and would not like to sell. Olive (27), a depressed, unassertive person both in adolescence and adulthood, told stories with feelings of unworthiness, inadequacy, disillusionment, guilt feelings, and masochistic fantasies. Sibling rivalry experienced in fantasy shows itself today in vague comparison of herself with others in regard to intellect. Dorothy (30), with little aggression in her stories, is described as a nervous person who does not want to have to boss others. Edwin (33) in 1940 told one story of a man who unfeelingly murdered his best friend. On the whole his stories were anxious and depressed, containing feelings of inferiority, timidity, and expectations of rejection. As a man he is lethargic and utterly without ambition. Seymour (36) told dependent stories of being the recipient of aggression. As a man he is easy-going with a nervous stomach. Jimmy (37) told stories rich in Oedipal themes. In general he is a mild, permissive man, but will

Adolescent Fantasy and Subsequent Experience 73

assert himself under provocation. Nancy (31) whose stories are remarkably free from aggression, has cyclic tendencies. On the whole happy, she has occasional spells of depression.

Then there are three subjects who are on the aggressive side. Wallace (1) told stories with themes of aggression toward both father and mother figures as well as sibling rivalry. Today Wallace shows strong rivalry and competition with men. John (39) who told stories in which subjects used aggression constructively to reform others and were ambitious in reality drives the men under him hard and is annoyed when they fail to come up to his expectations. Barbara (20), who told stories of hostility toward father figures and expressed themes of sibling rivalry, has strong masculine identification and competitive relationships with men.

From this survey it is difficult if not impossible to generalize about the correspondence of character and fantasy. Wallace (1) includes aggression in his stories and he is also aggressive and competitive in real life. Dorothy (30) includes little aggression in her stories and she says that she does not like to have authority over others. Roger (8) who told stories with much aggression is described as a mild person, but there will be sporadic outbursts of anger. Ralph (2), who showed much aggression in his stories, apparently exercises it by hard work and the struggle to succeed.

One may safely say that aggression in fantasy means that the individual has aggressive impulses. How they will be expressed in reality cannot be definitely predicted. One may be sure that they will find expression in one form or another. In some instances the aggression will find expression in the aggressive personality (Wallace, subject 1). But in many others the open expression of aggression is inhibited, displaced, or disguised. In many instances rebellious tendencies may be repressed, only to find expression eventually when the provocation is great—as in the case of marriage against the mother's wishes (Laura, 13; Viola, 14; and Pansy, 29).

It would be reasonable to assert that other themes in fantasy likewise represent impulses in the life of the person. Sometimes these impulses find open expression in personality—in other instances they are repressed, and will be expressed rarely or sporadically in impulsive fashion or in disguised or displaced mechanisms.

5. Change in Fantasy Related to Experience

In Chapter Three statistical facts regarding the shift in fantasy from 1940 to 1953 were presented. In the present chapter we will look closer at these changes in fantasy and attempt to relate them to the intervening experiences. Like the attempt to relate adolescent fantasy to subsequent personality, this is a highly speculative undertaking. Not only would it be speculative with wholly satisfactory data to try to determine cause-and-effect relationships between shifts in fantasy and intervening experiences, but the data themselves seem coarse and crude for this purpose.

It should first be stated that our main observation concerns not the change in fantasy from 1940 to 1953 but the remarkable constancy of fantasy over this thirteen-year interval. Taking cases almost at random the following are typical comments made by Dr. Jensen in comparing the stories:

Seymour, subject 36. In 1953 there is a remarkable repetition of the 1940 themes of passivity, being a victim of circumstances and being rescued from his difficulties. The easy come, easy go philosophy leads to failure.

Pansy, subject 29. The 1953 stories represent the same themes that are present in the 1940 stories with very little change. However, in 1953 the dynamics are expressed more directly and with less need for defensive tactics.

Celia, subject 28. There is a marked repetition of themes in the 1953 stories. Father figures are again represented as inadequate, mother figures as strong, strict, and ambitious. Themes of ambition and the need to be successful are again present. The attitude toward marriage comes more clearly out of the shadows; there is a desire for security and children, but the adequacy of the man is also important. There is again reference to religious themes which would indicate that religion seems to be a strong bulwark to Celia in helping her to resist some of her impulsive nature.

Change in Fantasy Related to Experience

We present the hypothesis that *if the situation does not change the fantasies will not change;* and conversely, that *change in fantasy is a function of change in environment.* If a man or woman continues to live at home, if members of the family remain constant, if there is little or no change in occupation or marital status, then fantasy will change but little. Fantasies change only when there is a change in the conditions of living. Having experiences leads to change in fantasy. A boy or girl is helped to change his fantasy if he goes away to college, has Army or Navy experience, secures a new job, and especially if he or she gets married. These experiences will lead to shifts in fantasy if they force the person to adjust to new relationships, if they require that he change his self-concept, or if they solve old problems or present new ones.

Most of this chapter is devoted to a discussion of the factors which lead to a shift in fantasy. Only one illustration will be given in which fantasy persists due to the continuance of living conditions. Ralph (2) told stories with obvious castration themes. In 1953 Ralph's stories retain the fear of the dominating and castrating female. Ralph lived at home for several years. He was never called to the service because of a lame leg. More recently he has belatedly sought a college education and is also engaged to a girl, but his experiences have not been sufficient to enable him to break through his fear of the phallic woman.

There is good reason to believe that all fantasy represents "unfinished business"—old wishes yet unsatisfied, old conflicts not yet resolved, old anxieties that persist. Fantasy will remain unchanged if nothing in the day-to-day experiences satisfies the wish, resolves the conflict, diminishes the anxiety. But fantasy will change if experience gratifies the wish, resolves the conflict, or reduces the anxiety. New fantasy may be produced if new wishes are created, if fresh conflicts are aroused, or if anxiety is increased. The following principles cannot be proved, but evidence will be presented that goes far toward supporting them.

Principle 1. If a tendency is expressed in reality there is less need to fantasy it.

In at least four of the subjects there was a decrease in themes of aggression, hostility, and excitement. Wallace (1) now finds outlets for his aggression in competition in business, for he works as a salesman, which requires assertiveness. Themes of wild aggressive adventure with excitement, murder, and robbery disappeared from the fantasies of Ralph (2) and these trends found expression in real life over the intervening years in ambitious striving, determination, and hard work. Roy (6), whose fantasies formerly included these same themes, says that he drives himself harder than most people do. Roger (8) also no longer expresses the same hostile aggressive fantasy that was present in adolescence and we suggest that these fantasies have been absorbed by his struggles to go through college and his continuing struggle in the world of business.

This principle shows itself very clearly in the case of Wallace (1), with reference to another theme. As an adolescent there were many themes of giving, receiving, and taking (by force). As a boy he showed his immaturity by his need to be given things. But this need receded in his adult fantasy and in its place is the give-and-take of business competition. In story A-4 in 1953 we read: "So he comes to get his money and first he's got to get the guts to go for it. The boy has grown up and become very successful in business."

Mabel (22) told stories in 1940 with themes of escape, but these themes are absent from her 1953 stories. The need for fantasying escape from restraint and supervision evidently have vanished since she left home to be married. We are told that her husband is a mild man, unlike her father who was strict, demanding, and punishing.

Laura (13), too, no longer has the need to fantasy separation from her family as she has accomplished this, in part at least, in reality. In the case of Laura themes of one person exerting an influence over another are no longer present in 1953. Laura, as may be remembered, defied her mother by marrying against her wishes. Apparently through the overpowering strength of her erotic desires she was able to exert her will in making decisions and hence had less need to fantasy doing it.

Another clear illustration of the decrease in fantasy where the trend has been expressed in reality is found in the case of Nancy (31). In adolescence there were themes of dating, marriage, pregnancy. As a woman having experienced these in reality she feels less need to fantasy them and there is actually a lower frequency of these themes in 1953.

As a final illustration of this point, Seymour's (36) 1953 stories show a decrease in themes of separation, orality, being the victim of circumstances, and accidental death. Seymour claims that he is happily married, speaks admiringly of his wife, and is proud of his children. He lets his wife make most of the decisions. So the security of the family situation has decreased his need for oral supplies and allayed some of his anxieties of being aggressed against.

Principle 2. If a tendency is expressed in reality there is less need to romanticize, glorify, or symbolize it in fantasy.

It was also observed that if a trend was expressed in real living some of the earlier distorted expressions of that trend in fantasy have decreased. Wallace (subject 1), for instance, told stories in 1940 with silly, embarrassed, rather unfeeling references to love and marriage. These have disappeared in 1953. In the meantime Wallace has married and there is one daughter in the family. His stories no longer have these silly references to marriage.

Laura's (13) 1940 references to the spooky and mysterious with obvious sexual implications do not appear in 1953. Apparently Laura's marriage experiences have taken the mystery out of sexual relationships and it is no longer necessary to fantasy it.

In one other subject the mystery of sex apparently has disappeared from fantasy. Roy (subject 6) included themes of mystery—which probably had a sexual reference—in his 1940 fantasy. But this mystery is not present in 1953. Roy is married with two daughters and life's experiences have taken away the mystery and spookiness of sex.

Albert (subject 40) was another subject who included in his 1940 stories themes of marriage and eroticism which are no longer present in 1953. Albert is not married, but credits his psychoanalysis with helping him to change his attitude toward heterosexual relationships. Earlier he had highly neurotic notions about marriage, also he was afraid of marriage. Now he believes that his relationship with the girl to whom he is engaged is not a case of romantic love—he simply likes her, respects her and feels good with her. So with this changed attitude toward women he no longer has the need to introduce erotic themes into his stories.

In two instances the trick or joke seemed to have a hostile or sadistic reference. Margaret (24) told stories in 1940 in which a boy or girl would play teasing jokes on another figure. These jokes are absent from the 1953 stories. Margaret had strong Oedipal tendencies, and although there is no indication in the record that she ever worked through her hostile feelings toward her mother, she does refer to difficulties with her mother-in-law. "Margaret says that her husband's mother was very hurt and bitter when they married, and it was quite some time before his mother accepted her. She says that now everything is all right, but at first her mother-in-law caused her a good deal of heartache." Having worked through this hostility in reality there is no longer need to refer to it in fantasy.

In Margaret's 1940 stories there was also a need to become attractive and popular, which is not present in 1953. In place of this striving, in 1953 there is a fatalistic acceptance of herself as she is. Thus marriage seems to have reduced the necessity for romantic striving because she has already reached the goals that this striving attempted to accomplish. It is of some significance in this connection that Margaret's 1953 stories showed an increase in feminine identification.

Barbara (20) omitted in 1953 the type of story she told in 1940 in which the hero is the innocent victim of a crime with themes representing a sadistic conception of sexual relations. Barbara has not married, but increasing maturity has brought her closer to the reality of sexual relations to which she reacts with fear and revulsion.

Nancy's (31) erotic themes have already been discussed. In 1940 Nancy's stories also included themes of striving and success. "Steve knocked at the door of the house long not seen. He had been very successful during those years away from home." Since there is no corresponding striving and success in Nancy's life in reality, one must surmise that success to Nancy had an erotic significance. Now Nancy is married and feels that life is dull, restricted, and prosaic. Here, reality of marriage has removed the romantic element from life and it is no longer necessary for her to fantasy success romantically and symbolically.

John (39) had frequent references to automobiles with obvious sexual symbolism in his 1940 fantasy. Since that time John has had direct experience with women and is disillusioned with regard to them, so it is no longer necessary for him to fantasy sex through the symbolism of the automobile. His former distrust of automobiles had been replaced by a more direct distrust of women.

Principle 3. If a tendency is expressed in reality the opposite active trend may appear in fantasy, or the opposite passive trend may disappear from fantasy.

This principle goes a step beyond principles 1 and 2. Not only will a fantasy disappear when the trend is worked out in real living, but this may make it possible for the opposite trend to appear in fantasy. Apparently opposite trends do not exist side-by-side in the conscious life. It is very difficult for a person to be both active and passive, to love and hate or to strive and submit simultaneously. While one form of expression is ascendant its opposite lies dormant. Apparently there are many more trends lying dormant—and which may appear in either fantasy or acting out—than are expressed at any one instant. Therefore the acting out of a trend in reality removes the need to express it in fantasy, which makes it possible for the opposite trend to appear in fantasy. This trend shows itself in at least two of the subjects by a shift in sex identification. Two of the male subjects showed greater feminine identification in their 1953 stories. Wallace (1), who included a larger number of feminine identifications in his 1953 stories, has been mentioned several times as a man who has an excessive need to demonstrate his masculinity and who adopts an aggressive, competitive role in life—characteristics which were earlier present in his adolescent fantasy. Feminine identification was probably present in latent form in adolescence but could not be expressed then because of his great need to express the masculine side of his personality. Now that he has learned to express masculinity in reality he no longer needs to express it so strongly in fantasy, and the feminine identification can find expression in fantasy.

Wallace's 1953 stories also show an increase in themes of wishful thinking, of having things come one's way without effort, a kind of passive-receptive trend that undoubtedly was also present in 1940, but was overshadowed at that time by the need to demonstrate his competence.

The same comments also apply to Roy (6), who incorporated much aggression in his adolescent fantasy. As a result of subsequent release of aggression in work he could permit himself greater feminine identification in fantasy, and his 1953 stories showed the principal characters playing a more passive role.

Another illustration of this principle is to be found in the case of John (39). In his 1940 stories success depended on hard work and the characters were enterprising. Since then John has been able to work out his success fantasies in reality. In their place there are themes of shiftlessness and indolence. One may speculate that the latter themes were present in latent form in adolescence but could not appear because there was such a great need to master anxiety through his fantasies of striving and success.

In the case of Jimmy (37), in adolescence his fantasy was concerned with tragic Oedipal themes. Because of the guilt of his Oedipal wishes his fantasy took this tragic tone. Jimmy saw grueling action in the front lines of the infantry during the war and apparently was able to work through in action his guilt for some of his tragic fantasy. Now his fantasy can include more direct love and sexual themes that look forward to a happy consummation.

Stella (19) illustrates a trend that is the reverse of what one normally finds. Typically, in cases involving sibling rivalry one finds that a child can only experience sibling rivalry in fantasy and that with increasing years the fantasy subsides as the hostility comes more out into the open. But in the case of Stella during adolescence she openly expressed her rejection of her younger sister as described in Chapter Four, in the section on aggression. The sibling rivalry in later years was more openly expressed in fantasy.

Catherine (12) could only say the best of things about her father and mother as a child, whereas in fantasy most subjects showed strong hostility toward parents, especially rejecting, punitive mothers. But partly as a result of psychotherapy, as discussed in the section on dependency, in Chapter Four, she has more recently been able to express negative feelings toward both father and mother in reality. Interestingly enough, in 1953 Catherine can also fantasy parents who are good, and one may attribute this to the fact that the earlier negative feelings now expressed in reality remove the necessity of expressing those feelings only in fantasy, which permits the opposite feelings to break through in fantasy.

To illustrate the disappearance of the opposite passive trend, Ralph (2) shows a decrease in themes of being aggressed against. As he turns his aggressive impulses from fantasy into realistic striving, there is less fear of attack from authority figures and this results in a shift of fewer themes of being the recipient of aggressive attack in fantasy.

Principle 4. Life's experiences sometimes remove a person from a punishing, forbidding figure, which enables him to break through repression, and as a result of these experiences he can better verbalize hostility or love in fantasy.

In five of the subjects there is an increase in aggressive fantasy expressed in themes of hostility. Stella (19), whose hostility was covered up in 1940 by a highly moral attitude, permits the hostility to come out more openly in 1953 and expresses sibling rivalry more openly. Somehow the vicissitudes of life helped her to break through the wall of repression behind which she kept locked aggressive feelings when she was younger. One may surmise that devotion to her mother and reconciliation with her younger sister have lessened guilt about her aggressive impulses and she can now express them more openly in fantasy.

Olive (27) is another subject who is better able to express hostility now than in adolescence. Olive was depressed in adolescence and still is at the present time. But her life experiences have enabled her to face her sibling rivalry and hostility more openly, together with guilt about them. Probably being away from home and consequently not being so close and hence threatened by retaliation have contributed to this greater freedom.

This last statement may also help to explain in part why Natalie (21) also can express hostility more freely. As an adolescent she was quiet and withdrawn and there was much anxiety in her fantasies. Now married and no longer living under her parents' roof and with her mother and dreading retaliation, she is more free and has gained courage to express her hostility more openly in fantasy—"they have a fume about it."

There is a shift from the passive themes of castration fear in adolescence to stories with more themes of anger and hostility, conflict and retaliation.

Viola (14) eloped and married against her mother's wishes. These and other expressions of independence have helped break through the wall of repression. Viola's life has been an alternation between hostile impulses and guilt because of them. So her fantasies in 1953 show a more clear expression of both aggression and sex, but also a sense of guilt because of them. One of Viola's 1953 stories shows a sharpened conflict between being at home and being away from home. In 1940 Viola managed guilt in one of her stories by not marrying, by living and dying alone; in 1953 sex is not disguised, but there is the same guilt, this time managed by returning home. In real life, of course, she worked out the better solution by marrying. Her marriage has made it possible for her to free herself of dependence on home and mother, but there is also increased guilt because of this.

Jimmy (37) also indicates that the struggle over securing independence has come into sharper focus. He gained the courage to face this decision from his army experience and while away from home. So in one 1953 story the man deserts the older woman for the younger woman, indicating some progress in asserting his independence. Also in the case of Jimmy there are more themes with direct sexual reference.

It is of considerable significance that this same trend toward a freer expression of active themes of aggression and less passive themes of being the recipient of aggression should have appeared in the two subjects who have undergone psychotherapy—Catherine (12) and Albert (40). This is precisely what one would expect from therapy. A psychotherapist places his client in a relationship where he is not subject to threat, pressure, hostile reactions, negative criticism, and the like. Albert reacted to this experience by telling stories in which there is less passivity and in which the hero is less the object of aggression from authority figures. And in real life Albert has begun to make more mature adjustments to authority figures. Catherine, for her part, as a result of psychotherapy, tells stories in which the central characters are less passive and helpless and in which they are able to assert themselves by their own efforts.

Principle 5. Fantasies are frequently in keeping with life's experiences posing problems that have not been wholly and successfully worked through.

There are some shifts in fantasy that are very realistic reflections of the changes in life's experiences. A person frequently fantasies what one would expect him to fantasy by common sense.[1] Usually in such

---

[1] In contrasting a common-sense interpretation of fantasy with the dynamic interpretations which are used throughout these discussions, we have in mind the naïve approach to projective techniques that characterized the work of many clinical psychologists in the early days of the movement. They tended to interpret a fantasy theme as though it had its exact counterpart in behavior. The themes found in fantasy were interpreted as characterizing the individual's overt

Change in Fantasy Related to Experience

cases the individual is faced with some new problem of immediate urgency or of a traumatic nature in reality, and his fantasies are his attempts, in part, to solve the problems with which he is confronted.

This is well illustrated by several of the subjects whose stories include a larger number of themes of depression. These subjects have met with reverses and disappointments. They have suffered disillusionment concerning some of their adolescent hopes and expectations. Life has become tragic or humdrum.

Normally this might lead to an increase in aggression—taking one's grudge out on somebody—but society does not countenance expression of ill will, with the result that the aggression is turned inward as depression. Jerome (7) is dissatisfied with his work and hoped for occupational guidance from the interviews in this study. Sam (9) although more successful in reality is also dissatisfied with the progress he has made in his work and he explains that the rewards are not commensurate with the effort expended. Edith (17) is justifiably depressed because of the loss of her infant son. Albert (40) expresses a sense of futility in that he has not seen the fulfillment of some of his adolescent dreams. John (39) in adolescence envisioned sex as joyous and exciting, but his life experiences have disillusioned him about sex and now he views it as disappointing and hopeless. Karl (11) has found rebuffs in the world of reality from which he was protected as a child and as an adolescent and this has produced a strain of depression in his stories. His educational, military, and work experiences have sobered him. Dorothy (30) whose marriage is unhappy inasmuch as she is not able to achieve satisfying sexual relations also experiences depression. However, the mere presence of disappointment, disillusionment, and the sense of futility are not sufficient by themselves to explain the increase of themes of depression in fantasy. These subjects who have found life disappointing have also found it necessary to deal with the increased aggressive impulses which these disappointments aroused.

To illustrate principle 5 further, reference to trends in fantasy other than depression follow. In each of these the situation is on the negative side and the response is one of discouragement and disillusionment.

Jerome (7) is vocationally unsuccessful and unhappy. He has never

---

behavior and personality. Such one-to-one correspondences are by no means the rule. But under principle 5 we are providing illustrations of fantasies that do reflect the current feelings and impulses that the person is experiencing.

been able to find the right employment, and is discouraged about his vocational future. This is reflected in his stories. There is a lowering in his self-concept and an increase in feelings of inferiority. Gone is his adolescent jauntiness and in its place are anxiety, despair, and feelings of incompetence and failure.

An obvious way of thinking about Jerome's shift in fantasy is to attribute it solely to his vocational dissatisfaction. But the evidence also suggests that his vocational failure may in part be due to his passivity and low self-concept and that his lack of success contributes to the attitude of helplessness. In a case such as Jerome's it is difficult to determine how much of the shift in fantasy is due to life's experiences and how much to the elaboration of earlier personality trends. Undoubtedly the recent experiences interact with the personality trends brought down from childhood and adolescence.

Edwin (33) is another subject who has been unsuccessful vocationally. At first he worked for his father but without satisfaction. Then with his wife's money he bought a grocery and this was a failure. Now he is a salesman. The themes of independence, self-sufficiency and self-confidence that characterized his adolescent fantasy have disappeared and in their place are themes of helplessness, impotence, and castration. There is an increase of themes of illness and accident, while themes of hope, planning for the future, and competence have disappeared. But at the same time there is an increase in themes of wishful thinking and immediate fantasies of success and greatness.

Nancy (31) is another whose life today is anything but ideal. Although married and the mother of two children, she feels that her life is restricted and confined by her marriage. Her husband is a "pain in the neck" to her, is tight with money, and has the disgusting hobby of raising pigeons. As a result her fantasies include themes of disagreement, misunderstanding, leading to anxiety, anger and finally separation.

Karl (11) who was much overprotected as a child finally received hard knocks when he went away to school and later entered the Army, serving overseas. He has come up against discipline in adulthood that he did not experience as a child and there are themes of punishment in his 1953 stories that were not present in adolescent fantasy.

In many instances leaving home has provided a subject with wished-

Change in Fantasy Related to Experience 85

for independence and has served to free him from previous inhibitions in the expression of aggressive and erotic impulses. But in the case of Pansy (29) her hard-won independence seems to have boomeranged and has made Pansy feel isolated, insecure, and rejected, and has led to increased feelings of insecurity.

Principle 6. Some individuals with increasing age face new problems or old problems with increasing intensity, and these problems may find expression in fantasy.

One of these problems is marriage for those who "missed the boat" in their early twenties. This seems to reach a peak in the late twenties, for women particularly. Part of the reason for this is cultural. Family and friends expect one to get married and increasing pressure is put upon the woman, not directly perhaps, but by side remarks and insinuations. Friends of earlier years have found new interests in marriage; the unmarried individual feels lonely, isolated, and left out. Whereas in earlier years men approached her with the natural spirit of mutual friendship, coupled with a rise in passion, in later years men make approaches that have more direct sexual implications and less indication of sharing mutual interests.

This increase in fantasy is illustrated by two of our subjects, both commented on before. Barbara (20), who had strong masculine identification, in 1953 is 27 years old, finds marriage life's most intense dilemma. She both desires marriage and at the same time fears and retreats from it. There is a noticeable rise in the theme of marriage in her stories.

Celia (28), also unmarried, is ambivalent toward marriage. Story A-10 (given on page 291) shows that marriage was a central theme in her fantasies. She both yearns for and protests against it. But the fortuneteller in the story held a promise: "They are hoping all the good things he says will come true—happy marriage, security, nice children."

On the part of the man, sometimes the most pressing problem is vocational adjustment. Illustrations have been given in previous pages concerning men who were unhappy about their vocational careers and showing the parallels in their fantasies.

Principle 7. Fantasies reflect the rise or fall of the level of anxiety and guilt according to the success with which a person has found adequate defenses against these affects.

In all the following illustrations, anxiety and guilt seem to stem from earlier hostile and aggressive fantasy. Undoubtedly there is a sexual component to this anxiety but it does not reveal itself in obvious terms, and the fantasy that has been reported as giving rise to anxiety in adolescence concerns aggression.

In two cases there is a noticeable rise in anxiety. Roger (8) produces four more stories with themes of anxiety in 1953 than in 1940. On the other hand his aggressive, hostile themes show a marked drop. As has been stated before, his aggression has gone into vocational striving. But the outcome is not sure and he is beset with doubts as to whether he can achieve his ambitions. As a result he has become exceedingly sensitive over his status with possible competitors. The blank card (B-11) in 1953 gave him an opportunity to verbalize his conflict over continuing this struggle or "being satisfied with the life you're living now."

Ralph (2) shows very similar dynamics. He has given up the aggressive, hostile fantasy of adolescence in favor of ambitious striving. But in spite of this outlet there is an increase of guilt because of the hostile fantasies of the past expressed in depression and a new moral, conforming attitude.

On the other hand, there are cases where the adoption of suitable defenses decrease anxiety and guilt. Some have accomplished this through altruism and reparation. In two instances the guilt over earlier hostile and sexual fantasies is contained by reparation by becoming a good wife and mother in reality. In one story told by Viola (14) the girl thinks of herself "as a servant of other people." In another story a young man will eventually recognize the "satisfaction of doing for other young people what was not done for him."

Mabel (22) is another who shifted from themes of defying father figures to helping them. In her case, too, adolescent death wishes toward father have changed to altruistic themes expressed toward her own children. "All I can see here is my own future. I see children playing happily with no worries or thoughts in the children's minds. The parents are preparing for their future in watching them grow."

Care for their children in some instances represents a defense against the hostility held toward parent figures in adolescence. Having now left home, she feels less hostile toward her parents and is better able to accept their point of view.

These two cases illustrate one of the positive outcomes and shifts in fantasy from negative adolescent fantasy to positive beneficent fantasy in adult years. And it came about through the process of reparation which Melanie Klein and Joan Riviere have emphasized in their writings.[2]

Another instance of this shift toward altruism and reparation is to be found in the case of Stella (19). Actually, in this instance there is no statistical reduction in anxiety or guilt in fantasy and we also find anxiety expressed in real life. Stella describes herself as a tense, anxious, worrying person. She shows much concern over her mother who "had a nervous breakdown" and Stella gave up her work in order to be with her mother. She also feels that her brother is "spoiled and undependable." Stella is making a strenuous effort to cope with the guilt which comes now from earlier hostile impulses which she could never express in adolescence and had to cover over with a highly moral attitude.

In two instances anxiety has apparently been brought under control by living a carefully regulated life. Celia (28) shows a marked decrease in anxiety in her stories. In part this may be attributed to her success in her work which has given her self-confidence. And in part it may have come about by the bolstering influence of the Catholic religion, of which she is a devout follower. Her religion may have given her support and relief rather than the increasing anxiety it sometimes brings by making requirements which add to the individual's strain because his impulses and wishes render it difficult for him to meet these requirements.

Isabel (18), too, is unmarried, lives at home, and is a devout Catholic. She has isolated herself from life by finding refuge in the shelter of the parental home. She avoids anything that might bring on her censure or criticism and in this way avoids anxiety. The school phobia present in her 1940 fantasies was really anxiety over relations with her parents; she manages this in the present by giving no cause for offense.

[2] See contributions by Melanie Klein and Joan Riviere in *Love, Hate and Reparation* (Psychoanalytical Epitomes No. 2; London, Hogarth Press, 1937). Recently reissued by Hillary House (New York, 1953).

But Natalie (21) has reduced her anxiety in quite a different way, as described in discussing principle 4. One may conclude that there is a decrease in anxiety in her stories as a natural concomitant of her increase in the ability to express and feel anger and hostility in real life.

Principle 8. Fantasies sometimes shift as there is need for a shift in the defenses against anxiety and guilt.

It is well known that a considerable portion of fantasy is concerned with defenses against anxiety. Ordinarily a person keeps his defenses in remarkably intact form over long periods of time. But life's experiences occasionally alter the balance of forces which permit or require a shift in the defensive structure. If anxiety or guilt diminishes, defenses may be lowered, or if they increase, defenses may be raised. As a person's life experiences provide him with greater outlets of expression or restrict his expression still further, he shifts and adjusts his defensive structure.

Principle 8, dealing with shifts in fantasy that are related to the defenses against anxiety and guilt, will be taken up under specific topics: depression, endings to the stories, realism in fantasy, and themes of escape.

DEPRESSION

As the statistical data show, one of the most prominent shifts in the fantasy themes is an increase in *depression.* In most of the cases in which this is true, it can be closely related to the need to turn aggression inward. Sometimes this is the case because it becomes unwise to express the full extent of hostile aggression outwardly; in other instances life has been disappointing and, since anxiety does not permit a person to express his resentment openly, his recourse is to turn it upon himself in the form of depression. There are other instances where overt expression of aggression has aroused guilt, which has backfired by an increase in depression.

The dynamics for the appearance of depression in fantasy cannot be summed up by a single formula. In some of the subjects depressive fantasies take the place of aggressive fantasies in adolescence. Ralph's (2) shift from adolescent fantasy aggression to ambitious striving in real life has already been commented on. As a person Ralph impressed the examiner as "a pleasant sort of person with nice manners." But hard work has not taken care of all of his aggressive impulses. He has to repress some of them or manage them by reaction formation in reality and by depression in fantasy. Almost the same things can be said about Roy (6) who is described as overcontrolled and rather tense and inhibited in his speech and manner.

In two subjects, Roger (8) and Sam (9), this turning aggression inward and having its appearance as depression is even more clearly revealed. Roger is described as a soft-spoken man, but when challenged in his work he will become violently angry and "shoot off his mouth." This is followed by periods of depression in real life, a depression which also appears in fantasy. Sam describes himself as even-tempered, but says that on occasion he will "blow his top." Although there is nothing in the record stating that Sam is depressed in reality, he is described as a nervous person, and there is a definite increase in depression in his stories. He has good reason to suffer from depression by identification inasmuch as his mother has had several severe depression episodes.

In some instances the increase of fantasy depression is coincident with a decrease in aggression in real life. Stella (19), whose 1953 stories show an increase in themes of depression, states that she used to be active in sports, but has no time for that now. Dorothy (30) also shows an increase in depression themes. Unhappy in marriage, she claims she is better able to endure frustration as a result of her turn to religion, which serves as a support against being overwhelmed by desire. But this resignation is accomplished at the expense of greater fantasy depression.

Inability to express aggression may be correlated with an increase in fantasy depression. Margaret's (24) inability to feel hostility toward her mother as discussed on pages 58–59. There was strong hostility toward mother figures in adolescent fantasy and now in 1953 we find an increase in fantasy depression. Apparently hostile fantasies not expressed in behavior lead to guilt, which finds later expression in fantasies with themes of depression.

Pansy's (29) case illustrates a variant of this. But in spite of her apparent success in expressing her independence there is still guilt, which finds expression in depression in fantasy.

In concluding this section on depression it should be added that one subject showed a decrease in depression. In the case of Catherine (12), as a result of the release of aggressive impulses she is free from some of her earlier depressive fantasy.

STORY ENDINGS

Shift in the endings to the stories frequently has dynamic significance. Of the subjects in this study there were some who showed an increase in positive endings and a decrease in negative endings, and there were some who showed the reverse—an increase in negative endings and a decrease in positive endings.

Of those whose stories showed an increase in positive endings, two subjects told stories which showed an increase in unrealistic wishful thinking. Barbara (20), who never married, indulges in unrealistic fantasies. Since she does not permit herself to enjoy sensual pleasures in reality she substitutes by fantasying them. Celia (28), also unmarried, shows a decided shift from negative to positive endings in her stories. Apparently Celia is making her adjustment to life by repressing rather than living out her impulses, and by permitting them to be expressed only in unrealistic fantasy. In both these instances a relationship with a person of the opposite sex has terrors or disagreeable features which block any action in that direction.

In the case of Edwin (33), increase in positive endings is clearly a denial of the negative, as a defense against the anxiety that arose from conflict over his strivings. On the one hand, his stories contain masochistic themes expressing unworthiness, insufficiency, and inferiority; on the other hand he indulged in unrealistic fantasies of success and greatness.

Viola's (14) stories show some decrease in themes of depression and also show fewer negative endings. Viola is one who achieved independence over her mother's domination through her marriage. She has managed her guilt in fantasy by themes of altruism and reparation and possibly this also is a governing motive with respect to her family and in raising her children. Defending herself against anxiety in this way permits her to add a new positive note to the endings of her stories.

Roger (8), whose adolescent fantasy also includes hostility, has to contend with much anxiety and guilt as a result. He also manages these trends by denial of the negative, evidenced by a pronounced decrease in negative endings coupled with more themes of repentance and reform. It is significant that whereas there is no increase in depression in fantasy he is described as subject to depression on occasion in reality and suffering from feelings of failure and inferiority.

Mabel (22) is another who has managed hostile fantasies primarily by shifting them to themes of nurturance and altruism. This is indicated by a decrease in the negative outcomes to her 1953 stories.

Catherine (12) again is an exception to this shift from negative to positive endings as a defense. As a result of psychotherapy Catherine is now able to accept the positive, not as a defense against anxiety and guilt but as a result of being freed of anxiety and guilt.

But in an equal number of cases there is an increase in negative endings to the stories. In a number of these instances the increase in the negative endings can be related to a decrease in anxiety and guilt and to more open expression of aggression.

Wallace (1), as will be remembered, is the assertive salesman and business man. Since he has learned to express his aggression openly he has less anxiety to contend with and hence has less need for his stories to end happily—he can tolerate a less happy, more realistic, ending. The same comments also apply to Roy (6). Life has enabled Sam (9) to accept his fiery temper and he too has less anxiety and less need to defend himself against it by incorporating a happy ending to his stories. Laura (13), who defied her mother by her marriage, is better able to tolerate her aggressive impulses with the result that she has less anxiety, less need to defend herself against it, and hence a greater number of unfavorable endings.

In two cases, however, an increase in the unfavorable ending accompanied a greater tendency toward depression. Edith (17) has suffered repeated frustration and discouragement which resulted in a retreat from her adolescent exuberance and a relinquishment of adolescent dreams and ambitions. In 1940 there was hope; in 1953, resignation. Her depressed and pessimistic outlook shows itself in part in a decrease of favorable endings. Dorothy (30) is another whose unhappiness (in this case marital) results in depression and fewer positive endings. Dorothy's case is complicated by the fact—and quite reasonably—that there is an increase in eroticism in her 1953 stories, which follows quite naturally from the fact that she is not getting sexual satisfaction from the marriage relationship.

A somewhat different set of factors seems to be present in the case of Julia (25). Her 1940 stories showed some anxiety and defense against it by the positive ending to her stories. Julia married early and happily and her anxieties seem to have diminished. As a result her stories have lost their wishful thinking character, are more realistic, and also have an increase in negative endings.

REALISM IN FANTASY

The shift in fantasy also indicates differences in the degree of reality or wishful-thinking character in the fantasy. Some of the stories show a greater amount of control, some less. This again can be referred to the anxiety that is present and methods used to defend against it.

In some instances where fantasy becomes less realistic and there is greater indulgence in unrealistic wishful thinking, these changes can be attributed to disappointments in life and the search for substitute satisfactions in fantasy. Some of these cases have already been referred to in the discussion of story endings because the reality or unreality of the fantasy is frequently exhibited in the nature of the ending.

Edwin (33) tends to daydream success, but he is not a success in life. Margaret (24), who has married, finds that marriage does not fulfill her adolescent dreams of exciting romance. She has settled down into the prosaic existence of the housewife, but continues to derive pleasure from her endless and unrealistic daydreams. Margaret told the longest stories and showed the greatest increase in story length of the stories of any subject. Her fantasy life is a substitute for working out her impulses in real life. On the other hand, Olive (27) has in part submitted to the dismal style of life which is her lot, and has turned instead to unrealistic daydreaming as a retreat from the struggle and as a revolt against it.

Celia (28) has already been mentioned as one who has compromised with life by repressing her impulses, and rather than live them out has adopted the substitute of expressing them only in unrealistic fantasy. This has been accomplished without too much strain probably because feelings of guilt have receded. Her greater control is due in part to the confidence which she has gained through success in her work and in part from the support of her religious (Catholic) devotion. Because of this outer control and freedom from guilt, she can afford to gratify her wish life by indulgence in unrealistic daydreaming.

Barbara (20) is another who in part substitutes daydreaming for reality. Barbara is the young woman with strong masculine identification who has not married and has a fear of intimate sexual relationships. As the cultural pressures increase Barbara yields to more daydreaming of marriage with erotic themes and this is coupled with an increase in positive outcomes to her stories. But these 1953 stories do not have the distorted, passive, sadistic conception of sexual relations of 1940 and come closer to reality. In short, there is an increase in fantasies of the pleasures of sex but a decrease in fantasies of the danger of sex. Finally, Dorothy (30) has already been mentioned as one who fantasies the erotic pleasures which she is unable to gain in reality through the marriage relationship.

There are subjects in whom fantasy has become more controlled and more realistic with less wishful thinking. Laura's (13) 1953 stories are measurably shorter than those told in 1940; they indicate repression and denial by more matter-of-fact endings. Laura is one of those who defied her mother by marrying against her mother's wishes. The examiner described her as insipid and colorless. One may surmise that to have opposed her mother as she did caused much guilt which she is now trying to manage by extreme repression that carries over into fantasy. And her actual personality shows the same repression and reaction formation by being prim, sweet, overly polite, and submissive.

Julia (25) is a person whose experiences have disillusioned some of her unrealistic and flighty adolescent fantasy. She found through her experiences in modeling in a department store and in the Navy as a Wave that real life did not always have the same exciting glamour conjured by fantasy. She is now happily married. Although she lives in a shabby part of town, apparently she is willing to settle for a very ordinary way of life if she can have occasional flashy indulgence in real life of her earlier fantasies. Her fantasy life, too, now partakes of the same drabness and lack of wishful thinking that characterizes her actual mode of life.

The case of Roy (6) contains an apparent inconsistency: he shows greater realism in his 1953 stories, but also an increase in wishful thinking. Roy has been mentioned several times earlier as one who has given up his wild and unrealistic fantasy in favor of more sedate, overcontrolled, stereotyped stories, as he has transferred his aggressiveness from fantasy to real life. But his 1953 fantasy also shows an increase in wishful thinking. This is an apparent paradox. His adolescent stories were full of action—his adult fantasies have become more passive; in place of activity is a wistful, wishful thinking. So rather than a shift to greater reality, the unrealistic fantasy has shifted from the active to the passive.

THEMES OF ESCAPE

One defense that frequently finds expression in fantasy is the wish to escape. As is well known, one of the struggles of adolescence is to secure the independence which characterizes adulthood. These strivings are symbolized in fantasy by themes of escape. But, as is so often the case, the shift in fantasy can take either of two directions—toward fantasy of more escape, or of less escape.

Roy (6), who used escape as a real method when a child, by running away from home, incorporates more themes of escape into his stories as an adult than as an adolescent. He tells a story in 1953 about a girl "wondering when she might get away from it [the small seacoast community where she lives] for to her it is dreary and dismal and without much hope of any further cooperation from life." Roy suffers from the disillusionment of frustrated hopes so common in young adults and he fantasies how he might escape from the life which he feels restricts his efforts.

But Mabel (22) had less need to escape (see page 76), and Catherine (12), who has undergone psychotherapy, apparently has been able to work through her feelings of separation and rejection. She can tell a story in 1953 that deals with the theme of separation, but it ends by having the persons united. She has been able to break through the barrier of the threat of separation and rejection and accept a relationship in spite of its potential threat (of failure) to her.

6. Relationship between Adolescent and Adult Personality

One of the goals of this follow-up study has been to compare the relative significance of fantasy with overt personality in adolescence for predicting personality in later years. On the one hand, it might be supposed that the overt, surface, describable personality in adulthood might best be predicted from the same overt personality characteristics in adolescence. That is, an adult might be expected to display the same or similar characteristics that he showed as an adolescent. But, on the other hand, there is a possibility that the underlying trends revealed in fantasy during adolescence might be more predictive of personality in later years.

The evidence for the similarity or dissimilarity of adolescent fantasy and later adult personality may be found in Chapter Four. The present chapter presents the evidence concerning similarities or dissimilarities between adolescent personality and later personality in early adulthood. This evidence is given in tabular form at the beginning of each section.

The material in the original study and in the follow-up are quite inadequate for this purpose. Ideally, on both occasions there should have been an elaborate schedule which would have included all the items on which comparisons might be made and an effort should have been made on both occasions to secure answers to the questions on such a schedule, either from testimony from the subject himself, or from others who knew him, or from judgments which an interviewer might have made from talking with and testing him. Such data are not available. Both times a rough schedule was used by interviewers, but only as a guide to the larger topics to be covered, and as a result the records include only what the subject brought out in the interview and what the interviewer recorded. This means that there are many questions on which it is desirable to make comparisons for which the evidence is available for only some of the subjects.

What has been done is to go through the material and select those items of personality for which there is clearly stated similarity (or dissimilarity). This is a dangerous procedure, for there is a possibility that one may conclude what one is looking for. To illustrate, if the record states that a person speaks slowly and distinctly in the interview, both in 1940 and 1953, that may be a chance coincidence. If one could get a rating of the speed and distinctness of speech for all subjects on both occasions, then it would be possible to determine the degree of similarity (or dissimilarity) for the total group. But this is not possible with the data at hand. The best that can be done is to report the similarities or dissimilarities as they can be culled from the records.

PERSISTENCE OF GENERAL PERSONALITY CHARACTERISTICS

Subject	Comments from interviews, 1940	Comments from interviews, 1953
Wallace (1)	Likes a man's man	Emphasizes strength and power
	Cocky, self-assured	Same
Ralph (2)	Meek, mild, hesitant	Same
Jerome (7)	Sexual exhibitionism, exaggerated lettering on autobiography	Exhibitionistic features in his dress and bearing
Roger (8)	Nice boy with charm—friendly and cooperative	Made a better impression than any other man in the study
Sam (9)	Friendly	Friendly, at ease
Karl (11)	Lies	Cannot distinguish fact from fantasy
	Queer	Same
Laura (13)	Sweet and well-mannered	Very sweet and polite
	Cannot stand people in pain, crying, or in trouble	Very sensitive, cannot stand bickering or fighting
Viola (14)	Much fantasy in autobiography	Lives a kind of fantasy life
Edith (17)	Cheerful personality, flashing smile	Pleasing smile, very nice teeth
	Quiet and reserved	Same

Adolescent and Adult Personality

PERSISTENCE OF GENERAL PERSONALITY CHARACTERISTICS (*Cont.*)

Subject	Comments from interviews, 1940	Comments from interviews, 1953
Barbara (20)	Dislikes feminine activities, make-up, dressy clothes, parties	Energetic, athletic
	Plain, tailored clothes; uses no make-up; does not fuss with hair	Neatly, attractively dressed; neat hairdo; uses no fingernail polish
Natalie (21)	Quiet and colorless; never becomes very excited or exuberant	Same—not assertive, drab and lethargic
	Does not have initiative	Marriage ties her down and she has no time for things she is interested in
Margaret (24)	Good disposition	Same
	Makes friends easily	Likes being and working with people
Olive (27)	Tight and tense	Same
Pansy (29)	Critical of everyone; chip on the shoulder	Critical of neighbors
	Hang-dog attitude	Very little self-esteem
Nancy (31)	Nice disposition—friendly, noncritical	Friendly, casual
Edwin (33)	Inadequate, sloppy	Lazy, inadequate as a person
	Easy to get along with, obedient, no rebellion, very considerate	Very easy-going, calm, sleepy, relaxed
Seymour (36)	Lazy; takes his time when asked to do something	Has very little ambition
Jimmy (37)	Does not like assignments that have to be done at a certain time	When he came home from the army he did not take a job for three years
John (39)	Likes to have helpers when he works, and enjoys being their boss	Same—now a factory foreman
	Has ideals of hard work	Is a hard worker himself and drives the men under him
	Likes to have his own way	Likes to have freedom in his work
Albert (40)	Wrote a disorderly autobiography	Calls himself a disorderly person
	Lazy	Same

DIFFERENCE IN GENERAL PERSONALITY CHARACTERISTICS OR NONE MENTIONED

Subject	Comments from interviews, 1940	Comments from interviews, 1953
Laura (13)	Gets depressed Very obedient	Does not get depressed Obedient until she defied her mother about marriage
Edith (17)	Peppy	Listless
Olive (27)	Cannot take criticism; believes she is mistreated or slighted	No sign of this
Celia (28)	Homeroom president	No mention of leadership
Pansy (29)	Bad temper	No mention
Dorothy (30)	Friendly, ready smile, pleasing manner	Looks old, dried-up; uses much make-up; tense and nervous
	A tactful, patient, thoughtful person, easy going and good-natured	Occasionally blows her top, but only at home and it requires great provocation
Edwin (33)	Always active, playing	No mention of this; called a sleepy personality
John (39)	Not the worrying type	No mention

General Personality Characteristics

Similarities in personality, as tabulated above, were noted in twenty subjects. The types of similarity were diverse, but it was obvious that many of the persons seen in 1953 had characteristics that were similar or identical with those in 1940. The individual described as friendly, cocky, quiet, queer, hesitant, or tense in 1940, was classified by the same or synonymous adjectives in 1953. In eight cases either there was dissimilarity, or a characteristic mentioned at one time had no counterpart at the other time. In one or two instances the personality seemed quite different. Edith (17) was described as peppy in 1940 and as listless in 1953; Edwin (33) was described as always active and playing in 1940, but as sleepy in 1953. There is a possibility that personality in these two instances changed or that an individual actually impressed an observer as having different characteristics on different occasions. But even in describing overt personality it is difficult to escape from the underlying dynamics. As an adolescent Dorothy (30) was described as friendly, with a ready smile and pleasing manner. In 1953 the interviewer did not contradict this impression, but neither did he state it in exactly those terms. He did find Dorothy tense, and she

Adolescent and Adult Personality

herself stated that she would "blow her top" under provocation. Laura (13) was called very obedient as an adolescent. And she still is obedient, as an adult, but the one big episode in her life—when she married against her mother's expressed wishes—shows that at least on one occasion she could rebel and be disobedient.

The net impression is that personality characteristics have a strong tendency to persist and that a person tends to be characterized as an adult with the same terms used to describe him as an adolescent.

PERSISTENCE OF AGGRESSION

Subject	Comments from interviews, 1940	Comments from interviews, 1953
Roy (6)	Little initiative, little aggression; tentative and hesitating; follows the leader	Overcontrolled
Karl (11)	Temper spells	Same
Laura (13)	Repression of both sex and aggression	Same
	Not easily angered	Takes slaps from mother rather than fight back
Barbara (20)	Mean, ugly, argues continually	Likes a good fight or argument
	Fights with boys	Wants men to know she is as good as they are
	Temper spells—ugly before menstruation	Quick and bad temper
Natalie (21)	Quiet, placid, self-contained, never excited; if angry will not yell or fight	Not at all assertive
John (39)	Has a mean temper	Has had squabbles and arguments with men above him at work
Albert (40)	Excitable, loses temper; likes a good fight	Always fighting with his analyst
	Passive with people but claims he would like to get into the competitive business world	Not aggressive enough to make a good salesman; cannot high-pressure people

CHANGE IN AGGRESSION

| Jerome (7) | Came from very difficult home; a tough and bully | Now working out passably well as an adult |
| Celia (28) | Hot-tempered and fiery | Afraid of hurting people's feelings |

Aggression

Special instances of similarity of aggression were noted for seven subjects and two instances of dissimilarity in aggression. Aggression, in these two cases, in 1940 refers not to the subjects' own self-report in autobiography or interviews but to reports given by parents or teachers. But in 1953 one naturally has to take the subject's own self-report as the only evidence available. In general, if a person is hot-tempered and quick to anger or is placid and self-contained as an adolescent, he also describes himself in these same terms as an adult. The only exceptions are Jerome (7), who was reported to be a tough and a bully or hot-tempered as an adolescent but apparently has satisfactory relations with others as adults, and Celia (28), who was said to be hot-tempered as an adolescent but afraid of hurting people's feelings as an adult. These are not necessarily contradictory.

PERSISTENCE OF PHYSICAL CHARACTERISTICS

Subject	Comments from interviews, 1940	Comments from interviews, 1953
Ralph (2)	Injury to leg	Leg bent and a handicap
Karl (11)	Lack of motor coordination	Slight motor peculiarities
Catherine (12)	Wanted to change her face	Has had operation on her Fallopian tubes
Laura (13)	Lost weight following her "breakdown" as a child	Lost weight following opposition to her mother about marriage
Edith (17)	Short and sturdy	Stocky build
Pansy (29)	Poor health as a child—had convulsions, appendicitis	Still has health problems—sinus trouble, adhesions in uterus
	Uses no make-up	Tired, run-down, looks old for her years, stoop-shouldered, hollow-chested, sallow complexion
Nancy (31)	Short	Short, slightly stocky
Seymour (36)	Large, pleasant, dull	Large, robust, heavy-set, slow-moving
John (39)	Health good but becomes nervous	Says he is healthy

PHYSICAL CHARACTERISTIC NOT MENTIONED

Laura (13)	Migraine headaches	No mention

Physical Characteristics

Similarity was noted in physical characteristics of nine subjects, as tabulated above. In some it was a matter of general impression. Short and stocky in 1940, the same in 1953; large and robust in 1940, the same in 1953. Some of the characteristics mentioned obviously had to be identical in both years—a deformed leg, lack of motor coordination. In some it is a matter of general good health or a history of illness. In one case there seemed to be functional similarity of losing weight when faced with a traumatic situation. The possibility that the dissatisfaction which Catherine (12) expressed with regard to her face in 1940 might have been related to a sense of sexual inadequacy that has been mentioned in her case before. In one instance (Laura, 13) headaches reported in 1940 were not mentioned in 1953.

About all that can be said with regard to similarity of physical characteristics and conditions over the thirteen-year interval is that in at least nine subjects mention was made of a physical condition that had persisted over the interval.

SIMILAR RESPONSES TO INTERVIEW AND TO TESTS

Subject	Comments from interviews, 1940	Comments from interviews, 1953
Wallace (1)	Fights with teachers, indulges in heckling behavior, but is likable and has established good relationships with many teachers	Heckled the interviewer, but later established good relationships with him
Roy (6)	Each sentence deliberate, hesitant	Very slow in telling stories
Catherine (12)	Speaks quickly, in a somewhat excited fashion, but seems well-poised	Same
Laura (13)	Speaks in a very precise way	Same
Viola (14)	Ability to verbalize ideas and feelings. Much pleasure in expanding on ideas	Fluent speaker. Same
Isabel (18)	When she speaks she seems always to be asking a question	Her voice goes up at the end of every sentence as though asking a question

SIMILAR RESPONSES TO INTERVIEW AND TO TESTS (*Cont.*)

Subject	Comments from Interviews, 1940	Comments from Interviews, 1953
Natalie (21)	Quiet—does not verbalize	Has to be drawn out more than most people
Julia (25)	Offered much resistance to taking tests and refused to write an autobiography	Refused a second interview
	Seemed very reluctant and talked about herself with difficulty	Inhibited in her talk
Olive (27)	Had difficulty in telling stories	Same
	Some teachers call her lively, talkative, but she impresses different people differently	Hesitant in her speech
Nancy (31)	Stories lengthy and elaborate—a literary exercise	Inhibited and controlled in telling stories
Albert (40)	"I can talk for twenty-four hours straight"	Speaks fluently and expresses himself well

NO EVIDENCE OF SIMILAR RESPONSE

Pansy (29)	Argumentative	No evidence

Response to Interviews and Tests

In eleven subjects, above, the interviewer (Dr. Jensen) in 1953 noted the same responses and attitudes in the interview and testing situation that were noted by the interviewers (Dr. Wexler or Dr. Silverman) in 1940. No two subjects approached the interview situation in exactly the same way. Some were fluent and expressive in speech, others were hesitant and reticent. Some had peculiar speech habits such as ending a sentence with a rising inflection, or being very precise. These distinctive speech characteristics persisted for thirteen years. While there is no specific evidence for seventeen of the subjects as to similarity in the way they impressed the interviewer, in these eleven cases there is a high degree of similarity and there is reason to believe that there is essential similarity in the others for whom precise characterizations are not provided in the interview reports.

Heterosexual Interests

It is typical of adolescence, especially early adolescence, to find that boys are not interested in, and in fact tend to shy away from, girls. The avoidance may be taken as a sign that there are underlying impulses which perhaps in early adolescence are too overwhelming, too frightening to be countenanced openly. This is probably more true of boys than of girls.

PERSISTENCE OF HETEROSEXUAL INTERESTS: SUBJECTS MARRIED IN 1953

Subject	Comments from interviews, 1940	Comments from interviews, 1953
Roger (8)	Shows interest in opposite sex	
Sam (9)	Goes with girls	
Edith (17)	Boy crazy	Married about ten years after junior high school
Stella (19)	Boy crazy	
Margaret (24)	Had love affair with boy	Married this boy
Julia (25)	Keen about boys and dancing	Married early
Dorothy (30)	Has had several boy friends	Married a man she had known for three years; had previously gone with another fellow
Nancy (31)	Likes to dance, listen to radio; collects pictures of movie stars	Husband impotent

CHANGE IN HETEROSEXUAL INTERESTS: SUBJECTS MARRIED IN 1953

Subject	Comments from interviews, 1940	Comments from interviews, 1953
Roy (6)	No interest in girls except to tease them	Happily married
Jerome (7)	Doesn't mix with girls	Happily married
Catherine (12)	Excited over possibility of being kissed by a boy; sexually disturbed	Was frigid in early married life; at first was indifferent toward sex; now much more keen about it
Stella (19)	Afraid to go out alone at night	Married

CHANGE IN HETEROSEXUAL INTERESTS: SUBJECTS MARRIED IN 1953 (*Cont.*)

Subject	Comments from Interviews, 1940	Comments from Interviews, 1953
Edwin (33)	No interest in girls; shy with girls	Met six or eight girls in service; now happily married
Seymour (36)	Does not go out with girls	Happily married; before marriage went with five or six girls
Jimmy (37)	Did not go out with girls	Happily married

HETEROSEXUAL INTERESTS: SUBJECTS NOT MARRIED IN 1953

Subject	Comments from interviews, 1940	Comments from interviews, 1953
Isabel (18)	Talks about boys all the time; interested in clothes, fixing her hair, etc.; raises the question of getting along with men; against coeducation ("it makes girls rougher"); afraid of the dark	Not successful with the opposite sex; hardly a trace of feminine glamour in her appearance
Barbara (20)	Does not talk about boys; does not have crushes on them	Aggressively competitive attitude toward men
Celia (28)	Prudish attitude; no sexual curiosity; little contact with boys	Negative attitude toward marriage; strict standards of premarital behavior
John (39)	Shy and bashful in presence of women; goes out with girls, but always in the company of several couples	Peculiar notions about women
Albert (40)	Does not go out with girls; does not dance; feels uncomfortable with girls; very modest—does not like to see girls exposed; finds many things wrong with girls	Calls girls distractions; always some barrier that would prevent marriage (but married one month after interview)

It will be noted that of the seven subjects in the tabulation of those who did not show interest in the opposite sex when adolescent, only two are women, and one of these is Catherine (12), who although apparently sexually disturbed as an adolescent, has had the subsequent

Adolescent and Adult Personality

benefit of psychotherapy. It should be noted that three of these subjects are older adolescent boys, so from this brief sample it would appear that fear of the opposite sex persists into the later teens among boys. We may conclude from this tabulation that lack of interest in the opposite sex in adolescence is by no means a sign of sexual disturbance and that these seven subjects are married and apparently happily married.

Another group of eight subjects who did show an interest in the opposite sex in adolescence are married in 1953. It probably is not a coincidence that six of these eight subjects are girls, giving added evidence to the point already made that girls are more precocious than boys in showing interest in the opposite sex.

Finally, there is a group of five subjects who were unmarried in 1953. Three of the five unmarried subjects are women. If one inspects the 1940 material of these three subjects he will note signs of disturbance in heterosexual relationships even at that early age. Barbara (20) and Celia (28) had little to do with boys in adolescence. They avoided them and had prudish attitudes toward relations with the opposite sex. Isabel (18) talked about boys, but there was much concern and anxiety in connection with relations with them. The two unmarried men apparently had a normal adolescent aversion to girls. John (39), an older adolescent, went out with girls but was excessively modest and was uncomfortable when a girl exposed herself. Albert is still unmarried, although by the aid of psychotherapy he has become engaged and is looking forward to his marriage (which took place about one month after the interviews). But, apparently, disturbance in normal sexual relations expressed itself as early as adolescence (and possibly before).

RELATIONS WITH PARENTS

Subject	Comments from interviews, 1940	Comments from interviews, 1953
Wallace (1)	Good relationships with parents—an aggressive mother and an indulgent father	Happily married
Ralph (2)	Does not dare express rebellion against mother	Resisted counselor's advice in high school, but went through college just to prove that he could
	Mother very dominating and controlling	Closer to mother than to father

Adolescent and Adult Personality

RELATIONS WITH PARENTS

Subject	Comments from Interviews, 1940	Comments from Interviews, 1953
Catherine (12)	"My family is the best in the whole world"	Critical of father and mother
Laura (13)	Difficulty with mother	Same
Viola (14)	Parents ideal, but occasional skirmishes with mother	Parents not ideal; opposed mother in marrying
Natalie (21)	Gets along well with father; he is best person alive	Critical of her husband
Mabel (22)	Mother not interested in talking about daughter	She tells maid to take away her child (daughter) during interview
	Mother has a maid	Has a maid
Pansy (29)	Ran away from home	Married so as to be removed from family
	Mother says daughter is a disruptive influence in an otherwise peaceful family; daughter "fresh" to her mother	Married against her mother's wishes
Seymour (36)	Affectionate with mother	Speaks admiringly of his wife; happily married
Jimmy (37)	He states that mother lets him make plans; parents advise him and he consults them	Mother dominates him
Albert (40)	Father is "phony"	Bosses are "phonies"

Relations with Parents

In the material of eleven subjects it is possible to relate early (adolescent) expressed attitudes (as contrasted with fantasy attitudes) toward parents with later attitudes toward parents.

In only three subjects (2, 13, and 29) is there a correspondence between the attitude toward parents in the earlier and later years. In two of the instances the attitude is one of hostility and antagonism. Ralph (2) did not dare express rebellion against his mother in adolescence (although she was very dominating and controlling) and in later years he believes he is closer to his father. In three of the subjects (12, 14, and 37) there is a shift in attitude. In adolescence three of these subjects could openly express only the most extravagantly favorable attitudes toward parents, but in later years they can openly express criticism and defiance.

In six of the subjects we have taken the liberty to report a displacement of attitude from father or mother to some other figure, as described below. Of course this does not represent a real correspondence in attitude because trends which may be repressed in adolescence can probably find expression in reality through displacement.

Two subjects (1, 36), both men, who apparently had excellent relations with their mothers, report later that they are happily married and have good relationships with their wives. Albert (40) could call his father a "phony" in 1940, and apply the same epithet to a string of bosses in his various jobs in later years. Ralph (2) could not express rebellion against his mother, but he could refuse to take the advice of a school counselor. Natalie (21) called her father the best person alive in adolescence, but is now critical of her husband. Finally, Mabel (22) identifies with her mother in having a maid and giving over to the maid some of the responsibility of caring for her children.

To summarize, we find that attitude toward parents represents one of the difficult aspects of life that adolescents face. If they are critical of parents in adolescence, this same freedom may persist into adulthood. More typically, however, the adolescent is not able to admit and face his hostilities toward parents in adolescence. There is a possibility that this repression may persist into adult years, but again life's experiences may have made it possible for the individual to break through the barriers of repression to express his hostility and antagonism openly. And where this is not possible, one may find these negative feelings expressed obliquely toward other figures in adult life by a process of displacement.

RELATIONS WITH SIBLINGS

Subject	Comments from interviews, 1940	Comments from interviews, 1953
Stella (19)	Sisters squabble	Had double wedding with sister
Pansy (29)	Always at cross purposes with her younger sister	Has not seen her younger sister for over six years
Jimmy (37)	Says he gets on well with sister	Tells about arguments with sister; very close to sister but no signs of affection

Relations with Siblings

What was said about relationships with parents seems to apply equally to relationships with siblings. Typically, an adolescent tends to minimize difficulties with his siblings. To be sure, they may say that a brother or a sister is "a pain in the neck," but when they are questioned further, loyalties receive predominant emphasis. The three cases for which we have evidence illustrate three different combinations of relationships and from them no definitive conclusions can be drawn. Jimmy (37) believes that he gets along well with his sister in adolescence, but strains in his relationships with her appear in the 1953 account. Stella (19) has the unusual ability to express sibling conflict in adolescence, but apparently the relationship between sisters is a comfortable one in 1953. Pansy (29) is the only one who shows consistency. At cross purposes with a younger sister in 1940, she had not seen her for over six years in 1953.

FRIENDSHIPS

Subject	Comments from interviews, 1940	Comments from interviews, 1953
Julia (25)	Friendly with girls	Has no close girl friends
Dorothy (30)	Has close girl friend	No mention of friendship with women
Seymour (36)	Pals with two or three boys—fairly sociable	No friends

Friendships

The material of three of the subjects permits us to make comparisons of their friendships. In these cases the friendships of adolescence seem to have evaporated and no close friendships are reported in later years. One has the impression that this is a pretty general state of affairs. Intimate relations in the adult years are confined to the family. One meets others, to be sure, in business, in church, in social groups, but the relationships, by and large, tend to be remote, superficial, and perhaps transient. It seems unusual in the cases reported in this study to find capacity for deep friendship persisting into the adult years.

Adolescent and Adult Personality

COMPARISON OF EDUCATIONAL PLANS WITH ACHIEVEMENTS

Subject	Aspirations and plans, 1940	Achievements, 1953
Wallace (1)	Would like to go to college that has good medical school	Had three years of college, majored in business
Ralph (2)	No statement	B.S. in mechanical engineering
Roy (6)	No statement	Entered twelfth grade but did not graduate from high school
Jerome (7)	Vocational high school	Eleventh grade, two years in dental technician school
Roger (8)	High school No great intellectual interest—school is used for social contacts	B.S. in civil engineering Had difficulty getting through college
Sam (9)	No statement	B.A. in economics
Karl (11)	No statement	One year in junior college
Catherine (12)	High school and business college	Twelfth grade
Laura (13)	Nurses' college	Twelfth grade; one year in business school
Viola (14)	Coed college Says she is stupid (as a denial), but her teachers call her bright	B.A., majored in English Emphasizes her high I.Q.
Edith (17)	Dramatic school, preferably Carnegie Institute Excellent school record, high I.Q.	Twelfth grade Did not go to college
Isabel (18)	Business college	Twelfth grade
Stella (19)	Is not planning on college; anxious to get out of school	B.A. in retailing and advertising
Barbara (20)	Wants to get out of school as quickly as possible; does not wish to go to college	Twelfth grade
Natalie (21)	Will take any course of study to help her become a nurse	R.N. (three years of training beyond high school)
Mabel (22)	Since brother is in college and only one in family can go, she has given up plans to go to college	Twelfth grade; two years business school at night

COMPARISON OF EDUCATIONAL PLANS WITH ACHIEVEMENTS

Subject	Aspirations and plans, 1940	Achievements, 1953
Margaret (24)	Hopes to go into nurses' training in general hospital	Twelfth grade
Julia (25)	No statement	Twelfth grade; two months in modeling school
Olive (27)	Business school	Twelfth grade
Celia (28)	No statement	Twelfth grade
Pansy (29)	Nurses' training school	R.N.; three years in nursing school
Dorothy (30)	No plans beyond high school; good student, giving much attention to school	Twelfth grade; in upper third of high school
Nancy (31)	Not interested in college, plans to go into nurses' training	Twelfth grade; six months in beauty-operators' school
Edwin (33)	Would take photography course in high school if they offered it; no college ambition	Eleventh grade; had two months in photography school
Seymour (36)	No college ambition	Twelfth grade (finished after service in the Army), six months in vocational school
Jimmy (37)	College; wishes to take a liberal arts program	B.A., majored in English
John (39)	Night college; after two years would go to college during day	Night college; also equivalent to a B.S. degree in engineering from an auto industry institute
Albert (40)	Wants to get job and go to night school, then to junior college until he can enter a good college; has in mind Wharton School of Finance "as I must work to go to college"	B.A. in sociology; went to the University of Maryland

Education

The records are more complete for education than for some other topics because a question about educational plans was asked as part of the routine in 1940. Most of the boys and girls in junior high school were very vague about their plans. While it was generally assumed by a boy or girl at that age that he or she would go through high school, few had thought beyond that; two of the girls expressed a wish to leave school as soon as possible. The boys at this age had less definite objectives than the girls.

One would say that expression of educational plans at the junior high school level was practically meaningless. Two of the boys who had given no thought to the matter went on to graduate from college. Another who wanted to go to a college with a good medical school only went three years to college, majoring in business.

Although the junior high school girls had better formulated educational objectives, one cannot find much agreement between these objectives and the actual outcome. One girl wanted to go into nursing but stopped at the end of high school, and afterward spent a year in a business school. But another girl with a lower I.Q. had a deep-seated ambition to become a nurse and later received her R.N. One girl who did not plan to go to college and was anxious to leave school as early as possible went on to receive her B.A. in retailing and advertising, whereas another who wanted to leave school as early as possible went on to finish high school. One girl who noisily proclaimed her wish to become an actress stopped going to school at the end of high school.

The picture is not too much better with the twelve girls who were in high school. One who hoped to become a nurse received her R.N. after three years of nurses' training following high school graduation. But another with ambition to become a nurse never went beyond high school. None of the girls who were taking the commercial course in high school went on to college.

But three of the five boys in high school went on to complete a college education or its equivalent. It was obvious that economic conditions were an important factor in plans for a college education. Two of these older boys could see their way through college only if they earned their way through by working while they studied in a part-time or evening program. Actually, they were able to secure their college education more easily than they anticipated.

One may summarize by saying that the correspondence is very low between statements of further educational objectives and plans, and actual educational experiences.

COMPARISON OF VOCATIONAL PLANS WITH EXPERIENCES

Subject	Aspirations and plans, 1940	Experiences, 1953
Wallace (1)	Medicine	Traveling salesman
Ralph (2)	Mechanical engineer, inventor	Student in engineering
Roy (6)	Aeronautical engineer	Worker in auto-repair shop
Jerome (7)	Cartoonist	Manager of retail liquor store
Roger (8)	Airplane pilot	Civil engineer
Sam (9)	Journalism, flower broker, electrical engineer	Is in father's business as electrical contractor
Karl (11)	Businessman	Delivers automobiles
Catherine (12)	Movie actress, private secretary	Housewife; last job was as a statistical typist
Laura (13)	Nurse	Married, but still working as secretary
Viola (14)	Not decided	Housewife
Edith (17)	Actress	Housewife; formerly merchandising manager of magazine
Isabel (18)	Secretary, piano teacher	Secretary
Stella (19)	Stenography	Housewife; formerly a secretary
Barbara (20)	Private secretary	Private secretary
Natalie (21)	Nurse	Housewife; formerly a nurse
Mabel (22)	Secretary	Housewife; formerly a secretary
Margaret (24)	Nursing, commercial artist, veterinarian	Housewife; formerly a bookkeeper
Julia (25)	Not stated	Housewife
Olive (27)	Secretary	Housewife; formerly a mail clerk
Celia (28)	Secretary	Purchasing agent
Pansy (29)	Nurse	Housewife; formerly a nurse
Dorothy (30)	Stenographer	Married, but still working as secretary
Nancy (31)	Nurse	Housewife; formerly a beauty operator, made no effort to become a nurse
Edwin (33)	News or movie photographer	Salesman

Adolescent and Adult Personality

COMPARISON OF VOCATIONAL PLANS WITH EXPERIENCES (*Cont.*)

Subject	Aspirations and plans, 1940	Experiences, 1953
Seymour (36)	Electrical engineer	Mail carrier
Jimmy (37)	Writer, advertising personnel manager	Inside salesman; quit work for three years to write but has had nothing published yet
John (39)	Chemical or electronics research, machinist, electrical engineer	Foreman in factory
Albert (40)	Business	Advertising manager

Vocation

The adolescent aspirations concerning vocation are no more significant and perhaps less meaningful than their statements about educational plans. As is well known, a child typically goes through a stage of vague and unrealistic thinking about his vocational future. In childhood there is identification with the glamorous and the spectacular without much thought as to what is required in the way of preparation. Some of these unrealistic aspirations are still present in adolescence, to judge from the data in this study. Jerome (7) wanted to be a cartoonist—actually he has become the manager of a retail liquor store. Catherine (12) thought she would become a movie actress but is now a housewife and her last job was as a statistical typist. Edith (17) also had ambitions to become an actress, but she too is now a housewife with former experience in the business office of a magazine. Jimmy (37) wanted to become a writer, and actually spent three years writing after he left the army. But apparently nothing came of the effort, and he is now an inside salesman.

Sometimes the vocation adopted is similar to the adolescent aspirations but on a lower level of competence. Roy (6) wanted to be an aeronautical engineer but became a worker in an auto-repair shop. Karl (11), who had aspirations to become a business man, delivers automobiles. Seymour (36), who wanted to become an electrical engineer, is now a mail carrier and apparently does not want a job with greater responsibility.

In the case of the girls in the study, vocational aspirations in adolescence do not have quite the same pressing reality as for the boys, inasmuch as a girl normally expects to work only for a few years before marriage, but actually it is difficult to tell that the girls are any less realistic or sincere about their vocational objectives than are the boys. Since all the high school girls were in the commercial curriculum it would be natural that they should think of going into some kind of office or secretarial work, and actually nine of the sixteen girls did state this as a vocational objective. Five chose nursing for a career. As it turned out, thirteen of the sixteen are married and of the thirteen, eleven are housewives, having given up working, while two of the married women are still working.

More women than men in the study pursued work in line with their adolescent objectives, perhaps because so many of them were in the commercial course in high school, which had definite vocational objectives and provided them with usable skills. But one who wished to be a nurse became a secretary, and another who had aspirations to be a nurse was trained to be a beautician.

In conclusion, although some are able to turn their adolescent vocational goals into reality, the relationship of adolescent vocational aspirations and the actual vocation followed is very low indeed. And where an individual follows a line of work it is typically on a lower level than was foreseen in adolescent hopes.

PERSISTENCE OF HOBBIES

Subject	Comments from interviews, 1940	Comments from interviews, 1953
Wallace (1)	Likes dogs	Says he wants to get a dog
Ralph (2)	Likes to work with tools	Went to engineering school; worked in father's machine shop
Roger (8)	Finds the Boy Scouts fun	Wonders if he should not help with the Boy Scouts
Sam (9)	Interested in photography	Main interest is photography
Laura (13)	Plays piano	Plays piano for her own amusement
Barbara (20)	Fond of sports	Same
Mabel (22)	Belongs to a girls' club	Belongs to Hadassah
Margaret (24)	Loves pets	Loves animals—has dog, cat, bird, fish
	Likes sports	Same

PERSISTENCE OF HOBBIES (*Cont.*)

Subject	Comments from interviews, 1940	Comments from interviews, 1953
Julia (25)	Concerned with clothes	Became a fashion model
Olive (27)	States that she likes to read	Reads—one book a year
Nancy (31)	Likes to sew; not interested in sports	Same
Edwin (33)	Photography	Same
	Baseball	Basketball
Seymour (36)	Interested in mechanical things—makes airplanes, likes to work on autos	Fools around with cars, woodworking
	Plays football, baseball	Does not go out for sports but likes to watch baseball or basketball games; no good at sports in school, was too heavy
	Movies	Television
John (39)	Fixes old cars and sells at a profit	Manager of auto assembly plant
Albert (40)	Not athletic	Says nothing about athletics
	Rather well read	Likes to read

DIFFERENCE IN HOBBIES OR NONE MENTIONED

Subject	Comments from interviews, 1940	Comments from interviews, 1953
Ralph (2)	Likes music a little	Not much interested in music
Mabel (22)	Plays horn in high school band, played piano, danced, sang	Golf, cards; knits, reads
Celia (28)	No mention of music	Likes to play the piano
Nancy (31)	No mention of music	Interested in opera

Hobbies

Data on hobbies for both the adolescent and mature periods were available for sixteen of the subjects. There is a remarkable similarity in hobbies over the thirteen-year period—much more than in vocational aspirations. In both 1940 and 1953 two persons liked pets, two liked to work with tools, two were interested in photography, one liked to play the piano, two were fond of sports, two liked to read, one liked to sew; one spoke of liking movies in 1940 and television in 1953. Two mentioned not being interested in sports at either time.

But there are four instances of a change in interest. In two cases interest in music is mentioned by the adult but was not by the adolescent, whereas the reverse is true for another subject. And Mabel (22) gives an entirely new list of interests as an adult.

One gathers the impression that on the whole there is a substantial persistence of adolescent avocational interests into the adult years. As a matter of fact one will be more accurate in guessing what a person's vocation will be by noting what he is interested in and what activities he pursues as an adolescent than by asking him directly what he plans or would like to do vocationally.

CONTINUING NERVOUS SIGNS

Subject	Comments from interviews, 1940	Comments from interviews, 1953
Ralph (2)	Shows lots of worries; thoroughly cowed by mother	Has nervous stomach; seems tense and anxious about school work
Roy (6)	Seems to have a feeling of impending doom; awful things happening or about to happen	Overcontrolled; has high blood pressure
Sam (9)	Mother has had several nervous breakdowns which required shock treatment; he is tense and nervous, like his mother	He describes himself and his wife as nervous; impressed examiner with being at ease
	Fearful about his health and his mother's health	During war was sent to hospital for battle fatigue; still worried about mother
Laura (13)	Worries a good deal	Gets tense and nervous
Viola (14)	Called tense, nervous	High-strung person with high energy level
Seymour (36)	Nervous, quick-tempered, excitable	Easygoing, has nervous stomach; gets mad at times but cools off; when angry shoots off his mouth
Albert (40)	Rather tense at times, not energetic, phlegmatic, bad tempered, always on edge, worries over little things	Nervous tension; listless; his bosses irritate him; fights with his analyst

INCONSISTENCIES IN NERVOUS SIGNS

| Celia (28) | Fits of depression | No mention of depression |
| Dorothy (30) | No mention of nervous symptoms | Nervous type—has butterflies in stomach |

Nervous Signs

Seven subjects show similarities in reported nervous symptoms at both periods. All seven of the subjects are described as tense, anxious, nervous, worrying. One subject was described as listless and phlegmatic in adolescence. But in two instances there is a discrepancy in the statements for the two periods: Celia (28) was described as depressed in 1940, but the 1953 report makes no mention of depression; Dorothy (30) calls herself the nervous type in 1953 and says she has butterflies in her stomach, but there was no mention of this in 1940.

MISCELLANEOUS SIMILAR TRAITS

Subject	Comments from interviews, 1940	Comments from interviews, 1953
Jerome (7)	Mother Catholic, father Protestant but converted to Catholicism; second mother was Protestant so father reverted to Protestantism	Wife originally Catholic; now he and wife are Protestants
Viola (14)	Went to Louisiana with grandmother	Went to Louisiana with husband after marriage
Dorothy (30)	When father died while she was a child, she and mother boarded with family; lived in one room	Still lives with mother, although married
Nancy (31)	Home rather plain and not at all tidy	Same
John (39)	Would like a fine home	Still lives with mother in lower-class neighborhood

Miscellaneous

Finally, there is a miscellaneous group of five items representing similarities over the thirteen-year interval. These can be called isolated instances of similarity in religious affiliation, similarity in experience, similarity in mode of life, and similarity in background.

Summary

From the foregoing detailed account of similarities and dissimilarities in the subjects in 1940 to 1953 one may make the following tentative generalizations.

There was a high degree of similarity in physical characteristics, in general personality characteristics including aggressiveness, in response to the interview situation and to the tests, in nervous signs, in hobbies, and in attitudes. These represent the more stable aspects of the overt personality. In general, one can say that a trend in one of the above areas observed in adolescence will be present thirteen years later, in early middle age.

The trends reported under the above headings represent either physical characteristics or observable behavior. In the case of relationships with others—parents, siblings, friends, or spouse—it is impossible to make an unequivocal statement. In some instances relations with parents or siblings carry over from adolescence to adulthood without change; in other instances the expressed attitudes have altered. In particular, several subjects are able to express antagonism and hostility toward parents or siblings in later years as they were not able to do in adolescence. Overt attitude toward the opposite sex in adolescence provides no basis for prediction concerning marriage. But disturbance in sexual attitudes of the few subjects who have not been able to form a marriage relationship or a satisfactory marriage was present in adolescence. Usually if a person marries he drops the friendship relationships that were common in adolescence.

No firm predictive relationship was found between verbally expressed educational or vocational plans or intentions in adolescence and the actual educational or vocational experiences of later years. Apparently there is a much closer connection between earlier and later hobby interests, expressed in actual behavior, than between interests expressed verbally.

7. Analysis of the Rorschach

This chapter presents an analysis of the Rorschach given to the subjects of the study in 1953. It is unfortunate that this instrument was not used in 1940 so that comparisons of the Rorschach at adolescence and in adulthood could have been made. The analysis of the 1953 Rorschach throws additional light on the personality structure of the twenty-seven subjects who took the test and comparisons are therefore made between the Rorschach, the Picture-Story Test, and direct observation of the subjects.

Dr. Jensen administered the Rorschach, electrically recording the responses, and from the transcription he scored the tests in the traditional fashion. These protocols were also scored and interpreted by Mrs. Stephanie Dudek. Her lengthy reports of three or more pages of interpretation for each subject serve as the basis of the analysis of the Rorschach in the present chapter. No attempt has been made, except for the section of this chapter which deals with the statistical analysis of the Rorschach, to make direct use of the basic Rorschach signs by which a protocol is usually scored. There is ample evidence that these signs by themselves have little significance and that the value of the Rorschach is to be found only in the comprehensive interpretation carried out by a psychologist trained and experienced in the use and interpretation of the Rorschach.[1] Mrs. Dudek has demonstrated her competence in Rorschach interpretation in another study.[2]

This may leave the reader with a feeling of utter subjectivity in the use of the Rorschach in this study and it must be admitted that the

[1] P. M. Symonds, "Use of the Rorschach in the Diagnosis of Teacher Effectiveness," *Journal of Projective Techniques*, XX (1956), 227–34.
[2] P. M. Symonds, "A Contribution to Our Knowledge of the Validity of the Rorschach," *Journal of Projective Techniques*, XXIX (1955), 152–62.

interpretation of the Rorschach at best is subjective. However, as one who is already familiar with the subjects of the study reads her interpretations he is impressed with the degree to which Mrs. Dudek's reports agree with the personality of the subjects as they have been reported by direct observation and from an analysis of the Picture-Story Test. In addition to describing overt personality, it is possible to diagnose from the Rorschach psychosexual, aggressive, and other trends which find expression in overt personality in many different ways. In only one case did Mrs. Dudek's personality description diverge from the picture of the individual derived from other sources. Mrs. Dudek described Olive (27) as an aggressive, lively, likeable, and exhibitionistic woman whose main goal is to display herself and to get attention and admiration. As we know her, Olive is drab, reserved, colorless, and restrained in her behavior, with pronounced tendencies toward depression. Mrs. Dudek found no reason to change her report after studying the protocol again, and one must conclude that in this instance there is a more than usual curtain of repression drawn over inner impulses and tendencies that are not permitted to find expression in the overt personality.

Coefficients of correlation were computed between certain of the variables which were analyzed out of the Rorschach reports and corresponding variables from the interviews and the Picture-Story Test.

For the Rorschach, five- or six-step ratings were made from the Rorschach reports, basing the ratings on the language with which a factor was described and also the positive and negative direction from a neutral point. If no mention was made of the factor in the Rorschach report it was given a middle position on the scale. When the report mentioned an individual as both having and not having a given characteristic, the rating was usually placed at a mid-point.

From the interview material Dr. Jensen systematically made ratings on 43 factors soon after his contacts with a subject. Some of these corresponded roughly with the factors used in the Rorschach and were used for the correlations.

For the Picture-Story Test the presence or absence of each of 38 themes was noted for each story, and the number of stories in which a given theme occurred for any subject was used as the measure of the strength of that item.

These correlations are highly attenuated and fail to indicate the true degree of relationship. Consider the following sources of error. On the Rorschach there is a sampling error due to the fact that the subject was seen on one occasion rather than another, and also a sampling error due to the subject's having responded to only ten Rorschach plates. Mrs. Dudek's interpretations add another large source of error. And the ratings of the strength of a factor from the Rorschach reports again are based on subjective interpretations which inevitably contain error.

Further, Dr. Jensen's ratings depend also on the fact that a subject was seen on one occasion rather than another and in certain surroundings. The willingness of the subject to reveal himself and the rapport between interviewer and subject are sources of error. Add to this the very subjective nature of the ratings made by Dr. Jensen following the interviews.

Similarly, on the Picture-Story Test there is a sampling error due to having the stories produced at one time and under certain circumstances, and a sampling error due to the fact that a certain twenty pictures were used rather than twenty others. Additional error arises from Dr. Jensen's subjective judgment as to whether a given theme is represented in a given story.

There are also a few factors which tend to raise the coefficients of correlation. There is a possibility that in making ratings the halo effect might have had some influence, but it is doubtful if this could have been very influential under the conditions of the rating.

With all these sources of error one wonders if any relationships are left; at any rate the coefficients of correlation reported are without doubt largely attenuated and the true relationship is much higher.

Rorschach Statistics

The statistical analysis of the Rorschach does not seem very valuable. The reliability measures of Rorschach signs is satisfactory though not high,[3] but Rorschach signs have not shown significant correlations with any other measures.[4] The validation of separate Rorschach signs with independent measures of the personality variables that they are claimed to measure have, on the whole, been disappointing.[5] Nor-

[3] Gertrude Gillenson Brady, "A Study of the Effects of Color on Rorschach Responses," *Genetic Psychology Monographs*, XXXXVIII (1953), 261-311.
[4] Joseph Zubin, "Failures of the Rorschach Technique," *Journal of Projective Techniques*, XVIII (1954), 303-15.
[5] M. R. Hertz, "The Rorschach Thirty Years After," in D. Brower and L. Abt, eds., *Progress in Clinical Psychology*, I (New York, Grune & Stratton, 1952), 119-29.

mative data on the twenty-seven Rorschach protocols obtained in this study are given in Table 15, and are to be taken for what they are worth.

TABLE 15. AVERAGE FREQUENCY OF RORSCHACH SIGNS IN THE PRESENT STUDY AND IN FIVE OTHER STUDIES PRESENTING NORMATIVE DATA

	Symonds	Cass and Mc-Reynolds[a]	Beck and others[b]	Wisch-ner and others[c]	Rapaport[d] 1[e]	2[f]	3[g]	Meili-Dworetzki[h] 1	2
R	22.1	24.6	32.6	18.5	12.1	18.7	16.8	23	29
W	8.0	9.5	5.5	9.2	7.0	9.9	5.4	8	10
D	12.1	11.7	22.8	7.1	8.8	7.5	10.2	14.5	26.5
d	0.7	1.1	3.0		0.2	0.1	0.2		
Dd	1.0	2.4			3.3	1.9	1.4	1	
S	0.3	0.9	1.9		0.9	1.2	1.4		
W%	36.4	48	19.8	60.2	45.6	50.9	34.0	37.8	24.5
D%	54.8	42	71.9	31.7	47.2	40.2	60.0	59.7	62.9
d%	3.0	3	8.2						
Dd%	4.4							2.5	12.6
S%	1.5								
M	2.9	3.0	3.5	1.4	1.0	0.5	0.8	2	3.5
FM	3.7	4.5		3.8	0.2	0.1	0.2		
m	1.2	1.0							
k	0.2	0.4							
K	0.1	0.2							
FK	0.6	0.5	1.8						
F	7.5	9.4		6.7					
Fc	1.4	2.6	2.0		1.5	2.8	2.2		
c	0.3	0.4		0.4	0.2	0.6	0.0		
C′	0.3	1.1			0.6	0.7	0.4		
FC	0.9	2.1	1.4	1.4	1.0	1.8	1.0	1.2	1.9
CF	2.2	1.8	1.4	1.6	0.7	1.3	0.0	0.7	2.4
C	0.2	0.2	0.6		0.0	0.3	0.0	0.1	0.3
F%	35.0	37.2	70.2	34.3	64.8	58.6	67.6		
P	6.1	5.4	6.8						
O	0.4								

[a] W. A. Cass, Jr., and Paul McReynolds, "A Contribution to Rorschach Norms," *Journal of Consulting Psychology*, XV (1951), 178–84.

[b] S. J. Beck, A. I. Rabin, W. G. Thiesen, H. Molish, and W. N. Thetford, "The Normal Personality as Projected in the Rorschach Test," *Journal of Psychology*, XXX (1950), 241–98.

[c] G. J. Wischner, J. B. Rotter, and R. D. Gillman, "Projective Techniques," in

Substantial normative data with which the findings in Table 15 can be compared are scarce. The most satisfactory data that are available are those provided by Cass and McReynolds.[6] The Cass-McReynolds study presents averages for 58 male and 46 female subjects, average age 34, typically high school graduates, selected, according to the occupational distribution, from a wide and representative sampling of the population. These Rorschachs were scored by the Klopfer system.

Another set of norms is provided by Beck, Rabin, Thiesen, Molish, and Thetford.[7] In the Beck study 151 normal adults are included, representing both college and elementary school graduates, but mainly high school graduates, and also a selection from 24 unskilled, 44 semi-skilled, and 48 skilled employees, and 38 executives. These were all employees in the Spiegel Mail Order House of Chicago.

Another set of norms is provided by Rapaport.[8] In the Rapaport study the normal adults consisted of 54 randomly chosen members of the Kansas Highway Patrol. These were rated 1, 2, and 3, 1 (N = 32) standing for cases in which neither pathology nor behavior indicative of maladjustment was present, 2 (N = 17) for those which were borderline, and 3 (N = 5) those which showed pronounced maladjustment.

A final study by Gertrude Meili-Dworetzki[9] included 20 adults of little education and 20 adults of high education.

The Psychological Program in AAF Convalescent Hospitals (Army Air Forces Aviation Psychology Program Research Report No. 15, 1947), pp. 144–57.
[d] David Rapaport, Merton Gill, and Roy Schafer, *Diagnostic Psychological Testing*, Vol. II (Chicago, Year Book Publishers, 1946).
[e] Cases showing neither pathology nor behavior indicating maladjustment.
[f] Borderline cases.
[g] Cases showing pronounced maladjustment.
[h] Gertrude Meili-Dworetzki, "The Development of Perception in the Rorschach," in Bruno Klopfer et al., *Developments in the Rorschach Technique*, Vol. II (Yonkers-on-Hudson, World Book Company, 1956).

[6] W. A. Cass, Jr., and Paul McReynolds, "A Contribution to Rorschach Norms," *Journal of Consulting Psychology*, XV (1951), 178–84.
[7] S. J. Beck, A. I. Rabin, W. G. Thiesen, H. Molish, and W. N. Thetford, "The Normal Personality as Projected in the Rorschach Test," *Journal of Psychology*, XXX (1950), 241–98.
[8] David Rapaport, Merton Gill, and Roy Schafer, *Diagnostic Psychological Testing*, Vol. II (Chicago, Year Book Publishers, 1946).
[9] Gertrude Meili-Dworetzki, "The Development of Perception in the Rorschach," Chapter 5 in Bruno Klopfer et al., *Developments in the Rorschach Technique*, Vol. II (Yonkers-on-Hudson, World Book Company, 1956).

The Wischner norms are based on 258 aviation students—all of whom had successfully passed psychiatric screening.[10]

Attempts to make comparisons are unsatisfactory, the major difficulty being variations in the meaning of the scoring elements. The Cass-McReynolds norms would seem to be the most satisfactory with which to compare the Rorschach data in the present study. Both were scored using the Klopfer-Kelly-Davidson system.

Beck's data involve a slightly larger number of cases, but Beck uses a somewhat different set of scoring signs, and one is never quite sure whether the comparisons are admissible. Beck counts as an F all responses including F whether the F occurs alone or in combination with some other determinant.

The Wischner data were secured during the war and only the main signs are reported.

Rapaport, following Rorschach's original scoring, has added refinements of his own which to him seem significant. Occasionally he follows the Binder scoring scheme.[11] Rapaport's W and D signs agree with Klopfer's. Rapaport's Dd is essentially what Klopfer means by d. Klopfer means by Dd unusual details, that is, details not included in his charts which define D and d. For Klopfer Dd includes tiny, edge, inside, and other rare details. Rapaport uses De for edge details, Dr for tiny and rare details. How Rapaport scores the inner detail could not be determined.

Klopfer uses F when it stands alone; Rapaport gives this measure but only in terms of percent; and Rapaport also gives an F% that includes all responses in which F is a determinant, whether standing alone or in combination with another determinant. It is in connection with the shading and texture responses that the greatest discrepancies and confusion lie. Klopfer distinguishes between texture responses which are determined by touch(c') and vista or depth responses(K). But Rapaport does not make these distinctions, and they all tend to be included under shading or chiaroscuro(ch) responses.

[10] G. J. Wischner, J. B. Rotter, and R. D. Gillman, "Projective Techniques," Chapter 9 in *The Psychological Program in AAF Convalescent Hospitals* (Army Air Forces Aviation Psychology Program Research Report No. 15, 1947), pp. 144-57.

[11] H. Binder, "Die Klinische Bedeutung des Rorschach'schen Versuches," *Schweizer Archiv für Neurologie und Psychiatrie*, LIII (1944), 12-29.

Meili-Dworetzki naturally follows Klopfer, since her paper is included in Klopfer's book. But even here there are inconsistencies. For instance, she places the S response in with the D or Dd according to the area indicated. Meili-Dworetzki also recognizes Rapaport's oligophrenic response(Do) which is a response in which only part of a body or person is seen where others see the whole body. Meili-Dworetzki follows Binder's rather than Klopfer's treatment of shading, and she provides no data with regard to the frequency of FM(animal movement) or m(inanimate movement).

So the comparisons of the tabulations in the present study with Rapaport and Meili-Dworetzki become more a question of comparing the method of scoring than of comparing the groups. The present study shows approximately the same R as the Cass-McReynolds study, considerably lower than Beck, and definitely higher than Wischner and Rapaport. The location analysis agrees fairly closely with Cass-McReynolds. The present study shows a much lower frequency and percentage of D than Beck and Meili-Dworetzki and somewhat higher than Rapaport. The frequencies in the other space areas are too small to make comparisons.

Our F and F% agrees fairly closely with Cass-McReynolds and Wischner. Apparently Beck and Rapaport define F differently than is done in the Klopfer system, and the results should not be compared with norms from these two authorities.

M and FM in the present study are close to the Cass-McReynolds norms. But our FC is noticeably lower than Cass-McReynolds, in fact, lower than in any other set of norms reported. On the other hand, CF is higher than any other group except Meili-Dworetzki's better-educated group. This difference in FC and CF is probably a real difference, and may indicate that the subjects in the present study are somewhat less emotionally inhibited than the adults used in these other normative studies.

Nosological Diagnosis

In this and in the following sections of this chapter the section is introduced by a tabular summary. The descriptions attempt to use the precise language that is used in the Rorschach reports themselves.

This may lead to some duplication, but there has been an effort to be inclusive so that a given subject will be characterized by the several terms used in the report to describe him.

SUMMARY: NOSOLOGICAL DIAGNOSIS

Subjects	Rorschach description	Number
1, 2, 7, 8, 9, 13, 14, 17, 18, 20, 22, 24, 27, 28, 29, 30, 31, 33, 36, 40	Normal	20
6, 12, 19, 21, 37, 39	Borderline schizophrenic	6
11	Paranoid schizophrenic	1
		27

Twenty of the subjects are reported to be in the normal range, although many of these show neurotic symptoms of one kind or another: fourteen are reported to be mildly depressed (1, 8, 9, 14, 17, 18, 21, 22, 24, 27, 28, 29, 31, 37); one is described as paranoid (13); seven have hysterical symptoms (1, 8, 11, 14, 27, 28, 39) variously described as hysterical character organization, hysterical overintensity, hysterical explosiveness; subject 14 is reported to be close to anxiety hysteria; the term compulsive is used to describe two subjects (29, 40); and subject 40 is said to have an obsessive-compulsive character disorder.

Other terms such as immature, excitable, ineffective, rigid, oppositional, and detached are adjectives used to describe other individuals, all apparently in the normal range.

Seven of the subjects are variously described as schizoid, or showing a mild, benign, underlying borderline schizophrenic process (6, 12, 19, 21, 37, 39), or as having a schizoid façade (36). Six of these are classified in the summary at the beginning of this section as borderline schizophrenic.

Finally, one subject (11) is classified as paranoid schizophrenic, not so deeply psychotic, however, as to be incapacitated.

It is significant that none of the subjects is or has been institutionalized or hospitalized for mental disturbance. Subject 11 had been receiving psychiatric treatment when first seen in 1940, and has struck all who have studied him as an extremely bizarre individual, but apparently as long as he can live in the protection of his parents' home he can manage to adjust to his surroundings.

Of the forty original subjects, one who was contacted in 1953 (Edgar, 10) agreed to participate in the study and made an appointment for an interview, but did not show up. A brother said that he was confused and somewhat irresponsible in his behavior. He had a record of hospitalization in a Veterans Administration Hospital in 1949.

Two of the subjects (12 and 40) have undergone or are undergoing psychotherapy. Both of them report improvement, but the Rorschach of one (12) indicates that she is still very disturbed. She received a tentative diagnosis of underlying schizophrenic structure; the other (40) received a diagnosis of obsessive-compulsive character disorder.

SUMMARY: PSYCHOSEXUAL ADJUSTMENT

Men	Rorschach description	Number
6, 7, 8, 9, 37, 40	Inadequate as a man	6
7, 11, 36	Immature psychosexual development	3
6, 7, 11, 17, 36	Lacks sensuality and eroticism	5
1, 6, 11, 33, 40	Afraid of women as sexual objects	5
6, 7, 8	Difficulty of control in sexual intercourse	3
1, 9, 36	Women as objects to be overpowered	3
2, 37	Ambivalent about women	2
11, 39	Narcissistic	2
1, 6, 9, 36, 37	Superficial psychosexual adjustments appear good	5

Women		
12, 18, 19, 20, 21, 22, 28, 30, 31	Unable to accept self as an adequate woman	9
12, 17, 19, 29	Wishes to remain a young girl	4
14, 17, 19, 22, 24, 28, 30	Sexually unresponsive (frigid)	7
14, 17, 20, 22	Fear of sexual contact in heterosexual relationships	4
14, 17	Phallus is dangerous	2
18, 21	Has suffered narcissistic injuries as a woman	2
17, 19	Little insight into sexual attitudes	2
13, 14, 17, 20	Feels paranoid and suspicious under pressure	4
18, 28	Helpless, inadequate, masochistic	2
12, 27, 30	Oversexualizes nonsexual situations	3
21, 27	Exhibitionistic	2
21, 22, 24	Superficial heterosexual adjustments appear adequate	3

Psychosexual Adjustment

The term sex means a number of different things. It may mean (1) orgasm, the climax of excitement in sexual intercourse. This is the meaning of sex as the term is used by Kinsey, who uses the term "sexual outlet" for both male and female, which he defines as "sexual activity or activities that lead to and culminate in orgasm." [12] It may mean (2) preparatory sexual reactions or fore play. Or it may apply to (3) the feelings that accompany sexual activity. Sexual reactions as understood in (1) and (2) may or may not be accompanied by feelings varying in degree of intensity. Also, there may be sexual feeling that is not accompanied by any observable sexual activity. A person may be called sensual, that is, ardent or eager for closeness, affection, bodily contact, without necessarily engaging in sexual activity as such. Another meaning is (4) sex-role identification, either male or female. This may be subdivided into (4a) acting the part of a man or woman. If the sex role is masculine an individual may act aggressively, with initiative and fervor, and he may wear male clothing and engage in active pursuits ordinarily engaged in by men; or if the sex role is feminine an individual may be passive, receptive, unassertive, wear feminine, soft, frilly clothing, and engage in the more passive and domestic pursuits of a woman. According to (4b) the sex role may exist in feeling, that is, an individual feels or wishes to feel like a man or woman. Naturally the feeling is usually accompanied by the corresponding behavior.

What aspects of sex are revealed by the Rorschach? The Rorschach primarily provides evidence for sexual feeling and sex-role identification as indicated by feeling. Also, the Rorschach indicates impulse tendencies, whether active or passive, and feelings, whether ardent or cold. The Rorschach also shows aspects of sexual adjustments that are expressions of other personality trends and expressions of the self—the need to demonstrate masculinity by overpowering women, the fear to assert oneself sexually, adopting a soft and yielding attitude, taking the sexual initiative, dread of the excitement of sex, etc.

The extent to which the Rorschach can diagnose actual sexual be-

[12] A. C. Kinsey, W. B. Pomeroy, and C. E. Norton, *Sexual Behavior in the Human Male* (Philadelphia, W. B. Saunders, 1948), p. 173. A. C. Kinsey et al., *Sexual Behavior in the Human Female* (Philadelphia, W. B. Saunders, 1953), pp. 510, 511.

havior is dubious, and any attempt to do so is speculative. Suffice it to say that, in general, impulses strive for expression, and the stronger the impulse the more certainly will it seek early and frequent expression. The Rorschach can also estimate the probability of overt expression of sexual impulses by knowledge of the freedom and constriction of response in general.

The tabulation at the beginning of this section undoubtedly has sacrificed complexity in order to present a picture of the situation that can be grasped at a glance. Only the complete Rorschach report would indicate complexities and interrelationships. The tabulation is startling in that apparently every one of the twenty-seven subjects in the study for whom Rorschachs are available shows some sign of sexual disturbance or failure to achieve maximum or even optimum sexual functioning. In the case of six of the men this is summarized as sexual immaturity or inadequacy as a man. Immaturity may mean wanting and giving affection but uninterested in more complete or intense sexual experience. Sex-role confusion or inversion is largely a matter of feeling or attitude, and certainly does not necessarily mean the overt expression of homosexuality. Inability to accept the female role in the case of the women means in some of the subjects fear of sex.

For seven of the subjects—four men (1, 9, 36, 37) and three women (21, 22, 24)—Mrs. Dudek has noted "good sex adjustment, superficially," but finds in the same Rorschach records signs of sexual inadequacy. That is, in each of these cases the subject is married, and apparently happily married. But subject 1 feels the need to overpower women in order to demonstrate his masculinity, subjects 9 and 22 feel sexually inadequate, subject 21 feels inadequate as a woman and tries to compensate by her exhibitionistic tendencies of wanting to be looked at and admired. Subject 24 finds little pleasure in sex relations. Subject 36, because of uncertainty about his masculinity, is not able to go beyond mild affectionate responses in his sexual relationships. Subject 37, because of close ties with his mother and the incest taboo, is unable to find normal libidinal pleasure in sex. These limitations in feeling do not mean that these individuals are unable to have normal sexual relations and to end coitus with ejaculation.

Seven of the twenty-seven subjects in the study are unmarried (2, 11, 18, 20, 28, 39, 40). Of the four men, two had homosexual tendencies and two were confused as to sex role, that is, they had partial identification with either sex. In the case of the three women each had difficulty or confusion in accepting her role as a woman. Apparently, from the few cases in this study, failure to achieve marriage is related to some disturbance in accepting one's sex role.

Of the twenty subjects who are married, six have no children, five have one child, eight have two chidren, and one has three children. Nothing in the Rorschach records could be found to indicate that those who had two or three children were better adjusted sexually than those who had one or no child. Subject 29, who has borne three children, is described as emotionally immature, and although the identification is feminine it is the feminity of a young girl, not an adult woman. Similarly, those with two children are variously characterized as immature, sexually repressed, having strong fear of sex, exhibitionistic, inadequate sexually. Apparently the ability to have children should not be confused with the capacity to have sexual experience with full capacity of feeling and libidinal involvement.

If one may generalize from this small sample, one must conclude that most people are far from experiencing the full enjoyment of sex. Some approach sex timidly, unsure of themselves and of their role in sexual relations. Some engage in sex reluctantly, with loathing and fear, some, because of their inhibition toward sexual experience, their distaste for it, and their lack of self-assurance, are driven to find sexual release in distorted ways such as in exhibitionistic display or in various perverse practices.

If this is true, and there is reason to believe it is true, what are the implications? Does it imply that such individuals are undersexed and lacking in normal potency? This conclusion cannot be drawn. But it does imply that the experiences of infancy, childhood, and adolescence have suppressed, cramped, and distorted sexual expression. Most of these individuals have been forced by experience to repress their sexual impulses and to find forms of sex-role identification that prevent them from enjoying and exercising their full sexual potentialities as adults. This may be in part a lack of sex education, but more importantly it represents attitudes that have been formed through interpersonal relationships, primarily in the family.

In general, this is not the picture that we have of people, and one could not draw these conclusions from the interviews in this study. It is not the custom or practice for people to discuss their sexual feelings or experiences with a stranger, certainly not in one or two contacts, and the general tendency is to give the impression of normality and satisfaction with regard to sex.

Of the seven subjects who are not married, Ralph (2) is all in favor of marriage but does not believe one should rush into anything so important. He has had serious intentions toward three or four girls and is now going steady. From the Rorschach one learns that Ralph has a mild homosexual orientation with paranoid fears and is ambivalent toward women. Karl (11) was candid in saying, "I don't mind telling you I hope to remain a bachelor, I have no love life; if you don't have no love life, you don't get married"; but he added, "I am not shy of girls, or stuff like that." The Rorschach tells us that he has a latent unconscious homosexual orientation and has much timidity with women. Isabel (18) claims she is in no hurry to be married, although she would "love to marry." She hates to be seen with a short man. She wants a man who is very good, from a nice family, who is religious, has a good job, is good to his mother, and is a good sport. From the Rorschach we learn that she has masochistic tendencies, and feels helpless and inadequate, but has strong penis envy. Barbara (20), who told of strong competitive attitudes toward men, talked much about marriage, but stated that she had not found the right man yet. She insisted that she has no objections to necking or petting and that she was not a cold person sexually. But from the Rorschach we learn of her fears of heterosexual relationships, phallic worship, penis envy, and a wish to have been a man. She avoids men because she fears she has little to give as a woman and is afraid of her aggressive impulses.

Celia (28) is not too anxious to get married, but has not yet met the right man. She would rather have an independent single life than make the wrong choice and spend the rest of her life regretting it. She believes she is normal in her emotions and reactions, but she has very strict standards about premarital sex behavior. The Rorschach indicates much sex role confusion, sexual unresponsiveness and frigidity, and sadomasochistic attitudes toward men.

John (39) has a poor opinion of marriage. He is looking for a goddess with both brains and beauty and has not found this combination. He claims that he has had much to do with models and actresses with plenty of opportunities to get married, but he can't see settling down to married life. The Rorschach indicates a strong feminine identification and an alternation between passivity and aggressive self-assertion.

Albert (40) is candid in saying that until recently he has been afraid of marriage. If a girl who was eligible showed any interest in him he would drop her. (Since the interview was concluded, Albert has married.) The Rorschach indicates a confused sexual identification with underlying homosexual conflicts and feelings of inadequacy as a man. There is castration anxiety and fear of sexual contacts with women.

Space does not permit detailed discussion of the other cases of those who have married. Wallace (1) states that he enjoys married life and gets along well with his wife. He says that has was never wholly in love with any other woman, but claims that they may have thought so and that he let them think so only so that he could get things from them, implying sexual conquests on his part. The Rorschach indicates a fear of women as sexual objects, and he reacts to them as objects to be overpowered because he is unable to handle them with a sense of adequacy.

Roy (6) speaks of a "harmonious marriage," but the Rorschach indicates sexual repression and difficulties of control in sexual intercourse. Jerome (7) claims that he could not have a better wife and that they get along very well together, that she is a devoted wife and mother. But the Rorschach tells of his being immature in psychosexual development, lacking in sensuality and eroticism and showing some of the effeminate traits of the feminine-passive character.

Catherine (12) was very frank in the interview about her sexual reactions. When first married she claimed she was frigid and sex was a real chore, but as a result of psychotherapy she now finds intercourse pleasant—"she practically needs two husbands." The Rorschach, however, is not so sanguine, finding that she is still unable to accept herself as an adult woman and has a tendency to oversexualize nonsexual situations. The Rorschach also points to much narcissism and need for body display.

Laura (13) talked at length about her mother's disfavor of her marriage. She and her husband are living with his mother. They practice birth control (against the teachings of the Church) until they are better established financially and can afford a child. There are no children as yet. The Rorschach indicates that she is hypersensitive to sexual demands, and becomes restless, nervous, or frightened, and tightens up in a man-woman sexual situation. She is not able to stand much pressure, and feels paranoid and persecuted if pressure is applied.

Viola (14), too, had much to say about resisting her mother with regard to marriage. She has been quite willing, on her mother's importunate demands, to leave her husband for short periods, but she always returned to him. They have two children, and she spoke of her "togetherness" with her husband. But the Rorschach tells of fear of sexual contact, and the unconscious fear of the phallus as a dangerous and destructive weapon.

Edith (17) talked about her husband with high praise and admiration. She described him as a quiet fellow, not at all aggressive. But the Rorschach indicates little evidence of sensuality. According to the Rorschach she is afraid of men and sex, and is sexually unresponsive (frigid), but is probably a compliant, dutiful wife.

Stella (19) seems to be very happy in her marriage. She claims that she likes housework. She thinks married life is much better than single life largely because she has such a good husband. But the Rorschach indicates that she is unable to deal with her sexuality with any deep or strong feelings. Her deeper identification tends to be masculine—or she is afraid that she is basically masculine.

Natalie (21) feels superior to her husband but also feels quite happy in her marriage. She claims her husband is a jealous man and one who cannot tolerate anything that is feminine or sissy. There was evidence of much difference between them about raising the children. At the end of the interview she commented, "I hope I haven't given you the impression that our marriage is not happy." The Rorschach indicates that she feels inadequate as a woman, that she feels damaged and hurt as a female and suffers from a castration complex, and consequently has a great need to be looked at and admired.

Dorothy (30) complained that her husband is impotent, never becomes aroused sexually, and never makes sexual advances. He is kind to her and they get along perfectly in every other way. But the Rorschach pictures her as sexually frigid and unresponsive. She is preoccupied with sex and finds it difficult to accept her role as woman and wife, although she adopts a pseudo-housewifely role. Sexual intercourse to her is something unclean. This case is a good illustration of the frequent tendency to project one's sexual difficulties and to place the blame and responsibility on one's partner.

Nancy (31) refers to her husband as disgustingly realistic, especially about money. She complained about feeling restricted since her marriage and stated if she could do it over again she would wait longer before marrying so that she could have more time to run around and have fun. The Rorschach also indicates dissatisfaction with her marriage, but attributes this to feelings of insecurity and failure as a woman and as a sexual partner.

Edwin's (33) wife is a cripple. He states that he does not have many interests in common with her, but they rarely argue about anything. They have one child and would like another. The Rorschach indicates a deep feminine identification on his part, and feelings of inadequacy as a man make him timid with women. He equates sex with annihilation, inasmuch as his feminine identification places him in the role of victim, not the aggressor. He feels sex is dirty.

Seymour (36) has married twice. His first marriage was not based on any real attachment, and actually he lived with his first wife only about a week because of the war. He says he wouldn't be a bachelor for anything now. He lets his wife make most of the decisions, and she has her way with most things. He claims that he has a very good sex life. But the Rorschach interpretation mentions lack of sexual identity. He is uncertain of his masculinity and hence overcompensates by overidealizing the masculine role, but he has very little capacity to invest libido in his relationships.

Jimmy (37) was so effusive in his interview that it was difficult to pin him down on any topic. He has evidently had a variety of experiences with women, but is now married and says the marriage has been happy from the start, with no difficulty in sexual adjustment. The Rorschach, however, pictures him as inadequate as a man and ambivalent toward women. He has difficulty in combining tender and aggressive feelings for the same woman. His Oedipal ties were never adequately resolved, and he alternates between passive feminine identification and aggressive masculine assertion. It is difficult for him to find normal libidinal pleasure, and the sexual act becomes overspiritualized and overidealized. The Rorschach indicates his tendency to deny disappointment and frustration in sexual contacts.

This brief comparison of the picture obtained from the interview and the Rorschach is sufficient to indicate how the interview fails to show the deeper underlying sexual attitudes. There is a tendency in the interview to disguise real sexual attitudes by projection and denial.

Psychosexual adjustment is not openly displayed in the stories from the Picture-Story Test. When one reviews the whole series of stories he finds plenty of direct reference to heterosexual relationships. Rare are the direct references to sex behavior as such, although this may be found in subjects 37 and 39. More common are the social adjustments and attitudes that are sexual in nature, as indicated by romance and marriage. There is undoubtedly much reference to sex that is symbolic, as was mentioned in *Adolescent Fantasy* (pp. 151–54). There we found sexual implications in themes of kidnaping, of being followed, hiding and being caught, passing an examination, automobile driving, collisions and crashes, robbery, particularly of jewels, and getting a job. Sexual attitudes are shown by aggressive activity or by timid and retiring passivity. Attitudes and relationships toward parents or parent figures frequently carry information as to sexual attitudes. Much general repression implies sexual repression, and general fear implies sexual fear.

On a superficial level, references to sex or to heterosexual relationships in the stories usually agree with and frequently amplify attitudes and behavior that were expressed in the interviews. Frequently the stories contain rather fantastic wishes that apparently play only a minor role in the individual's present and overt personality.

Isabel (18) incorporates the same romantic interests of love and marriage in one of her stories (A-10) that she expresses in her interview, but the interest is faraway and remote. Barbara (20), unmarried and with strong masculine identification, places much more of her sexual longings into her stories. She tells themes of a desire for love and marriage (A-1, B-3), fear of marriage (B-3), a broken engagement (A-9), and rejection of marriage (A-3). These are the same themes that she expresses in the interviews, but she expresses them with greater conviction and abandon in her stories. There is also confusion over sex role (B-3), with an emphasis on the weakness of men and the strength of women (B-10). The stories also present the conflict between marriage and a career (A-5), desire to be on one's own (A-9), work as an escape (B-9), and the loneliness of being single (A-3). Celia (28), also unmarried, tells a story (A-10) with themes of marriage, children, and security. But in story A-2 a girl's parents will not approve of a man because he does not have a good job. This is a patent projection in her stories. Apparently Celia is unable to accept the sexual frigidity and sadomasochistic attitudes toward men revealed in the Rorschach.

John (39) reveals his attitude toward women much more forcefully in his stories than in his interviews. The stories show strong hostility toward women, picturing them as fickle and untrustworthy, and he has a very poor view of marriage. In one story (B-7) a man cannot satisfy a woman sexually and she leaves him, but in other stories a man abandons a woman (A-5, B-10). In story B-9 sex and violence are confused with each other. On the basis of the Picture-Story Test Dr. Jensen tentatively diagnosed latent homosexuality. "There is a blatant rejection of heterosexuality. There is reason to suspect fears of sexual inadequacy. He seems to be a castrated male. Women are threatening to him and hence he fears them." The Rorschach mentions feminine identification, but stresses the aggressive elements in his personality and the sadomasochistic elements which cause an alternation between passivity and aggressive self-assertion.

The sexual implications in the fantasy productions of a few other cases will be commented on. Viola (14) incorporates masochistic tendencies in her stories that deal with relations between the sexes. There is guilt over sexual transgression (B-10) and a need for punishment. But there is mutual dependency of husband and wife, and the wife can change, reform, or rescue a man. There is denial of conflict in marriage (A-6) and the picture of an ideally happy family which is also mentioned in the interview. Neither the Picture-Story Test nor the interview indicate the sexual fear that is shown in the Rorschach. Apparently her moral attitude toward sex, present in conscious fantasy, is a defense against fear of sexual contact and the male organ.

Olive (27) fantasies a woman who feels neglected when taken for granted, and wants to be important to a man (B-10). In another story a husband is unfaithful (B-5), while in another it is the woman who wants to go out and have a good time, but the husband is timid and stays at home to do some of the housework (B-7). The Picture-Story Test depicts obvious marital dissatisfaction. There is nothing in the interview to suggest this. She stated that her husband was her first and only boy friend. They have interests in common. She is very much against petting outside of marriage. Although the Rorschach report mentions a repression of basic sexual energy, it emphasizes that sexual expression turns toward display and exhibitionism with little capacity to be sexually feminine, soft, or yielding. Discrepancy between the Rorschach and other evidence in the case of Olive has been discussed at the beginning of this chapter.

The main emphasis in the stories of Dorothy (30) is passivity. There is desire for marriage (A-10), men are watching her (B-10), the girl waits for a boy but the boy is shy and embarrassed (A-3). Dorothy pictures her husband in the interview as impotent, whereas the Rorschach report sees her as frigid and unresponsive. The Picture-Story Test in this case indicates her underlying wish life, the interview projects the difficulty onto the husband, while the Rorschach indicates sexual repression. Here the Rorschach reveals the defensive trend, the Picture-Story Test the wish life, while both of these are hidden by the defenses present in the interview.

Nancy (31) emphasizes in her stories how important it is to have support from a husband (A-3, A-9), and that a boy and girl should always be together (A-10), but there are themes of marital difficulties (A-6) and unfaithfulness (A-5), and of lovers separated (B-3). There is also an indication of sex guilt. This is quite contradictory to the interview, which indicates that if anything her marriage is too strongly cemented to suit her. She craves more freedom. She also states that whereas her husband is suspicious of people she is very trusting of others. Here is an unresolved discrepancy, but one suspects that there are unconscious fantasies of a promiscuous nature that are revealed in the fantasy productions.

The fantasies of Jimmy (37) are difficult to interpret, partly because his stories are long and involved. Sex is more unabashedly introduced into his stories than by any other subject. In two stories a younger person (a man in A-7, a girl in B-8) marries an older person. There is conflict between sex and certain more spiritual aspects of relationships between the sexes. A woman is horrified at the grossness of men in sexual relations (A-8). Jimmy's stories indicate clearly the unresolved Oedipus situation. In his interviews Jimmy, as has been recounted, discusses at length his struggle to achieve independence from his mother, intimates that he has had many sexual experiences, but that he is now happily married. The Rorschach pictures his ambivalence toward women, but also his inadequacy as a man.

It is difficult to summarize the contribution of these three kinds of evidence with regard to sex. Undoubtedly the Rorschach contains evidence as to basic sexual attitudes and feelings. The Picture-Story Test reveals the attitudes that can be expressed verbally in fantasy. These frequently pertain to the wish life, and may or may not agree with the underlying tendencies shown by the Rorschach. The interviews, of course, show only the attitudes and feelings that the individual himself is willing to admit to consciousness, and frequently, if not usually, they represent defenses against deeper, unacceptable feelings and attitudes. It is common for a person to deny difficulties, to claim that sexual adjustment is satisfactory, or to project his difficulties onto his partner.

SUMMARY: IDENTITY

Men	Rorschach description	Number
6, 36	Little identity as a person	2
6, 36	High regard for the masculine	2
1, 9, 36, 39	Need to test masculinity by self-assertion	4
7, 33, 39, 40	Feminine identification	4
2, 11, 33, 40	Homosexual orientation	4
7, 40	Feminine-passive character	2
7, 9	Lacks masculinity	2
2, 8, 36, 37, 39, 40	Confused sexual identity, concern with adequacy as a man; alternates between masculine and feminine	6

Women		
13, 21, 22, 30	Little identity as a person	4
20, 21, 27, 29	Feminine identification	4
21, 30	Pseudofemininity	2
14, 18	Gentle, yielding, compliant, submissive	2
19, 20, 28	Masculine identification	3
18, 20	Penis envy	2
30, 31	Difficult to accept role as wife	2
20, 28, 31	Not sure of femininity	3
12, 17, 18, 19, 20, 21, 22, 28, 30, 31	Cannot accept self as an adult woman	10
12, 17, 29	Identity as a young girl	3
28, 30, 31	Confusion and ambivalence about sexual identity	3

Identity

Although sex-role identification has been discussed in part in the section dealing with psychosexual adjustment, it will be given fuller treatment in this section dealing with identity. Identification is considered either in general terms as meaning personal identity or as sex-role identification. By personal identity is meant having a clear concept of self as a person, not being very dependent on others, possessing independence in thought and action. In the case of one subject it was said that "he has little feeling of himself as a person—he does not know who he is or what he wants," and for another that "he does not know where the world ends and he begins." The meaning of sex-role identification as adoption of a masculine or femine role should be clear.

The Rorschach indicated that two of the men and four of the women in the study have little identity as persons. These individuals also have feelings of inadequacy and inferiority and usually are weak, dependent, demanding individuals.

With regard to sex-role identification in general, if a man had made a masculine identification this was not commented on in the Rorschach report. Masculine identification among the men was mentioned only when it served as a defense against weakness or feminine tendencies, as was clearly the case for John (39) and less clearly for Sam (9). Feminine identification was mentioned for five of the women, but for two of these, Natalie (21) and Dorothy (30), this is called pseudofemininity, and for these two individuals this, too, served as a defense against underlying doubts about rejection of the feminine position.

Feminine identification was recognized in the case of eight of the men under such headings as feminine identification, feminine-passive character, homosexual orientation, and simply "lacks masculinity." For five of the men (including some already mentioned) there was confused sex-role identification, as an alternation between the masculine and feminine and concern for adequacy as a man.

In cases of the women, masculine identification was mentioned for three, penis envy for two, while three were said to be unsure of and confused about their sexual identity. The matter of maturity of sexual identity was mentioned for eight women.

As is the case with most of the other areas in which tabulations of the Rorschach interpretations have been made, there are overlappings and inconsistencies. For instance, Barbara (20) is said to have both feminine and masculine identification as well as inability to accept herself as a mature woman. Here as in other cases subtle distinctions are made in the Rorschach report. In the case of Barbara the identification is said to be mainly feminine, although she is not sure of her femininity. But there is also a secret penis envy and wish to have been a man. Her self-concept is slightly derogatory and certainly not a feminine one. She feels she has little to give as a woman. The report concludes, "She is capable of much richer and more rewarding emotional life if she could accept her feminity and sexuality more."

Although not specifically stated there seems to be an assumption that sex-role identification is in some way related to the adequacy of psychosexual adjustment. When the masculine role for men and the feminine role for women is adopted, without question heterosexual relationships tend to be normal, adequate, and satisfactory. But if the reverse identification is the case, a man lacks some of the assertion and aggressiveness for adequate sexual functioning and the woman lacks the gentle, yielding, compliant, submissive response necessary for her role in heterosexual relationships. But these same attributes also characterize to some degree nonsexual relationships. The man who lacks unconflicted masculine identification tends to be somewhat unassertive and lacking in aggression in his social and work relationships, or vice versa—the woman with masculine identification tends to be aggressive and bossy in her social and work relationships.

One has to read between the lines in order to get any hint as to sex identification from the interview reports. Among the men feminine traits may be expressed by the following. Ralph (2) "wore a fresh starched white shirt, a necktie, and a very clean white woolen sweater. He wore a heavy jeweled ring on the fourth finger of his left hand." Jerome's (7) "hair is extremely well brushed and combed. He gave the interviewer the impression that he is conscious of his theatrically handsome appearance." John (39), who tries to impress the world as a "he-man," does not drink or smoke. He once ran off five hundred copies of the Alcoholics Anonymous code on a ditto machine and passed them out to everyone he knew who drank. Albert (40) doesn't like selling because he feels that he is not aggressive enough to be a good salesman.

On the other hand, of the women with masculine identification Barbara (20) was a tomboy before she reached the ninth grade and used to beat up all the neighborhood boys. One of the male subjects in the study still carries a scar over his eye that he received from Barbara as a boy. Even today she wants men to know she is as good as they are. Celia (28) "often resents the fact that she has been doing a man's job but does not get equal recognition with the men in the company where she works. She believes that she is better qualified than some men who are promoted beyond her station in the firm." These illustrations were selected to show the correspondence between the Rorschach and the impression on the interviewer. In most of the interview reports such correspondence is not nearly as obvious, and one must conclude that in general sex-role identification as interpreted from the Rorschach does not have an obvious correspondence with the overt personality.

The Picture-Story Test, on the other hand, counts sex-role identification as one of its principal features. Every story is told from the point of view of either a male or a female character, and if the sex of the hero in the story is chosen from one of the minor characters in the picture or someone not present in the picture at all, the sex-role identification is especially prominent.

Feminine identification was specially noted in the stories of Roger (8). That he identified the figure in A-2 as a woman was quite unusual. Dr. Jensen comments, "In outward appearance Roger is probably the most masculine subject in the study. The girls in story A-8 with whom he obviously identifies are both sexually seduced."

These are two girls that were—that worked at a dime-a-dance dance hall. Probably they have a poor reputation. The dark-haired one possibly has been in the dance hall for a number of years while the blonde has just been introduced to the dance hall routine with in the last few months—the last three or four months. The brunette has hardened to the task of dancing and going out at nights with just anyone who seems to ask, with the—who has a large bankroll. The blonde is just probably, probably in this picture, being talked into going out with a twosome that the brunette has selected, found or been introduced to. They'll go out with the twosome, dance, have a few drinks. They'll probably end up in one of the girl's apartments. They'll make a night out of it and the men will leave the next morning. The blonde being possibly a slight tinge of conscience but as she gets hardened to it after a while there won't be any conscience left. (Roger, subject 8, Picture-Story A-8, 1953)

There is a possibility that Roger's anxiety over his ability is related to his concept of himself as a man. Of Roger the Rorschach report says: "His generally aggressive and slightly superior attitude may give the impression of masculinity and self-assurance, but his concept of himself as a man is far from sure and adequate." However, the Rorschach makes this more a matter of immaturity than of feminine identification.

Women in the stories of Barbara (20) are strong-willed and have tempers but show no signs of masculine identification.

Pansy (29) expresses some doubt as to sexual identity by being unsure whether the figures in pictures A-2 and B-9 are men or women. According to the Rorschach the identification is basically feminine, although somewhat immature.

In some of the stories, concern about sex-role identification among the women may be expressed by doubts about one's attractiveness. This was particularly noticeable in the stories told by adolescents. Dorothy (30) fantasies in story B-10 that a man is interested in the main female character, which may be merely a wish-fulfilling fantasy, but also possibly a fantasy on reassurance that she is sexually attractive. The Rorschach refers to her pseudofemininity and the fact that she is not sure of her femininity.

Edwin (33) shows a tendency toward feminine identification in his stories. The girl in story B-5 is concerned about her hairdo. Edwin is definitely credited with feminine identification by the Rorschach.

John (39), who adopts a very masculine persona in life, shows sex-role confusion in his stories. On card A-2 he says, "I am not sure if it should be a female or a male." On card A-10 he comments, "I was going to say two girls going down to a swami, but I will set this up as a girl and a guy." On A-2 he makes the male figure an artist, a somewhat feminine pursuit, "but he couldn't get to be an artist, he was just painting walls and ceilings, just trying to make ends meet." Being an artist is quite different from John's real job in life as foreman in an automobile plant. According to the Rorschach he has a definite homosexual orientation.

In the cases in which sex role stands out in a particularly striking way in the Picture-Story Test there is good agreement with the Rorschach.

Analysis of the Rorschach

SUMMARY: AGGRESSION

Men	Rorschach description	Number
1, 2, 9, 11, 39	Aggressive	5
7, 8, 39	Anger, rage	3
8, 37	Explosive	2
9, 40	Critical	2
7	Aggression turned inward	1
6, 9, 33, 37	Repressed aggression	4
2, 6, 9	Frightened by own aggression	3
11, 37	Dissociated from aggression	2
33, 40	Fear that people are hostile, critical	2
37, 40	Passive with authority figures	2
37	Low aggressive drive	1

Women		
13, 17, 20, 22, 24, 27, 28, 29	Aggressive	8
17, 21, 22, 28	Anger, rage	4
14, 21	Explosive	2
13, 20	Critical, rejecting of others	2
21, 22, 29, 30	Demanding, greedy, grabbing	4
19, 21	Oppositional	2
19, 30	Ambitious	2
18, 24	Spiteful	2
28, 29	Quarrelsome	2
13, 19	Suspicious	2
18, 21	Passive resistance	2
24, 30	Hostile toward women	2
14, 18, 20, 30, 31	Repressed aggression	5
18, 21	Passive, dependent	2
12, 14	Little capacity to fight, submissive	2
20, 22	Frightened by own aggression	2

Aggression

Admitting that aggression is present in everyone, the question remains—how is it expressed? The above tabulation is an attempt to summarize the Rorschach interpretations with regard to aggression. Again this attempt to summarize does injustice to the evidence which shows individual variations in the expression of aggression from subject to subject. Three of the men and six of the women are characterized as aggressive; in three of the men and four of the women aggression is repressed.

In the others aggression shows itself in specialized ways (oppositionalism, greediness, etc.), usually with aggression much under control; while in two subjects projected aggression was apparent. This general repression of aggression is to be expected in our society.

It is possible in the Rorschach to see some relationship between aggressiveness and sexual adjustment. Two of the men who have homosexual leanings are aggressive in a compensatory fashion. Of the three men characterized as sexually immature one is classified as having aggression turned inward, one is repressed aggressively, and one has low aggressive drive. In the women, on the other hand, inadequate sex is often coupled with aggressive tendencies. Of the five women whose aggression was repressed or who were submissive according to the Rorschach, two show sexual fear, two are unable to accept their sex role, and one is inadequate sexually.

As one reviews the themes of aggression in the 1953 Picture-Story material, one is impressed with the general lack of aggression. This is in marked contrast with the 1940 adolescent-fantasy material in which aggression is specially prominent. It is rare to have the hero in an adult story exhibiting overt aggression. But it is common to have both father and mother depicted as cruel, stingy, angry, and restrictive. Undoubtedly there is much projection in these characterizations. As one reviews the 1953 stories one is impressed by the passivity shown by the main characters, this again in contrast to the 1940 stories.

Of those who are characterized by the Rorschach as aggressive, Wallace (1), who is distinctly aggressive in real life, shows practically no aggression in his stories. Karl (11), who has an uncontrollable temper and frequently "blows his top," sometimes intentionally and sometimes because he cannot help it, tells very bland and unassertive stories in 1953. But there is one childish story of robbing a candy store, for which the man is punished, and parent figures are seen as dominating and punitive. John (39) boasted in his interview about his toughness and aggressiveness as a factory foreman. John depicted passive characters in his stories who desire to be taken care of and who need sympathy and succor, but his stories also include drives of ambition and persistence.

Among the women who are interpreted as being aggressive from the Rorschach records, Edith (17) was described by Dr. Jensen as listless, and there is nothing in the interview report to indicate any aggressiveness, except possibly in connection with the death of her son, which has been mentioned elsewhere in this volume. The fantasy material indicates envy and depression, but no sign of aggression. The aggressive drives described in the Rorschach report are "very deep and fairly well repressed, but there is a desire to express anger and hostility against the world in general."

Mabel (22) is said to have a temper at times. Nothing is said in the interview report about Margaret's (24) being aggressive. In fact, she is described as easygoing and not assertive. Although a mother figure is killed in one of her stories, in general the emotions in the stories are bland. The Rorschach report states that there is a good deal of resentment and spitefulness against society, and she feels particularly hostile toward women—an attitude which seems to stem from a good deal of hostility toward, and disparagement of, the mother. In the interview she stated that she is quite fond of her parents and visits them often, but her mother-in-law has caused her a good deal of heartache. If one can believe the projective material one must conclude that Margaret covered over much hostility in the interview.

Olive (27) has been mentioned many times before because of her unusual reticence and her difficulty in expressing her feelings. The 1953 stories continue the flatness and passivity observed in the earlier adolescent fantasy. Evidently aggressive impulses are thoroughly repressed, and the Rorschach report suggests that there is "a good deal of dissociation from the aggressive destructive drives so that she may think of herself as a pleasant and sweet person."

Celia (28) in her interview stresses her reluctance to assert herself in social relations, and states that she is afraid of hurting someone's feelings. Whereas in the interview Celia stresses her envy of men and her competition with them, in the fantasy material she expresses hostility toward women, although in the interview she claims that she is very close to her mother. The Rorschach report interprets these relationships as follows: "The attitude toward men is sadomasochistic with probably masochistic elements being more dominant, although the capacity to show strong outbursts of rage is there. . . . She is probably more at ease with men than with women, having felt very positive feelings for her father. The relationship to women is one of reserve and coolness beneath which is a hostile dependency on the mother."

The interview of Pansy (29) depicts a very masochistic, long-suffering woman, and the Picture-Story Test shows strong repression of aggressive tendencies, although father and mother figures are depicted as punitive and critical. But the Rorschach report refers to a "pervasive hostility" and an "attitude of rationalized dislike for and disgust with the world."

One may summarize and generalize this survey of nine individuals depicted by the Rorschach as aggressive by saying that this aggression is by no means reflected in the interviews or Picture-Story Test. Whatever underlying aggressive tendencies there may be are well repressed or are disguised, appearing either in ambitious striving or projected onto parent figures. It is generally true that sweetness, gentleness, and passivity seen in persons may be reaction formations against underlying hostility and aggressive impulses.

To take a quick look at the subjects who are described by the Rorschach as having repressed aggressiveness, Roy (6) is described as overcontrolled—tense and inhibited in speech and manner; a man with high blood pressure. The Picture-Story Test reveals fear of a parent's anger. Sam (9) describes himself as very even-tempered, almost too calm, rarely losing his temper but on occasions really "blowing his top." However, the Picture-Story Test contains more violent aggression than is found in any other adult subject. There are stories indicating the effort to hold his aggressive tendencies under restraint, but with difficulty, and there are conflicts between passive and aggressive impulses. The Rorschach report tells that in certain aggressive situations he becomes blocked and almost completely incapacitated from functioning. Edwin (33) is characterized as easygoing, calm, the most relaxed person in the study—"It takes a big strain to make him blow his top." Aggression is practically absent from the Picture-Story Test, being present in only one story, which expressed a death wish toward a sibling.

Among the women with repressed aggression on the Rorschach, Viola (14) spent much of her time in the interview telling of her mother's dominating tendencies and how she claimed her independence and rebelled by her marriage and by rejecting religion. She describes her husband's aunt as a "shrew." In the Picture-Story Test she reaffirms the attitudes that she expresses in life. There is attribution (projected) of hostility toward a mother figure and a death wish toward a father figure. There is a denial of aggressive intentions in the main figures in a story and the attitude of being the victim of aggression. The Rorschach states that Viola's main problem centers about the repression of aggressive feelings and that "the repression of aggressive and libidinal energy is a serious weakness in the personality and robs her of self-assertion and self-reliance."

Isabel (18) reports that she does not like to have to boss other people, and impressed the interviewer as being a quiet, retiring person lacking in vivacity. In fantasy mothers are disapproving and fathers are angry, but the main subject exhibits no aggression.

Barbara (20) departs from the aggressive pattern of the foregoing subjects. She has the male identification mentioned in earlier chapters, and claims that she likes a good fight or a good argument once in a while, regardless of what it is about. It is a means of letting off steam. She often gets into fights with fellows just to stir things up. In the Picture-Story Test a woman is described as strong-willed with a temper (B-10), and the man in the story is weaker than the woman. Mother figures (B-5) are castrating, and there are death wishes toward father figures (A-1, A-10). The Rorschach is interpreted in this case as showing curtailment of aggressive energy, resulting in accumulation of hostility and a feeling of rejection toward people.

Finally, Nancy (31) says that on occasion she is very short-tempered, but these periods last only a short time. The interviewer noticed that she showed "controlled patience" with her little girl who annoyed them during the interview. There is nothing in the Picture-Story Test that could be construed as aggression. The Rorschach report states that she is cut off from her own anger, but expects other people to be unpleasant and critical.

No attempt will be made here to review the other cases in which the Rorschach report mentions specialized forms of the expression of aggressive tendencies. Three of these four cases of repressed aggression on the Rorschach also show restricted, overcontrolled personalities. Barbara is the exception, but the chances are that she is not quite as pugilistic in everyday affairs as she gave the interviewer to believe. He found Barbara to be lively and vivacious, a dynamic person but not overly assertive.

One may summarize that on the whole the subjects in this study are not what would be called aggressive individuals, and most of them show a high degree of emotional control. This is what society expects and is certainly what their parents tried to produce. The fantasy material is also relatively free of aggression, in marked contrast to the fantasies of adolescence. But the Rorschach indicates that there is a strong undercurrent of aggression in most of the subjects, sometimes showing clearly and sometimes repressed.

SUMMARY: INTERPERSONAL (SOCIAL) RELATIONSHIPS

Subjects	Rorschach description	Number
1, 2, 7, 8, 9, 14, 17, 18, 20, 24, 28, 29, 30, 36, 39, 40	Social adjustment reasonably good	16
1, 7, 11, 13, 14, 17, 18, 20, 21, 24, 28, 30, 33, 37, 40	Good rapport, warm and accepting	15
13, 14, 31, 37, 39	Desire for closer interpersonal contacts	5
6, 18, 19, 27, 29, 30, 31	Poor social adjustments	7
1, 2, 12, 13, 17, 18, 20, 24, 28, 30, 33, 37, 40	Discomfort in social relationships	13
1, 6, 7, 12, 13, 14, 17, 18, 19, 20, 21, 22, 24, 27, 28, 29, 30, 31, 33, 36, 37, 40	Poor rapport	22
12, 13, 17, 24, 29, 30, 31, 33, 40	Fear of rejection	9
19, 24, 27, 28, 33, 39	Friction with people, irritable, quarrelsome	6
12, 13, 14, 17, 18, 20, 22, 24, 28, 37, 40	Difficulty adjusting to emotional needs of others; rejection and contempt of people	11
1, 11, 14, 18, 19, 21, 22, 24, 29, 36, 37, 39, 40	Dependent, submissive	13
1, 7, 13, 37	Conventional	4
7, 12, 21, 27, 29, 33, 39	Exhibitionistic	7
6, 13, 14, 24, 40	Paranoid, suspicious, distrustful	5
9, 19, 27, 39	Need to control or manipulate people	4
19, 21	Oppositional, stubborn	2
17, 27	Competitive, overambitious	2
13, 17, 33	Feeling of being concerned or pressured	3
21, 30	Demanding, exploitative	2
7, 22	Conscious of social status	2
17, 31	Tends to act cute	2

Interpersonal (Social) Relationships

The Rorschach in the interpersonal area, as in other areas, is better adapted to providing indications of underlying feelings and impulses than of describing actual behavior and the overt manifestations of personality. Mrs. Dudek, as a last statement in her reports, frequently added that an individual's social adjustments were reasonably good. This was intended to leave the impression that in spite of the limitations in social feeling mentioned in the body of the report the individual was undoubtedly able to find a place as an acceptable member of society, that he or she managed to get along tolerably well with others. Fifteen of these twenty-seven subjects were found to have the capacity for good rapport with others, for being pleasant, friendly, tactful, interested in people, warm, and accepting.

But the overwhelming impression from the Rorschach reports is the inability to maintain any kind of warm, comfortable rapport with others. Over and over again it was said that contact with others was remote, there was a lack of feeling and sensitivity for others, and no real empathy for understanding others (twenty-three subjects). In fourteen instances there was discomfort or actual fear of social relations. In six cases the capacity to be irritable and quarrelsome was noticed. In the case of eleven there was rejection and contempt of people, while in nine there was a fear of being rejected by others.

Sometimes opposite trends were attributed to the same individual. Good social adjustments might be a superficial trend, but on a deeper level there was coldness and loss of contact. Isabel (18), for instance, is said to have superficial good rapport, but to lack genuine feeling for and sensitivity to people. Of Pansy (29) it is said that social relationships appear adequate, but lack emotional investment, and there is a lack of subtle sensitivity to the emotional reactions of people. Dorothy (30) is said to be capable of being friendly and pleasant, but she seldom achieves a feeling of contact or ease with people. Her social adjustment is not conspicuously inadequate, but it is not a positive or happy one.

A relatively large number (13) of the subjects were described as dependent or submissive, but four showed a need to control or manipulate people, two were egocentrically demanding, two were competitive and overambitious. Six subjects expressed their needs by exhibitionistic behavior. Five were suspicious and distrustful, two were oppositional and stubborn. Four tended to be conventional and two were conscious of social status. Three expressed a feeling of being pressured or coerced, while two met the problem of social relations by acting cute.

The overall impression that one gains from the Rorschach is that these twenty-seven individuals have difficulty in their social relationships. While outwardly they may be pleasant and at ease, inwardly they feel considerable discomfort in their social relationships, and lack genuine warmth and feeling. There is distance between them and other people, to which they try to adjust by a variety of social stratagems which make them superficially appear to have good rapport with others.

An attempt was made to relate the interpretations of the Rorschach concerning interpersonal relationships with the interviews, but this was difficult to do. Individuals in the interviews seldom came out to discuss their relations with others in an evaluative way. The general impression of the interviewer may touch only the superficial attitudes and fail to penetrate to the underlying feelings. Nonetheless, the impression made on the interviewer may have some significance.

Indications of social adjustment from the interviews are provided for the seven individuals whom the Rorschach described as having poor social adjustment. Roy (6) impressed the interviewer as "on the spot" during the testing and the interview. "He attempted to keep from becoming too personal or expressing his true feelings." He was harder to draw out than most of the subjects, and seemed to be rather uncomfortable. Isabel (18) was tense, nervous, inhibited, and quite self-conscious at times. She gave the impression that her feelings could easily be hurt. Stella (19), on the other hand, was friendly and spoke easily. But Dr. Jensen described her as nervous and depressed under stress, moody and seldom elated. Olive (27) has been mentioned several times because of her inability to relate. Dr. Jensen found her repressed, friendly but in a very restrained way, a bit self-conscious and not at all vivacious. She was tense and nervous at first during the interview. Pansy (29) had a tired, run-down look, and lacked animation. She has always enjoyed being around sick people. She does not care for her neighbors, who are gossipy. Dorothy (30) was tense, inhibited, and nervous at the beginning of the interviews, although she loosened up later. Although outwardly calm she is inwardly tense. Nancy (31) tended to depart from this general picture of tenseness, reserve, and feeling ill-at-ease with a stranger. Nancy was friendly and casual, but she became inhibited and stilted in telling the stories. She stated that she can be miserable to live with when she becomes down in the dumps and becomes grumpy.

These, of course, are superficial impressions, and the picture is by no means uniform, but the general impression is that these seven individuals are not comfortable in a social relationship.

Let us look at two individuals whom the Rorschach described as warm and accepting. Viola (14) was tense, talkative, fluent, and went into everything in the interview with the same elaborateness that she showed on the Rorschach. She spoke of "togetherness" with her husband. Barbara (20), friendly, lively, and outgoing, also is a person of high energy level. Apparently she relates to others without much trouble. In the interview she emphasized her short temper and the fact that she gets into heated arguments easily. Possibly she overstressed this side of her personality and did not stress her warm, outgoing relationships. But Barbara is not married. Probably one must not confuse spontaneity in social relationships with good heterosexual adjustment.

These two subjects, who showed good social adjustment on the Rorschach, have vivid, lively, outgoing personalities in real life, as contrasted with the restrained, reserved personalities of those whom the Rorschach picked out as having poor social relationships.

It is difficult to estimate social adjustment from the fantasy material. Every set of stories depicts people relating to one another, and it is not possible to differentiate one story set as indicating more or less ease in social relations. The clearest differentiating factor is to be found in the formal aspects of the stories.

Ratings were made on interpersonal adjustment on the Rorschach and correlated with Dr. Jensen's ratings on (1) being pleasant and friendly in the interview, and (2) adjusting to others of his or her own age group. These correlations were .00 and +.27, respectively.

Factors in the thematic content which differentiate better from poorer socially adjusted subjects could not be isolated. At first glance it appeared that the poorly adjusted subjects showed greater depression, passivity, and dependence than the better adjusted subjects, and the poorly adjusted subjects rather regularly included stories with angry, rejecting, punitive father figures. But these same factors were also present in the stories of the better adjusted, so no conclusions can be drawn from content in the Picture-Story Test that would relate to social adjustment as shown by the Rorschach.

It was thought that social adjustment rated by the Rorschach might be related to psychosexual adjustment shown from the Rorschach, but no clear-cut relationship could be found. Of the seven individuals who were said to have "good sexual adjustment superficially," only four were said to have "reasonably good social adjustment." Of the seven unmarried subjects, six were said to have reasonably good social adjustment superficially from the Rorschach, but five of these show basically poor rapport in their social relations.

No definitive relationship was found between social adjustment and aggressive tendencies, both as shown by the Rorschach. Four of the six persons who showed friction in social adjustment were also classed as aggressive, and one showed oppositional tendencies. But of the seven who were said to have poor social adjustment three had aggressive personalities, while three showed repressed aggressive or oppositional tendencies. Apparently poor social adjustment may mean poorly directed aggression or the repression of aggression with consequent loss of social contact.

SUMMARY: AFFECT

Subjects	Rorschach description	Number
1, 8, 18	Warm and deep feelings	3
8, 9, 14, 17, 21, 28, 31, 33	Pleasant, gentle affect	8
1, 8, 13, 27, 39	Emotional sensitivity	5
1, 8, 9, 11, 14, 28, 31, 33, 37, 39	Emotional excitability, overintensity; intense and violent feelings, hysterical affect	10
1, 9, 28	Acting out	3
1, 2, 14, 19, 22, 27, 28, 29, 33, 39, 40	Explosion of affect; irritability, passion, rage	11
2, 6, 7, 9, 12, 13, 17, 18, 21, 22, 24, 29, 33, 36	Weak, shallow affect	14
17, 29, 30, 39, 40	Lacking spontaneity and warmth	5
2, 9, 13, 20, 37	Fear of strong emotion	5
2, 6, 7, 11, 14, 19, 20, 24, 27, 31, 33	Dissociation of affect, repression of feeling	11
8, 9, 11, 13, 33, 37, 39	Emotional lability, flexible, changeable	7
12, 19, 21, 31	Inappropriate emotion	4

SUMMARY: AFFECT (*Cont.*)

Subjects	Rorschach description	Number
11, 12	Lacking sensitivity	2
19, 21	Affect strained and forced	2
19, 36	Affect childlike and immature	2
1, 12, 22, 30	Egocentric, selfish	4
1, 2, 7, 19, 21, 27, 29, 33, 39	Exhibitionistic	9
9, 14, 37	Optimistic	3

Affect

Comments about affect and emotion on the Rorschach reports range all the way from extremely positive emotional excitability and over-intensity to dissociation of affect and repression of feeling. Ten individuals were said to have intense and violent feelings, and eleven showed an explosive type of affect with extreme irritability, passion, or rage. At the other extreme there were eleven who showed more or less repression of feeling, and fourteen who were described as having shallow affect.

Only a relatively few were credited with positive feelings under good control, three with warm feelings, eight with a feminine type of gentle, tender feelings, and five with emotional sensitivity to the feelings of others. One startling indication from the record is the difficulty people find in managing their feelings—they either repress them, or else express them in violent and uncontrolled bursts of passion or rage.

The careful reader should not be disturbed by overlappings in the tabulation. One would have to see the Rorschach reports themselves to appreciate the finesse of interpretations. Not infrequently repression of affect is coupled with episodes of explosiveness. Of Isabel (18) it is said: "On a superficial level she is able to express her positive feelings easily, but she lacks genuine feeling for and sensitivity to people. Her affect is generally superficial but pleasant." Of Mabel (22) it is said: "The emotional range appears to be narrow. Outside of anger, there is little capacity for strong emotion—though her affect is by no means shallow."

Again, as with the social adjustments, it is very difficult to check these interpretations against either the interview or the fantasy stories. But an inspection of Dr. Jensen's reactions to the subjects in the interview shows a remarkable correspondence with the Rorschach in regard to the expression of affect, as can be seen from a sample of individuals at either extreme in the Rorschach interpretations. Of those with intense or violent feelings as diagnosed in the Rorschach, Wallace (1), who gave Dr. Jensen a somewhat rough time, was hostile, resentful, and cocksure at the beginning of his interview. He seemed irritated and at times on the verge of losing his temper. In the second interview, however, he became very friendly, mixing a drink and offering to cooperate in the study in any way he could. Roger (8) was pleasant, cordial, aggressive in a quiet way, and he, too, took Dr. Jensen into his kitchen when he mixed highballs. Viola's (14) talk consisted mainly of describing her feelings and subjective states. Celia (28) had quite lively facial expressions, and laughed and giggled a good deal at various points of the interview. John (39), a forceful, high-energy person, spoke dynamically, bursting out into very loud laughter, pounding the table with his fist. He was an assertive, dynamic, vivacious, emphatic person, and a fluent talker.

Of those who were diagnosed as having weak, shallow affect, dissociation of affect, and repression of feeling in the Rorschach, Ralph (2) has been drunk only once in his life, and then had a terrific hangover the next day. He claims he will never drink that much again. He becomes depressed and has gastritis when under stress. Laura (13) seemed submissive, almost too "nice." She gave the impression of being a colorless, almost spineless, person. She was not at all assertive and was a person of rather low energy level. Margaret (24) spoke in a low, quiet voice, and gave the impression of being a stable, solid sort of person, not very "sensitive." She took longer to tell stories than any other subject in the study. Pansy (29) has already been described many times because of her drowsy, listless manner. She looked overworked, tired, run-down and without much energy, and lacked animation. Edwin (33) spoke in a slow, quiet voice. He was described as easygoing, not at all dynamic, having a sleepy personality.

One can see that the estimates of affectivity from the Rorschach correspond closely with estimates of energy level, vivacity, and dynamic quality as these factors impressed the interviewer.

In inspecting the fantasy material with respect to affect it has not been possible to differentiate subjects, at least not from story content. Stories of both those who were diagnosed as showing much and little affect on the Rorschach showed a variety of feelings in the stories. See page 174.

SUMMARY: MENTAL FUNCTIONING

Subjects	Rorschach description	Number
2, 7, 8, 11, 12, 17, 18, 20, 24, 28, 30, 37, 39, 40	Good intelligence	14
9, 27, 28, 37, 40	Thinking and reasoning excellent	5
9, 20, 37, 40	Logic excellent	4
9, 28	Fairly effective use made of intelligence	2
1, 2, 13, 18, 20, 22, 24, 28, 31	Judgment good	9
8, 9, 18, 28	Organizational ability good or excellent	4
9, 24, 28	Imagination good	3
20, 37	Keenness of perception	2
1, 13, 20, 22, 31, 40	Reality contact good	6
9, 22, 31, 33, 40	Able to see world as others do	5
6, 12, 19, 21, 27, 29, 33, 36, 39	Judgment poor	9
2, 7	Lacks originality	2
2, 7	Lacks imagination	2
2, 11, 18, 29	Lacks insight	4
1, 2, 9, 21, 27, 33	Reality contact poor	6
24, 27	Unable to think through realistically	2
1, 2, 7, 12, 27, 28	Little practical sense	6
18, 24	Reactions popular and conventional	2
7, 8, 22, 27	Intelligence not well used	4
21, 27, 36	Inefficient	3
6, 8	Fails to follow through logically	2
2, 6, 11, 19, 22, 33	Thinking confused and disorganized	6

Mental Functioning

On the whole the Rorschach report gives individuals credit for having good minds and using them effectively. Fourteen subjects are said to have from good to excellent intelligence and good to excellent thinking, reasoning, and use of logic. Nine subjects were credited with good judgment. Other comments in the reports stressed good to excellent organizational ability, good imagination, and keenness of perception. In six of the cases it was said that reality contact was good, and five were able to see the world as others do.

Few comments attributed low intelligence to these subjects. Eight were said to have poor judgment. Only scattered comments were made concerning absence of originality, imagination, and insight. Six of the reports mentioned confused and disorganized thinking. In others it was noted that there was intellectual blocking or that intelligence was not well used or was inefficient. Eight of the subjects were thought to have poor contact with reality, while six seemed to have little practical sense.

By and large, credit was given for commendable mental functioning, and in only a minority of the cases was it commented that judgment was poor, that inefficient use was being made of intelligence, that there was intellectual disorganization and confusion with poor reality contact. This more optimistic report of mental functioning is to be contrasted with the very negative conclusions about affect, psychosexual and social adjustment, and attitudes toward the self.

No systematic attempt was made to estimate intelligence or reality contact from the interviews. However, aberrations in thinking were noted in some of the interview reports. Roy (6) gave short and somewhat stilted responses to questions that were put to him. The mental peculiarities of Karl (11) have been commented on many times. Although extremely precise about dates, he evaded direct questions by wandering off to another subject unrelated to the question that was asked. But there was nothing in the interview reports of subjects 2, 19, 22, or 33 to indicate confused or disorganized thinking.

Subjects 9, 27, 28, 37, and 40 have I.Q.'s of 121, 86, 138, 112, and 134, respectively. The Rorschach report on Olive (27) is in error in many respects (pp. 286–87), particularly in crediting her with good thinking and reasoning. But Sam (9), Celia (28), and Albert (40), whose thinking and reasoning are excellent according to the Rorschach, have high I.Q.'s. Jimmy (37) is a particularly verbose individual and impresses one as being bright, but his mental test scores do not put him in a high intelligence bracket.

In some instances subjects quite obviously impressed the interviewer with their intelligence even though he did not make a precise note of his impression. He comments about Celia: "Her Rorschach seemed quite inadequate for a person of her intelligence." Of Albert he notes: "He appears to be well above average in intelligence, judging from his vocabulary and general knowledge."

Analysis of the Rorschach

The correlation between the intelligence-level ratings in the Rorschach and I.Q. was +.34.

Thematic analysis of the Picture-Story Test yields nothing that relates to mental functioning. However, the formal analysis of the stories sheds some light on mental functioning.

SUMMARY: CONCEPT OF THE SELF

Subjects	Rorschach description	Number
6, 7, 8, 12, 18, 19, 21, 22, 33, 37, 39	Feelings of inferiority and inadequacy	11
19, 20, 21, 24, 28, 30, 31	Inadequate as a woman	7
8, 33, 37, 40	Inadequate as a man	4
24	Intellectual inadequacy	1
12, 28	Physical inadequacy	2
18	Social inadequacy	1
6, 8, 18	Feeling of helplessness	3
12, 17, 21	Self-depreciative	3
1, 8, 13, 17, 20, 24, 28, 29, 40	Loss of self-esteem	9
1, 6, 22, 24, 40	Loss of self-confidence	5
13, 33	Weak ego	2
7, 17	Fails to take self seriously	2
22, 29	Narcissistic injuries	2
2, 27, 30, 36	No concept of role in life, little self-perception, little self-concept	4
11, 17, 29, 33	Vagueness about ego boundaries	4
13, 40	Expects and is afraid of criticism and rejection	2
2, 6, 12, 13, 19	Self-conscious	5
6, 9	Oversensitive	2
14, 40	Egocentric	2
11, 12	Little self-discipline	2
22, 39	Needs to compensate, strives for superiority	2
7, 28	Intropunitive, self-destructive	2
1, 6, 7, 22	Proccupied with status, prestige	4
9, 20	Self-confident	2
1, 14	Charming, attractive, likable	2
9	Happy, optimistic	1

Concept of the Self

When statements about the self in the Rorschach reports are gathered together, they produce an overwhelming impression that the individuals in this study are suffering from feelings of personal inadequacy and that they possess little self-esteem. This feeling of inadequacy may concern intellectual, physical, or social qualities, or the sex role. The subjects seem self-critical, self-depreciatory, and lacking in self-confidence. Several of them fail to take the self seriously, lose ego boundaries, and have vague concepts of one's role in life. Only two cases were described as self-confident, and two others show a brash bravado as expression of the need to compensate for feelings of inferiority.

No direct check could be made with the interview reports as these did not evaluate the subjects of the study in these terms. One may form general impressions of a person from the tone of the interview report as a whole, but this is probably not safe as a guide. Following are a few excerpts from the interview reports of individuals who were diagnosed from the Rorschach as feeling inadequate. Of Roger (8) the report says: "Roger's fear of failure probably goes back to his flunking out in college. He has something of an intellectual inferiority complex." Catherine (12) stated that she easily feels rejected. The case of Natalie (21) illustrates the difficulties of evaluating personality from the interview report. In the report it is said: "Natalie claims that she would like to be a lot more intellectual but that she has a long way to go. She wishes that she had more time to read and improve herself." The emphasis here is on the sincerity of her intellectual desires, but the statement may also indicate the depth of the feelings of inferiority. If Mabel (22) feels inadequate it certainly does not appear in the record. In fact, she gave the interviewer the impression of a person who feels secure, confident, and stable. Edwin (33) handled whatever feelings of inferiority he may have had by his extreme calmness, serenity, and unruffled disposition.

On the other hand, both Sam (9) and Barbara (20), who are diagnosed from the Rorschach as self-confident, give the same impression from the interview report although nothing specific is stated.

It is virtually impossible to make any comparison of self-acceptance or self-rejection between the Rorschach and the interview reports. On the other hand, the Picture-Story Test is helpful in letting one catch a glimpse of the attitude toward the self. It is not easy always to say that the Picture-Story Test agrees with the Rorschach or does not, but it does fill in details about the self-concept. In the stories of Roy (6), who was diagnosed by the Rorschach as having feelings of inadequacy, one finds themes of having to take second best. In story B-11 a man who comes in second in an automobile race is offered congratulations for a "good race." A woman (A-2) apologizes because she has come to believe that her point of view in an argument is stubborn or incorrect. Several of his stories have a depressed tone. Jerome's (7) stories showed anxiety and depression. Story A-9 tells of the self-pity of a housemaid. There is a feeling of disappointment and helplessness running through Jerome's stories. Roger's (8) stories also showed anxiety and depression. His concern about his ability and his need for achievement show out clearly. From the stories one can conclude that Roger "feels rather desperate about the fact that he sees himself as having just a limited number of chances to make good in life, and he may be anxious because he has not made the most use of some of the chances that have come his way." Catherine's (12) feeling of inadequacy concerns her physical appearance. B-4 is the story of a homely girl who is turned down because of her looks, and contains the following significant sentence: "If she didn't think she was so homely she wouldn't be so homely." Stella (19) invests her stories with much hostility, but they have a depressed tone. "Hostility turned inward helps to account for the depressed tone, guilt and sorrow in some of the stories." Natalie's (21) stories are also depressed. She feels that she is passed by (story A-3); the girl coming home from school is "in a bad situation" (story A-5). Edwin (33) tells stories in which the characters are unfortunate and pitiable. They are people who have been damaged in some way—who are homely, inferior, or incapacitated. In one story (A-6) the main character is blind. It is easy to conclude that Edwin feels psychologically castrated. It should be remembered that this subject married a woman who lost one arm in an automobile accident. John (39), who tends to compensate for any feelings of inferiority in real life by a driving energy in his work, tells a story (B-6) of a man "who sold his car and bought thirty acres of land in Kentucky, two hogs, six or eight chickens, just enough to keep himself going, and just enough food to keep himself alive. He had no wife. He was just shiftless and independent and just sits there and rocks his life away."

But on the positive side there is Sam (9). His stories contain far more aggression than usual. Hostility, bitterness, and depressive tendencies are repressed or denied. There are fairly strong achievement themes of a rather compulsive, inflexible kind. A more than usual amount of energy is directed into his "persona"—his social front, the appearance he permits to outsiders. Dr. Jensen was impressed by his poise during the interview, but his persona was threatened when he had to perform in a task (the Picture-Story Test) in which he had no practice or readymade ways of responding. Barbara (20) is another who shows some strength in the Picture-Story Test. Story B-10 tells of a woman who "lays down the law and brings things to a head," insisting that her husband go to church with her. Story A-9 tells of a cleaning maid with push and gumption "to really go out and get her own place—and I think she does." As has been told, Barbara is bewildered about love and marriage, but in spite of her inability to relate successfully in a heterosexual fashion she has self-respect and certain strength and independence.

The Picture-Story Test, it would seem, agrees rather faithfully with the picture presented by the Rorschach, and in addition, fills in some of the content or meaning of the personality trends which must be guessed from the Rorschach.

SUMMARY: ANXIETY AND DEFENSES AGAINST ANXIETY

Subjects	Rorschach description	Number
2, 8, 11, 13, 14, 29, 30, 40	Anxiety	8
1, 6, 19, 22, 24, 39	Strong anxiety	6
13, 14, 22, 24, 27	Defenses: Repression	5
13, 28, 29, 30, 39, 40	Projection of hostility	6
12, 27	Denial	2
6, 33	Intellectualization	2
6, 19, 31	Detachment	3
1, 8, 9	Ego defensive, combative	3
27, 39	Overactivity	2
13, 20	Sour-grapes attitude	2
22, 33	Somatization of conflict	2
27, 33	Intellectual blocking	2
12, 14	Little self-defensive ego	2
2, 6, 20, 28, 33, 39	Fear of emotion	6
29, 37	Fear of anger	2
12, 17, 18, 28, 30, 31, 37	Guilt	7
2, 28, 33, 39	Social situations anxiety-arousing	4

Anxiety and Defenses against Anxiety

Fourteen individuals were mentioned in the Rorschach reports as experiencing anxiety with more or less intensity. In six of these subjects the anxiety was spoken of as intense, acute, pervasive. Four individuals were made anxious by social situations which they would tend to shun. In eight cases there was fear of experiencing strong emotion, and in two of these cases the emotion was specified as anger. Four subjects gave evidence of guilt, largely for hostile impulses which were not overtly expressed.

Ten mechanisms of defense against anxiety were mentioned two or more times. One gathers the impression that more defense mechanisms could have been included in the reports, but Mrs. Dudek made no special effort to be exhaustive in this matter. Leading the list were *repression* and *projection*. *Detachment* and *ego-defensive reactions* (chip-on-the-shoulder attitude, combative, quarrelsome) were mentioned twice. Other defense reactions were *denial, intellectualization, overactivity, sour-grapes attitude, intellectual blocking,* and *somatization of conflict.*

It is very difficult to find direct allusions to anxiety in the interview reports. Anxiety in human affairs does not stand out separately as anxiety but becomes imbedded in the personality and pervades all reactions in various ways, either by the defenses that have been adopted, or somatically, or by character formations. In almost every one of the interview reports on the fourteen subjects whom the Rorschach reported to be anxious, it was possible to find some evidence of anxiety, but when the other thirteen interview reports were reviewed it was possible to find the same signs of anxiety. It was not possible to find evidence of any correlation between anxiety reported in the Rorschach and in the interviews. Ralph (2) has a nervous stomach; Roy (6) has high blood pressure; Dorothy (30) describes herself as nervous with "butterflies in the stomach" when interviewed. But Seymour (36), nonanxious by the Rorschach, also has a nervous stomach. Viola (14) is tense and high-strung; Stella (19) worries about her mother and becomes nervous when under stress. Yet Jerome (7), not anxious according to the Rorschach, worries over doctors' bills; Sam (9) worries over his mother's nervous breakdowns; Catherine (12) is anxious about her unborn child.

However, as one reviews the data there are a number of subjects not mentioned as anxious on the Rorschach who showed no sign of nervousness or tension in the interview. Natalie (21) was described as stable, realistic; Olive (27) said that she had no fears or anxieties; Seymour (36), in spite of his nervous stomach, was on the whole good-natured and easygoing, while Edwin (33) was perhaps too easygoing for his own good.

One may conclude that there is a barely discernible tendency for those diagnosed as anxious on the Rorschach to show signs of tension, strain, worry, or nervousness in real life, whereas the several not diagnosed as anxious on the Rorschach impressed the interviewer as stable, but there were too many exceptions for the trend to be very pronounced. The coefficient of correlation between ratings for anxiety on the Rorschach and from Dr. Jensen's ratings from the interview was $+.18$.

Likewise, no relation is discernible between anxiety as diagnosed from the Rorschach and anxiety evident in the Picture-Story Test. A comparison of the number of stories in which anxiety was expressed in the Picture-Story Test was made between those labeled anxious and nonanxious from the Rorschach, as shown in the accompanying tabulation.

COMPARISON OF ANXIETY IN STORIES AND IN THE RORSCHACH

Number of stories expressing anxiety	Number of anxious subjects (from Rorschach)	Number of nonanxious subjects (from Rorschach)
6	0	1
5	0	0
4	0	2
3	2	5
2	3	1
1	7	1
0	2	3
	14	13

If anything, more anxiety in the stories was found for those designated nonanxious on the Rorschach, but the trend was not marked.

The correlation between the Picture-Story anxiety and Dr. Jensen's ratings for anxiety was $+.04$.

SUMMARY: DRIVE AND ENERGY LEVEL

Subjects	Rorschach description	Number
1, 6, 8, 11, 12, 24, 28	Over-reactive, restless, dynamic, agitated	7
8, 14, 19	Impulsive	3
8, 9, 11, 12, 17, 18, 20, 27, 28, 37, 39	Assertive, active, energetic, animated, vigorous, lively, buoyant, enthusiastic, spontaneous	11
21, 22, 39	Explosive	3
22, 24, 27, 39	High drive, much energy, aggressive drive	4
19, 30, 37, 39	High ambition	4
39, 40	High productivity	2
21, 39	Compulsive	2
12, 14, 17, 20, 21, 22, 30, 33, 36, 40	Very little drive, aggression, or libidinal energy, little capacity to fight, little drive to be active, spontaneous, outgoing	10
9, 21	Passive	2
17, 36, 40	Little ambition	3
14, 18	Repressed	2

Drive and Energy Level

Rorschach evaluations of drive are about equally divided between statements of high drive level and low drive level. Eleven subjects were characterized as assertive and active, seven as overreactive, and three as explosive. On the other hand, ten were credited with low drive and energy.

Here, as with some of the other aspects of personality diagnosed from the Rorschach, there were contradictions and discrepancies. A person might give a certain impression, built as a façade, which could be the reverse of deeper trends in the personality. For instance, Catherine (12) "is overreactive but there is little evidence of spontaneous, outgoing affect. She is highly exhibitionistic with an overemphasis on physical appearance. She has little libidinal energy and is easily disturbed and coerced into submission where a fight is called for." Edith (17) is said to have little drive or ambition to get ahead. At the same time she is said to be reactive and responsive, but merely as a result of a superego feeling of the need to be friendly and pleasant. She is likely to be competitive in a cute, little-girlish way.

It was not possible to find a significantly high correspondence between these Rorschach evaluations of energy and the impressions made on the interviewer. Among the illustrations of those who were active, Roger (8) was soft-spoken but rather aggressive in a quiet sort of way; Karl (11) was said to have a medium energy level even though he was an assertive person and stated his ideas with great conviction, but the record stated specifically that he was not at all vivacious; Catherine (12) was described as a lively personality, rather vivacious; Margaret (24) was said to have medium high energy level, but not vivacious; Celia (28) was not assertive in manner or vivacious but was alert and interested.

On the other hand, of subjects with little drive according to the Rorschach, Viola (14) gave the impression of having a high energy level and was rather vivacious, in a nervous way; Barbara (20) was said not to be an assertive person but was described as vivacious and lively; Natalie (21) was a person of low energy level and not at all assertive; Mabel (22) was rather athletic-looking; Dorothy (30) did not have the fresh, youthful appearance of most of the young women of her age—on the contrary, she had the dried-up look of middle age; Edwin (33) had a sleepy personality, was extremely easygoing and not at all dynamic; Seymour (36) was easygoing, slow in speaking and moving, almost lethargic; and, finally, Albert (40) was not a very vivacious or energetic person.

With some exceptions it was possible to see a low correspondence between the Rorschach and the superficial impressions made on the interviewer in his contacts. The coefficient of correlation between ratings on drive and energy level from the Rorschach and Dr. Jensen's ratings of output of energy from the interviews was +.40.

It did not seem possible to attempt to evaluate drive and energy level from the Picture-Story Test.

SUMMARY: CONTROL

Subjects	Rorschach description	Number
13, 22, 40	Controlled	3
2, 6, 14, 18	Strongly repressed aggression	4
6	Tries to exercise control	1
14, 30, 33, 39	Attempts to repress emotional reactions	4
1, 19, 39	Wishes to control environment	3
13, 19, 24, 29, 39	Loss of control	5
7, 28	Frustration tolerance low	2
11	Uninhibited	1

Control

Although control is one of the main variables that the Rorschach is supposed to evaluate, there were only scattered references to control in the Rorschach reports. For ten of the subjects there were references to control or attempt to control aggressive, sensual, and emotional reactions. In six cases loss of control and inhibition were mentioned. Again there were inconsistencies which really turn out to be subtle differentiations between the wish and the actual reaction, the kind of discrimination that Mrs. Dudek is skilled at making. For instance, of Laura (13) it is said, "The attempt to repress instinctual and aggressive energy, although unsuccessful, has resulted in a great deal of inertia to spontaneous reactions to action." Later on in the report there is reference to her inhibitions and control. In the case of John (39) there is reference to his drive for power which is not a drive for status or prestige but for a certain kind of control which is essentially an unconscious attempt to control his own overintense emotions. But later it is said that he is afraid of the intensity of his emotional reactions, and he has reason to fear them, for his control is very poor indeed.

There are three references to the need to control the environment and especially people in the environment, and two references to low frustration tolerance.

In the interviews there was an attempt to assess aggressive tendencies and the control exerted over them. While this was not reported in every instance, many of the interview reports refer to this kind of control. Following is a tabulation of the comments on control from the interviews:

Subjects	Comments from interviews
6, 8, 9, 22, 27, 30, 31, 36	Overcontrolled, generally repressed emotion, but sporadic outbursts of temper
13, 18, 28, 40	Not aggressive, a poor salesman
21, 33, 36	Lethargic, relaxed
20, 39	Uninhibited
11	Uncontrolled

A comparison of this tabulation of control with control reported in the Rorschach indicates general agreement for the subjects showing control and inhibition. However, the Rorschach recognizes loss of control in subjects 13, 19, 24, and 29, for whom no mention of the matter of control was made in the interview reports. Evidently this type of loss of control shown on the Rorschach is unrevealed in the interview situation.

Ratings of control from the Rorschach correlated as +.34 with Dr. Jensen's ratings of inhibition in behavior from the interview, −.32 with the tendency to act impulsively, and +.16 with the tendency to show self-control under frustration.

From the contents of the Picture-Story Test it was not possible to estimate the degree or kind of control, but the formal aspects of the stories were quite revealing (see page 48).

SUMMARY: DEPRESSION

Subjects	Rorschach description	Number
1, 17, 29	Depression	3
8, 9, 14, 18, 21, 22, 24, 27, 28, 31, 37	Low-grade depression	11

Depression

Depression was mentioned in the Rorschach analysis of fourteen of the subjects. Eleven were characterized as having low-grade or slight depression. In subject 17 it was called acute, and in subject 29 fairly deep.

Depression was mentioned in the interview reports of nine of the subjects (2, 8, 11, 13, 17, 19, 20, 27, 31). Possibly it was present in some of the others without being specifically named as such—Albert (40), for instance, was described as listless. It is significant that of these nine subjects five were not mentioned as having depressed tendencies on the Rorschach. On the other hand, ten of the fourteen subjects who were depressed according to the Rorschach interpretations were not so mentioned in the interview reports. Actually, there were only four subjects (8, 17, 27, 31) who had depressed tendencies according to both sources of evidence. The tetrachoric r for this relationship is −.18, which is negligible.

The Picture-Story Test has been mentioned already as indicating considerable depression in the adult subjects in this study, with marked increase over the depression indicated in the adolescent stories. Actually, depression was a theme in the stories of twenty-three of the twenty-seven subjects for whom the Rorschach was available, leaving only four subjects (1, 11, 33, 39) in which depression was not observable. It was also not reported for three of these subjects in the Rorschach interpretations. On the other hand, the three subjects for whom depression was noted on the Rorschach had either no stories or only one containing a theme of depression. The correlation between the frequency with which depression appeared in the stories and the evaluation of depression from the Rorschach was —.13.

One must conclude that there is no relationship between evidences of depression from the Rorschach and depression as noted either in the interviews or on the Picture-Story Test.

Oedipal Relationships

Mrs. Dudek hazarded guesses about the Oedipal forces which may have helped to determine some of the personality characteristics, particularly the sex role, of fifteen of the subjects. No effort has been made to tabulate these interpretations or to draw general conclusions from them, nor has any effort been made to relate these interpretations to the interview material. The Picture-Story Test, of course, provides much evidence as to attitudes toward parent figures, but this is not of a nature permitting comparisons with these speculations from the Rorschach. Just a few illustrations are given to serve as samples of the kinds of Oedipal interpretations that were made from the Rorschach data.

Ralph (2) has been described as an ineffectual person, still unmarried and attempting to graduate from an engineering school. An only child, he claims that he feels closer to his mother than to the stepfather he has had since he was 11 or 12. His mother impressed Dr. Jensen as being very protective. The Rorschach gives him a confused sex role identity with a homosexual orientation. With regard to Oedipal relationships the Rorschach report mentions inability to identify with a weak father. The mother tried to play both masculine and feminine roles, neither one consistently.

Roy (6), also an only child, drives himself in his work in his father's auto-repair shop and has high blood pressure. Roy is happily married and has two children. Overcontrolled, he seemed tense and inhibited in the interview. The Rorschach report finds that he has little identity as a person, with high regard for masculinity which he must demonstrate by self-assertion. As to Oedipal relationships, the Rorschach report says that he has had very little warm and positive contact with his parents. His relationship to his father is probably warmer than to his mother, but he fears aggression from his father.

Roger (8) is another man with feelings of inferiority and confused sex-role identity, alternating between the masculine and feminine position. He has a stepmother with whom he has had some friction and by whom he has never felt wholly accepted. He claims that he gets along well with his father. The Rorschach report estimates the Oedipal situation as follows: "He finds it difficult to accept and feel accepted by a cold and powerful father who gave him no sense of humanity or importance (made him feel small and rejected). His feelings toward women (the mother) appear to be much more friendly." This, of course, is in direct conflict with his own statement. But his feelings of inferiority are real and there is no basis for explaining them from his own statement. One must give the Rorschach interpretation some credence as it provides a possible explanation for his lack of personal security.

Catherine (12) has been mentioned many times because of her antagonism to her mother. In adolescence this appeared only in fantasy, but as an adult she can express her hostility openly. She also speaks unflatteringly about her father. The Rorschach refers to the immaturity of her psychosexual adjustment. With regard to the Oedipal situation, the Rorschach report says: "Oedipal conflict. Desire to please father and a fear of rejection and disapproval by him. Mother may have made her feel unacceptable and unattractive." Here the emphasis is on the relation with the father, whereas in the interview Catherine concentrates her feelings on her mother. Here, as elsewhere, the interview may soft-pedal the relationship which actually has been most influential.

Nancy (31) complains that marriage is confining, dull, and uninteresting. The Rorschach mentions that she is not sure of her femininity and finds it difficult to accept her role as wife. She falters between masculine and feminine attitudes. With regard to the Oedipal situation, the Rorschach report suggests an unresolved incestuous relationship with her father, whom she seemed to idealize. Her father disappointed her by not giving enough acceptance and acknowledgment. Her conscious feelings are more positive toward the mother, but basically it was her father's love that she wanted. If this is true it may help to explain her present dissatisfaction with marriage.

Seymour (36) is another person who is confused as to sexual identity and concerned with his adequacy as a man, who needs to test his masculinity by a show of self-assertion. In the Navy he was tattooed on the arm. Actually, in real life a letter carrier, he avoids any pretense of being ambitious ("Why strain yourself?") and lets his wife make most of the decisions. The Rorschach says of the Oedipal relationship that Seymour never resolved the Oedipal tie with his mother. The relationship to her was close and sensually stimulating, but he made little contact with her as a real person. His father was more of a human being, but of whom he was secretly contemptuous.

Jimmy (37) has been mentioned many times because of the strong dependence on his mother. He describes his mother as a dominating and strong character, but his father he speaks of with great respect as a fine and understanding man. Jimmy, too, is said by the Rorschach report to have confused sex-role identification. Of the Oedipal relationship, the Rorschach report says that his anger and opposition to his mother is repressed. He has strong fear of his father and of his disapproval of sex (the angry Oedipal taboo). There is a strong sense of dependence on his parents and of need to free himself of it. He has never resolved the incestuous tie to his mother.

These speculations from the Rorschach reports on Oedipal relationships are parallel to the life history material in many instances, but sometimes run contrary to it. There are some indications that these Oedipal speculations may contain a germ of truth that helps to explain personality trends better than direct evidence from the interviews. As is well known, a person may not wish to reveal to the interviewer some of the deeper feelings and relationships to members of his family, or, as is probably more often the case, the individual is not aware himself of the depth and direction of his feelings.

8. Summary of Comparisons between the Rorschach Reports, Interview Material, and Fantasies

This chapter attempts to summarize comparisons between the Rorschach reports, the interview material, and the Picture-Story Test. This ought to describe in broad perspective the values of each of these three kinds of data, although it should be noted that evidence as to the relationships between them leaves much to be desired.

In general the Rorschach provides information about impulses and underlying tendencies, but such tendencies may have only a low relationship to the overt personality observed by the interviewer. Most persons have ways (mechanisms) for hiding or disguising their impulses and the expression of their underlying tendencies, especially in superficial contacts with a stranger. There is a natural tendency to put one's best foot forward and to hide, disguise, or omit expression of impulses about which there is shame or guilt.

This is particularly true with *psychosexual adjustment, sex-role identity, aggression,* and *interpersonal relationships.* The Rorschach may give a picture of sexual feeling and sex-role identification in so far as this is a matter of *feeling* or *impulse,* as well as of sex-related personality characteristics (masculinity-feminity). But the Rorschach apparently cannot diagnose overt sexual *behavior* with assurance of accuracy. Nor is sex-role identification as revealed by the Rorschach necessarily closely related to the overt personality. Not infrequently a man with feminine wishes may disguise these by an exaggerated overt masculinity.

This lack of correspondence between the underlying tendencies and their outward expression was particularly true for *aggression*. The Rorschach sometimes indicated strong aggressive or hostile tendencies which were not revealed in the interview. It is well known that those individuals with the strongest reaction formations of politeness and courtesy may have underlying aggressive tendencies. Likewise, a person may seem outwardly to be at ease in his social relations, but may experience discomfort in his relations with others and lack genuine warmth and depth of feeling. However, those with vivid, lively, outgoing personalities tended to show good social adjustment on the Rorschach, while those with restrained, reserved personalities showed poor social adjustment on the Rorschach.

There was a more pronounced correspondence between *affect*, *drive*, *control*, and *mental functioning* as diagnosed from the Rorschach and as observed in real life. Estimates of affect from the Rorschach showed some correspondence with the interviewer's estimates of energy level, vivacity, and similar "dynamic" qualities of personality. There was low but recognizable agreement between control as diagnosed on the Rorschach and control or emotional restraint as diagnosed in the personality. Similarly, there was a definite correlation ($r = +.40$) between drive and energy level as diagnosed from the Rorschach and as observed in real life. The Rorschach has long been known to be useful in estimating level and quality of mental functioning, intelligence, judgment, organizational ability, and imagination, and although the relationship was not as high in the present study as has been reported elsewhere,[1] there was definite agreement with intelligence estimates of the interviewer, and there was also a correlation of $+.34$ with I.Q.

Little relation was found between the Rorschach and independent estimates of *self* or of *anxiety*. It was not possible to find agreement concerning attitudes toward the self as diagnosed from the Rorschach and interviewer's reports. This is mainly due to the fact that the interview reports did not summarize specifically the observer's impressions of self-confidence or feelings of inferiority, and trying to make estimates from snatches of self-reference phrases that a subject might have used and which were included in the report were entirely too un-

---

[1] P. E. Vernon, "The Significance of the Rorschach Test," *British Journal of Medical Psychology*, XV (1935), 199-217.
W. D. Altus and G. M. Thompson, "The Rorschach as a Measure of Intelligence," *Journal of Consulting Psychology*, XIII (1949), 341-47.

trustworthy as evidence. One cannot say that a relation between Rorschach and observer estimates of attitudes toward the self does not exist, but only that evidence was insufficient to assert it.

One usually thinks of the Rorschach as providing evidence concerning anxiety.[2] Here again the observer's reports concerning anxiety leave much to be desired. Anxiety in most persons does not take the form of a state of panic, but has been directed into personality characteristics by a variety of defense mechanisms. It is indeed difficult to estimate a person's anxiety by a single interview with him. Rorschach estimates of anxiety may not correspond with the superficial impressions left on an interviewer.

The same can be said about *depression*. But here one wonders that the relationship is not closer. Depression was diagnosed in fourteen subjects from the Rorschach and was noted by the interviewer in nine subjects, but there were only four subjects who had depressed tendencies from both sources of evidence.

If one might hazard a broad generalization he could say that there is definite agreement between the Rorschach and direct observation in those aspects of personality which make a definite impression on an observer—the liveliness, animation, intelligence, spontaneity. But in the tendencies about which the subject may be sensitive and which he has repressed, disguised, or brought under control—psychosexual adjustment, sex-role identity, aggression, anxiety, relations with people—the relationship may be low. This is not to deny the value of the Rorschach. On the contrary, it may even enhance the value of a Rorschach diagnosis because it may point to trends which find expression only when stress brings them into play. They may nevertheless still be very important ingredients in the underlying personality structure.

It is possible that a finer differentiation of the Rorschach diagnoses according to whether the interpretation comes from formal analysis or content might indicate that those two kinds of interpretation may have their own distinct contributions.

The Picture-Story Test also furnishes evidence as to the latent, underlying impulses and wish life of a person which may or may not correspond to his observable behavior and personality. The Picture-

---

[2] Abraham Elizur, "Content Analysis of the Rorschach with Regard to Anxiety and Hostility," *Journal of Projective Techniques*, XIII (1949), 247–84.

Story Test, in addition, can portray only those wishes and impulses that a subject can put into words to characterize another person (projection). Because of this projective factor the picture-story method may reveal traits and impulse tendencies which a person might deny as pertaining to himself but which he may not be able to hide on the Rorschach.

In general, content in the Picture-Story Test reveals considerable information about the *sex wish-life, sex-role identity, self-attitudes,* and *Oedipal relationships*. In some respects this material is closer to the surface in the Picture-Story Test than in the Rorschach reports. On the Picture-Story Test a person may reveal his attitudes and feelings toward the opposite sex, the same sex, or marriage, even though he may not express these feelings in his real-life adjustment. One can tell whether the subject identifies with the male or female figures in a picture, but this does not necessarily tell one whether there is masculine or feminine identification in real life. A man may clearly identify with female characters in the pictures and betray this interest in his dress, gestures, or mannerisms—but give the world the impression that he is a rugged masculine type of individual by his activities, occupation, and interests. The Picture-Story Test also reveals feelings of inferiority or self-confidence as well as Oedipal material.

Content from the Picture-Story Test yields little concerning *social adjustment, affect, control, drive,* or *mental functioning*, but these may be diagnosed from the formal aspects of the stories. However, even if such diagnosis shows that these factors are present in the impulse and wish life of a person, one cannot be sure how they will be expressed in personality. As has been observed before, the relation may be inverse: if a person can express himself openly and freely he may have little need to fantasy and his stories may be meager and restricted, but if his behavior is inhibited, then his impulses may find free expression in overelaborated fantasy.

The same comments also apply to *anxiety* and *depression*. Depression was a theme in the stories of twenty-three subjects. In some of these depression came out clearly in the interview reports, but in others there was no mention of depression, although it might have been noted if one were alert to its manifestations. This is also true of anxiety and the comment about anxiety with reference to the Rorschach applies equally to the Picture-Story Test.

Though there was some agreement between the diagnosis from the Rorschach and the Picture-Story Test, in many instances this agreement was very low or altogether absent. The Rorschach provides evidence as to basic psychosexual attitudes and feelings whereas the Picture-Story Test tells how these attitudes and feelings work themselves out with reference to social adjustments and marriage. The Picture-Story Test provides content that must be guessed at from the Rorschach. On the other hand, whereas the Rorschach presents a very discouraging over-all picture of psychosexual adjustment, this would not have been guessed from the Picture-Story Test.

In general, where *sex role* is prominently revealed in the Picture-Story Test there is good agreement with the Rorschach. On the whole, the Picture-Story Test agrees rather faithfully with the Rorschach diagnosis of attitudes toward the *self*, and fills in some of the content or meaning of the Rorschach estimate.

When the Picture-Story Test is interpreted from its formal factors, agreement with the Rorschach is most apparent. Rorschach indicators of good social adjustment, for example, are correlated for the most part with richness of fantasy, elaborateness of plot, and absence of restriction or stereotype in the Picture-Story Test. Also, with regard to *affect* there is some indication that those who show repression and dissociation of feeling on the Rorschach also show paucity of feeling on the Picture-Story Test. Some slight relationship was also noted between elaborateness, freedom, and spontaneity of a set of stories, and the quality of *mental functioning* as diagnosed from the Rorschach.

But for other factors little or no relationship was noted between the Rorschach and the Picture-Story Test. Very little correspondence was found between short, stereotyped, stimulus-bound stories on the Picture-Story Test and *control* as diagnosed from the Rorschach. Likewise, whether a story was long and animated or short and restrained seemed to have little relationship to *drive* and *energy level* as diagnosed on the Rorschach. More surprising and difficult to explain is the complete lack of relationship between ratings on *anxiety* or on *depression* in the two tests.

Still more difficult to understand is the discrepancy among ratings on *aggression*. According to the Rorschach these subjects possess a great deal of underlying aggression and hostility although it may be bottled up in various ways and not permitted direct expression. The

The Rorschachs, Interviews, and Fantasies

1953 stories on the Picture-Story Test were noteworthy for absence of aggression, which was noticeably different from the amount of aggression in the stories of these same individuals in adolescence. Apparently, control and repressive tendencies influence the expression of aggression on the Picture-Story Test to a considerably greater extent than on the Rorschach.

One may summarize by saying that both the Rorschach and the Picture-Story Test provide evidence as to the underlying impulse and wish life of a person. In some ways the Rorschach, because of its unstructured nature, furnishes evidence that may be a little more basic but is often difficult to translate into terms that have meaning in actual personality. The Picture-Story Test, on the other hand, presents the wishes and impulses that the subject can put into words. If wishes and impulses are unacceptable they may not find expression even in fantasy. This may mean that often they are not as basic as the trends revealed on the Rorschach but they have the advantage of showing how the trend is thought of with regard to life situations, even though it may not find open expression in personality.

9. Prediction of Mental Health

One of the questions which it was hoped that this follow-up study of *Adolescent Fantasy* would answer is whether it is possible to predict general adjustment or mental health from the data which were gathered in 1940. Unfortunately, the Rorschach was not given in 1940, but there are available from the earlier period the results of the Picture-Story Test, the subjects' autobiographies, interviews with the mother or guardian, statements from teachers and other school officials, and general observations by the workers in the study.

In 1940 rankings were made of adjustment by Symonds, by Wexler and Silverman combined (Wexler ranking the boys and Silverman the girls), by Mrs. Muriel I. Chamoulaud; and then a composite was made from the three sets of rankings.

In 1953 rankings were made by both Jensen and Symonds separately on general adjustment from the material in the interviews, adjustment as judged from the Picture-Story Test, and adjustment as judged from the Rorschach. In addition, Mrs. Dudek ranked the subjects from her evaluations of the Rorschach. It is not known how much contamination there is in the rankings of Symonds and Jensen. The Symonds rankings were made several months apart; even so it is difficult to make an unbiased estimate from one set of data when one is familiar with the other data on the same subject. Composite rankings were also prepared by combining the rankings on adjustment as gathered from the interviews, the Picture-Story Test, and the Rorschach reports.

Rank difference intercorrelations, computed from the 14 variables, are presented in Table 16. From this table of intercorrelations one learns that the correlation between the composite of the 1940 rankings for adjustment and the composite of the 1953 rankings for adjustment

Prediction of Mental Health

is .54. This is the figure that comes closest to answering the general question posed at the beginning of this chapter. Whether this is a high or low relationship depends very much on one's point of view. It is far from a perfect relationship and also far from a chance relationship. It compares very closely with the level of relationship which is found in predicting college achievement from the best tests that are available today, and as a measure of prediction is quite creditable. This means that predictions made of mental health from evidence available during adolescence have considerable significance some thirteen years later.

TABLE 16. INTERCORRELATIONS OF RANKINGS ON ADJUSTMENT

	1.	2.	3.	4.	5.	6.	7.	8.	9.	10.	11.	12.	13.
2.	.64												
3.	.79	.48											
4.	.89	.80	.90										
5.	.39	.52	.35	.44									
6.	.55	.20	.40	.50	.34								
7.	.49	.41	.49	.54	.81	.79							
8.	.55	.44	.49	.54	.45	.36	.51						
9.	.55	.14	.36	.42	.09	.46	.35	.75					
10.	.58	.26	.43	.47	.32	.46	.47	.93	.94				
11.	.53	.24	.51	.44	.15	.38	.34	.68	.63	.69			
12.	.55	.28	.50	.47	.17	.41	.37	.65	.66	.69	.84		
13.	.25	-.03	.22	.15	-.07	-.05	.11	.53	.49	.54	.37	.31	
14.	.55	.15	.50	.44	.16	.28	.27	.77	.72	.79	.86	.88	.67

Key

1. 1940 Symonds rankings on adjustment. *2.* 1940 Wexler-Silverman rankings on adjustment. *3.* 1940 Chamoulaud rankings on adjustment. *4.* 1940 composite rankings on adjustment. *5.* 1953 Jensen rankings from interviews. *6.* 1953 Symonds rankings from interviews. *7.* 1953 composite rankings from interviews. *8.* 1953 Jensen rankings from Picture-Story Test. *9.* 1953 Symonds rankings from Picture-Story Test. *10.* 1953 composite rankings from Picture-Story Test. *11.* 1953 Jensen rankings from Rorschach. *12.* 1953 Symonds rankings from Rorschach. *13.* 1953 Dudek rankings from Rorschach. *14.* 1953 composite rankings from Rorschach.

The correlations of the Rorschach made by Mrs. Dudek are considerably lower than the other correlations in the study, and one is forced to conclude that Mrs. Dudek based her judgment on factors which differed from the other two workers who studied those data.

The correlation between the rankings of Jensen and Symonds on the Rorschach was .84, and on the Picture-Story Test .75. But the correlation between their rankings on general adjustment from the interviews was only .34. This will be the subject for later comment.

The correlations between general adjustment from the interviews and adjustment from the Picture-Story Test were in the middle range, those between the rankings of Symonds being .46 and Jensen .45. But the correlations between general adjustment from interviews and from the Rorschach tended to be lower, those for Symonds being .41 and for Jensen .15. The correlations between the rankings on the Picture-Story Test and the Rorschach were considerably higher—.66 for Symonds and .68 for Jensen. Apparently there is considerable correlation between the results on the two projective techniques.

The low correlation of .34 between the rankings of Symonds and Jensen on general adjustment from the interviews deserves a further look, because if it is not possible for two individuals using the same data to agree any better on what is meant by adjustment than this figure indicates, then the possibility of prediction is open to grave question.

With regard to the rankings on general adjustment, Jensen has made the following statement.

My initial rankings were made without consideration of the test materials. They were influenced perhaps too much by the degree to which the subject was living the kind of life expected of an adult and seemed to be meeting adult responsibilities successfully. For this reason some of the still unmarried subjects are ranked lower than they would have been otherwise. Also an element of "success" entered my ranking—those who seemed to have managed their lives well, have gotten good jobs, assumed the responsibility of a family of their own, have been able to acquire a house and car and have become responsible citizens of the community were ranked higher than those who have not taken on as many adult responsibilities or have not been as successful in meeting the demands of such responsibility. All of these are rather superficial criteria of "adjustment" perhaps, and any ranking would have to be considerably changed if it were based on my knowledge of the whole case including the test materials.

Symonds based his rankings on three criteria: (1) success in terms of well-rounded living, (2) happiness, and (3) ego strength in terms of freedom from neuroticism. Each of these requires extended definition, of course, and I did not have the necessary data to make entirely accurate rankings on criteria of this sort. It soon became evident that ratings on the three criteria did not agree, as far as the evidence permitted me to judge. Probably the evidence was clearest with regard to the external and superficial tokens of success—whether or not a person was married and there were children in the family, his education, the level of his occupation and roughly his success in it, the kind of community and house he lived in, and whether or not he owned a car.

But when it comes to the matter of happiness, the data do not permit such easy judgments. One does not wear his unhappiness on his sleeve, and many of the subjects tried and were successful in giving Dr. Jensen an impression that all was going well with them when, if the truth were known, there was much unhappiness that was not revealed. As it was, a large number of the subjects showed evidences of depression in one way or another. It was obvious that Ralph (2), who had not yet finished his education and was unmarried, Jerome (7), who complained about dissatisfaction over his job, Roger (8), who felt that he was capable of more than the world gave him credit for, Dorothy (30), who complained that she did not receive sexual satisfaction from her husband, and both Natalie (21) and Nancy (31), who complained that life was dull and drab, can all be classed as unhappy.

But what about both Barbara (20) and Celia (28), neither of whom is married, although they are vaguely concerned about it, but have vigorous, outgoing personalities and are successful in their work—are they unhappy? Or John (39), who is obviously very disturbed sexually and is unmarried, but prides himself on his feminine conquests and is apparently successful in his work—is he unhappy? Or Mabel (22), who lives in a better-than-average home and is able to have a full-time maid to do all of the housework and look after the children, but who admitted tensions between herself and her husband. Is she happy? And is Seymour (36), a postman with little ambition whose wife makes all the major decisions, unhappy? Should Pansy (29), who married out of her race and religion against her parents' wishes and lives in a very inferior neighborhood with obvious poor relations with her neighbors, but who has three children, be termed unhappy? Isabel (18), unmarried, lives quietly at home with her parents, has worked ten years in a bank, likes to sew, enjoys music, is a devout Catholic and has very little to do with men. Is she unhappy? These are difficult if not impossible questions to answer. In fact, I doubt that these individuals themselves could give an unqualified answer if the question were put to them. There may be vague currents of unrest and dissatisfaction, but on the other hand each of them enjoys many aspects of life that give considerable satisfaction and which they would not willingly change. With all of the complexity of human living, it is impossible to state unqualifiedly for oneself that one is or is not happy, to say nothing of assigning such a designation to another person.

The question of ego strength and freedom from neurotic tendencies is the most difficult of all. Except for Karl (11), who was diagnosed on the basis of the Rorschach as paranoid schizophrenic and who impressed the observers as very queer, none of the subjects of the study can be classified as being neurotic or psychotic in the sense that they have pronounced symptoms. Two subjects have undergone psychotherapy, indicating that their problems have been serious enough to prompt them to seek professional assistance. Catherine (12) consulted a psychiatrist because she had become very nervous and found it difficult to sleep. She was also concerned because she was frigid. Psychotherapy has removed these difficulties and Catherine is quite satisfied over the outcome. Albert (40) was undergoing psychoanalytic therapy at the time of the study. He sought help because of his difficulty in holding a job, but he also stated that it has helped him in his relations with girls. None of the subjects can be said to have anxiety neurosis, phobia, hysteria, hypochondriasis, neurasthenia, obsessive-compulsive neurosis, or character disorder. None has a serious psychosomatic disorder. Except for Karl none can be called manic-depressive, schizophrenic, or paranoid.

But isolated signs or symptoms of all of these can be found among the subjects. Ten subjects reported that they are tense, nervous, worriers. Ralph (2) has a nervous stomach which gives him gastritis when under stress, particularly the stress of examinations. Roy (6) had high blood pressure while in the Navy and it is likely to recur now when he is under stress. Sam (9), although in many respects making a good adjustment, reports that he is basically a rather nervous person, had "battle fatigue" while overseas in the Army, and now tends to worry about his mother, who is a very nervous person. Laura (13) is reported as tense and nervous, and Viola (14) tends to lose weight under stress. Stella (19), a frequent worrier, becomes nervous and depressed under stress. Dorothy (30) speaks of butterflies in her stomach. Seymour (36) has a nervous stomach and suffers attacks of indigestion under stress.

Albert (40) refers to his nervous tension and smoked nervously during the interviews.

Nine of the subjects reported that they were subject to more or less severe depression. Two of the subjects, Stella (19) and Nancy (31), reported cyclic tendencies—alternating periods of hyperexcitability and good feeling with more or less severe depression. Margaret (24), an otherwise healthy person, reported fear of high places and going up and down stairs, and Seymour (36) a fear of snakes.

While most of the men cautiously admitted that they would take a social drink now and then, none would admit that he drank heavily at the present time, except Albert (40). However, Karl (11) boasted about his drinking prowess and his ability to hold his liquor; and Edwin (33), Jimmy (37), and Albert (40) each stated that he drank heavily during the war while he was in the service.

From these scattered bits of evidence, it is not possible to tell how stable any individual is. Apparently at the present time all are able to function in a fairly satisfactory manner. But what any individual might do in a state of emergency or under severe stress is hard to say. All of the above symptoms were taken into account in making the rankings, but just how much weight they should have in connection with estimates of success and happiness as measures of mental health is debatable.

The relatively low correlation of .34 between the rankings of Jensen and Symonds points up the difficulty of estimating the mental health or adjustment of an adult. It was believed that some of the factors which might be responsible for the low correlation could be isolated if close inspection was made of those subjects for whom there was the greatest discrepancy in the rankings.

Wallace (1): Jensen ranking 23, Symonds 2, discrepancy 21. Jensen had difficulties in the two interview and test sessions with this subject. He found Wallace hostile, critical of psychology, and resentful, although he became more friendly by the end of the second session. Jensen described him as an "authoritarian personality." Symonds, on the other hand, from the record judged Wallace to be fairly successful, having a good job and living in a new modern house with his wife and child. His aggressiveness could be counted an asset, even though it may betoken an underlying inferiority.

Viola (14): Jensen ranking 25, Symonds 9, discrepancy 16. This subject also gave Jensen a difficult time in that she took more time in her interviews and tests than any other subject except one. She tended to be very exact and compulsively accurate, and spent much time hunting for the right word. Jensen found that she lived in a world of fantasy; he did not believe that she had her feet firmly on the ground. He called her a poetic type. Symonds, on the other hand, noted that she was well mated, had two children, and was pregnant at the time of the study. Her high energy level tended to give her a dynamic quality.

Edwin (*33*): Jensen ranking 10, Symonds 26, discrepancy 16. Jensen found Edwin to be very relaxed and not bothered by much of anything, which gave the impression of a high degree of stability. He is married and has one child. Symonds noted that Edwin was very ineffective and easygoing, had a mediocre job as inside salesman, and possessed pronounced feelings of inferiority.

Roger (*8*): Jensen ranking 2, Symonds 16, discrepancy 14. Jensen found Roger a soft-spoken, pleasant man, not openly assertive, with whom he felt comfortable. Symonds noted from the record that he was anxious and depressed. Although trained as a civil engineer, he holds an inferior job and has strong feelings of inadequacy. His wife teaches to help augment the family's earnings.

Olive (*27*): Jensen ranking 9, Symonds 23, discrepancy 14. Jensen found Olive robust and friendly, but she was very inhibited and for this reason difficult to interview. Symonds noted especially her repressed, depressed personality, her limited intellect, and pretensions above her capacity.

Seymour (*36*): Jensen ranking 11, Symonds 24, discrepancy 13. Jensen found Seymour good-natured, easygoing and happily mated. Symonds noted that he lacked ambition and was ineffectual vocationally. He tended to have gastritis under stress.

Celia (*28*): Jensen ranking 22, Symonds 11, discrepancy 11. Jensen observed that Celia was not married, was afraid of men, and held prudish sex standards. She was afraid of hurting other people's feelings. Symonds noted that she was attractive, refined, successful in her work, and competitive with men.

Catherine (*12*): Jensen ranking 15, Symonds 5, discrepancy 10. Jensen found Catherine subjective, self-centered, vague, with excessive fantasy. She was somewhat anxious about her pregnancy. Symonds

Prediction of Mental Health 183

noted that although she had earlier not been able to show hostility toward her mother, as a result of psychotherapy she was able to verbalize this and the treatment had also helped her to overcome a condition of sexual frigidity.

TABLE 17. SPECIAL SETS OF INTERCORRELATIONS OF RANKINGS ON ADJUSTMENT, TAKEN FROM TABLE 16

Symonds

Interviews	Interviews	Picture-Story Test		
1940	1953	1953		
.55			Symonds, Interviews	1953
.55	.46		Symonds, Picture-Story Test	1953
.55	.41	.66	Symonds, Rorschach	1953

Jensen

Interviews	Picture-Story Test		
1953	1953		
.45		Jensen, Picture-Story Test	1953
.15	.68	Jensen, Rorschach	1953

Composite

Interviews	Interviews	Picture-Story Test		
1940	1953	1953		
.54			Composite, Interviews	1953
.42	.41		Composite, Picture-Story Test	1953
.44	.27	.75	Composite, Rorschach	1953

As one reviews the discrepancies it becomes clear that these evaluations of mental health are based in part on personal likes and dislikes and on personal preferences and tastes in what is acceptable in people. Jensen, for instance, undervalues persons with push and nervous energy, who illustrate the "authoritarian personality"; and he tends to overvalue persons who are relaxed and easygoing. Apparently, in spite of what Jensen stated, he gave less attention to position and worldly success. Jensen tended to give poorer rankings to women who had not made good sexual adjustments. Symonds, on the other hand, tended to overevaluate men who were assertive, and gave poorer rankings to men lacking ambition, who were vocationally less successful, and who showed signs of feelings of inferiority. Symonds also tended to give better rankings than Jensen to women with neurotic tendencies which showed up in sexual repression. This comparison and analysis indicated clearly that evaluations of mental health are a function of the evaluator's own predilections and may be indicative of basic trends within his own personality.

It is interesting, in view of the subjectivity of these 1953 rankings of adjustment by Jensen and Symonds, that the correlation between the composite of their two rankings and the 1940 composite ranking was .54. There is an element of contamination in this correlation, inasmuch as rankings by Symonds appear in both factors, although thirteen years apart. But the correlation of Jensen's rankings with the 1940 composite is .44. One must conclude that taking an average of two or more evaluations tends to strike out the personal idiosyncrasies in the rankings of any one individual, with the result that the composite picture is not only more accurate, but also yields higher predictions of adjustment.

The lack of perfect correlation between the three measures was to be expected, and naturally part of the discrepancy can be attributed to the unreliability of the judgments. But a closer inspection of the discrepancies may throw further light on the different things that the judgments measure.

First, let us look at some of the larger discrepancies between rankings on adjustment from interviews and from the Picture-Story Test.

Dorothy, Barbara, and Celia may be studied together, as they show marked characteristics in common. *Dorothy (30)*: interview ranking 22.5, PST ranking 4, discrepancy 18.5. *Barbara (20)*: interview ranking 16.5, PST ranking 4, discrepancy 12.5. *Celia (28)*: interview ranking 16.5, PST ranking 4, discrepancy 12.5. All three are sexually maladjusted in real life. Barbara and Celia are unmarried and are repressed sexually. Dorothy, although married, complains of the impotence of her husband, although there is reason to believe that she may be inhibited in her own sexual responsiveness. The Picture-Story Test of all three shows a good deal in common. Each told stories of longing for love, romance, and marriage, which are interpreted as indicating normal, healthy longings. There is sibling rivalry in each. Celia's stories show a good deal of ambition and striving, while those of Barbara depict a strong-willed woman who is stronger than a man. Dorothy's stories, although showing a yearning for romance, are more subtle and sensitive but depressed and helpless, with an emphasis on sweetness.

John (39): interview ranking 9.5, PST ranking 25, discrepancy 15.5. Although he is obviously sexually maladjusted, his adjustment ranking is good because of his success in his work. But his stories lay bare his sexual inadequacies, with strong hostilities toward women. Jensen said that they had a psychopathic flavor with indications of latent homosexuality.

Mabel (22): interview ranking 1, PST ranking 14, discrepancy 13. She was given a good ranking from the interviews because she had a good home, was married, and had three children, although there were indications that there was tension with her husband. The stories, however, depicted a cruel father, rejecting mother, and sibling rivalry, and were meager, showing much repression.

From this brief comparison of large discrepancies between the rankings on adjustment from the record and from the Picture-Story Test, one can conclude that there is a tendency to overestimate adjustments from the Picture-Story Test when normal, healthy longings are depicted, which may only be wishes that have not been fulfilled in living. There is also a tendency to underestimate the adjustment when the stories show much aggressiveness, hostility, and violence, which may be finding release in fantasy and are not characteristics of the person in real life. On the other hand, there is perhaps a tendency to overestimate some of the superficial indications of successful living in real life, which may hide some of the conflicts, tensions, and anxieties underneath.

The same individuals appeared at the top of the list showing discrepancies between the rankings for adjustment as based on general interview observation and the Rorschach reports. *Dorothy (30)*: interview ranking 22.5, Rorschach 7, discrepancy 15.5. *Barbara (20)*: interview ranking 16.5, Rorschach 2, discrepancy 14.5. *Celia (28)*: interview ranking 16.5, Rorschach 3, discrepancy 13.5. *Isabel (18)*: interview ranking 24, Rorschach 7, discrepancy 17. The Rorschach ranking of each of these was well up toward better adjustment. Dorothy was described in the Rorschach reports as ambitious, having strong drives for prestige, status, and power, but sexually frigid; Barbara was noted as having high vitality and buoyancy, with good social and personal adjustment; and Celia was spoken of as intelligent, interesting, and imaginative, but with a vague concept of herself as a woman. Isabel, on the other hand, was described from the Rorschach as a restrained, controlled, and proper person, somewhat passive and dependent. All four of these are unmarried women who have obvious sexual inhibitions, which gave them low rankings on general adjustment. But *Mabel* (*22*)—interview ranking 1, Rorschach 21, discrepancy 20—who shows external signs of successful living, although with some marital tensions, is spoken of from the Rorschach as immature, anxious, with an aggressive drive and concern with prestige. *Stella* (*19*)—interview ranking 4.5, Rorschach 17.5, discrepancy 13—said to be happy in marriage although she gets nervous under stress, is described by the Rorschach as oppositional, immature, unpredictable, and suspicious, with an underlying schizophrenic process. And *Natalie* (*21*)—interview ranking 12, Rorschach 25, discrepancy 13—although her interview ranking is not particularly good since she is described as drab and listless, finding life dull, is described in the Rorschach as having poor contact with reality, as oppositional and demanding, with a mild schizophrenic process.

There is a tendency to overestimate adjustment on the Rorschach when the Rorschach record is a good one, having many W, M, FC, and F+ responses, even though there may be signs of sexual or aggressive inadequacy. On the other hand, the Rorschach may underestimate adjustment when there are indications of pathology as, for instance, a possible schizophrenic process or when there are FM signs of immaturity. But, as stated before, there may be a tendency to overestimate superficially good marital or aggressive adjustments in work as indications of good emotional adjustment, and to underestimate nervous signs or difficulties in social adjustment as possible indications of poor emotional adjustment.

This method of studying the discrepancies in the rankings cannot be applied to a comparison of the Picture-Story Test and the Rorschach because the correlation between them is so high—.79. Most of the discrepancies are small, and an inspection of the two highest does not suggest any significant trends. In the case of *Isabel* (*18*), the Picture-Story-Test ranking is 13.5 points lower (less creditable) than for the Rorschach; whereas for *Catherine* (*12*) the ranking is 11 points higher on the Picture-Story Test. In both instances the discrepancy apparently is due to nothing more than differences in judgment and interpretation of the records.

In summary, a coefficient of correlation of .54 was found between the estimates of adjustment made when the subjects of the study were adolescent and those made on twenty-seven of the subjects thirteen years later. This is a highly creditable measure of prediction. But the correlation of only .34 between the rankings of Jensen and Symonds from the 1953 data indicates the difficulty in making valid judgments about mental hygiene. There are difficulties in assessing the significance of surface indications of success and love life, in estimating happiness and the contributions of neurotic signs to mental health. There is evidence that evaluations of mental health are influenced by the likes, dislikes, and personal preferences of the judges. One gets somewhat different estimates of adjustment from the projective techniques than from the direct estimates of personality. Direct observation puts emphasis on external evidences of success in work and love life, whereas projective techniques provide evidence on underyling trends, impulses, conflicts, and anxieties.

10. The Significance of Fantasy

Since the Picture-Story Test was used in both the original study of *Adolescent Fantasy* and in this follow-up study on twenty-eight of the same subjects thirteen years later, it is possible to come to some conclusions concerning the role of fantasy in personality.

The first thing that our inquiry revealed was the remarkable similarity in fantasy over the thirteen-year interval between the two studies. In instance after instance it was found that subjects told stories with identical themes to the same pictures. Instances were also found where practically identical stories were told to different pictures by the same subject over the thirteen-year span. It was possible for judges to match the sets of stories of a subject told thirteen years apart even when they were interspersed with the stories of other subjects. This matching was based both on the formal characteristics of the stories and the thematic content. Fantasy, then, is a somewhat stable aspect of personality. Although evidence has been presented by many investigators to show that fantasy can be influenced by temporary states of hunger, fear, or ambition, and by stimuli impinging on a person from without, these are somewhat superficial aspects of fantasy. Beneath these temporary fluctuations lies a substratum of modes of fantasy expression and thematic content that persist year after year. However tenuous and shadowy fantasy may appear to be superficially, it is something that is a sturdy, substantial, firmly established part of the personality. And one might assume on theoretical grounds that something which is so indubitably a part of personality is no mere epiphenomenon, but plays an important role in the development and in the expression of personality.

But in spite of these tendencies toward the stability of fantasy, changes were noted both in the group as a whole and in individuals. The most striking change was a general increase in *depression* and a decrease in the *happy endings* to the stories, signifying that adolescent exuberance has given way to discouragement. This is a reaction to the fact that realities of romance and success have been disappointing and have failed to measure up to the shadowy hopes and expectations of adolescence. On the other hand, many of the distinctive characteristics of adolescent fantasy have been lost. There are fewer themes of violent *aggression, punishment* for it, and *reform*. Adult experiences have taken the *mystery* and *magic* out of *sex*. There is less need to fantasy *escape* since most of these adults to a greater or less degree have established emancipation from parental authority.

The trends which were noted in *Adolescent Fantasy* as one moves from earlier to later adolescence are continued and reinforced in early adulthood.

A study was made of the factors that are related to these changes. As the evidence was summarized it seemed possible to assert that change in fantasy is a function of change in environment. If environment does not change fantasies will not change; and the greater the change in environment the greater the change in fantasy. The fantasies of youths or maidens who remain at home, do not go on to college, find work of a routine nature, and do not marry are likely to continue without change into adult life. But if a boy or girl goes to college, has military experience, finds work that requires resourcefulness, marries and establishes a family, there is likelihood that his fantasies will change and lose their adolescent flavor.

Eight general principles (see Chapter Twelve), describe the conditions which seem to govern change or lack of change in fantasy.

Fantasy was found to have an impact upon later personality in five areas: dependency, erotic impulses, aggression, self-striving, and anxiety with its defenses. It has been shown that adolescent fantasy is lived out in reality in an almost compulsive fashion. Adolescent yearnings for independence find fruition as the young person leaves the home for college, for military service, and especially for marriage. Erotic fantasies find expression in marrying and establishing a family. Aggressive impulses find expression in work or in rebellion against the parents or in other ways. Fantasies of self-confidence frequently result in successful, competent adults, whereas fantasies of incompetence are often reflected in individuals whose doubts about themselves lead to lack of ambition and failure to move ahead vocationally.

But sometimes these fantasies never move out of the realm of fantasy. In some cases the struggle for independence is still a struggle in later years and possibly has been channeled into daydreams of independence not yet realized. Perhaps the erotic fantasies have become intensified as hopes for marriage recede. Fantasies of success may become unrealistic wishful thinking as success in reality becomes unattainable.

Fantasy may have many vicissitudes. If direct, open expression of the fantasy in realistic living is denied either by circumstances or more generally by interfering, contradictory impulses within the individual, the impulse may find expression in devious other ways. Various mechanisms of displacement, projection, and the like may permit an oblique expression of the impulse. If anxiety grows intense, then defenses appear in fantasy and defense mechanisms translate these repressed impulses into behavior in disguised form.

The evidence points strongly to the conclusion that fantasy attitudes expressed in adolescence play a major role in determining decisions to be made in later life. If erotic impulses are strong and are not contradicted, almost inevitably the result is marriage. But if there is at the same time fear of sex, then at times of decision the individual makes a choice that may lead away from marriage. Aggressive fantasy may lead to an aggressive personality if there are no interfering factors, but in general aggression has been so thoroughly punished and suppressed in our culture that at best it can only find sublimated or displaced expression. Frequently, attitudes that in adolescent fantasy are directed toward parents may in later years be directed toward a spouse or toward one's children.

There is a tendency for anxiety expressed in adolescent fantasy still to be present in adult years. Mechanisms of defense against anxiety expressed in fantasy in adolescence may help to determine the basic personality patterns of later years. Psychosomatic or psychotic trends that become sharpened in adult years may have been presaged in adolescent fantasy.

In regard to the correspondence between overt adolescent and adult personality, it was found that later personality reflected with great fidelity the personality characteristics of the adolescent years. This was true with regard to physical characteristics, general personality characteristics, and nervous signs. The mode of response in the interview situation tended to be the same at the two periods. There was a repetition of interests, hobbies, and attitudes.

But when it comes to *social relationships*, it was not possible to predict adult adjustments in personal relationships from adolescent attitudes. Adolescence is a time when interpersonal relationships arouse so much anxiety that frequently the trends are repressed. In particular with young adolescent boys, there is an absence of interest in the opposite sex that by no means predicts the interests and relationships in later years. Boys and girls frequently cannot express in words their resentment and hostility toward parents and siblings which they are able in later years to express in word and in deed. Correspondences are present between adolescent and adult attitudes toward other persons, but these correspondences are irregular, and are not 100 percent perfect.

Finally, one would judge that the correspondence between verbally expressed ambitions and intentions with regard to education and vocation is little better than what results from chance. Apparently what a person *does* has considerable predictive significance, but what he *says* has little predictive meaning.

In spite of the apparent fragile and intangible nature of fantasy the evidence from this study and from psychodynamic theory leads to the conclusion that fantasy is an expression of the basic stuff from which personality is made. The author has referred to fantasy as the "unfinished business" of personality. That is, when one constructs a story with a picture as its stimulus, he weaves the story about his own active impulses and tensions which represent unsolved problems or which indicate the presence of unresolved conflicts. According to theory, if a person finds a satisfactory solution to a problem situation, the impulses and tensions that have been aroused are dissipated. When he meets that situation again, his previous learning is called upon and he reacts to it successfully. But if the solution has not been found in previous trials, then old impulses, tensions, and conflicts are aroused again. This has been called the Zeigarnik effect because of the experimental demonstration by Lewin and Zeigarnik that incompleted tasks are remembered better than completed tasks.[1]

[1] Kurt Lewin and Bluma Zeigarnik, "Untersuchungen zur Handlungs und Affektpsychologie, III; Das Behaltenerledigter und unerledigter Handlungen," *Psychologische Forschung*, IX (1927), 1-85.

Consequently when a person tells a story to a picture, the themes that he incorporates into that story represent his "unfinished business." As the vicissitudes of living provide opportunity, a person may attempt to express these fantasy themes in behavior, and if he finds a successful resolution of the problem or conflict that they represent they become part of his personality. That is why fantasy themes relating to dependence-independence, eroticism, aggression, and self-striving find expression in personality in later years. But if a satisfactory solution is not found later these same themes may persist in fantasy, perhaps in exaggerated form, while the personality is still immature and undeveloped.

Personality, then, from this point of view is a precipitate of the working out and resolution of fantasy. Personality includes the habits and skills that a person has acquired and which represent his adjustments to daily living. Personality also includes the defenses against anxiety and guilt that have been built up. Adolescent personality represents the adjustments and solutions that have been made to the requirements of living in infancy and childhood.

Personality, in general, represents a stable form of adjustment. In other words the habits, skills, and defenses used today will be used tomorrow and next year for the same situations which they have served in the past. It is for this reason that the best prediction of future personality is present personality.

But personality is constantly being molded and modified through the working out in actual experience of fantasy. Fantasy is the testing of experience in anticipatory form before the right solution can be incorporated into the reality of personality. The little child does this in imaginative play as he tries out roles that he anticipates he will meet in later years. The five-year-old boy receives football togs and helmet with which he can anticipate experiences of high school and college sport; the five-year-old girl dresses up in adult finery or plays with her dolls to anticipate the adult role. Later on, the growing child becomes sensitive to the distinction between fantasy and reality and fantasy recedes to become a more private, inner affair. But the adolescent still anticipates his future roles as he fantasies erotic and aggressive situations, as he shifts between dependence and independence, and as he searches for a concept of himself. Later, when he experiences college, military service, work, and marriage, he has an opportunity to test his

The Significance of Fantasy

fantasies in reality. It is then that new aspects of personality may develop that were not evident in adolescence but were present in fantasy if one knew how to bring them into open expression. But conflicting fantasy trends may prevent any given fantasy theme from finding permanent expression in behavior, and it may be relegated to a continuing place in the world of fantasy.

Fantasy, then, has predictive value for later personality, but that value is uncertain. Whether or not fantasy will emerge into expression in behavior and personality depends on several things: it will depend on whether there are requisite experiences and whether there are not competing, inhibitory fantasies. Having experiences—leaving home to go to college, to military service, to work, to marry—helps a young man or woman to translate fantasy into personality. Being denied these experiences means that personality does not mature and that fantasy may actually be intensified. One may say that fantasy is a dynamic force within the individual, but the precise form in experience that fantasy will take cannot be predicted with assurance. Personality, being a precipitate of the working out of previous fantasy, represents a more stable form of adjustment and is a safer basis for the prediction of later personality.

11. Growing out of Adolescence into Adulthood

As the data in these studies are reviewed, the concept of adolescence as a seperate period in life with distinctive characteristics recedes, and in its place one is impressed with the idiosyncratic nature of the individual personality. It has become customary today to think of the adolescent boy or girl as being a creature with strange and incomprehensible characteristics, difficult to understand and hard to manage. The instability of the adolescent has been often noted. The following quotation from Anna Freud represents fairly the common, current concept of adolescence.

Adolescents are excessively egoistic, regarding themselves as the centre of the universe and the sole object of interest, and yet at no time in later life are they capable of so much self-sacrifice and devotion. They form the most passionate love-relations, only to break them off as abruptly as they began them. On the one hand they throw themselves enthusiastically into the life of the community and, on the other, they have an overpowering longing for solitude. They oscillate between blind submission to some self-chosen leader and defiant rebellion against any and every authority. They are selfish and materially-minded and at the same time full of lofty idealism. They are ascetic but will suddenly plunge into instinctual indulgence of the most primitive character. At times their behavior to other people is rough and inconsiderate, yet they themselves are extremely touchy. Their moods veer between light-hearted optimism and blackest pessimism. Sometimes they will work with indefatigable enthusiasm, and at other times they are sluggish and apathetic.[1]

This apparently is a composite picture. We found no individual in this study that could be said to possess all these characteristics, but all these characteristics were found in different individuals. Wallace (1)

[1] Anna Freud, *The Ego and the Mechanisms of Defense* (London, Hogarth Press, "The International Psychoanalytical Library," No. 30, 1937), pp. 149-50.

Growing out of Adolescence into Adulthood

was cocky, self-assertive, and self-confident; Olive (27) was depressed and restrained. Barbara (20) was self-confident as an adolescent, but Ralph (2) was unsure of himself. Julia (25) was mature and outgoing sexually, but Celia (28) tended to be prudish. Isabel (18) tended to be somewhat secretive, but Jimmy (37) talked about himself with great gusto. To be sure, Nancy (31) alternated between periods of hyper-excitability and depression, but it is recognized that she has a special "cyclic" disposition, and there are others who seem to be highly stable.

It is unfair and misleading, therefore, to speak of "the adolescent personality." Characterizing an age group in this way prevents one from attending to all the variations in the personalities of adolescents and the factors that are responsible for these differences. It is much more helpful to think of personality as a form of adjustment that has been acquired from responding to the vicissitudes of living. So the personality of the adolescent is an outgrowth of experiences of infancy and childhood, and it is not so much a matter of growing out of adolescence as it is reacting to life's experiences with the personality equipment and reaction tendencies with which the earlier years have equipped one.

It is possible, of course, that the conditions of the 1940 study did not make it possible to observe the chameleon-like changes that Anna Freud describes. One would have to live with an adolescent day in and day out to be able to observe the shifts in mood that she describes. But in the 1940 study each individual was seen five or six times over as many weeks, and any marked shifts in mood should have been observed in these several contacts. Jack (4) was one who did oscillate between obstinate and tractable behavior, but the majority of the subjects impressed the workers by the consistency of their personalities.

One of the outstanding findings of this study is the remarkable persistence of personality trends over the thirteen-year period. Growing out of adolescence does not mean giving up certain personality trends and taking on others, but rather meeting life's experiences with the same personality equipment one has been provided from earlier years. Wallace (1) is as aggressive and cocksure as a man as he was when an adolescent. Karl (11) is just as peculiar as a man and in the same way that he was as an adolescent. Laura (13) is just as overly polite as a woman as she was as a girl. Barbara (20), who was described as quick-tempered as an adolescent, described herself in the same terms in 1953.

Natalie's (21) teachers complained that she was so withdrawn that they could not hear her when she recited in class; the interviewer in 1953 commented on her low energy level and low, soft voice. John (39) impressed the interviewer with his energy and forcefulness in 1953 just as he impressed the worker in 1940. And so it goes. Becoming an adult does not mean shedding one personality for another, but rather using the personality that one has to meet the exigencies of adult years.

Relations with parents assumed greater importance as it became possible to review the present in terms of the past. An adolescent with a united home and strong, stable parents has the best chance for making a good adjustment in the early adult years. An adolescent boy needs a father with whom he can identify, and who will give him strength in meeting the problems that arise in connection with education and work. An adolescent girl needs a mother with whom she can identify, and who provides a pattern for the solution of problems in human relations. Ralph (2) as an adolescent had a divorced mother and a stepfather as of two years. The fact that his mother was very strict and his own father was conspicuous by his ineffectiveness during the formative years may account in part for Ralph's ineffectiveness as a man. Jerome's (7) mother died when he was five and his father remarried when he was eleven. During the intervening years he lived with his grandmother, and later he rebelled against the new stepmother. Jerome feels that he has never found himself vocationally. Roger's (8) mother died when he was a baby. He, too, lived with grandparents until his father remarried when he was five. He was much overprotected by his grandparents. Now he has pronounced feelings of inferiority. Olive (27) has a stepmother. She is the youngest in a family of seven girls, three of whom are stepsisters, and she has never outgrown the rivalry and depression engendered in this home situation. Dorothy's (30) father died when she was seven and there is no evidence of her mother remarrying. Dorothy, although now married, still lives in her mother's home and it appears that she married a man who is eleven years older than herself as a kind of father substitute. Albert's (40) mother died when he was four years old and he went to live with grandparents and aunts. Although his father remarried four years before the 1940 study, Albert continued to live with his grandmother. Certainly his various deprivations as a child have something to do with his hot temper, feelings of inferiority, and inability to give himself in a love relationship.

But the success of later adjustments often depends more on the relationships with those with whom one has contact than it does with real parents. Although Jack (4) lived in a foster family, he was given real strength to make satisfactory later adult adjustments because these foster parents were strong, devoted, stable people. And if the parents do not provide strength and good models, then later adjustment is not good. Seymour's (36) father, described as very easygoing, told Seymour to choose his own life. Now Seymour is a man without ambition, content with his present work as a letter carrier, letting his wife make most of the decisions.

The study shows decisively the difficulties of the adolescent in attaining emancipation from the family, especially the mother. This is noticeably true with the women in connection with their marriages. Catherine (12), Laura (13), Viola (14), and Pansy (29) all married over their mother's violent and bitter protests. Catherine described her mother as very domineering and easily upset when she did not get her way. Her mother used to take her window-shopping in the afternoon after school to prevent her being with boys. She did not approve of Catherine's marriage and today she does not approve of her husband. Laura's mother strongly opposed her seeing the young man whom she later married, and Laura became so upset and nervous over her mother's attitude that she broke off her engagement. When she later met her fiancé secretly and her mother heard about it, she gave her daughter an ultimatum: "I will give you three days in which to decide whether you love me or S (her fiancé) more." When Viola's (14) mother heard that she (Viola) was going with a Jewish boy she "had a fit" and tried to "break it up." Pansy (29) states that she married partly to get away from home. Her parents were "very narrow-minded people with very old-fashioned ideas. They always demanded that she [Pansy] be in by twelve o'clock." They were horrified when they learned that she intended to marry a Catholic. Her mother stated that she (Pansy) had ruined her (the mother's) life. Viola's parents were outraged when they learned of her marriage and they would not let her bring her husband home. Now they have disowned her and she has not seen or heard from her parents for five years.

But it is equally true that adolescents cling to their parental home. Ralph (2) has always lived at home and as a twenty-six-year-old man he now returns home from college at vacation time. Karl (11) claims that he would like to be more independent, but he is hopelessly dependent on his parental home, where he still lives. Viola's (14) experiences have been related in detail in Chapter Four.

Isabel (18), unmarried, has always lived at home. Stella's (19) nervousness has been described in Chapter Five. "She said she might as well have lived at home, she was at her mother's home so frequently." Barbara (20) and Celia (28), both unmarried, live with their parents. Dorothy (30), as has been stated above, although married, still lives in her mother's home. Jimmy (37), in spite of three years of strenuous military service in the infantry, never broke his close dependence on his mother and returned home to live for three years after the war. It is obvious from this that emancipation from family ties has been only partially accomplished by a substantial number of the subjects of the study.

Until the follow-up study was made, the full extent of feelings in adolescence was not realized. But adolescence is a time when feelings expand and run strong and deep, and adolescents rarely display their feelings openly. As I pass the adolescents that I know in school halls and on the streets, I am impressed by their reticence, reserve, and withdrawal. When a group of adolescents are together there may be a release of feelings expressed in orgies, riots, or "panty raids." But adolescent fantasy touches upon the strength of underlying feeling. We have learned how strong are the adolescent aggressive feelings expressed in hostility and death wishes toward parents and siblings, also how strong are the feelings for closeness, belonging, and romance. But these feelings are frightening, and the adolescent must do something to mitigate their strength by telling deadpan stories with endings that erase all the violence that preceded, or in real life by holding himself stiffly in control.

In later adult years there is also repression. The stories told by young adults have lost the adolescent flavor of adventure, excitement, and mystery. The aggressive themes present in the adolescent stories have virtually disappeared in stories told by adults. Adult fantasy is more matter-of-fact and stimulus-bound. At the same time, however, there is greater freedom to face human relations and sex realistically. Life's experiences have removed some of the reticence and reserve of the adolescent period. The young adults in this study were able to meet the interviewer, on the whole, easily and forthrightly, even if this openness was to some extent false and forced and a cover to other emotions and attitudes underneath.

We are shown clearly how becoming an adult is a disillusioning experience. In adolescence, fantasy lacks the checks of reality testing. The future is wide open and holds untold possibilities. It is easy to fantasy climbing to a high position in the firm in which one works, of marrying the boss's daughter, of finding jewels hidden behind the portrait in the livingroom, of robbing a bank. Success is attained—perhaps with difficulty and only by overcoming hardships—yet it is attained, in the fantasies of adolescents. But life itself scatters these rewards only in the newspaper headlines. All the young adults in this study were struggling to find themselves vocationally, and if some reached a degree of success it was through very hard work. But wealth, comfortable living, and leisure had not been achieved. Mabel (22), with two television sets and a full-time maid, is the exception.

Marriage has not provided all that adolescent romantic fantasies have conjured. Edith (17), who had fantasies of a theatrical career, found that the theater lost its glamour when she tried it out. Nancy (31) expressed the man's point of view: "Tom was listless and dejected. It seemed to him that life had been very cruel indeed. He sat in his room by the window not caring to do much. He had tried so hard and he had failed so bitterly that it seemed to him that he just didn't care what happened." And Natalie (21) expressed the woman's point of view: "This girl is walking home from work. She is tired and discouraged with life in this dirty little town, very drab, and it's the same old thing every day. You just go to work and come home and eat and go to bed and the next day do the same thing over again."

On the other hand, the things feared in adolescence are less fearsome after they have been experienced. Life's experiences provide a kind of reality testing, as illustrated by both Laura (13) and Roy (6), who, as adolescents, told stories marked with mystery, strangeness, and spookiness which was not present in their 1953 stories. This has been interpreted as meaning that the experiences of marriage have taken some of the mystery and fearsomeness out of sex. Likewise, Seymour (36) told stories in adolescence in which the subject became the victim of circumstances and was aggressed against. "He was struck over the head with a police club . . . he made enough to go home and his mother was very glad to see him, and he said he'd never run away again." Although the same fantasies are present in 1953, they are less pronounced, and the realities of life have made him less apprehensive of being the victim of circumstances.

In some instances life's experiences have helped a person to accept himself more realistically. Edith (17) told stories with an unusual masculine identification when adolescent, as though she were unable to have the world accept her as a girl, rapidly becoming a woman. It was easier for her at that time to perceive things from the point of view of her father—a man. As an adult thirteen years later, she is able to relate stories expressed from a woman's point of view. Adolescent feelings may be so frightening that they are difficult to acknowledge. Edith has had some very maturing experiences—she has given up her theatrical ambition, has married, has had two children, one of whom died. But there is still enough unrealistic wishing, anxiety, and depression present in the adult stories to indicate that many if not most of the subjects have drawn a curtain enabling them to avoid facing directly the unpleasant aspects of themselves and their circumstances.

The increase in depression from adolescence to early adulthood, mentioned many times in this report, is one of the clear-cut findings of the study. This is a natural result of the disillusionment of adolescent fantasy and expectation. It probably also points to the mystery of what has become of adolescent hostility and aggression. If young adults have lost the aggressive content of their fantasies, some of it may have been directed into work, but some of it, otherwise unexpended, may have been turned inward to appear in the form of regret, discouragement, and surrender.

It is a typical human attitude to wish to avoid assuming responsibility for what happens to one and to ascribe it to fate, circumstances, and the machinations of others. The schoolboy does not think of the marks on his report card as something that he earned, but something his teacher has given to him. So it is customary to think of life as being like a grand lottery with prizes being awarded to each as though from the chance turn of a wheel. But connections between early fantasy and later developments in experience and in personality make it seem that events may be unconsciously sought and chosen. Without being fully aware of it, a person makes turns and decisions according to imperceptible, slight factors which indicate that the direction chosen will harmonize with his inner wishes and fantasies. A man becomes attracted to a woman by her hair, skin, coloring, size, and shape, if one believes the current love songs, but the chances are that he is also attracted by her assertiveness or passivity, by her willingness to take responsibility, to be submissive, to listen, to answer, and a thousand other subtle personality nuances that mean she is like some other important person in his life, and hence continues to fill an old need, or is unlike someone whom he has resisted in the past. Similar considerations determine choice of vocation, employer, school or college, hobby, and indeed, every direction of a person's activity. Growing out of adolescence therefore means the unconscious exercise of choice that helps a person to find individuals and experiences which permit him to elaborate and work out satisfying experiences of childhood and to avoid the unpleasant experiences. One has to select his experiences from those presented to him by circumstances, but life offers a wide selection from which to choose.

Two other points should be added here. One is that expressing wild and aggressive fantasies in adolescence by no means precludes good later adjustment. Having aggressive fantasies, death wishes, and Oedipal fantasies is entirely normal; it does not mean that the adolescent expressing such fantasies is delinquent or mentally disturbed. In fact, those fantasies may be a prelude to excellent adult adjustment in that the adolescent telling them possesses normal vigor and energy which may be put to effective use later on as an adult in work, if a man, or as a mother, if a woman. Illustrations have been given earlier where the hostile, aggressive fantasies of an adolescent have been turned into altruistic, moral characteristics of the adult through the mechanism of reparation. All depends on the channels into which the aggressive fantasies are directed. With the right kind of encouragement and support from the adults in family, school, church, and community, these aggressive fantasies presage highly satisfactory adjustment in adulthood.

Finally, a person may make good adjustments in one area and at the same time poor adjustments in another. Mabel (22) has achieved her ambition of comfortable living, but apparently there is tension in the marriage relationship. Jerome (7) claims that he could not have a better wife, but vocationally he is quite unhappy. Celia (28) believes that she is as competent in her work as any man, but she has not been able to get married. Viola (14) is intelligent and dramatically talented and she has two fine children with another on the way, but she is in continual conflict with her mother. Wallace (1) is apparently successful in his work, but is opinionated and prejudiced. It is, indeed, difficult to find an individual that has made an all good or all bad adjustment. It is this variation that gives each person his own unique personality.

Becoming an adult requires making an adjustment with respect to three important areas—education, vocation, and marriage. The autobiographies told in adolescence have been reviewed, and they do not show that our subjects as adolescent boys and girls had given much thought to those important future adjustments and decisions.

As one reviews the statements of ambitions of these subjects when they were adolescents, he is impressed by the almost complete lack of planning. As adolescents they lived very much in the present. They were concerned with their homes and school, their friends, sports, hobbies, vacations, clothes, and other activities and interests of immediate concern; when it came to the future, they became vague and dreamy. As a rule the junior high school subjects assumed that they would go on to high school. Beyond that, their thoughts became unclear. One boy spoke of going to college with a good medical school, yet he actually attended only three years of college in a business program. Two of the junior high school girls stated that they did not want to go to college, while one felt that she could not go because of family finances. Two planned to go into nurses' training, two had in mind going to business school, one had aspirations to attend dramatic school. But one who did not care to attend college did in fact go and has a B.A. in business. One who wanted to go into nurses' training went to business school; and neither of the two who wanted to go to business college achieved this ambition. Apparently the statements of educational ambition were stereotypes—answers that one had to have ready to satisfy nosy interrogators. It was not much better for the high school subjects. To be sure, they had given more definite thought to future education, but their plans often miscarried. Three of the high school boys—Jimmy (37), John (39), and Albert (40) spoke of going to college, and they were able to achieve their ambitions.

One cannot attribute lack of educational plans to the educational system because both junior and senior high school had excellent counseling programs, and the counselors attempted to help boys and girls to think ahead about their education. Apparently, choice with regard to education is made when one is within months of having to make a decision. Economic considerations outweigh the vague aspirations of adolescence. It is unusual that subjects such as Pansy (29) and Natalie (21) knew that they wanted to become nurses, and that the three boys mentioned above knew they wanted to go to college and achieved this ambition by overcoming obstacles.

Of the eight who received college degrees, two—Viola (14) and Jimmy (37)—went to college directly after high school because it was what they most wanted. Viola stood second highest in her high school class. Three—Roger (8), Sam (9), and Albert (40)—entered college after they had finished their war service, apparently stimulated to further their education by their army experiences. Two—Ralph (2) and John (39)—went to college part time at first in order to advance themselves in their work. Stella (19) was one who insisted during junior high school that she would not go to college, but it was her father's wish that she go, and she entered at the same time that her younger sister started going. She actually enjoyed it more than high school. The average I.Q. of the eight going to college was 118, while the average I.Q. of those not going to college was 110, so intelligence was a factor that helped to decide who would go to college.

There is some curiosity as to why Edith (17), with an I.Q. of 142, and Celia (28), with an I.Q. of 138, did not go to college. In the case of Edith, her father lost his grocery store in a fire at about the time of her graduation from high school, and the financial loss was a blow to the family. Edith's mother decided that she should not go to college. Celia graduated fourth in her class, and has since regretted not having gone to college, but at the time she left high school she had no college ambitions as she had taken the commercial course. Neither of her parents had gone beyond elementary school, so that higher education was not a tradition in her family.

As for vocation, the story is very similar to that of education. Although almost every subject had some vocational goal as an adolescent, it seemed not much more than a matter of chance whether that goal was realized, and one gains the impression that the vocations mentioned in adolescence were either childhood fancies or stereotypes that an adolescent must have ready these days to give to his inquisitors. All of the high school girls were taking the commercial course, and it was natural for them to go into work of a clerical nature.

Work was apparently accepted as something expected on leaving school, and every subject (except one) took up some form of work when his formal schooling was over. Economic considerations were an important determinant in vocational choice. Several of the boys went to work with their fathers—Ralph (2), Roy (6), Sam (9), Karl (11), and Edwin (33). Others would try their hand at whatever was available providing that they had the necessary competence. Sometimes it was necessary to give up ambitions and take any opening that they could find. Jerome (7), who had trained himself as a dental technician, could not find a position in this field and took a job as filer in a factory. In almost every case there was some trial of several different kinds of work before settling down.

Apparently the girls in this study had less difficulty in getting clerical positions, and several of them have held the same position for many years. After marriage some became closely involved in their husbands' work but usually they ended by deciding that being a homemaker is a full-time job. Stella's (19) husband has his own business—selling infants' clothes. Stella works in the store on certain days, but her home prevents her from devoting much time to this. All have worked except Viola (14), who met her future husband during her senior year in college and married him the next year.

There seems to be a distinct difference between the men and women in the study as to the extent to which formal education served as preparation for their work. Of the twelve men, nine apparently entered work for which they had received no formal training in school or college. The three who were trained for their work went to an engineering college or its equivalent. Yet of the sixteen women, thirteen were definitely trained for their work in school—nine graduated from the commercial course in high school, one attended a secretarial course after high school, two went to nurses' training school, and one took a course for becoming a beautician. But in this sample, at least, formal education had little to do in perparing the men for their work.

Marriage, like education and work, seemed to come about naturally, with little or no preparation. Following the pattern described in textbooks on adolescence, the junior high school boys in the study had little interest in girls in 1940, but the junior high school girls were often concerned with dating and were sometimes termed "boy crazy." The 1940 records of the five boys who were in high school indicate a beginning interest in girls, yet little mention is made of this in the autobiographies. Edwin (33) and Seymour (36) were said to have no interest in girls. As for Jimmy (37), his mother wanted him to take his sister out, but this did not appeal to him. He thought his sister's friends silly even though they hung around to see him. In spite of his mild embarrassment about the topic, it is clear that he was becoming interested in girls in high school. John (39) was beginning to take interest in girls in high school and said he sometimes went out with a group of boys and girls together. In his autobiography, however, he made the queer statement that he was "quite bashful in the presence of a lady." Albert (40) was said to feel uncomfortable with girls.

On the other hand, the 1953 material indicates that the majority of these men had girl friends in high school, and one, Jerome (7) said that he was engaged while in high school. Most of the men had a number of affairs while they were in the service, and all eight who are now married testified that they had been interested in other girls before they selected the one whom they married. Two of the men married the year after graduating from high school, two four years after high school, and the others six, seven, and nine years after leaving high school.

Four of the twelve men have not married. The evidence would indicate that these individuals also have had girl friends, but for one reason or another they have not been able to make the decision to get married. They seem to be particularly choosy or critical, and the projective data indicate that there are psychological blocks which prevent normal sexual interests and relations.

The women's stories about marriage differ somewhat from the men's. The thirteen who married made much less of their premarital affairs than did the men. Seven left the impression that their husbands were the only men whom they ever knew. They spoke of loving their husbands and of the length of the period of the engagements. Three said they met their husbands while they were still in high school. Another met her husband while in college, another on a blind date, and Olive (27) said that her husband had been her first and only boy friend, that they lived next door to each other, and she had known him since she was fourteen. The others wished to leave the impression that their experiences had not been promiscuous—"had few dates," "thought of another man in college," "became engaged to her husband's roommate, but they did not make out," "went with another fellow in the service, but he lost interest in her," "had a few boy friends in high school." Two married two years after graduation from high school, one three years, three four years, three five years, and one each six, seven, and nine years after high school. The girls in this study were forced to wait in many instances for their future husbands to finish their terms of military service and/or to finish college. Julia (25), who was engaged while in high school to the man whom she eventually married, waited until six years after graduating from high school while her husband served three years in the Navy and then finished his college career. One gathers the impression that young people today are more impatient than the subjects of this study.

Nothing was said in the records to indicate that there was any kind of formal preparation for marriage. Courses were not given in either junior or senior high school in homemaking, and nothing was done to orient the subjects of the study towards an understanding of the psychological factors in marriage or in raising a family. Little was said about receiving sex instruction. Marriage counseling was not mentioned. Apparently the community was willing to assume that all the intricacies of marriage and establishing a home come quite naturally and do not require formal instruction. The point of view of S. R. Slavson—that "One of the major errors of our culture is the assumption that everyone who can bear children can *ipso facto* also rear them.... If parenthood is to be considered a skill and not entirely a series of instinctive responses as it is in other animals, then obviously training for it is essential" [2]—has not only not been accepted but not even considered by the community in which this study was conducted.

The general impression gained from reviewing the experiences of these twenty-eight individuals as they progressed from adolescence to young adulthood is that their maturing was on the whole a blind, trial-and-error process. Little or nothing has been done to help them to anticipate and plan the next steps. Every problem had to be met and dealt with whatever resources the individual had available when he came face-to-face with it. Formal education gave almost no help in preparing a person to meet the problems of education, vocation, and marriage that he must inevitably face. A century ago, when a trade

[2] S. R. Slavson, *Child Centered Group Guidance of Parents* (New York, International Universities Press, 1958), pp. 308, 297.

was learned through apprenticeship and when the arts and skills of homemaking were learned in the parental home, such skills were passed along from one generation to another without difficulty. Now, with the complexity of modern living and the lessening cohesion of family life, these older institutions can no longer be depended upon to provide necessary instruction. There is need today to plan for the induction of adolescents into the skills of adult living through formal education.

12. Summary and Conclusions

This is a thirteen-year follow-up study of twenty-eight young men and women who were among the forty originally seen as adolescents and reported in *Adolescent Fantasy*. In the initial study there were twenty boys and twenty girls who at that time (1940) were in junior and senior high school. Now (1953) they are young men and women who have finished (with one or two exceptions) their formal education, have served in the armed forces in World War II, have established themselves in some vocation, and have in many instances married and begun to raise families. The twenty-eight who could be located and who were willing to be interviewed and tested represent a random selection of the original forty subjects; at least, they do not deviate in any important way from them as a group. One subject (Jack, 4) was located and tested after the data for the main group had been studied, and he is not included in the tabulations. These subjects were given the Symonds Picture-Story Test and the Rorschach and were also interviewed during two sessions. The interviews were mechanically recorded and summarized by Dr. Jensen.

A theme count was made from the twenty stories in the Picture-Story Test on a thirty-eight item schedule for both the 1940 and the 1953 sets of stories. A dynamic classification of the themes in the stories was made for each subject telling stories in 1953, and this classification was compared with a similar classification of the themes in the same 1940 stories. A similar comparison was made of the formal factors in the stories and a descriptive summary of the outstanding characteristics of each set of stories was prepared.

Dr. Jensen rated each subject for personality characteristics on a forty-item graphic rating scale based on his personal observations and impressions following each interview. The Rorschachs were administered by Dr. Jensen and were scored and interpreted by Mrs. Stephanie Dudek. Both Symonds and Jensen ranked the twenty-eight subjects for adjustment based on general impressions from all the data, and separately from the Picture-Story Test and the Rorschach; and Mrs. Dudek, in addition, ranked the subjects on the Rorschach.

From this material a number of conclusions can be drawn. There is a marked persistence of themes in fantasy over the thirteen-year interval between this study and its predecessor, enough to make it possible to identify the narrator and match stories told thirteen years apart when they have been mingled indiscriminately with the stories of other narrators.

There are general changes in the thematic content of the stories over the thirteen-year interval. There is an increase in themes of *depression* and *wishful thinking*. There is a decrease in themes of *violent aggression, punishment for aggression,* and *reform*. There are fewer themes of *mystery, trick,* or *magic,* and fewer themes dealing with *escape, giving-receiving,* and *orality*. There is a decrease in *masculine identification*. All of this points to a lessening of the stormy, violent factors of adolescence expressed in stories of adventure and excitement containing much hostile aggression and romance; in their place are much less exciting and more matter-of-fact stories tinged with depression.

Comparisons made in five areas—dependency, eroticism, aggression, self-striving, and anxiety—between adolescent fantasy and later real life behavior, attitude, or personality, led to the following conclusions. In many instances it was clear that adolescent fantasy has worked itself out into open expression in behavior and/or personality in later adult years. Frequently there is displacement from the members of one's own family, toward whom the fantasy was directed in adolescence, to wife, husband, or children in later years. In some instances where independence has not been achieved, the theme of independence still persists in fantasy. Later attitudes toward sex were anticipated in adolescent fantasy. Fantasies of confidence in adolescence foretold a person with confident, self-assured personality as an adult; but ineffective adults who strove to compensate for real or imagined deficiencies had fantasies of inferiority as adolescents. There is a marked parallel between anxiety in adolescent fantasy and anxiety in personality in later life. The defense against anxiety shown in adolescent fantasy becomes the pattern of defense adopted in later years. Psychosomatic or psychotic trends that appear in adult years may be foreshadowed in adolescent fantasy.

It is hypothesized that change in fantasy is a function of change in environment; if the situation does not change, in general, the fantasies do not change.

Changes in fantasy have been related to changes in experience and these are summarized in eight principles.

1. If a tendency is expressed in reality there is less need to fantasy it.

2. If a tendency is expressed in reality there is less need to romanticize, glorify, or symbolize it in fantasy.

3. If a tendency is expressed in reality the opposite active trend may appear in fantasy, or the opposite passive trend may disappear from fantasy.

4. Life's experiences sometimes remove a person from a punishing, forbidding figure, which permits him to break through repression, and as a result of these experiences he can better verbalize hostility or love in fantasy.

5. Fantasies are frequently in keeping with life's experiences, posing problems that have not been wholly and successfully worked through.

6. Some individuals with increasing age face new problems or old problems with increasing intensity, and these problems may find expression in fantasy.

7. Fantasies reflect the rise or fall of the level of anxiety and guilt according to the success with which a person has found adequate defenses against these affects.

8. Fantasies sometimes shift as there is need for a shift in the defenses against anxiety and guilt.

There is a high degree of consistency in overt personality over the thirteen-year interval in (a) physical characteristics; (b) general personality characteristics, including aggressiveness, in response to the interview situation and to the tests; (c) nervous signs; (d) hobbies; and (e) attitudes.

With regard to interpersonal relationships, it is not possible to predict adult attitudes from adolescent attitudes.

No firm predictive relationship was found between verbally expressed educational or vocational plans or intentions in adolescence and actual educational or vocational experiences in later years.

Summary and Conclusions

With regard to the Rorschach, several conclusions were reached. A comparison of the Rorschach signs with normative data indicate that these subjects do not differ significantly from people in general. However, a lower FC and a higher CF indicate that the subjects in this study are somewhat less emotionally inhibited than the adults in other normative studies. This conclusion does not agree with the detailed Rorschach interpretations, conclusions from which are given below. From the Rorschach, twenty of the subjects were diagnosed as normal although this group shows some neurotic symptoms including depression, hysteria, compulsion, and such character disturbances as being immature, excitable, ineffective, rigid, oppositional, or detached. Six are schizoid and one is classified as paranoid schizophrenic. Every one of the twenty-seven subjects for whom the Rorschach is available showed some sign of sexual disturbance or failure to achieve maximum or even optimum sexual functioning, as indicated by such descriptive terms as immature, inadequate, unresponsive, and unable to accept his or her sexual role. Two of the men and four of the women in the study were said to have little identity as a person, with feelings of inadequacy and inferiority. Feminine identification was recognized in eight of the men in the study and masculine identification in three of the women; three other women were unsure of their sexual identity. The subjects of the study are not what would be called aggressive individuals and most of them show a high degree of emotional control, but there is a strong undercurrent of aggression in most of the subjects. The Rorschach indicates a general inability to maintain a warm, comfortable rapport with others. Contact with others is remote, there is a lack of feeling and sensitivity, and no real empathy for an understanding of others. Subjects in the study have difficulty in managing their feelings, either repressing them on the one hand, or expressing them in violent and uncontrolled bursts of passion or rage on the other. Credit is given from the Rorschach for commendable mental functioning, with good judgment, organizational ability, and reality contact. A large number of subjects in the study are suffering from feelings of personal inadequacy and possess low self-esteem. Repression and projection are common defenses against anxiety. Eleven subjects are characterized as assertive, over-reactive, and even explosive; while ten are credited as having low drive and energy. Depression is mentioned as present in the Rorschachs of fourteen of the subjects.

There is only a low relationship between impulses and underlying tendencies as revealed on the Rorschach and as observed in overt personality as regards psychosexual adjustment, sex-role identity, interpersonal relationships, self-concept, anxiety and depression. Overt sexual and aggressive behavior cannot be diagnosed from the Rorschach with assurance. Some correspondence was noted between affect, drive, control, and mental functioning as diagnosed from the Rorschach and as observed in overt personality.

From a thematic analysis of the Picture-Story Test one can gain considerable information about the sex-wish life, sex-role identity, self-attitudes, and Oedipal relationships.

Although agreement between the Rorschach and thematic analysis of the Picture-Story Test is low, in general the Picture-Story Test fills in some of the content which must only be guessed at from the Rorschach.

Fantasy attitudes expressed in adolescence play a major role in determining decisions to be made in later life. Fantasy is the "unfinished business" of personality—that is, it deals with unexpressed wishes and desires and unresolved conflicts. Personality is a precipitate, a working out, and a resolution of fantasy.

The correlation between rankings for general adjustment made in 1940 when the subjects of the study were adolescents and rankings for adjustment made in 1953 was .54, which may be taken as indicating a possibility of predicting mental health in later years from ratings of adjustment during adolescence.

Appendix A. Resumé of the Subjects of the Study

The main facts about each of the subjects of the study are presented here in summary form under six headings: (1) the subject as an adolescent; (2) synopsis of the main themes analyzed from the stories told in response to the Picture-Story Test in adolescence; (3) the subject as an adult, which includes observations made by the examiner, and a statement of the main events that have taken place in the subject's life since the original study; (4) correspondences noted between adolescent fantasy and the subject's adult personality—i.e., his wishes, fears, and behavioral tendencies as well as the events that have occurred in his life; (5) a tabulation of the changes in fantasy derived from the theme counts made from the 1940 and 1953 stories, accompanied by examples of some of these changes and an attempt to relate them to the subject's life experiences; and (6) an excerpt from the Rorschach report giving the main conclusions reached by Mrs. Dudek from her analysis of the Rorschach material. In the tabulations showing change in fantasy, each entry represents the difference between the theme count in 1940 and in 1953 for the given theme. A plus entry means that the theme occurred more frequently in 1953. Only differences of 3 or greater have been tabulated.

Many of the points made in these resumés have already been mentioned in the text to illustrate points which were made, but they are here brought together to make a more comprehensive picture of each individual. Three sections—on correspondence between adolescent fantasy and adult personality, on change in fantasy, and on the Rorschach report—have been omitted in the cases of Wallace (1), Roy (6), Jerome (7), Sam (9), Isabel (18), Margaret (24), Julia (25), and Edwin (33). In each of these cases the omitted material is of little significance, and the method followed in this study is amply illustrated by the material given for the other twenty-one subjects.

Although he is not one of the twenty-eight subjects who constitute the main population of the study, the case of Jack (4) is added. Jack was seen after the main body of data for the study was gathered. But because Jack was used in *Adolescent Fantasy* as an illustrative case and consequently there have been many inquiries since the publication of the book concerning what happened to Jack, and because his case is more than ordinarily instructive and interesting, the material concerning him is presented with greater fullness than is true of the other subjects in the study.

Since Jimmy, the other illustrative case used in *Adolescent Fantasy*, is one of the regular subjects of the present study, his case is presented in numerical order. Because his stories told as an adult are excessively long and rambling, only a few of them are presented in full, but there is included a comprehensive analysis of his 1953 stories.

Wallace, Subject 1

WALLACE AS AN ADOLESCENT

As a thirteen-year-old boy Wallace was small in stature, irresponsible, cocky, self-sure, with a need to assert his strong points. At school he was a troublemaker and a general nuisance, impudent and "smart-alecky." He was much overindulged and overprotected by his aggressive mother, who thought that he should not be repressed. There was reason to believe that his younger brother was favored by the mother, but his mother went to Wallace's defense militantly when anything went wrong at school.

SYNOPSIS OF ADOLESCENT FANTASY

His 1940 stories were very exaggerated and full of extravagances. He had a strong impulse to assert his masculinity and strength. He fantasied being the bold, bad man but he became easily hurt and retired to his mother. He was plainly hostile to the mother in his stories. It was suggested in *Adolescent Fantasy* that his aggressive personality might be a reaction against fears of inadequacy. It is possible that there was a connection between his being overprotected and overindulged by his mother and his unrestrained fantasies.

Appendix A. Resumé of the Subjects

WALLACE AS AN ADULT

As a man he still impresses others as being ambitious, assertive, aggressive, cocky, outgoing. On the other hand, he can be charming, attractive, likable, even if somewhat exhibitionistic. He is excitable, impulsive, and capable of acting rashly. He has an excessive need to demonstrate his manliness and adopts an aggressive, competitive role in life.

He attended several colleges but failed to graduate. He served a period in the Navy, but only within the continental United States. He has worked as a sales representative.

He is married and has one daughter, but would like a larger family. He says he enjoys married life. He goes in for sports and games, and smokes and drinks freely.

He is somewhat prejudiced and is conscious of class and racial distinctions. He is a good example of the authoritarian personality.

Ralph, Subject 2

RALPH AS AN ADOLESCENT

As a thirteen-year-old boy Ralph lived with his divorced mother, who worked during the day, and his stepfather, whom he had known for about two years. His mother was a very strict, even sadistic, disciplinarian and exacted obedience from him by threats and punishment. As a result, he was a meek, mild, hesitant, and lethargic boy and was afraid to talk in class. On one occasion he actually ran away. His mother allowed him to stay in jail overnight.

SYNOPSIS OF ADOLESCENT FANTASY

In adolescence his stories were wild and fantastic. There was much aggression, both against persons (killing) and property (robbery), followed by accidents, punishment, and remorse. Several stories showed him to be the victim of aggression. There were fantasies of running away. Story A-1 illustrates this so well that it is repeated here.

O.K. This boy lived with mother. Out in country he lived. Great ambition to go to city. Ran away. Stuffed $15 in pocket he had saved. Walked to city. Ran away from home. Here he stands wondering where to turn. Thought it was nice place to live in. Boys pile up on him. Take all but $2 from him.

He looks for work. Went in couple of buildings. Too young. No work. Slept in box in an alley. Next morning got few hot dogs and milk. Almost hit by car. He was cold. Following day his money all spent. Had nothing to eat. Read in paper all looking for him. Mother sick. He returns home and mother gets well. He never wanted to go to city by himself after that. (Ralph, subject 2, story A-1, 1940)

Note that "Boys pile up on him and take all but $2 from him." Also, when he is away, his mother becomes sick (is this because of his hostile impulses toward her?). Then he returns home (because of guilt?) and his mother gets well.

RALPH AS AN ADULT

This man went to a vocational high school, where he studied machine drafting and design. He started working for his stepfather in his machine shop. Later he wanted a college education but was forced to attend night school, where his grades were poor. A counselor told him that he was not college material. This seemed to be a challenge and he entered Carnegie Institute of Technology. Here he has worked very hard and plans to graduate next June, but has only a C+ average.

He lived at home until he went away to college in 1949. He has never been called to military service because of a lame leg which resulted from an automobile accident in childhood. He has been going steady with a girl for two years but is in no hurry to marry. His health is good on the whole, but he develops stomach ulcers when he is under stress.

CORRESPONDENCE BETWEEN ADOLESCENT FANTASY AND
ADULT PERSONALITY

The extravagant nature of his stories has not been reflected in his life experiences—indeed, he impressed the examiner as "a pleasant sort of person with very nice manners." Perhaps the bombastic nature of the 1940 stories is now exhibited in his hard work and struggle to succeed. In other ways, however, the 1940 stories anticipate the kind of man Ralph is. Story A-3, for instance, gives the picture of a girl who is ineffectual, just as he has been ineffectual in his struggles to get a college education.

What's this. Thought it was—pointing. She was playing basketball in gym in playground after school. Running hard. On side were sharp rocks. She

Appendix A. Resumé of the Subjects 217

had ball. Ran and threw it to other girl. Didn't look and fell on rocks. Ripped stomach open. Careless. Rushes to hospital. Doctors had to cut piece of rock out of stomach and sew it. Told she had to stay in for month or two. Stayed by window and read. Couldn't walk. Saw all other boys and girls having fun walking. Here she was thinking she'll never be careless again. After she recovers she never is careless. (Ralph, subject 2, story A-3, 1940)

The accident to the girl's stomach in this story may also be an unconscious foreboding of his later gastric disturbance when he is expected to prove himself adequate in test situations. It is true that he had this on his mind in 1940, for after telling story A-10 he added, "ulcers—my father had them a couple of years ago—now cured." And in story A-10 he told of a sick mother in bed: "What is that disease—you get holes in your stomach from eating sweets—I don't know. President Roosevelt's son had it and died."

His stories showed an obvious castration complex, illustrated by story A-6, of which one excerpt is given here. The boy in the story, who has been committed to the penitentiary for robbing a bank, is "determined to escape." The story proceeds as follows.

Slipped down stairs. Open window. Crawl down rope. Put pillows in cot. Got in boat. Sailed with aid of sheets. In jungle where savages were supposed to be. Boat—4 men in it—number 5—started to sink. Jumped. Sharks. One man lost foot, 3 fingers off right hand. Pulled to shore. In jungle. Made fire. Had meat. Fingerless man walking ahead. Cross stream. Water moccasin bit him in arm. Didn't dare shoot snake. Savages might hear. Four men left. Savages get them. Fingerless man had little life. Followed them. Burns village. Men escape. Get to mainland. Learn all four men to go free. Escaped for nothing. Did not commit crime accused. (Ralph, subject 2, story A-6, 1940)

It is possible that these obvious sexual fantasies with fear of castration are in part responsible for his delay and deliberation in marrying the girl he had been going with for two years. This must also be coupled with his 1940 fantasy of women as strong, masterful, castrating individuals. Story B-5, for instance, tells of a female FBI agent. Although she is hit over the head with a gun by the man in the story, through her efforts the father figure is eventually caught and she gets a job as a policewoman in the bank.

This man, bank robber. Going to rob bank. Disguised self as woman. Asked other girl to do something. He'd pay her. Name Sally Anne. She should talk to policeman while she did some business. He went in bank vault. Knocked guard unconscious. Money in brief case. Walked out with girl.

Police came. Took out pennies and threw it all over road. Poor people ran to get and stopped police car. Got to house. He took off rouge and make-up. Sally saw it was crook. Wants to tell police. He hit her on head with gun. Unconscious. Escape. But he drops license plate. When she recovers she takes plate, reports to police. Killer caught. Gets reward and job as policewoman in bank. Good salary. Later job in FBI as policewoman. (Ralph, subject 2, story B-5, 1940)

Ralph's case points out the value of leaving home to go to college, which permitted him to transfer hostile aggressive fantasy into ambitious energy and determination.

CHANGE IN FANTASY: RALPH, SUBJECT 2

Fantasy theme	Amount of change	Fantasy theme	Amount of change
Aggressed against	−7	Altruism	−3
Punishment	−7	Crime against person	−3
Positive outcome	−11	Escape	−3
Crime against property	−6	Jealousy	−3
Illness, accident	−5	Depression	+4
Eroticism	−4	Morality	+3
Reform, repentance	−4	Thinking, planning	+3
Trick, joke, plot	−4		

CHANGE IN FANTASY

The shift in nature of the stories told by Ralph in 1953 is more marked than with any other subject. All of the wild, aggressive adventure, excitement, killing, and robberies seem to have disappeared. Gone also is the need for punishment and the theme of being aggressed against and taken advantage of. In their place is strong depression with a kind of moralistic repentance well illustrated in story B-9 (1953), given on pages 41–42.

In 1953 there is apparent fear of strong emotions coinciding with Ralph's personality, which the examiner describes as passive, weak, and hesitant. The violent aggression which was fantasied in 1940 has found expression over the intervening years in the form of ambitious striving, determination, and hard work. This attitude, which has become his in real life, is reflected in his 1953 stories. Story A-2 is a good example. Note how the determination that appears in it is related to running away which still persists from adolescent fantasy.

By looking at this picture I get the impression that this is a boy who is in need, who isn't too well off, who seems to be knocking at the door about to do something, like perhaps ask for food or ask for a handout or something. From his appearance it looks like he's not dressed too well, he looks like he's almost doing something he doesn't want to do too much. I could make a story of someone who ran away from home and who has been away from home for awhile and finally in desperation goes to someone's house and seeks employment or seeks food of some sort, a sort of handout, or for some work, some food or clothing, perhaps a place to sleep, and one who seems to be determined, this boy, probably will make a success because he has the determination about him and from where he is now he might get a good start in life, get a job somewhere, make something of himself. (Ralph, subject 2, story A-2, 1953)

Apparently this shift is brought about in part by his loss of fear of aggression and attack from authority and sibling figures. As his striving becomes more prominent his feelings of being threatened become less prominent.

The case material does not provide us with detailed information as to what has brought about the change in the stories. One may speculate that his ambition to go to engineering school and the opportunity of throwing his aggression into this undertaking has adequately solved his aggressive needs. This permits a shift from the previously unrestrained aggressive fantasies into actual life and permits his fantasies to express guilt in the form of depression with moralistic overtones for his earlier hostile aggressive fantasies. Story B-3 indicates that he is at the present time in a conflict struggle between retaining his older rebellious attitudes and adopting more conforming, morally acceptable attitudes.

Well this reminds me of two different personalities altogether. The boys are about the same age. The one on the left looks like the kind of rough character, somebody who's pretty tough, whom we think is pretty tough. He smokes and drinks and what not, and hangs around with a rough crowd. The other fella looks the opposite. This picture suggests the theme that possibly he's trying to influence the other boy, trying to get him to change his ways to his. The other boy looks like he has a doubt on his face, whether he's doing the right thing or not. He looks like the clean-cut type of American boy. (Ralph, subject 2, story B-3, 1953)

He still, however, retains his fear of the dominating and castrating female.

Well, this reminds me of a man coming home late from a party with the boys, only this time it's a girl, it looks like she's coming home late from a big dance and probably her mother's there waiting for her to give her a big bawling-out and she looks rather hesitant going up the stairs. The clock says it's almost 3:30. Apparently it's past her bedtime, way past her bedtime. She looks rather cautious going up the stairs, rather expectant of what's coming. Apparently she enjoyed herself so much she doesn't know the time and she knows faithfully that she'll get a good bawling out and apparently be slightly punished for that act. She seems a little worried, apparently she's been bawled out before and she knows what's coming. She can't escape her fate. The shadow of her mother's on the top of the stairs, she'll probably get a talking to and then she'll go to bed and forget all about it. (Ralph, subject 2, story B-7, 1953)

His life experiences have not made it possible for him to change his attitude toward women.

EXCERPT FROM THE RORSCHACH REPORT

A self-conscious, immature, awkward, and ineffectual person. Is ambitious but has poor practical sense. Has an inadequate social persona and is likely to make a weak and unsympathetic impression. He does not know what he wants or needs. He drifts with the tide.

He is unable to assume a masculine or femine role. Mild homosexual orientation with paranoid fears. Ambivalent about women. Unable to identify with a weak father who has never taken a clear role. Mother tried to play both the masculine and feminine role for him.

Pervasive repression of instinctual and sexual energy—fear of all strong impulses. Capable of only shallow and superficial feeling.

Feels that he is a misfit. Generally self-conscious and awkward with people.

Roy, Subject 6

ROY AS AN ADOLESCENT

As a thirteen-year-old boy, Roy was on the fat side—stolid, calm, timid, retiring, hesitant, without aggressive assurance. He was polite, and spoke in a low voice, but he was always getting into trouble. Between the ages of two and seven he ran away many times, and was a kind of wanderer. He loved the out-of-doors and camping. His parents were strict disciplinarians.

Appendix A. Resumé of the Subjects

SYNOPSIS OF ADOLESCENT FANTASY

He related tales of his own adventures and the accidents and other misfortunes that happened to him. His 1940 stories were full of adventure, excitement, and criminal deeds. There were stories of mystery and danger. Mothers in his stories were strict. Anger was shown toward mother figures, followed by guilt and punishment.

Story B-9 illustrates self-punishment following guilt because of one's success. In *Adolescent Fantasy* (p. 145) it was stated: "His fear of self-assertion which comes to such a catastrophic conclusion in the story is also his pattern of adjustment in life."

ROY AS AN ADULT

He left high school before graduating, enlisted in the Navy in 1949 but was rejected because of high blood pressure. He went to work as a cost estimator in his father's automobile repair shop. He is married and has two children, both girls. He enjoys working around his ranch-type house and its three acres of land. He states that he believes he drives himself harder in his work than most people. It is evident that his life so far fits in with the first part of story B-9, but nothing had happened to parallel the catastrophe.

Jerome, Subject 7

JEROME AS AN ADOLESCENT

As a fourteen-year-old boy Jerome was called a bully, a tyrant, and a tough. His teachers spoke of him as disorderly. He was athletic. The school principal reported sex exhibitionism. His mother died when he was five and his father remarried when he was eleven. His grandmother, with whom he stayed in the intervening six years, resisted letting him go to his father. He has rebelled against his stepmother and has run away from home.

SYNOPSIS OF ADOLESCENT FANTASY

His adolescent stories showed a desire for reform, along with repentance and apology. He wanted to do well in school and be a president. His heroes left home but returned homesick. He felt strong guilt for hostile fantasies. The upperdog felt guilt for his successes, repented, and let the underdog have a chance. He was afraid of being a sissy. "Maybe if I had been home, mother would not have died." Many stories involved orphans, and religious conflict played a part in his stories. In *Adolescent Fantasy* (p. 101) it was said: "It seems clear that in this boy's case there is a conflict between his resistance to authority and his guilt for these impulses and a tendency to defend himself against his guilt by fantasies of reform and repentance. It is significant that he does not control his feeling of guilt by punishment fantasies. This boy's stories indicate strong superego conflict, however, the fantasies of repentance and reform do not show in the control of behavior."

JEROME AS AN ADULT

Now, as a twenty-seven-year-old man, he is described as tall, well-built, broad-shouldered. There is a somewhat exhibitionistic quality to the man. His dress, hair, general appearance leave a theatrical impression. After a period in the Navy he finished high school. He thought at one time of preparing himself as a dental technician but, after several jobs, now operates a retail liquor store. He married a childhood playmate and has two children, a boy of four and a girl five months old, with another on the way.

He showed dissatisfaction with the interviews because he had hoped to get vocational advice from them. There was real anxiety over his vocational and financial situation. He claims he never had time for sports as he has had to work even while he was going to school, and he says he is old before his time.

Roger, Subject 8

ROGER AS AN ADOLESCENT

After Roger's mother died, when he was eighteen months old, he lived in the home of his grandparents until he was five, when his father remarried. He was very much overprotected by his grandmother and was unable to dress himself at that time. He had a mischievous and happy-go-lucky, but pleasant, ingratiating personality. He was feminine in figure. He would not help at home and lacked perseverance. When fourteen, in 1940, had a stepbrother three years old.

Appendix A. Resumé of the Subjects

SYNOPSIS OF ADOLESCENT FANTASY

In adolescence his stories contained violence—murder, robbing, kidnaping, excitement—but no emotion. He was jealous of a younger brother and showed anger toward his stepmother. He put some emphasis on eating and had castration fears. He thought of getting what he wanted by force, to be followed by counteraggression and punishment. Underneath was considerable anxiety.

ROGER AS AN ADULT

He finished high school and became a radio mechanic. After military service he went to Rutgers and graduated in six years with a low record and after considerable struggle. He is now a construction and maintenance inspector for an oil company, but has unrealistic dreams of doing engineering work in Canada.

He is married to a high school teacher who is superior to him in ability. He stated quite frankly that there is friction between him and his stepmother and that he has never felt fully accepted by her. He states that he has a severe temper. He is sensitive to his standing in comparison to other men, gets depressed on occasion, and has a feeling of failure and a sense of inferiority.

CORRESPONDENCE BETWEEN ADOLESCENT FANTASY
AND ADULT PERSONALITY

Two stories will be given to illustrate his attitude toward life.

This mother had two daughters. Liked one, disliked other. One she liked always got what she wanted. Other had to work and buy what she wanted. One night she came upstairs and killed sister and mother through jealousy and ran away. No place to hide. Picked up by police. Sentenced to reformatory to 21, then executed in electric chair for murder. (Roger, subject 8, story B-4, 1940)

In this story we have a simple tale of sibling rivalry and great hostility toward both sibling and mother who favored him (his stepbrother).

Boy always sat alone in house. Didn't do anything. Never went to dances or washed dishes. Played hookey. Mother disgusted. Became notorious criminal. Gang, rob bank. Stool pigeon squealed. Police hid in vault with oxygen masks and torches in case locked in. Gang came in. Police close in. Blew gang right out. Two killed. One escapes, but later caught by G-men. (Roger, subject 8, story B-6, 1940)

This story indicates, however, that as an adolescent he showed his resentment to his stepmother by noncooperation and by indulging in hostile fantasies (for which he is punished in fantasy). Undoubtedly this tendency to resist has followed him into adult life and may be partly responsible for his difficulties in getting through college and his failure to rise in his present job. He still shows tendencies for his hostile impulses to get out of hand "especially at salesmen who try to be engineers and go over his head in making decisions." These occasions are followed by depression, just as his aggressive fantasies in 1940 stories ended with punishment.

CHANGE IN FANTASY

Roger is still another adult who has dispensed with his extremely hostile adolescent fantasy. For him, too, hostility has undoubtedly been absorbed by his struggles to go through college and his continuing struggle in the world of business. As a boy he was carefree and happy-go-lucky and showed his aggression by mischievousness and pranks. Life has become more serious for him and this shows up in his stories by more striving and more anxiety. Story A-1 illustrates this trend.

It brings to mind an immigrant boy coming over to either New York City or one of the big cities, trying to make up his mind either which way to go, not necessarily literally speaking, right or left, but which way to go—where is his future really leading him. Why did he come here and what for. He'll probably, being an average person, well maybe not being too average, instead of taking the path of least resistance being a shoeshine boy or working in a grocery store, he'll probably, because of his hesitation here in the picture, he'll probably, spend quite a bit of his time in a library of some sort studying for a goal he has in mind and possibly from there he'll go on to be one of the great men in his field. (Roger, subject 8, story A-1, 1953)

CHANGE IN FANTASY: ROGER, SUBJECT *8*

Fantasy theme	Amount of change	Fantasy theme	Amount of change
Criminal death	−9	Crime against person	−4
Positive outcome	−8	Crime against property	−4
Hostility	−7	Anxiety	+4
Aggressed against	−6	Reform, repentance	+3
Punishment	−5	Striving, effort	+3

There is increase in guilt shown by the fact that fewer of his stories have negative outcomes while more have themes of reform and repentance, and by his tendency to become depressed in real life. As in the case of others who have yielded aggressive fantasies, there is an increase in depressive themes. In 1940 there were six stories in which the hero was taken advantage of by others. In 1953 this direction of aggression has disappeared partly because in real life he "blows his top," and "shoots off his mouth" against those who attempt "to go over his head in making decisions." But when he does this he becomes depressed afterwards.

Roger's 1953 stories illustrate very well his anxiety over his inability to demonstrate a high level of competence. Story B-6, told in 1953, should be compared to the story told to this same picture in 1940 (see above). In the earlier period he showed immature aggression over parental rejection. In 1953 he is struggling over what he should do for himself—"one of those students who is not too bright."

This one I can remember. He had just turned sixteen or seventeen, whatever the age is where the question comes up for those students not too bright: should I stay in school or should I leave school and join one of the armed forces? His lot in life hasn't been too good, probably a three-room apartment with two or three brothers, mother and father. Not a happy home and the environment is very poor. He is debating himself whether he should, as I said, stay in school or join the Army. He'll debate this quite a while, not only in his room but also at school, falling further and further behind until the principal or his teachers bring him to task, so to speak, and have an after-school meeting on his case. The meeting, the teachers and the principal probably come to the conclusion after seeing his poor grades and the attitude and situation he has gotten himself into, the committee will probably recommend that he join the Army, get out of this rut, this environment that he is in and try to better himself in the Army and obtain the rest of his high school education in the Army and possibly find a trade that he would be suited for, because at this stage it would be difficult to help him with this indecision that . . . What will probably happen here is he will take the advice of the teachers and the principal and join the Army and get into some specialized training in the Army, finish his high school degree, and possibly stay in the Army for a number of years, whether he'll stay there until retirement from the Army or get out after three, five, or six years, but he will stay there for a number of years. Chances are he will stay in the Army until retirement. (Roger, subject 8, story B-6, 1953)

And story B-11, told to the blank card, permits him an opportunity to verbalize his conflict between continuing the struggle or to "leave the door shut and be content with the life one is living now."

One word—"blank." That's indecision right now as far as I'm concerned. The card is a closed door—the surface of a closed door—many doors that you reach in life. Whether you should open that door and find out what's on the other side or should we leave that door shut and be satisfied with the life we're living now. Maybe on the other side of the door there will be more headaches and troubles and worries than you are confronted with now. That's it. (Roger, subject 8, story B-11, 1953)

EXCERPT FROM THE RORSCHACH REPORT

A highly reactive person caught in a deep conflict between aggressive-assertive and passive-dependent needs. An impulsive, egocentric, generally assertive, and physically active man, but because of his dependency needs he may give an impression of timidity, caution, compliance, and helplessness in dealing with authority figures. His emotional reactions may change day by day.

He is not using his intelligence to capacity. He is frequently explosive, with inappropriate intensity and anger. He suffers from a chronic feeling of frustration. He is argumentative and ready to charge into open conflict. His problems appear to stem from a cold and powerful father who made him feel small and rejected. His feelings toward women are more friendly, but he tends to take women lightly.

He feels helpless and inadequate as a man. He has good sensual and erotic sensitivity but poor control over his sexual impulses. Has difficulty feeling gratified and has a sense of inadequacy as a husband. Has a generally aggressive and slightly superior attitude, may give the impression of masculinity but his concept of himself as a man is far from sure and adequate.

At present a low-grade depression and mild agitation. There are guilt feelings about his explosive but shallow outbursts of aggression. There may be short states of acute depression relating to his inability to meet authority figures without feeling helpless and small.

Sam, Subject 9

SAM AS AN ADOLESCENT

As a fourteen-year-old boy Sam—an only child—was described as calm, but tense and worrying. He was self-centered, and daydreamed. His teachers said he was lazy, careless, thoughtless, and a show-off, but he got good grades in school. He liked writing (poems and stories), reading, arguing, and music. His mother gave the orders; his father carried them out. His father was very strict and punitive, lectured him, and would not let him go out at night. His father at one time used to beat him, but at the time of the study used little restrictions and deprivation.

SYNOPSIS OF ADOLESCENT FANTASY

His 1940 stories were rich with fantasies. There was a masochistic tendency in the stories with a need to be rescued and helped. There was marked feminine identification. His heroines became blinded, crippled, sick, lived in seclusion, but later were applauded and rewarded. There were themes of running away from home and also dependency on the home. There were unrealistic fantasies of great wealth and wishing to be a movie star. His figures had severe, castrating superegos, exacted punishment, and had feelings of guilt. The conflict between good and bad appeared in many stories. Oedipal themes were common; the father figure was depicted as bad and eventually got killed. He wanted to make good in his mother's eyes in order successfully to take the place of his father. Sex was dangerous, closed, forbidden—the mother was the forbidding figure, the father the punishing figure. There was castration anxiety and conflict over masturbation. There was a fear of aggressive impulses that were projected onto others who became "enemies." But the endings were usually happy.

SAM AS AN ADULT

As a man Sam is tall, well-built, neat, well-spoken, friendly. He saw nineteen months' service with the infantry in the occupation forces in the Russian and American zones in Germany—and later graduated with a degree in economics from the Wharton School. He is now associated with his father as an electrical contractor. He married a strong-willed woman. They have one child—a girl.

In Germany he was in a hospital for battle fatigue and now has a fear of hospitals. He describes himself as a nervous person. He is generally even-tempered, but when he does lose his temper he loses control of himself.

Karl, Subject 11

KARL AS AN ADOLESCENT

As a fourteen-year-old Karl was described as a very odd boy and badly disturbed emotionally. He had a history of motor incoordination, which may have been due to a birth injury. His teachers were puzzled by him—he was queer, quiet and dreamy, different from other pupils. But he was very affectionate. His mother was much concerned about him and had taken him to a psychiatrist. But the mother, in spite of her interest, tended to cover up his strangeness and her disappointment in him. Karl himself told of parental strictness and punishment and indicated that an older brother was favored.

Of him his mother said: "Karl is very sloppy about his personal appearance. He has a dirty mind and has a string of vile stories, but he has never been curious." A teacher commented: "His mother tried to give him sex information, but he would titter and snicker. He has no modesty at all."

SYNOPSIS OF ADOLESCENT FANTASY

His 1940 stories were bizarre and confused in the extreme. There was fear of a rejecting father figure and actual killing of a mother figure. There was much emphasis on food, signifying an extremely primitive, undifferentiated affectional need, an immature dependency, and an arrested personality development. Fantasies overruled the picture stimuli and thinking was confused. There was obsessive-compulsive concern with numbers and small details.

KARL AS AN ADULT

Thirteen years later, in 1953, Karl is a heavy, strongly built, assertive man with square jaw. He expressed himself with conviction, deliberation, and assurance. He was still very precise about dates and facts involving numbers. He was curious about the nature of the study.

In school he got no further than the eleventh grade. He was drafted into the Army and was in the Philippines when the war ended. Later he entered the 82nd Airborne Division as a glider man and then transferred to the artillery. He tells of talking back to his officers. Afterward he entered a junior college in Georgia, where he got a high school diploma and a degree in business education. He also studied business in a technical college in Nebraska.

He was unemployed for a period, during which time he turned down many job offers for superficial reasons. Now he is working for his father in the automobile showroom. He is jealous of his brother, who is being advanced in his father's business.

He states that he will never get married and he has no steady girl friend. He became interested in a girl in Georgia but when he went down for a visit he was not permitted to see her.

His eyesight is poor, he has a bad leg, and he contracted malaria while in the service. He claims he is a heavy smoker. He likes dog and horse races. He takes part in VFW activities and is a member of a bowling team. He is afraid of heights. He gets depressed easily. He lives at home but would like to be more independent. He says he has a violent temper and once knocked into the street a tray of poppies which a veteran was selling. He claims that people listen to him respectfully when he speaks because they do not dare to oppose him.

CORRESPONDENCE BETWEEN ADOLESCENT FANTASY
AND ADULT PERSONALITY

The bizarre nature of Karl's 1940 stories carried over into the 1953 interviews. The preoccupation with numbers which was so outstanding in the stories was reflected in the interviews in his efforts to be exact in dates and ages. Story A-4 indicates this characteristic.

Here's a boy and his father. Father has $500—giving his son $250. "Now that you are going to college you will need this money. When you need some more money just write me and I will send it to you by mail." So he takes $250 and calls up railroad station. "What time is next train due for Norfolk, Va.?" Man down at railroad station says, "There's one due at 8:45 A.M. and also at 9:00 A.M. and due at 3:00 P.M. and one at 7:30 P.M." Boy decides to get 3:00 P.M. train which will get him in Norfolk, Va., at 8:00 A.M. next morning. He gets on 3:00 P.M. train and waves goodbye to mother and father 'till he is out of sight. (Karl, subject 11, story A-4, 1940)

In his 1940 stories the themes of orality showed his great dependence. Story B-6 illustrates this need.

This is no. 22? Boy sitting dopey in the chair. Why did I have to drink that 10 quarts of beer? So he's real drunk and walks upstairs to his mother and doesn't know what he is saying. He says to his mother, "Can I have a couple of quarts of beer to drink?" She says, "What are you crazy—you just had a couple." He says, "All right, I won't take 'em." And he goes downstairs and takes 'em. (Karl, subject 11, story B-6, 1940)

As a man Karl still lives at home, works for his father, apparently completely dependent on his parents. He boasted about his drinking prowess and claimed he could drink a whole bottle of liquor in one evening without becoming drunk enough to lose his self-control or self-respect or to have a hangover. In spite of his immaturity and dependence he fantasies leaving home and having his own apartment. But his parents tell him that if he were to leave home he would have a difficult time and he agrees with them. This present-day fantasy of leaving home is reflected in story A-6.

Boy sees his shadow on the wall. He gets real real scared. So he takes the flashlight and shines it on the stairs and he finds out it's his own shadow. Then he walks up the stairs and they creak like anything. He gets up in his room and finds a ghost up there. The ghost, "You will be murdered in one year from now if you are living in this house." But if he is living in this house and runs away the ghost will always be behind him. But if he moves away nothing will happen to him at all. (Karl, subject 11, story A-6, 1940)

His interviews reflect weak ego control. He tells episodes of losing his temper and doing bizarre things. Probably story B-9 is the fantasy counterpart of this lack of ego control.

Looks like a jail. Empire State Building in distance. Church where he goes and where his mother is buried. He wishes he hadn't murdered his mother. If he hadn't murdered his mother he would be in Hollywood and be a movie star. In jail for 3 years. (Karl, subject 11, story B-9, 1940)

This story is unique because of the blandness with which he relates the story of matricide. There is a nonsequitur in that the only reason for the character having regret for having killed his mother is that it prevented him from becoming a movie star. In the original stories story B-9 was followed by this story:

(Queer.) Trees fallen down. Lightning has struck the house. Puts all lights in house out of commission, including the telephone, and the water. They ran out of the house for help. Ladder is just about to fall down when they walk out of the house. (Karl, subject 11, story B-10, 1940)

Here we see that an outcome of the matricide in story B-9 is oblivion, as lightning blacks out all the lights.

Karl introduces boy-girl relationships into several of his stories but there seems to be no feeling for the relationship, which is overpowered by the strange fantasies his mind produces:

(Hard one.) Fortuneteller. Tells girl that she and him are going to be married in half an hour. Two days after they are married she is going to have 16 children—8 boys and 8 girls. A year goes by. Then she has quintuplets. They enter things in races and are on radio programs, they always enter things and they get 50 times as much money back as they put up. (Karl, subject 11, story A-10, 1940)

So in real life his interest in girls seems remote. In his interview he stated blandly: "I don't mind telling you I hope to remain a bachelor. I have no love life. If you don't have a love life you don't get married."

CHANGE IN FANTASY: KARL, SUBJECT 11

Fantasy theme	Amount of change
Punishment	+5
Negative outcome	+4
Orality	−6

CHANGE IN FANTASY

There can be no doubt that Karl's 1953 stories were told by the same person who told the 1940 stories. There are the same bizarre characteristics, the same illogical trends and nonsequiturs. There is the same hostility toward mother figures, but not expressed in the same extreme form as in 1940 in story B-9. Story B-8 illustrates the attitude toward the mother in 1953.

Looks like the father talking to a daughter, maybe 10 years old, telling her something that happened—trouble. She hasn't seen her mother in a couple of days. She came to her father and asks, where's mother, and he told her. And he says she's out for a visit, or something, or her mother and father are sick or something, and she goes to see how they're doing. She feels better now that she knows how her mother is, but she doesn't still like the fact that her mother went away without telling her. (Karl, subject 11, story B-8, 1953)

In both 1940 and 1953 there is a fear of a punitive father figure. Story A-6, told in 1940, has already been given above. Story B-7 expresses the same attitude in 1953.

Looks like a young lady carrying a coat in her arms, up the stairs, the clock says, I imagine the clock says, let's see, 25 after 3 A.M. She's probably coming home from a late date, maybe it's Saturday night. And when she gets half way up the stairs, looks like a man's shadow, looks like her old man's goin' to beat her. If she stayed out late, if she's a child, she's nervous-like, and she don't know what to do. Whether to run out of the house or take the beating and forget it or what, but I figure from the shadow, it's her father. (Karl, subject 11, story B-7, 1953)

On the other hand there are striking changes in the stories that are difficult to account for. For instance, punishment does not appear in the 1940 stories but occurs five times in the 1953 set. Story B-6 illustrates well this change. This 1940 story has already been given above. In 1953 he told this story to B-6.

Here's a fella, first of all, he needs a haircut, his hair's droopin' down to his eyes. Maybe that's the way his hair grows, I don't know, but, I'd say he's a kid about, well, he's a big kid for his age, about 14. Anyhow his folks, uh, he must have done something wrong because he's probably locked up in his room because he did something wrong. He's locked up there until well, he's locked up in solitary confinement. Because you can see the little light comin' in there. [Does it do him any good, does he turn out better?] He improves, not that it really does him any good. (Karl, subject 11, story B-6, 1953)

One notes here that the identification is with an adolescent character and that the attitudes expressed in the story are adolescent or childish. Apparently in 1940 Karl's fantasies are almost entirely oral. One can only surmise that as a boy Karl had been greatly overprotected and babied, perhaps as compensation because his brother was really preferred. But it was not until his Army experience that Karl really came up against discipline. So his superego was very late in developing and only as a grown man has he learned to think of the difference between right and wrong.

In similar fashion Karl tells no story in 1940 with a negative ending. Everything is bland and without point. But in 1953 frustration and tragedy enter into his fantasy life. Story A-10 is used for illustration (the 1940 story was given above).

Here's a fortuneteller and a couple of young lovers. They go in there to have their fortune told, they want to know what their future is. Naturally their present is that they are in love and they want to hear him. So he tells them it's written very bright, and the expression on his face is that they get married and they have a happy time for a while and they have a small family and someone in the family gets deathly sick and gets pneumonia and almost dies, but they get a break, but it's a long, long time before they recuperate, and someone else has a serious attack and the future isn't bright for him. (Karl, subject 11, story A-10, 1953)

In 1953 he introduces the theme of illness and the story ends with "the future isn't bright for him." This corresponds, no doubt, to the depressive trend observed in so many of the other adult stories. Un-

Appendix A. Resumé of the Subjects

doubtedly his army, educational, and work experiences have sobered him and taught him that life is not wholly a place of bliss, but in the world of reality misfortune can come as well as fortune.

These two trends must of necessity be paralleled with a decrease in themes of orality—and this turns out to be the case.

EXCERPT FROM THE RORSCHACH REPORT

An intelligent but childish, overexcitable, overreactive man whose thinking and judgment assume grandiose and omnipotent proportions and who is so lacking in insight that a paranoid-schizophrenic process is suggested, but in his environment remains an "eccentric" person, to be treated as one treats a child.

He is active, aggressive, overbearing, with an unreasonable ambition. His grandiosity and exuberance carry him away and he distorts reality situations to suit his wishes. His capacity to see the world as others do is defective and he makes inappropriate responses.

His main difficulty is in his relationship with his father; he is unable to give up his little-boy role and face maturity, and gives the impression of a brash, overconfident, insensitive teenager. He has a completely childlike tie to his mother resulting in a latent unconscious homosexual orientation. Because of his immaturity he can avoid facing hetereosexual conflicts and hence is uninhibited in his relationships with people. He is timid toward women. That is out of keeping with his generally blustering, aggressive approach. There is a denial or rejection of sensuality.

His frustration tolerance is low and he has little capacity for self-discipline. He would be lost without constant friction with his social environment. There may be feelings of unreality and his anxiety in dealing with authoritative figures may lead to a loss of contact with self.

Catherine, Subject 12

CATHERINE AS AN ADOLESCENT

As a fourteen-year-old girl Catherine was described as nervous, high-strung, and jumpy, with reports of upset stomach and vomiting spells. Although usually quiet and unobtrusive, she had a violent temper on occasion. At the time of the first contact she was "boy crazy," but her mother used to meet her after school every day to take her window shopping, thus depriving her of going to ball games and being with boys. In school she wore bright clothes, was stubborn, argumentative, spoke out of turn, and forgot to bring materials to class. In her autobiography Catherine said: "There are four in our family—my mother, brother and me, and the dog, all of whom I love dearly; my father is the best in the whole world. All in all we have a happy home life." (She left her mother out in the original typing and inserted a reference to her later.)

SYNOPSIS OF ADOLESCENT FANTASY

In 1940 her short, very imaginative and fantastic stories depicted subjects with strong hostility toward parents, especially the rejecting, punitive mothers. The stories were bizarre, wild, and disordered. There was a feeling that parents restrict social life and that one must please mother before being able to do as one wishes.

There was much interest in the opposite sex, but lack of self-acceptance. There was concern over physical appearance, especially size, and the feeling that one must change in order to be accepted by peers. This leads to a narcissistic self-concern—"if no one cares for me I'd better care a lot for myself." Her self-image was so distasteful she would like to destroy it.

There was a strong need to achieve and succeed.

CATHERINE AS AN ADULT

Now, in 1953, Catherine is described as large and robust, friendly, outgoing, and talkative. After graduating from high school she worked as a typist, secretary-stenographer, and statistical typist. She married in 1948. She continued to work after her marriage while her husband completed his college education.

She has had intensive psychotherapy. Partly as a result of this she is outspoken in expressing her hostility toward her mother and father. She reports friction between her mother and her husband. She describes her mother as domineering and as upset when she cannot have her own way. She lived at home when first married but could not get along with her mother and moved to an apartment—about which she still has feelings of guilt. She is protective toward her brother, whom she describes as backward socially and a heavy drinker. She has difficulty with her mother-in-law.

She is now pregnant and hopes to have a girl. Psychotherapy released her sexually; when she was first married she was frigid.

CORRESPONDENCE BETWEEN ADOLESCENT FANTASY
AND ADULT PERSONALITY

In one of her 1940 stories (A-7) Catherine, who was large for her age at the time, told of a girl who would not marry a man three inches shorter than she. She is described in 1953 as large and robust while her husband is described as "a small man, quiet, and soft-spoken."

Girl and boy used to like each other a real lot. Girl went away. Was gone for 3 years. She couldn't wait until she got home again to see her boy friend. When she finally got home and saw him she found he was three inches shorter than she was and she told him she would never marry a man shorter than she was and that she would never see him again. Tragic ending to a love story. (Catherine, subject 12, story A-7, 1940)

In 1940 she believed herself to be ugly:

Girl—funniest looking girl in whole town. One day blind boy came to town. She met him. Fell in love. We're going to be married. Boy found out a great surgeon was coming to town and could operate to restore his sight. Girl was afraid when he was able to see her he wouldn't love her any more because she was so funny looking. She went to New York and had her face lifted. Came back to town. Everyone thought she was beautiful. Boy's sight was restored. They were married. (Catherine, subject 12, story B-2, 1940)

The girl in this story had her face lifted. In actual life Catherine, who underwent psychotherapy reports that before therapy she was "an extremely plain girl and not very feminine," but that she has changed considerably in this respect after therapy. She also reports that she was treated for infection of the Fallopian tubes which had prevented her from having children, but now that that condition has been corrected her efforts have been rewarded and she is now pregnant.

Two short stories in 1940 (B-9 and B-10) depicted the mother as bad and punitive.

Girl lives with father. Mother was dead. Father thought girl should have mother. Went out and married a lady who had a daughter girl's age. Thought they would be happy. Mother treated stepdaughter meanly. Father died. Mother wanted to get rid of stepdaughter. Wanted to send her to an orphanage. Lady next door felt sorry for girl. Took her and moved away. (Catherine, subject 12, story B-9, 1940)

Girl coming home from school . . . 15. Was thinking about examinations. Had been told by mother that if she didn't get highest grade on algebra exam she couldn't got to prom. Passed exam—second in class. Got 99½ percent so mother said she could go. (Catherine, subject 12, story B-10, 1940)

Actually, in 1940 in her autobiography she stated that she had the best parents in the world. She believes that psychotherapy has removed the scales from her eyes and she now unabashedly refers to her mother as domineering, a possessive and selfish woman, a useless person—"there is not one thing I like her for." And yet she adds that in psychotherapy she discovered a great deal of her mother in herself. Likewise, she now can speak of her father in unflattering terms as a man who is selfish and thinks only of himself.

Her 1940 stories show a desire to get away from home:

These two boys are brothers. Parents are dead, live with uncle. Uncle doesn't like them and treats them real bad. One locked out on front porch. Decide to run away. Run away. Hop a freight train and go to a different town. A rich man likes the boys and takes them in. He sends them to a military school and college. Both are intelligent. One became a doctor, one an author. (Catherine, subject 12, story 16, 1940)

And in real life she lived in her parental home when first married but could not get along with her mother, and she and her husband moved into an apartment.

CHANGE IN FANTASY: CATHERINE, SUBJECT 12

Fantasy theme	Amount of change	Fantasy theme	Amount of change
Negative outcome	−5	Positive outcome	+4
Passivity—aggressed against	−3	Separation	+3
		Striving, effort	+3

CHANGE IN FANTASY

Catherine's stories in 1953 bear striking resemblance to those of 1940 in spite of the fact that she has undergone psychotherapy in the intervening period. There is the same hatred toward the father, and the

Appendix A. Resumé of the Subjects

picture of a strict, disapproving, punitive mother. There are still fantasies of getting away from home and a desire for achievement and success.

But the fact that Catherine is now openly able to express her negative feelings toward her parents makes it possible for her to fantasy also parents who are good. So in story B-1 a boy finds "a nice couple who lived on a farm who would take the boy and keep him."

> This boy lives in a brownstone house in New York City. He always lived in the midst of the city where there was never much trees or yard and place to play. He always dreamed about living in the country on a farm, but his parents had to live in the city and they didn't feel that it was necessary for his happiness that they move out of the city. When he was about fifteen years old, his father died and his mother had to go out and earn work and she didn't have any way of taking him with her. So, she had to break up her apartment in the brownstone house and she found a nice couple who lived on a farm who would take the boy and would keep him and let him work on the farm and go to school and live in the country. So, he is on his way to the farm. (Catherine, subject 12, story B-1, 1953)

This is a reversal of the usual treatment of picture B-1. Typically the subject in the story has left home to find his fortune in the big city. Perhaps the outstanding shift in the stories is from negative to positive endings. This accompanies her general tendency to accept the positive as well as the negative in life, following her psychotherapy. Story A-1 shows change from a feeling of being neglected and unhappy to the feeling of being accepted and happy. Catherine is one subject that goes contrary to the general rule of an increase in depression.

> Boy sent to a military school by his parents. Had never been away from home before. He was looking forward to go to the school, had a gray suit on. Boys had a rule that they wouldn't speak to a boy who had on a gray suit until he took the suit off. Boy was heartbroken because there was no one there to welcome him. But when he found out the rule, he put on a blue suit and hocked the other one. (Catherine, subject 12, story A-1, 1940)

> This is a boy that came from a town up in New Hampshire. A country boy and he came down to New York City to go to school and get a degree in psychology. He's looking for a place to stay because he can't find a room; quarters are very cramped in New York. He finds a club in New York where a bunch of young people all stay and live together and where his meals are served and he's very happy because he feels he could have been very lonely if he hadn't found a place where he could find other young

people to mingle with. While he's living at this club, he finds a girl and he falls in love with her and they get married and they get a little apartment in Manhattan and she puts him through college. (Catherine, subject 12, story A-1, 1953)

There is also an increase in themes of striving and a decrease in themes of passivity—of having things happen to one. Perhaps this is best illustrated in story A-9. In 1940 Catherine told a very adolescent yarn involving mystery and probably much sexual symbolism (the subject in the story is bound and gagged). In 1953 the subject in this story is still waiting to be chosen; but the difference is that this time she goes to work to improve herself in style so that "she can grace his home and be the kind of wife that a man of his means should have."

Girl was chambermaid in big hotel on top floor. Heard strange things through the keyholes. This was the strangest. One day was cleaning in room on top floor, found a diary. Was written in German. She wondered what it meant. Took diary to German chambermaid in same hotel. German maid translated it for her. Found it was a report. Had a blueprint in it of one of latest army airplanes. Became frightened. Didn't know what to do. Wanted to put it back and tell police. As she was putting it away, German spy came in and asked her what she was doing. He realized she had diary. Bound and gagged her. Packed his things. Lowered her from window. Put her in a submarine. German maid came looking for her, saw signs of a struggle. Called police. Covered trains and waterfront. Discovered she was on submarine. Got girl back and got spies. (Catherine, subject 12, story A-9, 1940)

This girl is a maid in a very wealthy home and she falls in love with the son of owner—the son of her employer. She never lets him know because she always feels that he isn't interested in her as he has lots of other girls that he goes out with, with lots of money and clothes and stuff like that. Finally one day, she's cleaning and she overhears him talking to his father and his father is saying, "When are you going to settle down and who is your choice for a wife." He says of all the girls he knows he likes the girl who works in the house the best and he is going to ask her to marry him. She's very happy about it and they get married and she finds that her background has been very different from his and it's a handicap in their marriage, but she's a very intelligent girl, very alert girl and she studies things—etiquette, clothes, and things—she really feels that she can grace his home and be the kind of wife that a man of his means should have. (Catherine, subject 12, story A-9, 1953)

Finally, there is a change in her attitude toward separation and rejection. There are actually more stories in 1953 dealing with the

Appendix A. Resumé of the Subjects

theme of separation, but they end by having the persons united, whereas in 1940 they did not. This is another outcome that can be attributed to psychotherapy—an attack on the problem of acceptance-rejection, which has finally been worked through so that she is able to break the barrier and accept a relationship in spite of its potential threat (of failure) to her. One may compare story A-7 in 1940, given above, with story A-7 told in 1953.

This boy in the picture is—that's his mother. He has come to her and told her that he wants to, he's just about to graduate from school, and he wants to go into the service and volunteer. She's very brokenhearted about the whole thing, about his going because she feels he's too young but she tells him that if it's what he really wants to do that she won't stand in his way. So, he goes off into the service and when he comes back, she realizes that his physical health and stamina are much better than they were when he went away and she feels that the service did him a lot of good and that his decision to go in was the best after all. (Catherine, subject 12, story A-7, 1953)

EXCERPT FROM THE RORSCHACH REPORT

A disturbed woman with uneven reality contact and a great sense of inadequacy and insufficiency. There is an underlying schizophrenic structure. She appears suggestible, has very little control over her thought processes and very little self-discipline. She is overreactive and projects readily, but there is little evidence of spontaneous, outgoing affect.

She is concerned with the impression she makes on others, is highly exhibitionistic and self-conscious, with heightened body narcissism. She compensates for feelings of physical inadequacy and inferiority by overemphasis on physical appearance through clothes.

She is frustrated in her attempt to make good rapport with people, and has psychic discomfort in her relations with people.

She is unable to accept herself as an adult woman. She is chronically afraid of criticism and rejection. She has a well-developed mechanism of denial and will avoid looking at the unpleasant nature of things. An Oedipal conflict is at the root of her exhibitionism, inversion of libido, and body narcissism.

She wishes to remain a young girl, enjoying the protection of her parents. Her approaching motherhood intensifies her conflicts about becoming a mature woman, with functions other than those of self-display. The relationship to the father seems to have been one of desire to please and a fear of rejection and disapproval by him. The mother may have made her feel unacceptable and unattractive.

She is easily disturbed and coerced into submission when a fight is called for.

Laura, Subject 13

LAURA AS AN ADOLESCENT

As a thirteen-year-old girl Laura was described as inhibited, quiet, overly polite, docile and conscientious, a worrier, willing, cooperative, and obedient. She had severe migraine headaches until she was nine. Her busy, able mother dominated her. She had two older brothers, and was the family pet. Her father was quiet and unobtrusive.

SYNOPSIS OF ADOLESCENT FANTASY

Her adolescent fantasy showed death wishes toward both mother and father, with yearning for the father to return. She was anxious about separation, getting lost, being alone, being an orphan, and being adopted. She feared retaliation from others for her aggression. There was jealousy because of her mother's fondness for her brother. There was conflict between wishing to leave home and searching for the mother. There were themes of the unpopular girl making herself attractive against parental opposition. There were themes of a mysterious big house and strange noises at night. The Oedipus complex showed clearly in her stories, as did homosexual implications.

LAURA AS AN ADULT

After leaving high school, Laura took a position as stenographer with an automobile sales agency, a position which she still holds. She claims that she is very close to a girl who works in the same office.

Laura is described in 1953 as prim, sweet, overly polite, cooperative, submissive and on the whole colorless and spineless. Although not interested in boys in high school she married a Catholic man three years her senior, over her mother's energetic protest. At one time her mother forced her to break off the engagement. Her mother will have nothing

Appendix A. Resumé of the Subjects

to do with her husband and has all but disowned Laura. Laura says she loves her mother deeply and is unhappy over the situation but she loves her husband and is happy with him. There are no children. She would rather take slaps from her mother than to fight back. Although her mother is prejudiced against people of other religions, races, or nationalities, Laura states that she gets along well with all kinds of people.

CORRESPONDENCE BETWEEN ADOLESCENT FANTASY AND ADULT PERSONALITY

Oedipal themes are prominent in the 1940 stories and it is possible that these Oedipal fantasies are the basis for her marrying against her mother's wishes. Hostility against the mother is a recurrent theme in the 1940 stories. This is evidenced by the fact that a mother (alive) is not a character in any of the 1940 stories. Story B-5 (1940) presages, in a vague way, later events.

Two sisters, one was orphan adopted into rich family. Daughter was lonely, adopted girl. Sisters made friends to each other. Adopted daughter found that Janet was up to something bad. Told Janet it was wrong, would hurt family's reputation. Janet began to doubt her own scheme. After school Janet thanked her for stopping her from doing what she planned, because if she had done it her family would never have forgiven it. [What was she going to do?] I don't know. (Laura, subject 13, story B-5, 1940)

In this story a girl is "up to something bad"—something that would "hurt the family's reputation." Whatever this was Laura could not voice it in 1940, but she knew that "her family would never have forgiven it." This same theme of rebellion against family wishes is shown in story A-1.

In New York. Boy who was interested in a sailor's life. Family disapproved; not a life to be proud of. Parents wanted him to have a good education. Boy's heart set on going to sea. Packed his suitcase and left. Went to docks. Got a job on a ship. Sent telegram to his folks saying he was at sea and at last had his wishes and was at sea. (Laura, subject 13, story A-1, 1940)

Story B-7 is a weird tale in which the mother dies and the girl is left alone with her father. There is a projection of guilt (disgrace) over a hardly veiled incestuous relation:

Girl's mother died, left rooming house to her. Saw shadow as she was going up to give man the trousers she had pressed. Thought it was man waiting for trousers. Delivered trousers. Came down, saw shadow again. Frightened. Went up again. Saw shadow. Investigated, found nothing. Girl's father was in Europe. Received notice that he had done something bad. Didn't say what. Wondered about shadow and father. Next day saw shadow was father. He didn't want to come out because of his disgrace in Europe. She said he was welcome despite what he had done. (Laura, subject 13, story B-7, 1940)

The implication in these stories is that you can't have a man without hurting mother. Story B-8 presents the same theme with an added homosexual implication.

Janet's father—lawyer. Called away on case. Mother dead. Father was leaving. Janet didn't want to be left alone. Father told her to get a girl to stay with her. Didn't know when he would be back. Had a good time with girl. Father away three weeks. Told them about experience. Told them innocent person was set free. Janet happy to see father again. (Laura, subject 13, story B-8, 1940)

Apparently a homosexual crush is a defense against the full impact of her Oedipal fantasies.

CHANGE IN FANTASY

In the 1953 stories, A-8 comes close to verbalizing the meaning of her demureness and passivity. Here she tells us that underneath the soft-spoken character is one that is "rather boisterous, aggressive, loud and outspoken." She has carried over from childhood a quiet, demure personality as a defense against the more turbulent forces underneath which sometimes erupt into overt action in a way that puzzles her.

Two sisters, one opposite from the other. One quiet, soft-spoken, and the other rather boisterous, quite the opposite in personality. I think the one that is quiet and demure and soft-spoken would like to be like her other sister, but she just can't be, and vice versa. The quietness of the sister impresses the one that is more aggressive and more outspoken, and therefore between the two of them, there exists not a jealous feeling or anything but a feeling of respect for each one, and probably the one that is more aggressive and loud will always defend the one that is more quiet and soft-spoken, as well as the one that is more timid is more apt to defend the one in action for her sister's outspoken ways. The quiet one gets married the earliest. (Laura, subject 13, story A-8, 1953)

One important change over thirteen years in the stories is from the good to the neutral ending. In 1940, even though Laura could tell stories involving unhappy incidents, she had to clear them up with

Appendix A. Resumé of the Subjects

a happy ending. Her experiences over the intervening years, perhaps her open defiance of her mother, has taken away some of the danger connected with her aggressive impulses and she is able to tolerate them more easily. One may surmise the strength of her erotic needs that helped her to override her deep-seated adolescent defenses against permitting aggression to find open expression. In later years the need for reaction formation toward mother hostility has been dispelled because she has defied her mother in reality.

CHANGE IN FANTASY: LAURA, SUBJECT 13

Fantasy theme	Amount of change
Positive outcome	−14
Crime against property	−3
Dominance—coercion	−3
Mystery, strangeness	−3
Separation	−3

There is a decrease in the length of the stories in 1953, indicating some increase in repression and denial in later years. Dr. Jensen described her as insipid, colorless, impressing one with her innocence and immaturity. The Rorschach describes her as a rigid, frightened, slightly paranoid person, afraid of close contacts, and with minor panic reactions. In real life she and her husband practice birth control in defiance of the teachings of the Catholic Church. One may compare story B-5, given in 1953, with the same story told in 1940 to see this trend.

Such a worried expression on this girl's face simply telling this other person some very bad news, describing some kind of event to her, must be something that has just happened with the expression of anxiety that's on her face. It could be an accident of some kind with the expression, her hand being shown as it is. (Laura, subject 13, story B-5, 1953)

Gone also are themes of one person exerting an influence over another. Apparently the exertion of her own will in making decisions has eliminated the need to incorporate this trend into her stories.

The mystery and strangeness (of sex) has also disappeared from her later stories, due to her more realistic experiences. Also, there is evidence that she is now sexually repressed.

Again, she no longer needs to fantasy separation from her family in 1953 because she already (in part) has accomplished this.

EXCERPT FROM THE RORSCHACH REPORT

Rigid, unimaginative, frightened, slightly paranoid. Ego is weak. She uses repression and a "sour-grapes" attitude. She finds social relationships unpleasant and difficult to handle. She is afraid of close contacts with people, is self-conscious, afraid of criticism and rejection. There is lack of outer and inner freedom and spontaneity. She is suspicious of people and looks for criticism and injustice—tends to reject her aggressive impulses. High level of anxiety makes her see danger where none exists.

She finds it difficult to maintain her composure in sexually challenging situations. Underlying irritability that suggests that she is hypersensitized in a negative sense to sexual demands and may quickly lose her temper or become restless and nervous, or frightened and tighten up in a man-woman sexual situation.

She may feel persecuted, rejected, and frightened under pressure.

Viola, Subject 14

VIOLA AS AN ADOLESCENT

As a fourteen-year-old girl Viola was well spoken of by her teachers, who respected her ability and described her as mature, dependable, and cooperative. She was a young sophisticate and talked philosophically and speculatively. Boys did not understand her because of her considerable ability to verbalize her feelings and ideas. But she was elected president of her homeroom. She was an only child, was alone a great deal and had a rich fantasy life, but she hid her emotions behind a passive exterior. Her father drank, her parents quarreled, and the family was not well off. Viola spoke of quarrels with her mother. Viola once had a nervous breakdown and went on a trip with her grandmother.

SYNOPSIS OF ADOLESCENT FANTASY

In her stories Viola was very much aware of her intellect, which was a source of pride and satisfaction. Story characters were aesthetes with a desire to write—but their intelligence was not harnessed to the real problems and affairs of life. There were pronounced death wishes toward both parents. Mother figures were stronger than the fathers, but were restrictive and religiously fanatical. Father figures were weak, ineffective, passive, and dependent.

There were schizoid aspects to her stories. Characters were withdrawn, lonely, lacking in capacity for self-expression and the enjoyment of life. There were feelings of isolation and withdrawal. Characters thought and felt, but were passive and ideational rather than vigorously active.

Characters suffered misfortune and there was much apprehension about impending dangers. There was considerable insecurity and feelings of being rejected, unattractive, a victim of circumstances.

Characters had ambitions, but on the whole they remained unrealized. There was much concern over moral conflict. She suffered because of this, was masochistic, and in her imagination endured punishment and extinction.

There were Oedipal themes and themes of sibling rivalry.

VIOLA AS AN ADULT

Now, as a twenty-seven-year-old woman, Viola is described as a tense, highstrung, secretive, poetic person in whom fact and fancy are not too clearly separated. She goes into detail about her feelings and subjective states. She had a considerable need to be exact and will elaborate, modify, or retract statements that she makes.

She reports that high school was the happiest time of her life. She graduated from college with a major in English and a minor in speech and dramatics. She loved her two minor subjects. She has never worked.

She eloped with a man she met on vacation while in college. She eloped partly as a protest against her mother's domination and in part because she was afraid her mother would not approve of her husband. After living in Louisiana she came back to the North to live with her husband's father and aunt. But her mother came and took her home and forced her to separate from her husband, against which she put up little opposition. She eloped with the same man to Chicago and for two years did not let her parents know where she was. There she had two children. Again they returned and moved in with her parents, but her husband could not get along with them so they moved out. She is expecting a third child.

CORRESPONDENCE BETWEEN ADOLESCENT FANTASY
AND ADULT PERSONALITY

The outstanding feature of Viola's life has been her opposition to her mother through her marriage. This attitude toward her mother was foreshadowed in story B-2.

Jane Cummins was an orphan. Lived with aunt who was official guardian. Worked as stenographer in law office. Pretty and gay—found it hard to live with aunt because of restrictions upon her. Loved pretty clothes—was hopeless because she never had enough money. Aunt Jane didn't like Jane associating with other girls and boys of her age because they weren't serious about things. Aunt was fanatic, religion was all important. One Christmas Jane's boss gave her a gift, was delighted. Aunt asked Jane for it. Jane rebelled against this. Jane wanted a dress, went and bought it. Was gay about it. Was pleased with success of Christmas gift. Aunt very displeased. Jane didn't care. Always kept the dress as a reminder that not everything in life was gotten through virtue. Jane got married. Could afford new clothes but always treasured the old one. Aunt died. Jane was sorry but thought Aunt had been wrong about the dress. (Viola, subject 14, story B-2, 1940)

In this story the mother figure, an aunt, placed restrictions on the heroine, against which she rebels. The story ends by the heroine marrying and the aunt dying. So even as an adolescent Viola has fantasies that she acts out in real life later.

Another story tells of rebellion against a mother figure:

Pat Windsor—spoiled child when young. Parents gave her everything. Both parents died at same time. Only relative left was father's sister, who became legal guardian. Pat didn't like her but didn't mind her. Aunt restricted Pat's time. Pat conformed to aunt's wish. One night came home at 2 o'clock. Pat's spirit of rebellion was up. Came in at 3:30. Then thought it might not be so wise. Saw aunt at head of stairs. Aunt scolded her until she was ready to let her out. Pat angry. Outwardly they got on well. Pat seething inside. Ran away. Realized she didn't have much money with her. Was embarrassed. Aunt had upper hand. "I told you so" attitude. Pat settled down. Got along well with aunt. Pat married but never forgot aunt had taught her there were two ways to do a thing—the way one wanted to and the right way. (Viola, subject 14, story B-7, 1940)

In story B-1 she depicts a man as weak and ineffective:

Nice residential section, average people lived there. One summer day refined peddler came along. Had usual type of things to sell and a story of failure. Had wife, three children. Wife had job as housekeeper. He wanted to do what he could. Wife really earning money. Man lost confidence in

Appendix A. Resumé of the Subjects

self. Took up peddling as a last resort. Was putting up a front so people couldn't see how he felt. Discouraged, despondent. One day was walking through entrance of a house. Stumbled over a black case. Went inside with it. Husband had dropped case containing material which could not be duplicated. Was thankful for return of papers. Promised man a job. Next week was given a job as night watchman. Wasn't much of a job, but it helped financially. Also lost despondent air, got pride back. Didn't advance but didn't care because he got feeling of attaining. After he died, children carried on. Had memory of gay, light-hearted father. Transformation from dejected into glad-to-be-alive person was wonderful to see. (Viola, subject 14, story B-1, 1940)

This not only reflects the father but also the man she married. Her 1953 interview, in describing her husband after they had returned from Louisiana and her mother forced her to leave her husband and come home to her, tells us that "she was cut off from her husband. She just let this happen to her and didn't put up much opposition and her husband didn't even come to see her. Her husband lived just a few blocks away. They could meet on the sly. She and her husband used all kinds of subterfuges in order to see each other. He never took matters into his own hands, he only pleaded with her, but she would ask him where they would go to live and what did he have to offer." It was after this that they eloped for a second time.

Story B-6 shows that Viola had intellectual and aesthetic interests.

Boy of an average family. Got fairly good marks, fairly well liked. Underneath he had one desire—was thoughtful, conscientious, studious—to be a famous author. Daydreamed about it. Wrote very well, but never let anyone see the things he wrote well. Didn't waste his real talent on school work. Kept it to himself. Went up to attic, and thought. Sat down to exercise his mind. Tried to get thoughts organized into stories. One day mother arranged to sell desk and chair in attic. Movers came and got it when boy was in school. All his work was in desk. Boy came home, went to attic. With desk had gone all of his work. Great loss to him. Waste of his work. Mother came home and he asked her about it. No one ever took trouble to return stories to him—didn't have name on. People who got desk threw stories away. Boy never bothered to write again, discouraged. Should have been more practical. Grew up, got job doing something else. Didn't want to bother writing. With loss of desk went source of inspiration to a mind that could have turned out good work. (Viola, subject 14, story B-6, 1940)

Viola majored in English in college and throughout school was interested in dramatics. While in Louisiana she joined an amateur theater group. In her interview Viola placed stress on her intellectual ability.

CHANGE IN FANTASY: VIOLA, SUBJECT 14

Fantasy theme	Amount of change
Accidental death	−7
Negative outcome	−3
Altruism	+3
Guilt	+3

CHANGE IN FANTASY

In Viola's 1953 stories there is a remarkable persistence of the themes expressed in 1940. Story B-7, for instance, shows the same feeling of obligation to and dependence on the mother that was expressed in the earlier stories, notably B-7 (see above).

Here is a highschool girl coming home from school . . . at exactly the time she is expected. Each day she returns to her home at 3:20 to her semi-invalid mother, who waits anxiously for the daughter's return. Never has the daughter dared to upset this precise routine of "come right home," for she has all her life been made to feel the burden of responsibility for her mother. Her mother has always maintained that she lives only through her daughter, that she needs her daughter's presence constantly. And the girl, trained for years to accept this formula, adheres to it. Her occasional longings for any personal freedom are far outweighed by the sense of guilt such thoughts incur. So she lives in this rigid pattern, neither unhappy nor resentful. She will never realize the tragedy of her own arrested development, for even after her mother's death she will look back on her years of unquestioning subservience as a time of "doing all I could for Mother." (Viola, subject 14, story B-7, 1953)

But in 1953 one feels that Viola comes closer to recognizing her impulses and tendencies than in 1940. In story A-10, for instance, the conflict between being at home and being away from home is sharpened: "the danger of going home is much greater than the danger of staying."

[Do you remember this?] I think so, yes. It's so old, it's been a long time. Two young people want an answer to a question, very, very, much. It's very, very important to them to know what to do. They've come to this fortuneteller hoping to get some sign so that they'd know which way to turn. Although I think each of them does know, what he'd do as a solution anyway. I wonder what the problem is? I think it's a problem of a young married couple—we'll say in the depression era, because money is the problem and it's a very, very, very real problem. They are living in a city where his skill as a laborer is absolutely not needed, she can help not at all. They are newlyweds. They've been married less than a year. They did it against the wishes of their parents, from both sides. They live in a town where they are not known, and try to make out, knowing that it would be hard financially. They belong together, they've been living together with great happiness, with the simple things in the customary way, but no matter how much together they feel there is an adjustment in everyone's life. He has no money, the problem of eating, of finding a place to sleep is an impossible one. They must seek help someplace. They get very reckless, and feel things are unfair, and they see the old fortuneteller, to perhaps give some solution. The problem in their own minds as they approach them is whether for each of them to go back to their respective homes because while the parents of the boy and the parents of the girl did not condone that, neither home would welcome them as a married couple. They don't know what to do. They just feel that it's unfortunate that they have to be in this situation together. I'd like to find someone that—well, that some visionary remarks that the fortuneteller can throw out to them that they could just take unto themselves and twist their own minds just enough to mean that only in being together would they find the way. That the danger of going home is much greater than the danger of staying. And somehow, I'd like them to find that life together and that the fortuneteller can give an omen that they shall stay together, that they must struggle together, and that in struggling together they can find a life to live happily ever after. (Viola, subject 14, story A-10, 1953)

In 1953 there is a marked decrease in the number of stories in which a parent figure accidentally dies. But there is also an increase in themes of guilt in 1953, as illustrated in story B-7. So as her fantasies become clearer and are acted out they bring with them a sense of guilt and a need to backtrack and make amends for her fantasies and needs. Viola's life has been an alternation between her hostile impulses and becoming overwhelmed with guilt because of them.

There are also fewer stories with negative endings in 1953. Story B-6 told in 1953 should be compared with the story told to the same picture in 1940.

Dejection because of rejection. Here is a young man who has sat up the whole night, brooding about his own sense of inadequacy. The day before, he received a letter from the state university rejecting his application for admission on the basis of unsatisfactory preparation. During his teen-age years he had often dreamed of the bounties of education, determined to attain the "glory" of a college degree. But, fearing the accusation of presumptuousness, he let no one know of his goal. Consequently, he just drifted along at the lower level of his class—classes in a very inferior high school in one of our poorer states. He is sure the failure is his, and knows no solution. Turning to the occupation where his is more than adequate—his father's fishing fleet—he is able to prosper, mature, and gain community approval. After some years, marriage, and fatherhood, he begins to realize that early refusal to the university was partially the result of a poor school system. He becomes the local champion of reform in the little town's schools, and will eventually recognize the satisfaction of doing for other young people what was not done for him. (Viola, subject 14, story B-6, 1953)

In 1940 this story ended "boy never bothers to write again, discouraged." In 1953 the main character "will eventually recognize the satisfaction of doing for other young people what was not done for him." This represents definite growth. The earlier depression has been replaced by a thought of making amends by helping others. It is possible that Viola sees a way of doing reparation for her earlier negative fantasies and deeds through her own family and children. This theme of altruism appears in at least two other of the 1953 stories. The girl in story A-3 "thinks of herself as a servant of other people . . . I think there isn't any sacrifice that this person makes that isn't a full one because the element of giving is a valuable one to her, and to everyone."

Her guilt, however, is not wholly over her hostile impulses and fantasies. Part of her guilt is because of sex. This is clearly indicated in story B-5, as told in 1940 and in 1953.

June Clark—when 17 was in auto accident. Face and body scarred, burned. Doctors didn't expect her to live. She did. Mentally she was still shaken up about it. Face covered with bandages for several weeks—hadn't seen self with them off. Didn't anticipate anything as horrible as she turned out to be. Was determined to take up her life where she had left it, promised self she would not be sorry for self. Will power pushed self-pity out. Startled everyone because it was so awful to see her. Knew everyone was talking about it. Doctor thought plastic surgery would not help. Didn't marry. Had many friends. Lived and died alone. Was not sort of person who liked to be alone. After she died several people marveled at her courage and how she faced her problem. These people were ones to be blamed. Were ashamed of selves. Realized they shouldn't have excluded her from their group. (Viola, subject 14, story B-5, 1940)

This is the moment of a shocking revelation. Here are two girl-cousins, who have been reared together by the parents of the blonde, "Plain Jane." Her curly-headed cousin "Silly Sue" has always lived with this family, being trained to the pattern of dutiful daughter and useful citizen. The contrasting personalities of the two girls complement each other—they are boon companions, until a man enters the situation. This man is unlike all the usual high school friends of Jane and Sue—he is older, more worldly . . . and of a world neither has ever seen. Sent to the girls' small town on an engineering project, he paid enough attention to Sue to capture her dreams. And when he speaks of life in a big city . . . its many pleasures, she begins to see herself there with him. He eventually asks, in the interest of satisfying his own sex pleasures that she arrange to go off with him on a certain Saturday night . . . for a week-end. Sue, here in the picture, is telling her cousin of what she considers to be her approaching elopement and marriage. She is ready to go to the life her hero has mentioned. Jane tries to dissuade her. Cannot do so, off goes Sue, meets her idol, makes a few pointed remarks about their future, and then is hastily and brutally informed that she was chosen not for a lifetime but rather for a clandestine week-end. She beats a hasty retreat, returning to the safety of her home, feeling foolish but wiser. (Viola, subject 14, story B-5, 1953)

In 1940 she manages her guilt by a masochistic fantasy. One should note that she paid the penalty because she didn't marry and lived and died alone. In 1953 the theme of sex is not disguised, but there is the same guilt, managed this time by returning home. It is obvious that the 1953 story is in part autobiographical, but she has actually worked out in real life a more healthy solution than that of the individual in the story. But it took her at least two attempts in real life before she found the better way.

EXCERPT FROM THE RORSCHACH REPORT

A highly sensitive woman who lives in a world of fantasy with some depression present. Artistic. Her emotions are aesthetic and ethereal. She tries to direct her feelings into religious or spiritual channels. Her repression of aggression and sexuality are the result of deep Oedipal conflict. A person of softness and gentleness, beneath which are strong aggressive impulses never directly expressed except in sporadic outbursts. She distrusts people and finds it difficult to understand them. She is basically compliant and submissive.

Oedipal fantasies deep and conspicuous. She idealizes her father but is afraid of him as an authority figure. She has strong fear of sexual contact and she may find it difficult to be sexually responsive. Fantasies of rape and prostitution. She has a soft affect and wants physical closeness.

Relationship with mother strained, with much unexpressed conflict and resentment. But mother has given her physical and emotional closeness. She is capable of strong attachments to people in which dependency plays a large part, but she is impulsive in spite of her submissiveness. Repressions rob her of self-assertion and self-reliance.

She has many of the characteristics of a narcissistic character disorder, but may be closer to anxiety hysteria.

Edith, Subject 17

EDITH AS AN ADOLESCENT

As a thirteen-year-old girl—short, sturdy, and plain-featured—Edith received high praise from her teachers, who said she was a leader and an organizer, intelligent, efficient, and popular with other pupils. She was independent, did excellent work, was cooperative, well-poised, and nonaggressive. She had two younger sisters; three in-laws lived with the family. She was popular with boys—was said to be "boy crazy." She liked active sports. Her mother said she was obedient but did not care for housework. She wanted to be a musical comedy actress and was excited over her conquests as an entertainer, but so far had been given only a second lead in a school play. She hated the thought of death, was moody, lacked a sense of humor, and was easily embarrassed.

Edith came from a family in moderate circumstances. The mother was devoted to the family and was proud of Edith, whom she would have liked to see attend college.

SYNOPSIS OF ADOLESCENT FANTASY

The stories showed anxiety and depression and a fear of failure. There was much concern over the need to be popular and she showed rivalry with competitors. There was envy of others. There was a passive theme running throughout the stories—of yearning, wanting others to make advances to her, and passive acceptance of fate. There was some anxiety and guilt over sex wishes and possible loss of parents, and the theme of returning home occurred twice. The stories were short and unelaborated.

EDITH AS AN ADULT

Thirteen years later she presents herself as an attractive, poised woman, somewhat listless. When she graduated from high school she started a dancing school of her own. She tried going to a dramatic workshop but did not like the kind of people she met, and withdrew from it.

She held secretarial positions until she married a quiet man in 1951. She has one child, a daughter, but lost her first-born son when he was sixteen months old through a virus infection. This was a very traumatic experience for her.

Now her home is her main interest. She is a devout Catholic and is against practicing birth control.

She describes herself as an idealistic person. She speaks affectionately of her father, admiringly of her mother, and with enthusiasm of her sisters.

CORRESPONDENCE BETWEEN ADOLESCENT FANTASY
AND ADULT PERSONALITY

Correspondence between the 1940 stories and later life experiences or the present personality of Edith are difficult to discern, partly perhaps because the stories are so short and matter-of-fact. However, story B-6 contains themes that reverberate in her present life.

This man attempted to do something in new surroundings and failed to do it. Probably he has someone depending upon him. He's now very worried about what will happen to them if he doesn't make good. (Edith, subject 17, story B-6, 1940)

Even in 1940 Edith's fantasies had a depressed tone. That Edith is now depressed seems very reasonable because of the death of her infant son. For a long time after this event she had difficulty sleeping and lost interest in food, which resulted in her losing weight. Her family feared that she would break down as a result of the experience. In the story the man failed. Edith states, with regard to her son's death, that this has been her greatest failure. She thinks that perhaps she was too confident that he would pull through his illness. She believes that if she had not been so confident in her own ability to care for the child that she might have changed doctors sooner. She says that she still has doubts as to her own role in her son's death.

In Story B-6 it is also said that the man has someone depending on him. This is a trait that Edith displays in her own life. She describes herself as a very idealistic person and says that she always wanted to do something humanitarian.

Appendix A. Resumé of the Subjects

Story B-5 contains a reference to death, which may be put in juxtaposition to her recent experience.

Girl brought other one startling news which she can't believe. Member of family (mother or father) died or was killed. Naturally it upset her very much. Because of this she doesn't stay where she is but goes back home to other members of family who need her. (Edith, subject 17, story B-5, 1940)

This story shows that as an adolescent Edith could fantasy death to some member of her family and that this helps to strengthen the bonds with others members of her family who need her. One is reminded that Edith speaks of her family at present in most affectionate terms and that she expresses responsibility for them.

Without clearer evidence it is perhaps presuming too much to suggest that the death of her infant son in some way was the working out of some deep need, but as she relates the incident she goes half way in assuming responsibility for the death. Perhaps an event of this kind was necessary to her to provide the situation where she could atone for her life-long envy and jealousy of her sisters.

This feeling of responsibility for others is clearly shown by Edith in story B-9.

I think this man or woman is condemned to die. This is the morning [of the execution]. This person isn't sorry for himself but for someone who depends on him or her and what will happen to that person after he is dead or she is dead. But I think just before he is to be taken away, they find him innocent and he is freed. (Edith, subject 17, story B-9, 1940)

Two stories, A-5 and A-8, show the strength of sibling rivalry.

I think this girl would be doing her homework if not for something that is troubling her. She can't get her mind on school work. It's probably about a rival girl friend. I don't know if she would be a friend in that case. I think everything turns out in her favor. She doesn't have to worry very much longer. (Edith, subject 17, story A-5, 1940)

Two sisters, dark-haired. One is envious of the blond. Perhaps one has boy friend. Is trying to figure out a way to get even with her sister. Whatever she tries to do fails. (Edith, subject 17, story A-8, 1940)

CHANGE IN FANTASY: EDITH, SUBJECT 17

Fantasy theme	Amount of change
Positive outcome	−7
Male identification	−3

Appendix A. Resumé of the Subjects

CHANGE IN FANTASY

Themes of depression and pessimism, although present in 1940, are more frequent and pronounced in 1953. This is to be expected from the recent, tragic event of the death of her son.

Story B-6, given below, may be compared with the same story told in 1940, given above.

What a sad character. This looks like a picture of a very lonesome man. Looks like a man who might not have any friends, which is probably the lonesomest kind of person. He looks like, aside from being lonesome, he might be disappointed about life all together and may not have succeeded in what he wanted to do. Probably has no family. Looks like he's in total despair over something. He looks like he's not so old that life may not have some new openings for him. It makes me pity him, looking at him. (Edith, subject 17, story B-6, 1953)

Of similar import is the fact that there are fewer stories with positive outcome. Whereas in 1940 there is hope, in 1953 the attitude has changed to resignation. Story A-3 illustrates this difference.

The girl was an unpopular type and she feels downhearted when she sees girls going out with boys and reads. She thinks how she can make herself more popular. [Does she succeed?] I think in this case she does. She cares less about her books and more about her social life. (Edith, subject 17, story A-3, 1940)

This looks fairly obvious to me. Looks like a lonesome woman, who is perhaps a bit envious of the couple outside of her window. She's about half-way through that book, no doubt she'll finish that and many more. Looks like she's going to stay lonesome. (Edith, subject 17, story A-3, 1953)

This change is in part a natural retreat from the exuberance of adolescence to the acceptance of reality in later life, but in the case of Edith it represents a relinquishment of her earlier dreams and ambitions because of repeated frustrations and discouragement. Her ambitions for a theatrical career did not have the same glamour when she tried them out, and the death of her son squashed her dreams of family life.

There is a shift away from masculine identification in the 1953 stories. Story A-2 illustrates this shift.

This young man has a date. He's calling on his girl. He has for a long time wanted to go out with the girl and she has finally accepted. He is naturally quite happy about it. (Edith, subject 17, story A-2, 1940)

It looks like a woman knocking at a door. The only thing I can make out of this one, and that's only by the expression on the woman's face, is that she might possibly have some good news for whoever is going to open that door. She has a faintly happy expression on her face. But what a large fist she's rapping with. (Edith, subject 17, story A-2, 1953)

It is difficult to explain this shift in identification. The figure in card A-2 is actually seen as female very rarely and there must be a strong need for one to so see this figure as female. One may surmise many things. In adolescence masculine identification seems predominant. As, for instance, in story B-8.

I think this man has had some hard luck. He is telling this to her now. He's explaining the situation. She stands by him. She appears to me as though she might be the very loyal type. And I think they overcome the difficulty or the situation or whatever it might be. Maybe some trouble with his business. (Edith, subject 17, story B-8, 1940)

It is almost as though in adolescence Edith could not accept herself, but saw herself through identification with her father. But in 1953 she is able to accept her feelings and impulses as a woman as her own.

This looks like a picture of an old man, an older man, older than the girl, that is to say, giving advice of some kind to this young girl. She is listening to it. Reminds me of that one I saw last week where a woman was talking to a boy, at least that's the way I looked at them. He looks like a nice person, so does she. It maybe her father or someone she has a great deal of respect for, the way she's looking at him. I think that she probably accepts whatever he tells her. (Edith, subject 17, story B-8, 1953)

In short, in adolescence her own feelings and impulses were too exciting to her for her to accept them as her own and she had to see them through the eyes of another person. But the experiences of life have enabled her to face her inner self directly and she is able to accept her feelings more realistically.

EXCERPT FROM THE RORSCHACH REPORT

This person is in a reactive depression. Has little drive or ambition.

She finds it difficult to be interested in social relationships and to have warm, positive feelings toward people. She fears that life can be unpredictable and cruel. There is a fear of being deprived of someone she loves, also fear of dying. She is cut off from deeper feelings and can express only surface emotions and worries.

Her attitudes are unrealistic, colored by a basically childlike fantasy.

Appendix A. Resumé of the Subjects

This prevents her from seeing people as they really are and from establishing a good adult rapport with them. Afraid of people whom she expects to be unpleasant and rejecting. The self-concept is self-depreciatory. Assumes an attitude of "cuteness." The affect is shallow. There is no evidence of warmth or outgoingness.

Unable to accept her feminine role. Self-image is that of a little girl. She is afraid of men and of sex. Sexually unresponsive. Is a compliant and dutiful wife. Regards men as carnal and to be avoided. Has desire to express anger and hostility against the world in general but sense of guilt and fear of punishment are strong, which prevents her from being more direct in her expression of aggression.

Isabel, Subject 18

ISABEL AS AN ADOLESCENT

As a fourteen-year-old girl Isabel was characterized by her teachers as immature, impulsive, nonaggressive, and a bluffer. She bit her nails. She showed little leadership. But teachers also called her capable. Her critical mother said she was nervous like her father, had facial mannerisms, was dominating, and nagged and teased at home until she got her way. She got on well with an older sister. She was noisy and played the drum in the school orchestra.

SYNOPSIS OF ADOLESCENT FANTASY

Her stories depicted parents who are anxious, strict, protective, and restrictive, but also disapproving and rejecting. Mother figures were punitive but also dependent on their child. There was a repeated fantasy of returning to home and mother. There were feelings of inadequacy with regard to school and a desire to please teacher. Fear was denied. There was a passive acceptance of loneliness, boredom, and inactivity.

ISABEL AS AN ADULT

As a twenty-seven-year-old woman Isabel is described as plain, old-fashioned, without glamour, lacking in spontaneity, vivacity, and self-confidence. During the testing she was tense, inhibited, and nervous—telling stories was an ordeal to her.

Following graduation from high school, where she made the honor roll, she went to work in a bank and has been there ever since. She is unmarried and lives at home. She does not take the intiative and has little interest in men. The man she would marry must meet exacting specifications. She sews, belongs to a girls' club, has many interests with little conviction in any of them. She is a devout Catholic and if married would follow the rules of the Church about birth control. Smoking is a filthy habit—she is prejudiced against Negroes and Jews and is stanchly Republican. She does not want to have to boss other people.

Stella, Subject 19

STELLA AS AN ADOLESCENT

When fourteen years old Stella had a good reputation with her teachers as dependable, a good worker, quiet, not overly aggressive, conscientious, and with leadership qualities. Sometimes she impressed others as wistful and a little pathetic. There was an older brother, a sister a year and a half younger, and a still younger brother. She tended to be somewhat hostile to her sister, associated with an older set and resented having her younger sister go with her. The family was the social center for the neighborhood. About herself she said that she did not like school and was selfish.

SYNOPSIS OF ADOLESCENT FANTASY

Her stories at that time were short, prosaic, commonplace, and lacked the fantastic quality so often found in adolescent stories. Characters were under superego restraint—they were upright and respectable and avoided aggressive behavior, although they might feel hostility. There was a lofty moral tone to the stories. There was an unusual amount of conflict between female characters, and girls in the stories were belligerent, rivalrous, and disagreeable. There was a need to be appreciated by others and a fear of losing loved ones. There was a strong wish to be independent. There was a clear feminine identification. She was ashamed of quarreling with her family and was anxious about it, but there was strong family loyalty. There was concern about success with school work.

Appendix A. Resumé of the Subjects

STELLA AS AN ADULT

Thirteen years later Stella was found to be a personable young woman—neat, sensible, rather attractive.

Her father was insistent on her going to college after graduating from high school, so after a short experience working in a bank she enrolled in Rutgers, where she majored in retailing and advertising, and graduated in three years by attending every summer session. After college she obtained a secretarial position, which she kept until her mother had a nervous breakdown and she wanted to be near home.

Stella met her husband while in college. Apparently the marriage is a happy one, although her mother objected to the match. They now have a ten-month-old baby. Her husband has set up his own business—selling baby clothes—and she helps in the store on certain days, but believes that being a good mother is a full-time job. Usually she is a cheerful, outgoing person but becomes depressed at times when under stress. She has a tendency to worry about things. Her mother had a severe breakdown and she is afraid that this may be her fate, too, as she is like her mother in many ways. Her husband is a stabilizing influence.

Stella had much to say about her brothers and sisters. She is most concerned about her younger brother whom she describes as spoiled and undependable. Her mother's breakdown was due in part to worry over this son.

CORRESPONDENCE BETWEEN ADOLESCENT FANTASY
AND ADULT PERSONALITY

The case of Stella is a good illustration of the influence of unduly high superego standards. Story B-3 shows a very loft moral attitude.

There are two young boys, one is the toughie of the community and the other doesn't approve of his habits. Rough boy probably wants to make the other one just like him. Puts on an act of smoking. Other boy doesn't pay attention to him. In later life he finds out it was better that he didn't because the other one wasn't good for anything. (Stella, subject 19, story B-3, 1940)

Story A-4 not only shows the repression of aggression through the adoption of a polite attitude, but the guilt that follows from even asserting oneself politely.

Boy probably worked someplace where he delivered papers after school. On payday he went for his money. Boss tried to cheat him but in a polite way he got around to get it all. But when the boss gave it to him he wasn't pleased about it. Boy decided to leave his job instead of causing any more trouble. (Stella, subject 19, story A-4, 1940)

In later life Stella describes herself as a tense, anxious, worrying person with the fear that the same thing may happen to her that happened to her mother. She does not want to let things get her down, she doesn't want to get involved in too many things because of this fear.

The only negative feelings that Stella could permit herself in her 1940 stories concern sibling rivalry (story A-8).

Two sisters. One plain, one enjoys all riches and luxuries of life. Both keep trying to tell each other that their way of living is better than other. Arguments are caused for nothing. Both girls leave each other, go on with their own likes and dislikes and find out it is better to be away from each other and let each other have their own lives. (Stella, subject 19, story A-8, 1940)

So it is significant to find that actually she and her sister went to the same college, graduated at the same time and had a double wedding. Apparently experiencing strong emotion in fantasy in adolescence does not interfere with good relations in later years.

In story B-6 longing to go to college is expressed.

Young boy who is depressed. Wants to go to college. Finds his parents can't afford it. Thinks of different ways he might secure money for it. None of them work out. One neighbor might lose her son who she was preparing to send. Might send this boy instead; give him everything she planned to give her own son. Plan might work out very well. Becomes a lawyer and in a speech he might say he owes it all to the neighbor. (Stella, subject 19, story B-6, 1940)

Actually Stella did go to college and made a good record there. In her interview she makes it appear that she went to college largely because her father wanted her to. But this story would indicate that it was her own deeper ambition, and in the interview she practically admitted the same thing, "When her sister graduated from high school and went on to Rutgers, Stella wanted to do likewise."

Stella stressed several times in the interview how important marriage is to her. "She can't imagine now not being married. She thinks married life is much better than single life. She thinks this is largely because

Appendix A. Resumé of the Subjects

she has such a good husband." This attitude is foreshadowed in one of her 1940 stories (B-8).

Lady's husband is going away to settle a business dispute. She is sad at his leaving her. Makes him promise he'll be back as soon as he can. Probably stays away for a few weeks. She begins to worry. He returns. She decides next time he has to go, she is going with him. This gives him a great deal of satisfaction to know he is appreciated. He is sorry she had to worry about him. (Stella, subject 19, story B-8, 1940)

CHANGE IN FANTASY

The tabulation of themes shows little change from 1940 to 1953, perhaps partly because the total of themes is so low.

Sibling rivalry is still expressed, in 1953 perhaps in more pronounced form than in 1940.

This is the picture of a mother and two daughters. The one who is all dressed up probably is the favorite. It looks like she is going to a party and her sister in the background is supposed to stay home, and she resents it and is sort of very bitter about the girl, her other sister who is going. She is very sad. I imagine that may be her sister who is going to the dance. Probably feels sorry that she is going and the other one isn't, and maybe —I wouldn't say that she is the favorite though—I think that she is being punished for something, and she is not allowed to go out, but I don't think she goes to the party, but I think that the sister talks to the mother and she is forgiven for whatever she did. Everything runs smoothly from then on and the sister suspects that she is being punished for something. (Stella, subject 19, story B-4, 1953)

Story B-11 told to the blank card reports with somewhat different emphasis the story told in B-8 in 1940.

What is this—a blank card? [Yes, you can make up your own story, you have all the freedom in the world on that.] I don't know. I don't have a very good imagination—I don't think I ever did. I'll have to imagine a picture. Somehow I imagine a nice trip to Florida. I can picture myself going on the train—not flying, I wouldn't want to fly. Oh, I can just picture myself relaxing on the beach and having a wonderful time. I wish my husband could go with me, but probably he couldn't. Then I'd come home all rested, and I think I would be able to go on with whatever I'm doing. It would give me a good pickup. That's about all I can think of. (Stella, subject 19, story B-11, 1953)

In 1940 it was the husband who went away and the wife yearned to be with him. In 1953 the wife goes to Florida and then adds (autobiographically), "I wish my husband could go with me but he probably couldn't."

Actually, when one inspects the two sets of stories there are striking differences. The hostility which almost certainly was present in 1940 but was covered up by a highly moral attitude, comes out more openly in 1953.

This looks like a story of a girl who is a shut-in. She is looking very lonely, a healthy girl approaching by the window, probably dreaming of being out there, being able to do everything that they do. She also looks very well in white. Looks like her books don't interest her, and she just sort of has it open to, so it idles the time away, and she sort of looks like the girl that would never, who doesn't think that they are able to get back on the top. I would think that she probably never does. She just becomes very bitter and drops the whole thing. She looks sort of mean, probably taking out her loneliness on everybody who would come in contact with her. I think it's like one of those stories you see on television, you read about these girls who try to break up the lives of people they live with and they don't know how to take out their own way with somebody else just to make trouble. Want me to finish the story? Well I think probably in the end something would happen in one of her malicious feelings come on her and she should be made to see that she is just acting as she does out of her own hatred for people because of her difference probably doesn't do her any good. Somebody else who does the right will probably win out in the end. (Stella, subject 19, story A-3, 1953)

The statement "she looks sort of mean, probably taking out her loneliness on everybody who would come in contact with her," is certainly a more open form of expression than one finds in the 1940 stories. Somehow the vicissitudes of life have helped her to break through the wall of repression behind which she kept locked aggressive feelings when she was younger.

There are two stories told in 1953 indicating closer relationships with the mother figure.

This would be a girl who is returning from the dance, had a wonderful time and she is coming upstairs to tell her mother all about it, I think her mother is waiting for her, and is very anxious to hear about everything she did, and I think they spend a very nice time together and she probably tells the mother about all the people who were there, just what they did there and her mother must have enjoyed waiting up for her daughter everytime she goes out, so she can hear these things, they probably make her relive some of the good times she had when she was younger and I imagine that there is a very nice relationship between them, and she is probably very happy at home. (Stella, subject 19, story B-7, 1953)

It strikes me as this girl's living with her mother. She is about to go to a dance. She is admiring herself in the mirror, and I think that her mother is probably a little sorry that her daughter is so vain. I guess she thinks she is just wonderful, and that there is nothing like her mother. She is probably thinking to herself, well she just doesn't know that things aren't always so terribly bright and eh, what difference, she is just like the other young girls. Goes to the dance and has a very wonderful time. Her mother was sort of bitter, maybe because she might have felt the same in her youth, and things might not have turned out for her as they do for her daughter who thinks they will. I imagine someday the girl feels the same as her mother, and looks at her daughter going to a dance and might have the same idea in the back of her mind. (Stella, subject 19, story B-2, 1953)

There is no parallel to these stories in 1940. (Indeed, there are only two references to mother figures in the 1940 series, one in which a mother is solicitous over a wayward son and one in which a boy expresses disappointment with his parents because they cannot send him to college.) But the 1953 stories show a high degree of identification with a mother figure. One can only surmise that there is guilt over earlier hostility toward the mother and that Stella takes pleasure in being solicitous for her mother's happiness and welfare. In the interview we are told that Stella gave up her work to be with her mother when her mother had a nervous breakdown. One can surmise again that the mother's illness precipitated her guilt over the possibility that she could have been in part responsible for her mother's illness because of her earlier hostile fantasies.

Another of the 1953 stories (A-3; see above) displays these negative feelings openly so that the foregoing speculation has some basis in fact. If one goes back to the 1940 story A-3, one notes that the same negative feeling is expressed, but that it is less elaborated and the guilt that it causes is expressed by failing a test and not through altruistic attitudes toward others, as is true in 1953.

The girl is indoors, is going to study. Another girl walks by with her best boyfriend. She decides to do something about it instead of studying her lessons. She goes out and has a squabble with this girl. She convinces the other girl to let the boy alone. The next day she fails her Latin test. She decides the boy wasn't worth it and that next time she won't bother about him. (Stella, subject 19, story A-3, 1940)

In 1953 Stella is able to face reality and does not have to disguise her feelings by using symbolic fantasy.

EXCERPT FROM THE RORSCHACH REPORT

This is an uneven, unpredictable, immature, oppositional person with poor judgment and reality contact. An underlying schizophrenic disease process has to be considered.

The neurotic defenses are both compulsive and hysterical.

She is detached from people but wants to manipulate persons. She has an ambitious drive and concern with status.

Her perception of the world is childish and eccentric. The core areas of disturbance center about her inability to deal with sexuality or with any deep and stormy feelings (aggression and passion). She has no concept of herself as a woman. Her deeper identification tends to be masculine. She feels anxious, insecure, and self-conscious in situations where her feminity is challenged and she suffers from a sense of emptiness and isolation.

There is an explosion of affect (a minor scene) that follows situations of fear or mild emotional shock—and this explosion is a defense against the strong anxiety which she feels when such explosion is not possible.

She generally feels not understood and her main wish is for protection and understanding that one would get from a family. Her secret attitude is that the world is a dangerous, bad, deceptive place.

She can be pleasant and lively but generally prefers a more quiet front.

Her aggression is expressed largely by oppositionalism and a suspicion of people. Men especially are villains.

She is likely to be a difficult person to live with. Her main pleasures come from romantic fantasies about herself and occasional exhibitionistic displays of affect.

Barbara, Subject 20

BARBARA AS AN ADOLESCENT

As a fourteen-year-old adolescent Barbara was a tomboy who played boys' games with boys, striving to be first and bossing the girls. But

Appendix A. Resumé of the Subjects

teachers called her quiet, demure, efficient, solid. One teacher called her sweet but not her sister's equal. Another found her nervous and quick-tempered. At home she was mean, headstrong, ugly, argumentative, difficult to handle, lacking in affection, and unwilling to help her mother. She took advantage of her father, who was good to her.

SYNOPSIS OF ADOLESCENT FANTASY

Her adolescent stories were long, expressive, emotional. She had a strong urge to be successful, at the top, ahead of others. She would have liked to be lax and let her studies go but feared the consequences. There was ambivalence toward mother figures but father figures were depicted as cruel, against whom there were death wishes. A masculine flavor was prominent in the stories with contempt for anything sissy or feminine. Her stories contained such sentences as "She told me the children had a pet fish and the cat had eaten the fish and when Danny went down to feed the fish it was dead" (story 7, original series); "Joe gives the policeman a dirty look and passes out" (story B-9); "Look as if they are in some sort of a mess that they have to get out of" (story 16, original series); "Mr. D.: 'Take this bottle of medicine over to Riverside Drive, this box of pills to Mrs. Greenberg, these magazines to Walnut Street, this Coca-Cola to the P.O.' Boy 'What? All for 15¢? Those places are all in different parts of town!'" (story 15, original series); "Kissed mother; wished her a happy birthday and gave her a big box of candy!" (story 40, original series). The exact significance of this anal interest is not clear, being locked up in symbolism, but there is evidently both anal erotism and anal sadism, with penis envy and castration wishes.

BARBARA AS AN ADULT

Now Barbara is a young woman of twenty-seven, unmarried, living at home with her mother and older brother. She never went to college, but graduated from high school in the upper third of the class. She is described as a good-looking, vivacious, dynamic woman having good rapport with others. After high school she had a number of office jobs and is now manager of an office for a trucking firm with two girls under her.

She is much concerned over the fact that she is not married. Her denials give away the secret when she says that she is not afraid of getting married and is not frigid. She also denies that she is dissatisfied with her sex but she wants men to know that she is as good as they. She has a quick, bad temper which she lets off frequently, and she has a tendency toward perfectionism and order.

CORRESPONDENCE BETWEEN ADOLESCENT FANTASY AND ADULT PERSONALITY

Many of these trends were foreshadowed when she was an adolescent. Her stories have a strong masculine identification and many of them resemble the stories told by young adolescent boys. Story A-4 is an example.

"Son," called a man sitting on park bench, "are you in any hurry?"
Tom: "No sir."
Man: "Would you mind going to the drugstore and getting me a pack of cigarettes?"
Tom: "All right, sir," taking the $20 bill offered him. In drugstore clerk looked at him strangely when given the bill. Asked him where he got it. Tom said from man who wanted cigarettes. Clerk said bill was counterfeit. Called for policemen to check on it. Kelly came, looked at bill. Said it was counterfeit, wanted to see man who gave it to him. Told Tom to give him cigarettes, would follow. Tom did. Man asked for change. Tom was going to say he didn't have it when the policemen came up and nabbed him. He was taken to a police station where it was discovered that he had been passing counterfeit bills. (Barbara, subject 20, story A-4, 1940)

As a woman she openly questions whether she is satisfied with her role as a woman. In her 1940 stories she definitely despises what is sissy. In story A-10 a boy and girl are passing by the fortuneteller's tent. The girl protests that she does not want to go in—"I am afraid to go in there"—to which the boy retorts "Aw! Why not? You girls are such sissies." And in story A-7 a boy who is asked by his mother to do an errand at the grocery store retorts: "Gee, that's sissy stuff."

As an adolescent Barbara was concerned with her appearance, as illustrated by story B-2.

Janet's mother brought home a lovely new dress for her to wear to party. Janet thought it wasn't as nice as other girls' dresses. Dissatisfied with it. Janet's mother gave her some money, said if she wasn't satisfied with what she brought home she could go and shop for herself. Went into one store, not satisfied. Went to another, found nothing there. At end of day wound up by bringing home same blue dress mother had. Was so tired

Appendix A. Resumé of the Subjects

she went right to bed. Mother said, "Now you know how I feel when I shop for you." (Barbara, subject 20, story B-2, 1940)

And in story A-3 a girl pitied herself because she was sick and felt that others did not like her as she did not have fine clothes and a rich home. Actually, as a young woman she is a "smart" dresser, stylish but in good taste.

Perhaps her 1940 stories give some inkling as to her later sexual attitudes and difficulties. The fortuneteller in story A-10 told the following "fortune."

I see a large ocean with waves. On it there is a boat, a very large boat. On this boat there are many people. Out of this crowd I single two people which are you. There will be a great misfortune in your life. I see a car driving along a highway at night. In this car there is a man hurrying home to his wife and child. It is raining and the highway is very wet. All of a sudden, the car skids and jumps off a steep embankment. This man is your father. He is killed instantly. (Barbara, subject 20, story A-10, 1940)

This excerpt from story A-10 should be considered along with story B-10.

Virginia, 15. Lived on farm with stepfather. Cruel to her. Wanted her to stay home and cook for him. Kept her home for a year. Someone heard about it. Reported it to Board of Education. Said she would have to go to school. Father tried to keep her from going. Only time she could call her own was at school. At home feared stepfather would beat her. Knew he didn't have to stay on farm—had money. Heard him counting his money when she was in bed. He was killed in an accident. She went to orphan asylum. Was told she was to get all the money. So she could go to school wherever she wanted. Though she knew she should feel sorry for stepfather, she wasn't at all. (Barbara, subject 20, story B-10, 1940)

Her father in real life was described as a quick-tempered man who would "blow up" with anyone he really knew, such as family and friends. She identified closely with him. In her interview she stated that "she would want a man to be something like a boss, someone who would put his foot down sometimes and keep her in line. She would not want a man who would give in to her too easily." Apparently, then, she fantasies a man in sex as being somewhat sadistic, but at the same time there is sexual rivalry and competition and she has castration fantasies and death wishes against the male. In her interview it was said: "She claims that she likes a good fight or a good argument once in a while regardless of what it is about . . . she claims that she often gets in fights with fellows just to stir things up . . . she has never wanted to be a man but she wants them to know that she is as good as they are." But one of her stories indicates that she fantasies the man as weak.

Man traveled about, didn't care to work. Gave name to employment agencies and waited for them to call him. Would work just long enough to get something to eat and then would quit. Then when he went back to agency they said they couldn't give him any more jobs if he didn't do the ones he got satisfactorily. In one town worked for 4 weeks. Then was too lazy to work again. Went to his daughter's home and said he had to rest a bad ankle. She didn't know he was shiftless, wanted him to stay. He demanded everything just so until son-in-law told him to go to work. Had to start work over again. (Barbara, subject 20, story B-6, 1940)

The man in this story is weak and shiftless; he has to be told to go to work. In this way she fantasies herself as having the whip hand over the male. Actually, when her father died he left a number of debts and the whole family had to pitch in to straighten out his financial affairs.

CHANGE IN FANTASY: BARBARA, SUBJECT 20

Fantasy theme	Amount of change	Fantasy theme	Amount of change
Crime against property	−3	Positive outcome	+4
Hostility	−3	Passivity—erotic	+3
Neuroticism	+4	Pleasure	+3

CHANGE IN FANTASY

The 1953 stories repeat many of the themes of the 1940 stories. There is an emphasis on the masculine and at the same time a contempt for the male. Story B-10 in 1953 illustrates this trend.

This is a young couple, farmers. They are in the village. The young wife is quite a church-going person, whereas the husband only went because his parents made him; but since he has been out on his own he hasn't—eh, he's given up going to church, and they had quite a few arguments about attending church. She feels that they should go and he has been very lazy, says, if you want to go, go ahead. I'm staying home. I have got work to do, and she has always gone off by herself. This Sunday I think she is going to lay down the law and bring things to a head; and told him that when they have children she wants them to be raised up to be good church-going people and that the only way that they will be church-going is that their parents should be the same way. She was tired of going to church by herself. She wants him to go too. She said it was something he should do or something he should want to do, and she popped off. She had gone ahead, hoping that he would follow; but she has time. She would wait. He thought it over and realized that she is right and that he just uses work as an excuse not to make the long trip into town, and he followed. They end up by every Sunday going to church and making their children to be good church-going people. (Barbara, subject 20, story B-10, 1953)

There is a noticeable rise in the theme of marriage. Apparently Barbara at the age of twenty-seven fears this as life's most intense dilemma. There is both a desire for marriage and a fear and rejection of it. There is confusion over sex role and conflict between career and marriage. She fantasies the pleasure of being single, yet also in a vague way she sees bliss in marriage. Two stories will illustrate these fantasies. There is no doubt but that Barbara puts into these stories persistent daydreams and musings with which she is much preoccupied.

I can't find much here. [Pause.] Well, here's a girl and she has the feeling that she doesn't know what she wants out of life. She doesn't know whether she wants to keep on with her studies, or go out and get a job, to get married, she's stuck and can't make up her mind what she wants to do. I think she quits college, gets a job, probably a secretarial job of some kind, she's pretty good at it, for a while I think she sticks at it. She enjoys her work, and she finally gets married, when she's 35, and lives happily ever after. (Barbara, subject 20, Story A-5, 1953)

Oh, there's nothing on it. [You can make up your own story.] Oh, oh! If I couldn't make up a story with a picture, what am I going to do with a blank one. [Laughs] That's a picture of my mind right now—blank. Are you kidding? Do I have to make up a story? [Laughs] [Yes, there are no restrictions; you can make up any kind of story you want.] This is the story of a young working girl. Her ambition has always been to go to the Hawaiian Islands. She's thought about it for several years—not seriously. But whenever people asked her where she wanted to go, she said she thought the Hawaiian Islands would be a nice place. The more she thought of it, she figured other people do it, why can't I. So she saved some money and took a trip across country to Hawaii. She had a wonderful time surfboard riding, going to the native feasts, and everything. And instead of going back home she stayed there she liked it so much. She had a little home of her own, and a lot of friends. She finally meets a man that she loves very much. They marry and live happily ever after. (Barbara, subject 20, story B-11, 1953)

There is a noticeable increase in positive outcomes in the 1953 stories, but this is not the typical defense that tries to soften anxieties aroused by thoughts of aggression; rather is it indulgence in unrealistic daydreaming. Apparently, since she will not permit herself to enjoy sexual pleasures in real life, she substitutes by fantasying them.

Themes of hostility and crimes against property that were present in 1940 do not appear in 1953. The 1940 crime stories have a distinct passive quality. The subject of the story does not commit a crime but is the innocent victim of a crime. Story B-3 told in 1940 illustrates this.

John was walking in front of bank. Suddenly heard shooting, didn't know what to make of it. Three men came dashing out of bank, to car at curb. Policeman rushed up and fell shot through the heart. John felt something sharp push into his side. Turned around, saw man holding a gun. Man pushed him into car and they drove off. Was blindfolded and he was tied. He was so surprised he couldn't let out a sound. Heard men talking but couldn't tell what they said. A black bag was thrown from the front seat to the back. Man in back seat opened the bag. In bag was a lot of green paper, size of dollar bills. Looking more closely at it it dawned on him—the National Bank had been robbed. "I guess they figure," said John, "that the police won't come after them while they've got me." They drove for nearly four hours. Just as John was beginning to fall asleep the car stopped short. Four men jumped out of the car but got no further. At that moment the police closed in. Soon after this, John was in police station telling story to reporter. When asked how he felt during the ride, he replied, "I wouldn't take another one of those rides for anything in the world. Gosh I was scared. I thought they'd kill me." (Barbara, subject 20, story B-3, 1940)

Story B-10 from 1940, given above, illustrates very clearly the counter-hostility that these fantasied threats aroused.

One can speculate that these stories represent a sadistic conception of sexual relations. With increasing maturity these fantasies have come closer to reality, and as Barbara is confronted with the reality of sexual relations with men, to which she reacts with fear and revulsion, her antagonisms increase toward any man who approaches her. In short, there is less need to fantasy reactions of danger toward sex relations when they must be reacted to in reality.

EXCERPT FROM THE RORSCHACH REPORT

This record shows many positive qualities. This woman is intelligent, with much psychic and physical vitality and buoyancy. She has the capacity for good social and personal adjustment. Her judgment and reality contact are good. She has a capacity to relate to people and to

Appendix A. Resumé of the Subjects

empathize with them. She has a capacity for good emotional relationships with people and probably has many friends. She shows a ready capacity for role-taking and a flexibility in shifting roles.

There is, however, a severe curtailment of self-assertive energy. There is discrepancy between endowment and self-imposed constriction and a meager use of her capacities.

Her identification is mainly feminine but she cannot function sexually as a woman. There is fear of heterosexual relationships and a fear of her own potential aggressiveness and destructiveness and there is need to keep out of deep and permanent involvements which would be threatening and challenging to her femininity.

There is a tendency to phallus worship and a secret penis envy and wish to have been a man. Her self-concept is a derogatory one and not feminine. She finds it difficult to give herself completely to any emotion mainly out of fear of becoming emotionally dependent and highly anxious. Her deep attachments to people are likely to have a transitory quality. Her fear of losing love is the result of her feeling that she has little to give as a woman and therefore could not expect to hold anyone.

In repressing her aggressive energy she has accumulated a certain amount of hostility and feeling of rejection toward people. As a result she makes herself not as pleasant or as yielding as she could be. She is basically a warm and intense person—capable of loving and hating —but by holding herself in she has become dissociated from her genuine emotions. She is capable of a much richer and more rewarding emotional life if she could accept her femininity and her sexuality more.

Natalie, Subject 21

NATALIE AS AN ADOLESCENT

As a thirteen-year-old girl Natalie was quiet, demure, unobtrusive, inhibited, and emotionally underdeveloped. She was not well known by her teachers because she was quiet and withdrawn. Some thought that she was dull. Others complained that they could not hear her when she recited. Her mother, who was dominating, was disturbed about Natalie and wanted to force her to show more initiative. Natalie was on good terms with her quiet father. Natalie spent much time in a fantasy world with imaginary companions, planning wardrobes for her dolls. She had a brother and a sister but did not get on well with her brother.

SYNOPSIS OF ADOLESCENT FANTASY

Her 1940 stories are another set that were somewhat meager. Anxiety was a prominent theme. There was anxiety over being kidnaped, of losing mother, of losing job; there were fantasies that life is dull, drab, and all drudgery. Mother figures entered many of the stories and anxiety was projected onto the mother. There was need for mother's approval and the fantasy of the good mother. Still, there were stories that expressed the wish for popularity and the desire to marry. Natalie showed a number of these sexual implications in her stories. Many of the stories were concerned over possible exposure if she should become more active (see *Adolescent Fantasy*, pp. 151–52).

NATALIE AS AN ADULT

In 1953 Natalie impressed the interviewer as being a particularly drab, lethargic, colorless, matter-of-fact, unassertive person with low energy level and a low, soft voice. She spoke fluently but did not elaborate.

As a girl she wanted to be a nurse, and after graduating from high school went into nursing school. She became a graduate nurse in 1948. She specialized in obstretics, pediatric, and psychiatric nursing, but did not care for operating-room experience. She has worked as a psychiatric nurse and likes working with mental patients and being kind to people. She continued to nurse after she married until she became pregnant. She would still like to work as a nurse and hopes someday to be able to teach nursing.

Natalie married a psychiatric aide, but since the pay was low he has changed to factory work. The husband is afraid of anything that might be called feminine. He has a severe temper and would like to be a tobacco farmer, or just go hunting and fishing. She claims that she is more intellectual than he. He has no interest in anything cultural and does not care what is going on in the world. He is reported to be a jealous man. She would like to bring up her children to appreciate the finer things in life, but she gets no encouragement from her husband. She has two children, a boy and girl, but finds life dull. She is again pregnant.

Appendix A. Resumé of the Subjects

CORRESPONDENCE BETWEEN ADOLESCENT FANTASY
AND ADULT PERSONALITY

Natalie continues in adult life the same characteristics which she adopted as a child in response to her dominating mother and easygoing father. In her 1940 stories there were themes of the dullness of life. Story A-5 is typical.

> Girl has come out of school in June. Will be out all summer. Wishes it were September instead of June. She thinks of all the things she likes to do in school and wishes it were school time. She never went anywheres in the summer so it wasn't much fun for her. (Natalie, subject 21, story A-5, 1940)

Now Natalie complains that her life is humdrum, drudging along in "the same old groove, day in and day out." Apparently this is an attitude that she adopted in childhood in response to and as a protest against her mother, who tried to force her to be more spontaneous and to have more initiative.

Several stories illustrate how her attitude toward her mother has helped to give her a characteristic mode of adjusting to the world. Story B-4, for instance, lets the deep-seated hostility slip through.

> This woman has two daughters, one her own and one her second husband's daughter. Hers is beautiful, other one is not. There is something on tonight and the mother is letting her daughter go but is keeping the other one home to do dishes, etcetera. Other girl wishes her mother was alive so she would not have to live with this selfish woman. (Natalie, subject 21, story B-4, 1940)

One naturally thinks of identifying her with the girl who is permitted to go to the party, but probably she is identifying in just as real a sense with the girl who stays home, for this serves as a defense and a protection against dangerous sexual fantasies. One also sees mother hostility and rivalry here, and there is probably some borrowed erotic satisfaction of a more remote nature. But story B-3 shows that a characteristic mode of adjustment is to forget self and yield to the importunate demands of the mother.

> Boy is walking to school with friends. He is bad, he is smoking. Friend tells him to smoke because it's nice. Boy said he wouldn't, what would his mother think. Friend says he never thinks of what he wants to do, and what his mother wants him to do. (Natalie, subject 21, story B-3, 1940)

Story B-8 portrays the conflict that Natalie lives out.

At a dance. Man is just asking girl to dance. Girl is too tired. Man offers to take her home. Girl says it's too early to go home. He says to sit the dance out, so that she'll be rested and will be able to dance the next dance. (Natalie, subject 21, story B-8, 1940)

In this story the girl obviously wants to dance because she says it is too early to go home. But at the same time she can't yield to pleasure and gives her characteristic excuse of being tired. Similarly, even now she wants to be wanted by her husband but she cannot yield for fear of disappointment. Her resolution is to project her difficulties on to her husband, to complain that he is not interested in anything cultural and to maintain that he is inferior to her. The interviewer reports that "Natalie's life is rather lacking in emotional and aesthetic satisfactions due largely to her husband's personality and meager range of interests."

CHANGE IN FANTASY: NATALIE, SUBJECT 21

Fantasy theme	Amount of change
Negative outcome	+4
Anger	+3
Anxiety	−3

CHANGE IN FANTASY

There is much in common with the stories that Natalie told in 1940 and those in 1953. There is reiteration of the theme of the dullness and drabness of life. Story B-10 illustrates this trend.

This is a mining village in Wales. This girl is walking home from work. She is tired and discouraged with life in this little dinky town, very drabby, and it's the same old thing every day, you just go to work and come home and eat and go to bed and the next day does the same thing over again, and back of her is a miner, he is following along and he feels the same way, just the same old thing. This grimy little town, that goes on and on the same old way. (Natalie, subject 21, story B-10, 1953)

The statistical count, however, shows three shifts. The most prominent is the increase in stories with unfavorable endings. This may be coupled with an increase in stories including the theme of anger. It is quite clear that Natalie is able to express negative feelings more openly in her fantasy, which may be taken as a sign of gain. One can surmise that no longer living under her parents' roof and with her mother, she is more free and has gained courage to express her hostility

Appendix A. Resumé of the Subjects

more openly. There is still a lot of projection. She states that she visits her parents about twice a month.

Boy works each day, comes in after a hard day. Sees a shadow and thinks it is his mother. But it looks like a man's. He gets frightened and walks right up to it. He discovers it is his mother and she just had her hair cut. (Natalie, subject 21, story A-6, 1940)

Young husband here he has come home late in the evening. He has been out with the fellows and he is late meeting his wife. He tries to sneak up stairs but she is already down there waiting for him. They have a fume about it. (Natalie, subject 21, story A-6, 1953)

In story A-6 in 1940 Natalie evidences her fear of her mother and then introduces the theme of castration. One may surmise that her listlessness and drabness is in some way connected with her castration fantasy applied to herself. But in the 1953 story there is a shift from the castration theme to one of conflict and retaliation—"they have a fume about it."

Girl is in Asbury Park—is walking through amusement house. Mother is behind her, doesn't want to go to amusement house, wants to go to the movies. Girl looking into funny looking glass, mother grows impatient. Tells her mother she will go with her as soon as she sees herself in all the mirrors. (Natalie, subject 21, story B-2, 1940)

The woman in the back looks like a prison matron, and this young girl is just going out on probation. She has civilian clothes on for the first time in a long time, and she is admiring herself in the mirror, but the matron has doubts as to whether the girl will turn out all right. [How does she make out?] Not so good, doesn't look as though she really cares, the only thing she cares about is how she looks. Why do these characters always look so mad? In all of the pictures they look that way. (Natalie, subject 21, story B-2, 1953)

In story B-2 told in 1940 Natalie depicts a girl and her mother in conflict. The girl is fascinated by distorted images of herself. The girl does not argue with her mother but says she will come when she is ready. But in 1953 by projecting her feelings on to the picture Natalie really expresses anger. This is coupled with a decrease in anxiety in the stories, which is a natural accompaniment to the increase in capacity to express and feel anger and hostility.

EXCERPT FROM THE RORSCHACH REPORT

The Rorschach indicates a mild schizophrenic disease process in an extremely immature, inadequate person. There is a tenuous psychic equilibrium and her contact with people and reality is very meager. Her judgment is poor, her reasoning infantile.

She is basically very oppositional, showing this through a passive resistance. She is capable of being stubborn and emotionally stupid. There is an underlying sporadic, unpredictable explosiveness and quick anger that is short-lived.

She is orally dependent—demanding. She is inadequate as a woman. There is evidence of traumatization and narcissistic injury as a woman. She seems to have suffered some very bad experience which has maimed her emotionally—perhaps a psychotic episode.

She is in a low-grade depression giving her a feeling of inner deadness and a sense of inadequacy, confusion, and the "uselessness" of life.

She has a very feminine façade, showing exhibitionistic tendencies, and wants to be looked at and admired. The superficial heterosexual adjustment seems adequate. Psychically she feels damaged and hurt as a female and probably suffers from a castration complex. She is likely to use hysterical symptoms to discharge conflict and tension. The ideational energy and capacity for fantasy living is low, as is the libidinal and aggressive energy. Genuine contacts with people are actually impossible. Her affect is shallow, superficial, and frequently strained and inappropriate.

Mabel, Subject 22

MABEL AS AN ADOLESCENT

Mabel as a fourteen-year-old junior high school student was called 100 percent normal. Her teacher described her as a sweet girl, demure, cooperative, popular, serious, neat, but one who did not work up to capacity. Her mother spoke of her as healthy, cheerful, sweet, poised, active, precocious, mischievous. She did not make advances. Her father was strict and punishing. An older brother, on whom the mother doted, was in college. She wanted to be a doctor but her parents did not approve and wanted her to prepare for a musical career. As a child she gave theatrical performances and was musical, but did not like to practice.

SYNOPSIS OF ADOLESCENT FANTASY

One outstanding characteristic of Mabel's stories was her fantasies of vulgarity—which may be contrasted in real life with her sweetness and demureness. "After all her excursions into romance and glamor, when she sees only one picture left, she retreats back into her protective encasement of demureness" (*Adolescent Fantasy*, p. 157). In the last story she runs home and locks herself in. There could be no more graphic expression of repression and reaction formation.

Coupled with these fantasies of vulgarity, romance, and glamor was the need to be successful. One recurrent theme was negative feeling toward the father—father figures were mean, stingy, punitive, brutal, and there were death wishes toward the father. Coupled with these themes, however, were Oedipal themes of being left alone with a father figure after the mother was disposed of. There were themes of leaving home and looking for parent substitutes. There was also a story which indicates castration anxiety.

MABEL AS AN ADULT

At age twenty-seven Mabel is married and living comfortably in a four-bedroom house with two TV sets and a full-time maid. She is described as businesslike, sophisticated, smartly dressed. She has two children, both girls. She likes to play golf and cards. She has had one miscarriage and has since been depressed. She gets angry when her husband complains about her spending money. She describes him as even-tempered.

CORRESPONDENCE BETWEEN ADOLESCENT FANTASY AND ADULT PERSONALITY

Mabel's 1953 interview tended to be strictly factual and it did not reveal much of the person. The fact that she lived in a well-furnished house in a good neighborhood and had a full-time maid seems to reflect the emphasis on success which was present in her 1940 stories (story A-8, 1940).

In her 1940 stories she fantasied being left alone without a father (B-7). She married a man who travels and she had a miscarriage on one occasion while her husband was away. Story B-6 tells of a boy who gets angry when his father says he can't go out. Mabel says that she gets angry when she is crossed by her husband over expenses.

Boy was eating supper while there was company. His father thought boy didn't have as good manners as he should have. Father says he can't go out. Boy has somewhere to go. Gets angry, goes to his room and sits down. Family goes out. He climbs out the window and goes out against his father's wishes. (Mabel, subject 22, story B-6, 1940)

CHANGE IN FANTASY: MABLE, SUBJECT 22

Fantasy theme	Amount of change
Negative outcome	−5
Escape	−3
Positive outcome	+3

CHANGE IN FANTASY

The 1953 stories repeat many of the themes of the 1940 stories. There are the strivings for success, Oedipal conflict, fear of being alone with father, leaving home for parent substitutes, sibling rivalry. Apparently her life experiences have not succeeded in modifying her fantasy life to any great extent.

One change is from negative to positive endings to her stories. Perhaps the most dramatic of these is B-8.

Man is talking to his daughter about a job she wants to take. He doesn't want her to take it because it's in the worst section in town. They are quite hard up. She takes the job. Her father disowns her and she leaves town. (Mabel, subject 22, story B-8, 1940)

This girl has just told her father that she wants to get married. Her father thinks she's too young and not ready for marriage. He wants her to finish school and wait 'til she's sure. She's a good girl and has always listened to her father when he's given her advice. She does listen to him and she's very thankful that she does. She finds it would all have been a mistake. She finishes school and meets someone else who she's much more in love with and does marry. (Mabel, subject 22, story B-8, 1953)

In 1940 the daughter in the story does not take her father's advice, her father disowns her, and she leaves town. In 1953 she does take her father's advice and marries a man she is in love with. Apparently now that she has left her parental home for a home of her own her hostility and resistance to her parents have softened and she is able to accept

Appendix A. Resumé of the Subjects

their point of view more readily. This may be juxtaposed with stories B-10 and B-11.

The nice quiet country town on a Sunday. This young girl is coming home from church. She takes a long walk on the way home—out to the country. She loves living there. It's quiet and peaceful. She takes care of her father. Her mother died when she was a baby, and she's devoted her life to taking care of her father. (Mabel, subject 22, story B-10, 1953)

All I can see here is my own future. I see children playing happily with no worries or thoughts in the children's minds. But the parents are preparing for their future in watching them grow. They get a good education for them and see them get married and see them have families of their own. (Mabel, subject 22, story B-11, 1953)

Here we see Mabel changing her role of defying her father to taking care of him. Then story B-11 shows that the shift or displacement is toward her own children. The dynamics here are probably too subtle to be read from the stories alone, but one can surmise that guilt has changed the adolescent death wishes to fantasies of nurturance displaced toward her own children. This indicates one of the healthy shifts in fantasy from the negative fantasies of adolescence to the positive fantasies of parenthood.

Themes of escape which were present in stories B-6 (above) and B-10 in 1940 were not present in 1953. The need to escape from restraint and supervision of the parental home seems to have vanished since she has left home. It is stated that her husband is a mild man. Since she did not marry a man who repeats the father pattern she is able to drop her fantasies of escape.

EXCERPT FROM THE RORSCHACH REPORT

A limited, immature person with poor capacity to relate to others. She is concerned with prestige and status as a means of compensating for lack of inner strength. Little drive or energy to do something about her social ambition or to be spontaneous and free.

Low-grade depression. She has feelings of inferiority and strivings for superiority. There are signs of anxiety. There is an unconscious delegation of responsibility to others. She depends on status or position to carry her through.

Her conception of people is on a very immature (little-girl) level. She feels inadequate as a sexual partner and sees men as castrative—based on fear of men.

She has a destructive, aggressive drive, exhibited by a sharp temper. Outside of anger she has little capacity for strong emotion. She wants to be taken care of and has little ability to adjust to the needs of others.

Margaret, Subject 24

MARGARET AS AN ADOLESCENT

As a sixteen-year-old high school girl Margaret, an only child, was charming, pleasant, popular, with a ready smile, full of life and fun. But she was also unreliable, irresponsible, the class clown, with plans that she could not carry out. She was large in stature, neat, careful about her appearance, but boyish and fond of athletics. At sixteen she was engaged. She identified with her father, who was ambitious for her as he had wanted a son. She was her father's pride and one may suppose that he would like to have her compensate for what he has not been able to achieve (he was at one time a circus clown). He had made plans for her future.

SYNOPSIS OF ADOLESCENT FANTASY

In her 1940 stories there was strong identification with as well as hostility toward father figures, and hostility toward mother figures. There was conflict between rebellion and authority. There was dissatisfaction with home and a desire to get away. Much personal inadequacy was shown in the stories as the characters tended to be masochistic and lacked self-confidence, were shy, lonely, and felt rejected. But there was a desire to be attractive and popular with peers as a defense against anxiety. Joking was a disguised way of expressing hostility. Marriage was a way out. She was attracted to shy men. Oedipal themes were prominent. In stories the mother was dead and the female figure lived with the father. Or she felt the mother's jealousy and would have liked to hurt or kill the mother, but was afraid.

MARGARET AS AN ADULT

As a woman she is robust, healthy looking, easygoing, friendly, warm, stable, and solid. She finished high school and wished to be a nurse but soon married. While her husband was away during the war she worked as an IBM operator but later gave up working because of her pregnancy. She hopes for a girl. She tends to be optimistic. She loves animals and has a dog, a cat, birds, and fish.

Julia, Subject 25

JULIA AS AN ADOLESCENT

As a sixteen-year-old girl Julia, an example of flaming youth, had long red hair, bright clothes, and flashy jewelry. She was called the best dresser in her homeroom and had quantities of clothes which her aunt made for her. She was not very bright in school and did poor school work. She was spoiled, undisciplined, and keen on boys and dancing. She went with an older group. She had one younger sister and several cousins. She did not write an autobiography and her parents would not consent to be interviewed. In her adolescent interview she appeared reserved and lacking in energy. Julia was concerned over marital difficulties between her parents and felt that she was left out of her parents' affections. She identified with her mother in wearing striking clothes. She tended to neglect school work in favor of clothes and self-exhibition.

SYNOPSIS OF ADOLESCENT FANTASY

Her adolescent stories depicted characters that were socially insecure, passive, dependent, and narcissistic. There was something selfish and self-centered about the actions of the characters. A girl married only for what she might get.

There were themes of self-elevation and status. One story told of a girl who was bright, successful in school, and looking ahead to college. She thought of moving upward in terms of acquiring education and money. But there was also a passive theme of not wanting to work hard for what one gets. There were also themes of being socially popular.

Father figures were seen as mean, punitive, lacking in understanding. The father was expected to give status through wealth and education.

JULIA AS AN ADULT

As a twenty-nine-year-old woman, Julia is tall, well-dressed, friendly, relaxed, with dreamy eyes—not assertive or vivacious. She did not go to college. After eighteen months in the Waves and a variety of secretarial jobs she is happily married and has a two-year-old daughter. At one time she served as a model in a department store.

She has feminine interests and is dramatically inclined. She is close to her parents but gets irritated at her mother-in-law. Although a devout Catholic, she would postpone having another child until they can improve themselves financially. She is not aggressive and likes to work with other people.

Olive, Subject 27

OLIVE AS AN ADOLESCENT

As an eighteen-year-old Welsh girl Olive, who was the youngest of six girls, was one of a family of whom only two were her own sisters. She was very reserved and taciturn to the point of depression. She was drab, sallow, stooped in posture, tight and tense in her behavior. Olive spent long weekends doing housework and caring for a small child. Her whole family was tense, reserved, hardworking. Teachers characterized her as nervous, soreheaded, resenting criticism, a disruptive influence, reticent and not outgoing.

SYNOPSIS OF ADOLESCENT FANTASY

Her adolescent stories, told with difficulty, contained themes of insecurity, anxiety, and depression. There was anxiety about school, one's work, the future. Characters saw a life of hardship, poverty, being aggressed against. There were themes of high standards of conduct and disapproval of one's inability to measure up to these standards. This led to feelings of unworthiness, inadequacy, disillusionment, guilt, and masochistic fantasies. She was concerned with appearance and wished to be popular and vivacious in order to be attractive to boys, yet she feared being a disappointment to others. There was a desire to help and console others.

She placed stress on intellectual values and described characters as intelligent, deep thinkers, poetically inclined. One character had a compulsive need to finish reading an uninteresting book.

There was sibling rivalry, which played an important role in Olive's life. Stories B-1 and B-3 illustrate not only the sibling rivalry, but Olive's method of repressing her hostile feelings by discontent and impersonality.

Appendix A. Resumé of the Subjects

Why would someone paint a picture like this? The older boy seems to have a grudge against something. He is looking at the younger boy with a vicious eye. The younger boy is not at all interested about the other. He seems to be listening attentively or is thinking about something very deeply. (Olive, subject 27, story B-3, 1940)

Young boy is leaving the school building, with an attitude that he is going to hit someone. His grudge seems to be very deep. Probably someone that said something and he, being in a high position, had been highly insulted and therefore his standards were lowered. But he is thinking if he hits anyone it will mar his high standards and that he will be worse off than by just letting it go. (Olive, subject 27, story B-1, 1940)

OLIVE AS AN ADULT

As a thirty-one-year-old woman Olive impressed the interviewer as being robust, drab, colorless, but restrained, repressed, and inexpressive. She spoke in a monotone and was hesitant in speech.

After high school she worked as a salesgirl and factory operator. After two years she married a factory worker and is now pregnant. She continued to work for eleven years after her marriage.

She has limited intellectual ability but expressed vague aspirations about getting a college education. She believes she is more intellectual than her husband.

She has the blues occasionally and feels sorry for herself. She believes that children should be brought up more strictly.

CORRESPONDENCE BETWEEN ADOLESCENT FANTASY AND ADULT PERSONALITY

Some of Olive's 1940 stories seem almost prophetic of the kind of person she is today and the kind of life she lives. Story A-10 is a good example.

Wonder why she chose to come to the fortuneteller. Why is her brother with her? Maybe it is not her brother. Information must be very sad from expression on her face. I wonder what the future was—death or some other misleading misfortune. Why did she choose to bring this boy along? Maybe they were supposed to get married and they want to see what their future plans would be. Fortuneteller said they could not get married. Very mysterious. Someone was going to distrust them. Wonder what they are thinking about. She seems to be very poor. Hands look as though she had gone through many hardships. (Olive, subject 27, story A-10, 1940)

In this story the subject looks sad. "She seems to be very poor. Hands look as though she had gone through many hardships." One wonders if there is not a compulsive, neurotic nature to her own drab life of moderate circumstances which is on the border of hardship.

Many of Olive's openly expressed thoughts about herself in 1953 correspond in detail with her adolescent fantasy, but these bear little relationship with her actual life condition. Today she fantasies herself as an intellectual person—as more intellectual than her husband because she reads *Look* magazine and one book a year. In 1940 she told the following story (A-3).

Mary sitting by the window. Her attention is drawn by a couple seeming to be interested in each other, making Mary think, "I can find someone interested in me." I wonder what the book is she is reading. It isn't a very interesting book because she is not so pleased with it. She is only half-way through. She has a wonderful atmosphere around her. The book is uninteresting. "I wonder if I shall finish it, I don't know, I might as well. Gosh, I wish I was that couple, they seem so happy. Well, I still have to finish this book." (Olive, subject 27, story A-3, 1940)

This story not only emphasizes her desire to be intellectual, but suggests some of the dynamics. Here she expresses a conflict between her aspirations and her accomplishments. This disappointment in reality makes her depressed and she expresses this disappointment in her appearance. However, these are probably symbolic aspirations and standards, symbolic of a deeper source of futility in her competition with her sisters and stepsisters. In 1953 she still expresses this same conflict. Stories A-1 and B-4 express this sense of inferiority and inadequacy.

The boy's attitude seems to be—"Shall I enter or not?" Probably some of his old friends that come to this school told him so many tales that he hesitates to enter. He probably is a good sport and is willing to take whatever comes to him from the older members. But why should he hesitate? (I forgot what I was going to say.) On his mind he has some things which he can't quite figure. Probably there are some friends in this school—he is afraid will take advantage of him because he is entering as a new boy. He is thinking about the storybook he read of Tom Brown's school days, where Tom enters into Rugby and is taking an awful punishment. He knew the boys of that time were glad to have a new boy whom they could take advantage of. Seeing that this is so long ago he made up his mind he would take what was coming to him and become a good sport. (Olive, subject 27, story A-1, 1940)

Mary stood behind her mother and her sister with a long face and a perplexed mind. She could not figure out why she never went any place and her younger sister who was so pretty was always invited. She thought that the boys did not care for looks, keeping in mind she wasn't pretty but for a good sport and one who would like to do things the other person liked. She couldn't estimate herself on these two quetsions, but in her sister she found these very common. She was full of pep and never thinking of herself always agreed to do the things that everyone wanted. This was a great difference between the two sisters and she found out that if she put a little pep in herself she would probably also be invited. She could not understand why her mother would favor her younger sister and always leave her in the dark. She found this extremely so just today when her sister Jane was going to a dance and her mother was so very proud of her and encouraged her and told her to have a very nice time. She seemed to be so pleased with her that there seemed to be a great change in her nature from the usual and everyday routine. She always heard that her mother never favored anyone but somehow found this to be a different day. (Olive, subject 27, story B-4, 1940)

There is a suggestion in story B-4 that basically her depression stems from the attitude of her stepmother, and perhaps the fantasy that she has been abandoned by her own mother.

CHANGE IN FANTASY: OLIVE, SUBJECT 27

Fantasy theme	Amount of change
Feminine identification	−3
Wishful thinking	+4
Guilt	+3

CHANGE IN FANTASY

There is much similarity between 1953 stories and 1940 stories. There is great depression, anxiety, and social insecurity. There is a poor self-concept—characters see themselves as helpless and victimized; they feel ignored and rejected by others. Life is weary and dull. One character is bored with being a housewife. They are passive and dependent; one would like to change but is so indecisive, perplexed, and anxious that she cannot venture out on her own.

If anything the stories have become less realistic and there is greater indulgence in fantasy. In 1940 the stories reflect despair; but in 1953 there creeps in unrealistic daydreaming. Story B-1, 1940 (given above), and 1953, illustrates this.

The gentleman is walking out the door. He looks rather weary. He's going to his job. His job is not very exciting—he seems to be shuffling his feet. He's just a young beginner at his trade. He is not a woodworker as yet, just an apprentice and he seems that he's never going to become a star in his job. He seems to be walking toward his job a little uncomfortably being as how each day he has to pace himself and stay within what he is instructed to do until he, in his own mind, sees what a woodworker can do. He has great plans in his own mind but being as he's suppressed by his superiors it's a task for him to go in every day. He's just biding his time hoping that it will soon end and they will allow him to do what he is imagining. He has huge ideas of building a beautiful home—the interior of a home—but, as yet, he cannot fulfill his own ideas. In his own mind, he is planning and he has it down on paper and as soon as they release him from his apprenticeship he will go and fulfill his ideas. (Olive, subject 27, story B-1, 1953)

This change may be the result of the continuance of her dismal style of life and her retreat from the struggle against it into the false satisfaction of her inner fantasies.

There was guilt in the 1940 stories, but it was expressed more in action than in so many words. The guilt that Olive feels can be verbalized better in 1953.

Dear Aunt Ruth: I'm glad I'm going to the junior prom. I feel so elegant all dressed up, but along side of me stands my little cousin, Bess, who feels that she would like to go, but being that she is a youngster, two years my junior, and won't be able to attend the dance until the future, makes me feel very bad going by myself. We've been playmates for a long time and I would like her to be with me at all huge occasions, but it's something that bars us from joining all the occasions. She is two years younger which means that I will be ahead of her in most of the scholastic debuts. She seems very forlorn and would like to be along with me. I just don't feel like going to this occasion being that we're always together. I wish she would occupy herself right now and I would go with a lighter heart. She makes me feel as though it were my fault that I'm going to a dance and she has to stay home, but I guess she'll get over it soon as I leave for the dance and she'll probably realize that, in time to come, she will be just as happy as I am this evening. (Olive, subject 27, story B-4, 1953)

This story reveals with clarity that Olive's problem stems from rivalry and competition with her sisters, and she expresses guilt from the hostility that she feels toward them. Here again the vicissitudes of life permit her to admit her feelings more openly. She has grown to be less afraid, to a slight degree, of her own aggression.

EXCERPT FROM THE RORSCHACH REPORT

An aggressive, exhibitionistic, emotionally seriously disturbed person. Little sensitivity to the needs of others and little insight into herself.

Lively, likable, hysteric with aggression as the main drive. Persona is animated, lively, and pleasant. Aggressiveness is competitive, grabbing, and possessive. Behavior not predictable or consistent. She is overambitious with a vague desire to manipulate the social environment. Her main goal is to display herself, to get attention and admiration. Feeling of being caged up and lacking the ability genuinely to express herself and find satisfaction as a human being. Repression of sexual energy and limited concept of her sex role in life. She sees herself as a decorative rather than as a functional person.

She tries to oversexualize all situations and to handle them through reductive exhibitionism. Overemphasis on femininity. She has little capacity to be sexually feminine, soft, or yielding. Her actual aggressive energy is always too close to the surface.

There is intellectual blocking due to anxiety, conflict over her exhibitionism and aggression, and some slight degree of depression.

Celia, Subject 28

CELIA AS AN ADOLESCENT

As an adolescent Celia was a pretty, Catholic Spanish girl, the third of four daughters, an honor student in the commercial course of high school. She was very well spoken of by her teachers and respected by her classmates. A leader, she was elected president of her home room. She had creative ability, played the piano and sang, but tended to underrate her own ability. She was hot-tempered and fiery, high-strung, and suffered from blue spells. Her mother was strict. She felt close to her second oldest sister but clashed with her oldest sister.

SYNOPSIS OF ADOLESCENT FANTASY

Her adolescent fantasies had a depressive trend, and characters were tired, pensive, disappointed in themselves and guilty, with a need for punishment. There were themes of immaturity and dependence, of being frightened and being away from home, and running to mother.

There were hints that she felt unlovable, unpopular, deprived. There was passive wishful thinking—of receiving without effort. But along with this was a philosophy that to get what you want you have to be independent and self-sufficient. Marriage was a means toward getting what one has been deprived of.

In her adolescent fantasies mothers were strong, dominant characters, while fathers were weak and undervalued. Children were dependent on the mother and feared her disapproval. Women perceived men as undependable, like small boys who had to be watched. There was sibling rivalry which led to punishment for which the girl in the story was not sorry. Religion apparently was important to Celia. She was anxious about school work as there were themes of school achievement and a desire to go to college.

CELIA AS AN ADULT

Now, as a mature twenty-eight-year-old woman, Celia is described as neat, attractive, refined, feminine, but listless. She went to work from high school and, now unmarried, is the secretary for the purchasing department of an oil firm. She compares herself with the men with whom she works and believes that she is as competent as they are. She resents that a promotion has been so long delayed.

She has never been away from home. Marriage seems increasingly remote. She is very choosy about the man she would marry. She believes that she scares men away and that the only attractive men are already married. A devout Catholic, she has strict standards of marital behavior.

She finds it more difficult to give orders than to receive them. She is afraid of hurting other people's feelings and finds it hard to say no. It is hard for her to boss others.

CORRESPONDENCE BETWEEN ADOLESCENT FANTASY AND ADULT PERSONALITY

In many ways Celia's adolescent fantasies foretold her mature personality quite faithfully. Celia has never been away from home except for one week, and then she became very homesick. This attitude was foreshadowed in story B-10, told in 1940.

Girl walking home from Sunday school. Might be walking through section of town not very nice and she is kind of frightened. Perhaps she doesn't know but there is someone in back of her. If she does know it she will be sort of scared and she will walk faster. She is thinking of the things that happen in the newspaper, kidnaping. She will run home and tell her mother and won't go out again alone through that section of town. (Celia, subject 28, story B-10, 1940)

Appendix A. Resumé of the Subjects 289

Celia states that her mother is the one who has been the driving force in the family. This same attitude was expressed in 1940 in story B-1.

Boy leaving house in the morning. Has to find a job. Looks determined. Thinking he won't come back unless he has one. Mother probably has told him to look hard as they will need it and the family needs the money he will bring in. Although he knows it will be hard to find it, he is determined—face set and his hand clenched. (Celia, subject 28, story B-1, 1940)

Celia is described as listless. Although she is not described as depressed it is evident from her discussion of marriage that she is disappointed and feels she has missed opportunities. Her claim that she is not anxious or concerned at not being married sounds like denial. So stories A-5 and B-6 reflect the mood to be found thirteen years later.

Young girl high school age—on way home from school. Perhaps she is tired—sat down to rest. Looks pensive. Thinks over some things in school. Thought she flunked test and is worried about it. Perhaps she hasn't studied for it and wishes that she had. Probably makes up her mind that she will study for the next one. (Celia, subject 28, story A-5, 1940)

Dejected high school boy. Sad about something. Fight with brothers and sisters. Probably started a family brawl. Taken a punch at one of his younger brothers or sisters. Mother has sent him into his room for punishment—got a good bawling out for that. Not sorry for what he did but is punished for it. Will probably do it again. He will stay there an hour or two until his mother says O.K. [Who was it?] Probably brother—wouldn't take sock at sister—would get worse punishment then if he did. (Celia, subject 28, story B-6, 1940)

Although Celia is described as being attractive and beautiful she tends to depreciate her charms. She claims that she scares men away and she wonders if there is something about her that is lacking. This same feeling was expressed in 1940 in story A-3.

Girl unattractive from her appearance. Takes to reading. Not popular with the boys. Sees girl passing, prettier girl than she. Wishing that she were as pretty—had that girl's personality. Would even like to change places. Envious of the other girl. Even though she stays in the house, would like to go out and have good times as the other girls do. (Celia, subject 28, story A-3, 1940)

The attitude expressed by the maid in story A-9 in 1940 is similar to her attitude at the present. She envies her friends who have gotten married—they seem to have found happiness. The theme of boredom and ennui appears here too.

Chambermaid—working in one of the hotels. Sweeping out the room. Nice hotel and nice room—luxurious. Yearning, envious. Might be wishing she had some of the things she sees. Doesn't get much in her position and not able to afford any of the luxuries of life. Probably tired and disgusted from her work. Probably wishing she could meet someone she could marry who would give her the things she wants. (Celia, subject 28, story A-9, 1940)

Her attitude toward men is well expressed in story A-6. They are despised as being like little boys, needing to be watched, scolded and suppressed.

Man coming in late at night, 2:00 A.M. Been playing cards with some of his friends. Doesn't realize how late it is. Tries to get in house without letting his wife know. Wife has been waiting for him—can see shadow. Gets a good scolding [giggles]. To soothe wife will have to compromise by taking her somewhere the next night and will not be able to go anywhere by himself for quite a while. (Celia, subject 28, story A-6, 1940)

Celia apparently prizes her independence—the fact that she holds a responsible position, earns her own money, and is hence not dependent on anyone for her support. This attitude was expressed in story B-8 in 1940.

Girl and her father—she is asking him for something. Might be a new coat or hat. She seems to want it—is sort of pleading. Father telling her right now they couldn't afford it. If she could work herself right after school she might make extra money and she could spend it for the coat and anything else she wants. Teach her to be independent. She is ambitious and wants the coat. She will go out and look for a part-time job, save up money, and buy the coat. (Celia, subject 28, story B-8, 1940)

CHANGE IN FANTASY: CELIA, SUBJECT 28

Fantasy theme	Amount of change
Anxiety	−5
Self-confidence	−3
Positive outcome	+5
Wishful thinking	+5
Eroticism	+3

CHANGE IN FANTASY

There is a marked repetition of themes in the 1953 stories. Father figures are again represented as inadequate, mother figures as strong, strict, and ambitious. Themes of ambition and the need to be successful are again present. The attitude toward marriage emerges more clearly

Appendix A. Resumé of the Subjects 291

from the shadows: there is a desire for security and children, but the adequacy of the man is also important. There is again reference to religious themes which would indicate that religion seems to be a strong bulwark to Celia in helping to resist some of her impulsive nature.

One of the outstanding changes is decrease in anxiety and concern about self. Three of the 1940 stories indicated anxiety about success in school. Apparently her success in her work has helped her to increase her confidence in herself. The report from the interview states: "She feels that she is as capable in her work as any man would be and that she knows more about various aspects of the business than many men in jobs over her." Now her masculine striving comes through to a successful conclusion. Competitiveness with men has moved more out into the open.

Another shift in the stories is from the negative to the positive. Several of the 1940 stories had tragic endings but these are not present in 1953. There was wishful thinking in 1940 but actually more of the 1953 stories have themes of wishful thinking. Story A-10 illustrates this shift as well as any.

Two high school children—gone to fortuneteller to find out what is going to happen. Fortuneteller finds out something about one that seems to have frightened him. Could it be a tragedy? Boy has hand around the girl. They have no happy looks on their faces. May be sickness in the family. Probably go home and tell their mothers and they will all be upset. All will be waiting for the tragedy to fall. (Celia, subject 28, story A-10, 1940)

Engaged couple tries to get this fortuneteller to open the door to them, and he was telling them all about these wonderful things that would happen to them, great wealth and happiness was in store for them, but the girl is a little timid because her religion says that she shouldn't go to fortunetellers or believe in anything like that, even though she was fascinated at such a thing, yet she felt a little reluctant but the boy however had no such qualms and they are very much engrossed in what the fortuneteller is telling them, and they are hoping that all the good things he does say will come true. Happy marriage, security, nice children, etc. (Celia, subject 28, story A-10, 1953)

In adolescence Celia reacted to her wishes and impulses with feelings of guilt and the need for punishment. But in 1953 this feeling of guilt has receded. Religion seems to be more of a supporting than a condemning factor in 1953. In story A-2 a young man "is saying a little prayer asking God to give him a little help and guidance," while in B-9 the young boy in jail "hears the church bells ringing on a Sunday morning and he is just wishing that he might, once he gets out of jail, be able to change to a good life and make amends for his conduct in society." There is nothing in her life story to indicate how this change came about. Apparently religion has become a source of strength and comfort to her because it helps her to keep under control impulses which otherwise would be disruptive. But her success in work may have helped to give her a sense of power and hence of self-control. Because she has her behavior under such firm control she can indulge in more unrealistic fantasy, as illustrated by story A-5.

Here a young schoolgirl in her junior year of high school. She lives in a small country town. She has put in her day's work at school and is on her way home and decided that she would like to sit down by the quiet countryside and think a little. She has the great ambition to leave the town some day and perhaps become a great actress on Broadway and have her name up in lights and she is just wondering if there is any chance for her to become something like that, and she goes away from school and tries to make up her mind whether she should remain there and get married and make a family. The other girls were doing so and were fine. (Celia, subject 28, story A-5, 1953)

There is no story in the 1940 series that represents quite such a flight into unreality. In 1940 not one story contained any reference to love. The story that came closest to it was A-9 (given above), but here the maid was "wishing she could meet someone she could marry who would give her the things she wants."

In 1953 at least three stories develop the theme of love openly, albeit in a somewhat juvenile fashion, well illustrated by story A-2.

This is a young man who has set out on very firm steps of life. He is knocking at the door of his fiancée's home and he is determined to ask her a very important question, in other words he is asking her to be his wife, and he is quite a little afraid because her parents do not exactly approve of him. He hasn't steady or a very good job but he is so much in love that he has decided that he will take the step anyway and hope that her parents will see their way clear to grant permission to marry their daughter, and he is saying a little prayer right then asking God to give him a little help and guidance. (Celia, subject 28, story A-2, 1953)

Apparently, with the greater reserves of strength to resist her impulses, she can permit herself to fantasy romance in a somewhat unrealistic fashion.

One pities Celia because apparently she is making her compromise

Appendix A. Resumé of the Subjects 293

with life not by living out her impulses, but by repressing them and giving them their only expression in unrealistic fantasy.

EXCERPT FROM THE RORSCHACH REPORT

Intelligent, interesting, imaginative person. Mildly hysterical character. Highly reactive and lacks distance from people. Tends to over-interpret or project feelings into situations that may or could be neutral. Frustration tolerance low.

High degree of aggressive energy poorly repressed and a confusion about sexual activity. Vague concept of herself as a woman—masculine identification. As a woman she feels inadequate and unnatural in that role. Probably frigid. Difficult to repress her hostility and irritability when under sexual pressure. Attitude toward men sadomasochistic with masochistic elements dominant. She is interested in contact with people and in making a heterosexual adjustment but her evaluation of people is unrealistic—divided into good and bad. Social contacts make her feel uncomfortable and panicky. This is in contrast with her easy structuring of work situations. Her social contacts present her with anxiety.

Mildly depressed. Phobic reactions to people when her femininity is challenged. More at ease with men than with women. Positive feelings for father. Relationship with women one of reserve and coolness which is a hostile dependency on mother.

Rushes headlong into situations providing friction and some sense of power in controlling the situation in this way. Runs away from emotional challenges and avoids permanent relations—marriage. Work adjustment excellent.

Pansy, Subject 29

PANSY AS AN ADOLESCENT

As an eighteen-year-old girl in the last year of high school Pansy was well spoken of by her teachers as a good student, conscientious, and a hard worker, but without great ability. Her mother, however, was critical of her, described her as argumentative, irritable, both critical and sensitive to criticism. She had epileptic convulsions at age thirteen. Removal of an ovarian cyst improved her health and personality. She felt anxious and wanted to make a better scholastic record in school. She wished to be a nurse and worked efficiently in a hospital during the summer. She admired an older sister but quarreled with a younger one.

SYNOPSIS OF ADOLESCENT FANTASY

Characters in her adolescent stories had a strong need to be liked and accepted. Parents were seen in ambivalent terms but mostly as bad, and there was a desire to get rid of parents. The need to be liked was related to hostility and resentment toward others. Acceptance by others could be won by being kind, pleasant, selfless, and by not being critical of others. There was a self-sacrificing, self-blaming masochistic tendency in the stories. She would have liked to change herself. A virtue was made of being plain and homely. There were themes of being falsely accused of a crime.

In *Adolescent Fantasy* many contradictions between Pansy's stories and her autobiography were pointed out. "Although she uses no cosmetics and pays little attention to her personal appearance, her stories show that she wishes to become more attractive and to change her clothes and appearance. She does not like to read, but her stories show an interest in reading ('Took up book again. Became interested in it. Became more interested in reading books. Spent half her time reading; whenever her father went to general store asked for books. Bought her a history book—enjoyed it. Got an education by herself!' —story 40). She wears sweaters and skirts—daydreams of feminine clothes. She is shy, but in her fantasies she meets many people. She does not go out with boys, but in her stories she has many friends. Here is the picture of an inhibited girl with many normal repressed wishes."

PANSY AS AN ADULT

As a thirty-one-year-old woman Pansy is seen as a tall, stringy, tired-looking woman, stoop-shouldered and hollow-chested, and has a sallow complexion. Straight hair and lines in her face make her appear older than she is. She was living in a dilapidated Negro settlement and her home had a barn-like appearance.

Pansy actually did go into nursing and liked being around sick

Appendix A. Resumé of the Subjects

people whom she enjoyed helping and caring for. She said she liked best the charity ward where people were most appreciative.

She first married a man whom she had nursed, a Catholic, although her parents were Methodist and strongly prejudiced against Catholics. They violently opposed her marriage. She believed she married in part to get away from home. Her husband insisted on practicing birth control and eventually she secured an annulment. She became Catholic during this marriage.

Following this she married another patient—a Negro Catholic priest. After their marriage he gave up his priesthood to take up factory work. Her parents have completely disowned her as a result of this marriage.

She has three children and states that she will have as many children as God gives her. Several of her teeth are missing, which she claims has helped to improve a bad sinus condition. Adhesions in her uterus were cured by having children.

CORRESPONDENCE BETWEEN ADOLESCENT FANTASY
AND ADULT PERSONALITY

In a dramatic way Pansy has worked through the fantasies which she expressed as an adolescent. In her 1940 stories she depicts the mother as scolding, dominating, critical, and distrustful. Stories A-6, A-7, and B-2 illustrate these attitudes.

Young fellow has been out. Don't know how he's spent his time. His mother has left a light (my mother does that when I'm out). He didn't realize how late it was. Just going upstairs—sees shadow of woman. It's his mother and she demands an explanation of where he was—he doesn't give one. Mother thinks he is too young to be out so late. Tries to discipline him by saying that he can't go out for a long time. He listens to mother and later explains where he had been. Mother forgives him and makes him promise he won't stay out so late. (Pansy, subject 29, story A-6, 1940)

Boy's mother thinks he has told a lie, he is trying to tell her exactly what happened. Is supposed to have wanted some money to go out somewhere—asked for it. Said he couldn't have it. He tried to figure out a way to get it. While mother was out—money was taken. Mother accused him. Boy had been out of house. She thought he might have taken it. Is trying to tell her he didn't do it. After much explaining she decides that he is telling the truth. Had just mislaid it. She gives him the money he wanted. (Pansy, subject 29, story A-7, 1940)

Someone had told the girl that she was quite attractive. Goes to her bedroom. Giving herself the "once-over" to see if this is true. Tried to make herself more attractive than she was. Mother came in. Girl explained what she was doing. Mother said she was foolish. Should stay as she was. (Pansy, subject 29, story B-2, 1940)

Then there is a hint that Pansy fantasies being freed from her parents, in story A-10.

Brother and sister at a fortuneteller's. First time, don't know how to take it. Are orphans—left in care of an old aunt. Want to see what future holds for them—if they'll become rich. Aunt is old, don't know how much longer they will be with her. Want to prepare for later. Engrossed in what fortuneteller tells them. Find they will inherit much money from aunt and parents. (Pansy, subject 29, story A-10, 1940)

This is confirmed in her 1953 interview. She states that her parents were narrow-minded and had very old-fashioned ideas. They always demanded that she be in by twelve o'clock. They never permitted her to have a date before she was nineteen. When she began to go out she began to feel quite independent and became resentful of her parents' domination. Becoming a nurse, marrying successively a Catholic and then a Negro Catholic priest expressed dramatically her defiance of her parents and her desire to show her independence of them. Story A-4 told in 1940 foreshadowed her masochistic tendencies.

Man is trying to teach son right and wrong. Didn't know how to go about it. Had money—asked boy if he had two piles of money—which he would take—one large pile, one small one. Boy said "large pile." Father angry, said he would be ungrateful. Should learn to take smaller things and leave larger things for other. Like cutting a pie, cut smaller pie for yourself, larger one for other. (Pansy, subject 29, story A-4, 1940)

Her selection of nursing as a career, her insistence that it excited her to see patients come in to the hospital desperately ill and then to see them make a recovery and to think that she had a hand in it, her preference for the charity ward illustrates this masochistic trend. This is further shown by her marriage and the circumstances of her living at the present time.

In 1940 she was concerned about her appearance and wished to make herself attractive, as indicated in story B-5.

Girl had nice personality. Got along well with people. Other girl wasn't pretty but had possibilities. Got together to give each other pointers. Pretty girl was trying to help other girl improve her appearance. Was always frowning (that's me), should smile. Attitude she took made her lose a lot of

Appendix A. Resumé of the Subjects 297

her friends. Worked at changing the girl around. Took her advice, changed hair-style, way she dressed. Tried to have pleasant expression on her face rather than going around with a sour look. Tells her friends she didn't think she could ever change her personality and her ways. (Pansy, subject 29, story B-5, 1940)

This tendency, however, was opposed by the mother figure in story B-2, above, which has had such an oppressive influence in her life. Now her appearance is decidedly shabby, and missing teeth leave visible gaps when she smiles. Guilt and the intropunitive tendency have gained the upper hand. It is of some moment that she attempted to improve her appearance for her second interview.

Story B-5 also shows her concern over the possibility of losing friends. This is to be compared with her present attitude that she has no close friends in the community in which she lives. This she projects by saying that they are gossipy and because she doesn't like to gossip they think she is a snob, stuck-up, and too good for them. But she says she has no hard feelings and would be glad to help her neighbors in any way that she could.

CHANGE IN FANTASY: PANSY, SUBJECT 29

Fantasy theme	Amount of change
Positive outcome	−10
Negative outcome	+3

CHANGE IN FANTASY

The 1953 stories repeat the same themes that are present in the 1940 stories with very little change. However, in 1953 the dynamics are expressed more directly and with less need for defensive tactics. Parental figures are unsympathetic. The father is punitive, the mother is critical. Hostility is revealed more directly and openly. There is still a desire to get away from her family. But a masochistic attitude appears, which serves as a defense against hostile impulses. There is still concern over physical attractiveness and an envy of more attractive women.

A depressed tone has appeared in some of the stories.

Apparently, in spite of the vicissitudes of her life and her achieving independence from her family she is still struggling with these relationships as a problem. Story B-1 illustrates this.

Appendix A. Resumé of the Subjects

This man has been told no about something. He's very angry and he has turned on his heels and he's about to go out the door. Apparently he might have asked one of the members of his family for a loan and was rejected and is going to seek to get it elsewhere or he has been told by one of his girlfriends no. Whatever it was, he is very angry and he doesn't wish to stay at the house. (Pansy, subject 29, story B-1, 1953)

Story B-6 indicates that she still feels rejected. Separating herself from her family, instead of solving her problems, has given her new ones of feeling isolated.

My impression is that the room or place where this man is is very barren and cold—I mean not in temperature but in the sense of friendliness and atmosphere. He is very rejected. He doesn't know what he is going to do. He probably might have just lost his job or lost his best girlfriend and he's just sitting there meditating and trying to figure out what he should do. (Pansy, subject 29, story B-6, 1953)

One would relate this to the fact that her present home is described as barn-like. There were no rugs on the floor. The furniture was crude, very worn, and stuffing was coming out of the cushions on the sofa.

Perhaps the clearest indication of change in the stories is in the nature of the outcome. Sixteen stories in the 1940 set had positive outcomes, none negative outcomes; none of the 1953 stories has positive outcomes and three have negative outcomes. Story A-10 illustrates this shift. Compare the following story told in 1953 with story A-10, given above.

The young lady and man have gone to a carnival or circus and they have gone to see the crystal-gazer or fortuneteller. They are very much in love and they want to see what the future holds for them. They would like to get married and they would like to find out whether or not things will go all right for them. [What did the fortuneteller tell them?] That he doesn't see things going right. There might be some disaster or some harm done to somebody, but whatever it is it wasn't good—what he foretold them. (Pansy, subject 29, story A-10, 1953)

This depressed trend toward the negative has been seen in many other subjects where aggressive impulses have been turned inward into fantasy. Life's experiences, in spite of Pansy's efforts to secure independence and doing so by expressing hostility, have boomeranged; at present she is feeling discouraged and sees the future darkly.

EXCERPT FROM THE RORSCHACH REPORT

This is a compulsive, immature, deeply disturbed woman with an irritable, aggressive, competitive manner. There are strong feelings of narcissistic injury and self-pity, and a need for concealment to hide an ugly and defensive psyche. There is a pervasive hostility.

There is a picture of quick irritability and a tendency to see imagined or projected hostility and to react quickly with feelings of rejection and resentment. She expects maltreatment from people, is ready to take the defensive, and carries a chip on her shoulder. She is afraid of aggression from people. She is so immature that her judgment is poor. Through detachment and emotional withdrawal she is able to effect relationships with people which lack emotional investment, rapport, and spontaneity.

There is evidence of a fairly deep depression which accentuates her critical, rejecting attitude toward the world and herself. Her self-esteem shows signs of serious damage. Her affect is deeply withdrawn and she has little capacity to get pleasure from life. She cannot give herself freely to her fantasy world. She might feel psychically very ill or there may have been a psychotic breakdown in the past.

The identification is essentially feminine. There is need for concealment and inconspicuousness.

Dorothy, Subject 30

DOROTHY AS AN ADOLESCENT

As a seventeen-year-old girl Dorothy, an only child, was described as mature, attractive, vivacious and pretty. She had a sense of humor and a quick tongue which at times could be sarcastic. Her mother said that she was pleasant and easygoing but also responsible. Her father died when Dorothy was seven and her mother worked after that event as manager of a store. At that time Dorothy planned to be a stenographer and had fantasies of owning a car and a fur coat, and she wanted a tall boyfriend with money.

SYNOPSIS OF ADOLESCENT FANTASY

Her stories at that earlier time indicated a certain dissatisfaction with reality and with herself. Characters adopted a "brave front" and stoical attitude and the feeling that "things are bad, but that's life and I must face it." She felt that she had been deprived and denied. She saw her mother as ambitious for her and coercive. There was distinct ambivalence toward the mother figure.

The stories showed a good deal of narcissism and self-centeredness. There was a wish to be popular and attractive, but there was much self-centeredness and self-gratification in the stories. One story (B-8) was Oedipal with the theme of living alone with the father and taking care of him even after marriage.

There was a distinct "sour-grapes attitude" in the stories and the necessity of accepting the real with a forced smile.

DOROTHY AS AN ADULT

As a mature woman of thirty Dorothy impressed the interviewer as appearing much older than she was. She had a dried-up look and her skin was full of fine lines and wrinkles. She wore heavy make-up and had the appearance of a person who had had a hard life. She spoke with a babyish voice. She was tense and nervous at the beginning of the interview.

She graduated from high school in the upper third of her class. After high school she went into secretarial work. She stayed with her first position only two years because she did not like her irritable, woman boss. Now she has been with the same company for ten years as secretary to the treasurer. She has two or three girls working under her but she does not like being a boss and having to correct people. She hates to hurt people's feelings.

She married a man about eleven years her senior who had been previously married. He is a Baptist, she a Catholic. There are no children and the husband is described as impotent. He is a kind, friendly, but outspoken person. He is very sensitive about his condition and will do nothing about it. Dorothy is perplexed as to what to do and she would like to have children. They live with Dorothy's mother.

She is sincerely interested in her religion (Catholic) but feels some guilt because she has married out of her religion and hopes some day to be able to have a marriage in the Catholic Church.

Outwardly calm, she inwardly is tense and nervous and has butterflies in her stomach. Occasionally she will blow her top but not at home.

Appendix A. Resumé of the Subjects 301

CORRESPONDENCE BETWEEN ADOLESCENT FANTASY
AND ADULT PERSONALITY

The dynamics of Dorothy's marriage adjustment are undoubtedly present in her 1940 stories but the interpretations are subtle and hypothetical.

There are two stories (A-1 and A-5) that indicate that she herself realizes that her outward attitudes do not express her inner feelings and desires.

Howard Johnson has a job in New York. Got it through the mail. Gets to New York. Always lived on farm. Hasn't seen much of city life. Big buildings dumbfound him. Seems so big to him. Stands there, feels lonesome. Sorry he's taken the job in New York. It doesn't look like a friendly place. Thinks he'll find a hotel and write to mother saying he likes it even though he doesn't. May get to like it. After a while he does. (Dorothy, subject 30, story A-1, 1940)

Sarah Brown goes to high school. Lives in country. On her way home she sits down and thinks about boy who asked her to prom—had to refuse. Said she didn't want to go, really did, but didn't have gown. Couldn't ask mother for gown—were hard up and mother would feel bad if she had to refuse. Thinks maybe next time she'll be able to go. Gets up and goes home. (Dorothy, subject 30, story A-5, 1940)

In story A-1 the boy wrote to his mother saying he likes his life in the city "even though he doesn't." In story A-5 the girl told the boy she didn't want to go to the prom, whereas she really did but she did not have a gown. One may surmise that Dorothy gives the world the impression that she is happily married, whereas in reality she is much distraught because she does not have satisfactory sexual relations with her husband.

There is no doubt but that her reaction to her father's death when she was seven has greatly influenced her life. Story B-8 (given on p. 38) gives a hint of this. Perhaps she married an older man as a father figure and the difficulty in sexual relations in some way is related to the incest taboo.

Story A-10 would indicate that Dorothy is self-centered and narcissistic.

Jean and Tom at country fair. Jean kept asking Tom to take her in to see fortuneteller. He felt like a sissy. Finally persuaded him. Fortuneteller tells her she will marry someone rich. Has gone off in a dream about it. Thinks about life she will have—have few cars—won't have to ride around in old family car. Tells her she will live long. Says in crystal ball he sees she will be very happy. When she gets outside she's dreaming. Tom asks her if she believes what he says. She probably does. (Dorothy, subject 30, story A-10, 1940)

CHANGE IN FANTASY: DOROTHY, SUBJECT 30

Fantasy theme	Amount of change
Positive outcome	−5
Anger	−3
Eroticism	+3

CHANGE IN FANTASY

Again there is remarkable similarity in the themes in Dorothy's 1940 and 1953 stories. Story B-7 in 1953 repeats the theme previously told in 1940 in story B-8. These stories have been given on p. 38.

Dorothy is still obsessed with the unconscious fantasy of caring for her father. There is still embarrassment about the opposite sex.

Joe Dunn is going to make his first call on Mary Lou Smith. She just moved here from Illinois. Thought it would be nice if he called on her. Mother thought he should go. Goes up to house. Undecided whether to knock on door. Knocks softly. No one hears him, has to knock louder. Mother comes to door. Asks for Mary Lou. She has gone downtown. Joe is disappointed. Thinks it was not so bad talking to her mother. Plans to come back next day. (Dorothy, subject 30, story A-2, 1940)

This looks to me like a young man, possibly going out on his first date. He's made a date with this young girl and has probably gotten her parents' permission to take her out and he has now reached the part of knocking at the door and waiting for her to answer. Well, since I'm assuming that it is his first date, I think he's going to be a little embarrassed, probably—sort of flustered and not have much to say. He doesn't look like the overwhelming type of fellow. He looks rather shy. I think he'll go out and have a good time. (Dorothy, subject 30, story A-2, 1953)

There is still a stoical attitude of passivity and nonresistance, which probably also has a masochistic element. In 1940 this was shown in story B-1.

Mr. Black had argument with wife because she wanted a new coat. Said they couldn't afford it. She said she could save up money. Argued until he walked out. He goes to a store where they sell sporting goods to talk to his friends and forget troubles. May think of a way to get coat. She doesn't need one.

When he gets home wife has calmed down, wife says she doesn't need coat, can do without it. Everything all right then. (Dorothy, subject 30, story B-1, 1940)

In 1953 this same tendency was shown in story B-6.

This fellow always sits and sits and sits. He dreams a lot—he's a big dreamer. He never seems to do too much. Today, he's sitting in the same chair, thinking about the same nothing. Later maybe he'll get up and go outside and see the rest of the fellows. He doesn't seem to feel that he has enough energy but maybe later on he'll get up and go out in the daylight. I don't think he feels that he's got too many friends. He feels as if everyone is against him and he can't understand why because he feels inside that he's a pretty nice fellow and he doesn't know why people don't like him just because he doesn't, isn't, always full of ambition like everybody else. He thinks that he's going to live longer by taking life a little easy and I think that he'll always be just the way he is. He won't change very much and all his friends will move away and go on to bigger things, but he'll just sit right where he is, right on the chair. (Dorothy, subject 30, story B-6, 1953)

But new elements enter in 1953. There is a depressed tone to some of the stories—and in story A-5 this sadness is related to heterosexual adjustment.

This young girl is in college. Right now, her parents are sending her to college to get a little knowledge. I think that she has met a very nice young man while at college that she feels rather fond of. This particular afternoon she feels rather worn out and she's just gone out into the park or some other quiet spot and she's sitting trying to think out all her dreams about this man and about life and wondering about whether this is the man for her or whether it isn't, whether she'll finish college or whether she won't, whether she'll get married before she does. I think that she looks a little sad to me, as if possibly the things that she knows herself aren't going to be the way she wants them to be. I think that she knows that this fellow that she's real fond of isn't quite the one for her. (Dorothy, subject 30, story A-5, 1953)

This story tells clearly that Dorothy is unhappy over the outcome of her marriage. Story B-10 is a projection of a possibly growing tendency to seek satisfaction in other men, fantasying that they are following her.

This young girl is coming home from school. She usually comes the same way every day after school. She follows one direct street and goes all the way to her home. There is a city loafer that is always hanging around this particular street. Every day she goes by he keeps watching her and watching her and watching her. She's never noticed him until today. Not that she's never noticed him, but she's never noticed that he's been particularly watching her. She keeps walking along and walking along and she goes past him and she doesn't want him to know that she even notices that he's watching her. When she gets home I think that she's going to tell her older sister about this boy and she's going to have her sister come and meet her and walk home with her tomorrow to see if he's watching her again. But, I think that tomorrow he'll still be there and he'll still be watching and when her sister walks by with her she'll go over and ask him what he is up to and what he thinks he's doing and he'll be afraid to hang around there watching this young girl any more. (Dorothy, subject 30, story B-10, 1953)

Referring to the tabulation of changes in themes there is an increase in themes of eroticism. Dorothy's marriage experience has resulted in frustration and more of her fantasy life is concerned with erotic themes. These were virtually absent in 1940. Although Dorothy was concerned with popularity and being attractive in adolescence she did not permit herself to fantasy erotic relationships, but subsequent life experiences have brought these into the foreground.

In three of her early stories characters become angry—a wife because she did not have a new coat, a girl because she was not invited to a party, and a boy who was asked by his mother to go on an errand. It was also Dorothy's picture in adolescence to have her stories end happily so that the negative emotions aroused would not continue to haunt her. But in 1953 these trends have disappeared. She is able better to endure frustration, but at the expense of depression. One would say that both of these changes are the result of her marriage experience and her clinging to religion as a support against being overwhelmed by her desires.

EXCERPT FROM THE RORSCHACH REPORT

This is the picture of an oversensitive, intelligent, and ambitious person whose sense of inadequacy as a woman seems to have resulted in a highly compensatory drive for status, prestige, and power. The overall attitude to life is that of an egocentric, passively demanding oral character who has need for physical and sensual closeness, but is ready to retract with phobic rapidity when a real and personal contact is offered. Because of a lack of sexual identity and definite concept of her role in life she has a deep problem in relationships with people and seldom achieves a feeling of contact and ease with people.

She is likely to be sexually frigid or at least unresponsive, perhaps preoccupied with sex and with a tendency to use it in relationships where it does not exist. She finds it difficult to accept her role as woman and wife. She has an unresolved Oedipal fixation on the father who seems to have treated her with much affection and apparently regarded her as a little fairy princess. There seems to have been some serious emotional traumatization in relation to her feelings about her father so that it is necessary completely to introject him. Positive feelings toward him and toward herself as an acceptable, lovely child have been repressed. Her attitude toward people is one of exploitation and subtle hostility—especially toward women. The rejection of femininity has made her feel guilty and anxious and there is overcompensation in the form of a compulsive housewifely pattern.

There is little individuality. She clings to conventional values and ideas of prestige and status. There is a chronic need to fill the inner emptiness with material goods and signs of success and adequacy.

Nancy, Subject 31

NANCY AS AN ADOLESCENT

This subject, the youngest of three children—there were two older brothers—of Russian Jewish parents, as a fifteen-year-old girl was described as well-adjusted, happy, normal, and with a good disposition. She was friendly and socially outgoing, got along well with her family and had many girlfriends whom she tended to antagonize by being critical. She was a B student with ambitions to be a nurse. Of this her mother was doubtful, but her father approved. She was somewhat aggressive in real life.

SYNOPSIS OF ADOLESCENT FANTASY

Her stories during adolescence were among the best in the series. They pointed to a person who was secure, happy, optimistic, and extroverted. Parents were described as good and nurturant. There were fantasies of dating, marriage, and pregnancy. She was concerned about acceptance by the opposite sex, popularity, and jealousy of other girls. She daydreamed about intimate relations but doubted whether she was lovable. There was both a wish for and a fear of sex. There was a theme of anxiety about being accepted on returning home. There were themes of returning home a success, which was rewarded by the parents. Ambitions about a career, however, were merely stepping stones to marriage. The Oedipus complex—going off with one parent and leaving the other—was evident. Story 37 (original series) illustrates this.

Joe was girl of seventeen—parents dead. Now on her way to uncle's home in California. Sat at station and waited impatiently for the train. Wasn't sure if she was happy, scared or anxious. Had met uncle only once; he was nice. Wondered if aunt and cousins would accept her. Finally got on train, found her seat. After day of riding she arrived at her destination. Uncle and family waiting for her. She was greeted very warmly, very happy, decided there and then she would like new home. (Nancy, subject 31, story 37, 1940)

There was marked passivity in the stories—a wanting to be wanted; a waiting attitude, submissiveness, with the corresponding emotions of longing and disappointment. Story 30 (original series) illustrates this.

Betty in room dressing for a date. Started extra early because it was a special date with someone special. When she was finished she walked downstairs nonchalantly. Clock tolled 8:00. Date should be there at any moment. Did not come. Thought he was delayed. Began to read. She had to do something or she would burst with anxiety. 8:20, 9:00 o'clock passed. Wondering where he was, what he could be doing. Had planned this for so long, wondered if he would disappoint her. Was miserable. Just as she was about to give up and go to bed, in walked her date. Didn't know whether to be angry or happy. His excuse was legitimate and she had a good time after all. (Nancy, subject 31, story 30, 1940)

NANCY AS AN ADULT

As a mature woman she is described as friendly but casual, and was inhibited and stilted in telling stories.

She never studied beyond high school and did not fulfill her ambition to become a nurse. Instead she worked in a factory, as a salesgirl and as a hairdresser. Then she married an industrial engineer, whom she describes as disgustingly realistic and very tight with money. She has two children—both girls. She feels that her life is very restricted and she cannot run around and spend money and have fun the way she would like to. She is very healthy and had easy pregnancies. She takes her religion casually. She says that she is very short-tempered and at times gets down in the dumps. She is a rather untidy person.

Appendix A. Resumé of the Subjects

CORRESPONDENCE BETWEEN ADOLESCENT FANTASY
AND ADULT PERSONALITY

The prediction offered from her 1940 stories—that Nancy would get married earlier than most of the subjects—has been born out in real life. Story B-8 shows the trend of her 1940 fantasies.

Nancy had just finished the dishes. Was going to change her dress and freshen up a bit. Doorbell rang. Answered it—in walked John. Young man who lived down the street. They had intention of some day being married. John was beaming—so happy he couldn't talk. Finally blurted out that he had a good job. Nancy stood there and gasped at him. Took her hand and said affectionately "You know what that means. We can be married immediately." (Nancy, subject 31, story B-8, 1940)

Most of the 1940 stories had a euphoric character, like B-8 above. But some stories had a depressed tone. Story B-6 illustrates this trend.

Bill sat slumped in his chair, head down, hands in his pockets and his feet sprawled in front of him. Was worried. Everything had gone wrong. Life seemed to him like one big mistake. He had been pounding the pavements for weeks and there was nothing for him to do. There were no jobs for those who had not completed school and had no experience. Wondered where he could get experience if no one would give him a job. Felt he had made a mistake by leaving school. Hadn't enough money to go to night school. There were not many things he could do. As he sat there he thought what a fool he was not to accept the opportunities given to him while attending school. He had learned what school meant, but the hard way. (Nancy, subject 31, story B-6, 1940)

This would indicate the possibility of a cyclic tendency. In her interview Nancy stated that she can be miserable to live with when she doesn't feel well, at which times she is very short-tempered, gets down in the dumps, and is grumpy. But these periods—which may correspond with the menstrual cycle—last only a short time and are rare. Nancy also complains that since marriage and especially since the children came she has less freedom and less time to run around and have fun and less money to spend on herself.

There are a number of stories with themes of returning home and of success which are not reflected in the interview, and the impression is gained that Nancy did not reveal many aspects of her life and personality in the interview. The theme of returning home probably reflects Nancy's yearning for closeness in personal relationships.

CHANGE IN FANTASY: NANCY, SUBJECT 31

Fantasy theme	Amount of change
Eroticism	−4
Feminine identification	−3
Striving, effort	−3

CHANGE IN FANTASY

In 1953 the same romantic themes of dating and marriage are present but they are not so frequent as in 1940. There is still a great deal of euphoria of a happy, optimistic, shallow type. Story B-10 illustrates this trend.

It was 5:30 and Mary had left the department store and was on her way home. It was quite a long walk, but after a day of being closed in it felt good to be out, so walk she did. As she walked, it gave her time to think of a pleasant homecoming and of a wonderful dinner and perhaps a movie that night. (Nancy, subject 31, story B-10, 1953)

But the depressed themes are also present, as illustrated by story B-6.

Tom was listless and dejected. It seemed to him that life had been very cruel indeed. He sat in his room by the window not caring to do much. He had tried so hard and he had failed so bitterly that it seemed to him that he just didn't care what happened. There was a knock at the door and his mother walked in. After listening to her for awhile he realized that the world didn't come to an end with one disappointment and there was always tomorrow. (Nancy, subject 31, story B-6, 1953)

In the 1953 stories there is a noticeable drop in the theme of eroticism. Obviously the erotic daydreams that filled her adolescent period have since been fulfilled in reality and she no longer has the need to indulge in this anticipatory wishful thinking of sexual and pregnancy experiences.

Likewise the themes of striving and effort are less frequent in 1953. One can only surmise that in 1940 these themes had a sexual significance as Nancy apparently in real life had very little ambition to be successful in study, work, or status. After graduating from high school she was too lackadaisical to go into nursing, which had been her announced ambition, and never got her application into a nursing school.

The shift in emphasis is perhaps best seen in comparing story A-6 told in 1940 with A-2 in 1953.

Appendix A. Resumé of the Subjects 309

Steve knocked at the door of house long not seen. It had been his home in his childhood, but in later years he moved away. Had been very successful during those years away from home. Now he was returning, to something close and near, for what was more dear to a man than the home which he was raised in. His knocks were not answered. Tried the door—it opened. Looked in, saw same old living room which he was so accustomed to play in. Walked in, walked around room, touching things to make sure they were real. While he was looking he saw a shadow cast on wall. But no one else was in the room. Didn't know what to think. Heard door close. Turned with a start. Before him stood his mother—almost the same as he had left her. Heard him enter and had come to investigate. Surprised. Looked at each other. He was where he always longed to be. At home. (Nancy, subject 31, story A-6, 1940)

It looks almost like a woman—I can't make my mind up. It has been a long time since Paul has been home. How would he be received? So much had happened in the years that had gone by. He didn't even know if his parents were still alive. The years had been long ones and tedious ones. When he left, he had the whole world before him and he was going to conquer it and it hadn't turned out that way. Here he was today almost afraid to knock on the door. He wondered how he would be received. Would they be glad to see him or had too much time passed? Well, there was no sense in prolonging the agony. Finally, after much hesitation, Paul did make himself knock on the door. There was a cheery greeting when the door did open and the warmth came out to meet him. And yes, there was Mom, still the same. A little older perhaps and a little more worn, but still the same. She greeted him warmly and with open arms. Paul asked how Dad was and he was told sadly that Dad was no longer with them. So, his coming home was very gratefully received for there was indeed much need for him. (Nancy, subject 31, story A-2, 1953)

In many aspects the stories are identical with the theme of returning home to mother. But in 1940 the youth who returned home "has been very successful during those years away from home" while in 1953 "he had the whole world before him and he was going to conquer it and it hadn't turned out that way." These fantasies may have some symbolic significance not readily apparent, but it is safe to say that they indicate that adolescent dreams have been deflected and she is struggling over the necessity of resigning herself to the rather unglamorous and unexciting role of housewife and mother.

The euphoria that was present in 1940 seems to have dimmed and in its place is some strain in relationships. The stories told to card B-8 illustrate this. The 1940 version of this story has already been given above.

Tom looked at Jane and wanted to know where she had been. She had been gone for hours and he had been waiting for what seemed to be days. He had paced the hall and the livingroom for what seemed to be miles and miles waiting for her return. There was so much he wanted to tell her. He had such wonderful news that it seemed that she would never get back. After awhile, his anxiousness became anger and when she finally did arrive, all he could do was rant and rave and demand an explanation. (Nancy, subject 31, story B-8, 1953)

In 1953 the closeness in personal relationships seems to be less than perfect. Separations are too long and eventually the separations, disagreements, misunderstandings lead to anxiety and finally to anger. In the interview she states that her husband's hobby of raising pigeons is a "pain in the neck" to her.

EXCERPT FROM THE RORSCHACH REPORT

An emotionally spontaneous person with an adaptive and sociable persona. Her capacity to relate to people on a mature level is disturbed by an unresolved incestuous relationship to her father whom she seems to idealize, and an ambivalent and unstable identification as a woman. She falters between masculine and feminine attitudes. Her efforts at emotional closeness are childish and lack seriousness.

She rejects her husband as inadequate and lacking in sensitivity as compared with her idealized image of her father. Her father has disappointed her in not giving her enough acceptance. Her conscious feelings are more positive toward her mother.

A sense of having made a mess of her life. She feels that she has been a failure as a woman and as a sexual partner. She has guilt over repressed hostility. There is mild depression and insecurity about growing old.

Edwin, Subject 33

EDWIN AS AN ADOLESCENT

A sixteen-year-old Jewish boy, Edwin had failed in his high school college preparatory program but was doing adequately in the technical high school. He was unobtrusive, immature, inattentive, but obedient and helpful. He pursued photography, earned money for his own clothes, did not go out with girls, and willingly gave money to his mother, of whom he was considerate. His father was ambitious for him and was disappointed in his school progress.

SYNOPSIS OF ADOLESCENT FANTASY

His fantasies in 1940 were those of a hurt and defeated adolescent with feelings of inferiority, timidity, and rejection. He saw himself as homely and unattractive but he desired to be independent, self-sufficient, self-confident, and socially popular.

He had little use for, but was observant of, girls, yet there were themes of strong attachment between boys and fear of sexual attack. Punishment and a masochistic trend were prominent in his stories, sometimes for possession of mother and fear of the threatening female. There was father hostility and secret aggressive fantasies, but overt fighting was avoided because of fear or retaliation.

EDWIN AS AN ADULT

As a twenty-nine-year-old man Edwin is chubby, lethargic, with a sleepy, drowsy, easygoing personality.

He quit school in the eleventh grade, subsequently had a night course in metalworking and a brief course in a photography school. He saw military action as an airplane gunner with twenty missions over Germany. He has worked for his father in the tailoring business. With his wife's money he bought a grocery store, which failed, and is now a salesman for a furniture company. He states that he had affairs with six or eight girls while in in the service. He is now married, with a four-year-old son who has deformed feet. His wife lost an arm in an automobile accident two years before their marriage, for which she received $7,500 compensation. He describes his tense wife as "terrific," an introvert who keeps her troubles to herself. Both in and out of the service he has drunk heavily.

Seymour, Subject 36

SEYMOUR AS AN ADOLESCENT

As a fifteen-year-old boy this man was described as good-natured, lazy, indifferent, and phlegmatic. His sister described him as nervous, excitable and quick-tempered. His teachers said he did not study. The examiner found him to be resistant, noncooperative, and disinterested. He felt inadequate and immature and tended to daydream and fear the supernatural.

SYNOPSIS OF ADOLESCENT FANTASY

His stories were fantastic, showing a strong Oedipus complex (striving with father for possession of mother, but father in control). Theme of killing father was followed by guilt and repentance (killing = crazy). Strong feelings for mother were displaced to sister. Mother was giver of food, but it was wrong to want mother. Fear of being eaten was described. Main theme was separation from and return to mother, and guilt and punishment for leaving mother were shown. Strong sexual conflict was apparent (jealousy of couple). There was a theme of saving the woman from aggression. He feels inadequate and immature, tends to daydream and fears the supernatural.

SEYMOUR AS AN ADULT

As a man Seymour is large, robust, heavy-set, slow in speaking and moving. His hands are dirty like a mechanic's and he uses poor English. He left high school to join the Navy, where he worked as a ship's welder and metalworker. After separating from the Navy he finished high school and started college, which he did not complete. After many different kinds of work he is now a letter carrier.

He has been married twice, the first time while he was in the Navy. He lived with this wife only one week and both agreed not to continue within a year. Now in his second marriage, he has two children—a boy and a girl. He is easygoing. His wife makes most of the decisions. He has a nervous stomach when under stress. He gets angry at times but cools off. He takes pride in his wife, children, and a home of his own.

CORRESPONDENCE BETWEEN ADOLESCENT FANTASY
AND ADULT PERSONALITY

The 1940 stories show the main figure as passive, the victim of circumstances, who tries independence but comes home to mother who supplies his oral needs. Story B-5 reports these fantasies.

Picture of two women. One's telling other about Jones boy, that he ran away from home. The boy boarded a train and went to Chicago. He got a job there and sending home money every week to mother. He lost this

Appendix A. Resumé of the Subjects 313

job after a couple of months and decided to go home. Didn't have no money left so he thought he'd hitchhike. Got a ride for a couple of miles. Then got another and kept on going for a couple of days. Decided this was too slow. Hopped freight at freight yard. This was a train just pulling out. He met a couple of tramps on train. He became good friends with one and several times they helped each other by sharing food. Came into home-town yard and he jumped off train. Police chasing all off and he was struck over head by police club. He left him there to chase after someone else. Just then train pulling out. His friends seen him lying on ground so he picked him up and put him on freight. When he woke he found he had passed destination. Soon as he could he hopped off. Went to town to get a job. Made enough to go home and his mother was very glad to see him and he said he'd never run away again. (Seymour, subject 36, story B-5, 1940)

This dependence on mother is also revealed in story A-6.

Picture of a boy going into old store in London. Curtains drawn so no light could go out. Blackout. Boy lived in store with mother. Every night went to air-raid shelter so they wouldn't be killed. In this shelter there was a plague. Everyone getting diseased. Mother afraid to go to shelter. Decided to stay in house. Soon hear sirens. Bombs bursting. House across the street hit. Rocks and bricks came tumbling. Boy tired of sitting in house all night so decided to go out. Mother pleaded with him not to. He says, "If I'm to be killed I'll get killed in house just as easy." Came back. Near house, sees bomb strike his house. Complete wreck. He rushed into wreckage to find mother. Gives her up for dead and walks sadly down street. Next thing he knows he sees mother standing on corner. Is surprised mother wasn't hurt and asked her how she got out of wreckage. She said she wasn't in there when bomb struck. She was worried about him and started out to look for him. Said he'd never go out and leave her again. (Seymour, subject 36, story A-6, 1940)

The interview presents the picture of a man for whom home is most important and who leans heavily on his wife for guidance. Actually he himself has little ambition and initiative. His earlier stories combine ambition with easy defeat and a tendency to turn around and go home to mother. Story A-5 illustrates this tendency.

Girl on way home from school. Sits down awhile to rest on grass, thinking. Daydreaming that she'd like to be actress. Pretty and had talent. Decides to quit school and go to Hollywood. She quit against her parents' wishes. Got job as waitress. Worked for couple about a year. Had enough money for Hollywood. Bought new clothes—train ticket—set out. Arrived couple of days later and decided to go to one of movie places. Went to first. No casting. Kept going back. No use. Went to other studios. Turned down. After about month she decided to give up and go back home. By this time money gone. Decided to get job and make enough to get home. Got job in restaurant. Worked 'til she saved enough to go home. Boarded train. At home. So glad and started school again. Said she'd never try to be actress again. (Seymour, subject 36, story A-5, 1940)

This anticipates a general attitude revealed in the interview: "He cannot see much point in advancement. You get more pay but you also get more responsibility and he claims he is not one who goes in for taking more responsibility."

Story B-6 is a fine illustration of irresponsible fantasy. The youth in the story meets a man who adopts him and leaves him his estate and fortune. Apparently his life has been governed by these fantasies of easy wealth without working for it.

Picture of boy sitting in house all alone. Wasn't really house, just a shack. Didn't have no parents and ran away from orphan asylum. Made living by picking junk and rags and selling to junk man. On Sundays he went to golf-course and caddied for men. One day a man came out to play golf. Asked boy to caddy. Boy says, "Yes." After they were through man said, "How would you like to caddy for me every Sunday?" Boy said he would. Man handed him $10. Next Sunday out on time. Man just starting to play. Got to talking. Boy told him he had no parents. Lived alone in shack. Man felt sorry for boy. Having no children of own, said, "How would you like to live with me?" Boy happy about this. Went to live in big mansion. Got everything he wanted. Everybody so good to him. One day man died and everything left to boy. Boy sold house and by this time about 20 years old. Took money and went into business. (Seymour, subject 36, story B-6, 1940)

CHANGE IN FANTASY: SEYMOUR, SUBJECT 36

Fantasy theme	Amount of change	Fantasy theme	Amount of change
Passivity—aggressed against	−7	Excitement	−3
Orality	−4	Separation	−3
Accidental death	−3	Success	+6

CHANGE IN FANTASY

In 1953 there is a remarkable repetition of the 1940 themes of passivity, being a victim of circumstances, and being rescued from his difficulties. The easy-come, easy-go philosophy leads to failure. Story A-6 illustrates this latter trend.

This is a young fellow—he's a writer. He has come to the big city to write plays and he is living in these cheaper tenements. He is pretty down on his luck. He's got a depressed look on his face—pretty shabby. Finally, he meets

Appendix A. Resumé of the Subjects 315

some people who help him get along and he finally makes a big success of himself. After he makes a success, he has a girlfriend home that he is supposed to send for after he makes a success in the city, but he got in with the wrong people and one thing added to another—a lot of drinking and a lot of parties. Finally, his plays weren't good anymore and he ended up going back to the home town just the way he came to the city—a failure. (Seymour, subject 36, story A-6, 1953)

Story A-7 in 1953 makes clearer the meaning of his real needs so copiously expressed in the 1940 series. A boy steals candy. His mother reproaches him, and "it ends up with him telling her that he missed something during his younger childhood."

This boy seems to be being reprimanded by his mother. He's been stealing candy from the candystore on the corner and stuff like that. Just picking up things. No reason at all. He comes from a good family. Word comes to his mother that he has been doing these things, but there is no positive proof on it, so she has a good heart-to-heart talk with him and it ends up with him telling her that he missed something during his younger childhood. He wanted these things so he just went to steal them. Finally ends up with his mother and his father talk this all over and they straighten him out and he pays up everything, etc.—pays it back. He finally straightened out. (Seymour, subject 36, story A-7, 1953)

Story B-10 is autobiographical inasmuch as in reality Seymour's father-in-law told him to "make good or get out and do not marry my daughter." His confusion and tendency to throw up his hands when he cannot see his way clear is well illustrated by the end of this story.

A girl walking down the street. Her father seems to be following her way back. She's going to meet this fellow that her father doesn't approve of at all, but she don't know he's following her. They meet at their secret rendezvous and decide that they're going to run away and get married. The father overhears all this and he is going to put a stop to it. So, when they go to meet to run away he steps in and grabs them. The fellow is a nice young kid but the father wanted her to marry someone that was well-to-do, that had a good position. The fellow was only just out of school and he didn't have a good job or anything. So, he says that the only way you'll get to marry my daughter is to make a success of yourself and all that stuff. He sends him out to the city to get a job and that. He finds a job and seems to be getting along pretty good when the young girl, her fancies turn toward another fellow that was there, who had a big job in the town. The father approved of him. When he came back and tried to prove that he had the stuff to marry his daughter, he found she was engaged to this other fellow. She realized that she once loved this other boy and it might come back to her again and she felt like for both boys.

So she says you'll have to try to prove which is the better man. I give up on this one—I'm all mixed up. (Seymour, subject 36, story B-10, 1953)

Dr. Jensen's survey of the formal characteristics of the 1953 stories is revealing: "The formal characteristics of these stories are striking and fit the rest of the picture beautifully. The stories are rather short but never inhibited or cramped. They really give the impression that the subject is intellectually lazy. Very little effort is put into the task of telling the stories. He won't exert himself. The stories are simple and effortless. The grammar is poor, indicating that he has no intellectual or social pretensions and that he is from a rather low socioeconomic status and satisfied to remain there. He tells his stories in a relaxed, easy, uninhibited, almost lethargic manner. His stories show no planning, he simply goes wherever the next thought leads him."

In spite of the persistence of the trends which he exhibited in adolescence, the theme count shows a decrease of seven in passivity, of four in oral themes and three of accidental death, and three in separation. On the other hand, there are six more stories in 1953 than in 1940 with themes of success. One would suspect that the vicissitudes of life have made him more sensitive to the problem of success and his lack of it. Also, the security of his present family situation has decreased his concern with problems of separation or the need for oral supplies. More extensive contact with the realities of life have made him somewhat less apprehensive of fate and being the victim of circumstances.

EXCERPT FROM THE RORSCHACH REPORT

Constriction of both intellectual and emotional life. His psychological environment is limited. The drive for achievement and for friction with the world is conspicuously low. Inefficient in the use of his intellect and energy.

Serious lack of identity. No feeling of himself as a person so is unable to make a mature contact with people. He compensates by overidealizing the masculine role. He seems to feel more at ease in the role of a clown.

Highly schizoid, immature personality, not far from the border of psychosis. No substance and very little resource for the complexities of living.

Emotional life repressed. The relationships he makes are likely to be those of dependency. He may be quite interested in making conquests with women. His relationships with women may be affectionate and may appear to be emotionally outgoing, but actually seem to involve only the sexual relationships and interests of a boy. His relationship with his mother was very close and sensually stimulating. The father was perceived as a real human being but one toward whom the boy may have been secretly contemptuous.

In contacts with people he is evasive, noncommittal, presenting an affectless, schizoid façade.

Jimmy, Subject 37

JIMMY AS AN ADOLESCENT

When he was an eighteen-year-old, this youth's home relationships were described as very fine. He did satisfactory work at school and was described as well-adjusted and a leader in school. He had a younger sister with whom he was close and he spoke in glowing terms of his mother. The father was a somewhat more passive, retiring person. Jimmy was liked by teachers and schoolmates.

He was an exceedingly introspective youth, and through the encouragement of an English teacher he was led to believe that he could write. He went through high school and college with a good record.

SYNOPSIS OF ADOLESCENT FANTASY

Jimmy's stories as an adolescent depicted very clearly the Oedipus conflict. There was hatred for father figures and love for mother figures. Stories show the dependency of a boy on his mother. Rivalry of one person for another was shown on the sibling level. But there were many contradictions in the stories. Father figures were admired and there was hatred toward and revolt against mother figures, and then there were themes of reconciliation. Because of the Oedipus conflict and attempts at its resolution, Jimmy was enmeshed in a number of conflicts, particularly between the good and the bad. The theme of love pervaded his stories. There were strong cravings for pleasure and fantasies of extramarital sexual relations. There was a search for self-realization. Jimmy revolted against his mother's ambitions for him and there was a reaction against success. In spite of the revolt against the mother he was very sensitive to the mother's wishes.

JIMMY AS AN ADULT

He saw active service as a first-line infantry man in World War II, which matured him greatly. In the 1953 material it appeared that his mother was a very dominating, controlling person, but she exerted her will through love rather than through conflict and opposition. When he returned to civilian life he resolved to become less dependent on his mother but because of her grip on him he has only partially accomplished this with difficulty. For three years he lived at home working on a novel. Now he is married with a four-and-one-half-month-old baby. After marriage he went to work for various industrial concerns—as office manager in one, in the service department of another—but his main interest is to continue writing. He strives through his writing "to find himself."

CORRESPONDENCE BETWEEN ADOLESCENT FANTASY AND ADULT PERSONALITY

The stories of Jimmy contain exceptionally clear illustrations of Oedipal fantasies.

This man works for rich farmer. Been working for him for years. Been underpaid, beaten, treated mean but for some reason he never left the place. Reason was when he was little boy he was first brought to this place by his father. He has grown up with present farmer, his boss now, and present farmer's sister. He had—as they grew up he grew to love farmer's sister and farmer hates him because of all the attention given him. He was strong, handsome. Farmer hates him, for he was frail and jealous of his strength. He lived under the cruel condition, beaten, all because of love for sister. Finally farmer, who had great influence over sister, was forcing her to marry some man to get his money. This was day of wedding. He had just heard farmer's sister was found dead in her room. She had killed herself to avoid marriage. Farmer had—he had come out and realized he had no reason to stay and at last he could have revenge without hurting one he loved. He went into house and killed the farmer he had grown up with—choked him to death with powerful muscles of his hand—muscles farmer had forced him to build. He did not try to escape from police after they found he had murdered farmer but confessed to crime and was hung on tree right in front of great house he should have owned. And he was buried alongside of farmer—farmer's grave separated his and girl's. They were separated even in death as in life. (Jimmy, story B-1, 1940)

Young man coming home from college on surprise visit. Been away for

Appendix A. Resumé of the Subjects

three years and has had to work way through. During three years only chance to come home. This is last year. Due to graduate in few months. Worked very hard. Saved few extra dollars. Wants to take mother back to see him graduate. Would be pretty lonely graduating not having anyone close around. Have to share happiness as you share sorrow. Comes home, just before exams. Surprise visit. Downstairs the same ole place. All familiar. Knocks at door. Doesn't know if to jump in and yell surprise or just walk in. Knocks. No answer. Tries door. Open. Walks in. Sees no one there. Opens closet. No clothes in them. Furniture still there but no one else. Goes upstairs. Inquires of landlord whereabouts of mother. Landlord amazed to see him. Says mother had gone to college to surprise him for graduation. Boy takes return ticket and starts back. Meanwhile at school mother encounters same situation. She, too, started back. Both riding on same railroad but never really met. Trains did meet but never got a chance to meet again. Trains crashed on way back and both killed looking for each other. (Where did that come from on a nice day like this?) (Jimmy, story A-2, 1940)

In another story (A-7, 1940), he platitudinizes as follows: "No matter how many times your mother tells you, advises you, she's had more experience . . . . the minute someone is in trouble or is frightened, they have a tendency to yell 'Mom!' or 'Mother!'" Another story, B-8, tells of conflict between the home that is formal and a home with love. At the beginning he tells of "a great fancy estate, with trimmings and ornaments. Mother never knew how to make a house a home. She couldn't put life into anything. Everyone must sit in certain chairs, eat in a certain room. All had set places." Mother's philosophy was "There's more than love to marriage. There's background, family." But after the vicissitudes of this story mother discovered that "it took more than four walls and furniture to make a home." This close relationship has been a matter of great struggle on the part of Jimmy. As a result of his war experiences he has struggled to emancipate himself from his mother. His search for himself was clearly already started in 1940. Story A-1 illustrates this well.

Here we have country lad coming to great, cruel, cold city. Heard all about it from people at home. Great and cold. That doesn't bother him. A dreamer. Sees city has heart and that blood that feeds into heart is love. Each building seems warm, not cold brick as described in home town. Idealist and he made up mind that while in city he'd live by proposition that heart of city pumped blood of love. Got himself inexpensive room in inexpensive part of town and proceeded to look for job. Looked for days and days and found nothing. Went back to hotel every night sad

320   *Appendix A. Resumé of the Subjects*

and began to think city cold. Struck thought from mind and said city must be warm for it pumps love. Met girl next day—cross out— Decided to do writing. No job. Thought job would keep him 'til he sold something. Wrote poems, short stories, novels. On for passing of years. Did odd jobs. Just enough to keep alive. Every poem and play about great city. Every theme was warm heart of city that pumped blood of love. When he finished play he thought no one could reject, best, he realized he had no money. Last hope to keep alive. Went from office to office. No one ever saw play. Couldn't get by first desk. Home. Weak from hunger. Dropped to bed. Wrote a letter to people back home still telling them city had warm heart but a cold, hard outer surface that must be penetrated before you can really love the city or have the city love you. Then next morning he was found dead. A few years later they uncovered his plays and they produced them and city loved them. He had penetrated outside covering of heart of city. Reached heart but too late for him to reach that. But always knew while alive that heart was warm but never realized it was he that was part of that heart. (In other words searching for self, I guess.) (Jimmy, subject 37, story A-1, 1940)

His desire to find himself through writing was present even in the early period. This story also indicates that his desire to write is equated with sex—writing is a substitute for or displacement of sex. Instead of meeting a girl, he switches the story to writing about love.

CHANGE IN FANTASY: JIMMY, SUBJECT 37

Fantasy theme	Change in fantasy	Fantasy theme	Change in fantasy
Negative Outcome	−9	Crime against persons	−3
Aggressed against	−6	Eroticism	+3
Accidental death	−5	Rejection	+3
Hostility	−4		

CHANGE IN FANTASY

As in 1940, Jimmy is reacting to his original Oedipal tendencies which still hold him in their grip and against which he is still struggling.

It is easy to find much in common between the 1940 and the 1953 stories—the length, the vague soul-searching, philosophizing, his feeling of having been smothered by his mother—but differences also are prominent. The earlier stories, for instance, were stories of tragedy. Quite baldly, many of them were stories of guilt for Oedipal wishes— wishes for the mother and for the destruction of the father. The son in A-2 (1940, given above), a college boy, is killed in a train wreck

Appendix A. Resumé of the Subjects

searching for his mother. And in B-1 (1940) he is executed for murdering the man (father figure) who separated him from the woman he loved. But in 1953 these tragic themes have largely disappeared, and in their place the love and sexual themes look forward to a happy consummation.

With his greater sophistication he presents Oedipal tendencies more symbolically, but they still underlie his fantasies. In several stories, however, his Oedipal ties are clearly revealed. In A-7 a boy and an older woman have an affair. A man makes friends with a whore who mothers him (B-4). A girl whose father is dominated by his wife marries an older man as a father substitute (B-6) and in a story in which a girl is afraid of her father and sex we find that later the father turns into a husband (B-7). And in the autobiographical story to the blank card (B-11) the subject searches through sex for a mother figure while on leave in some French Riviera community during the war.

Symbolically, in story A-1 the subject wants to get back to the soil, to feel close to mother earth. So at the beginning he announces his need for a close tie with mother. Throughout his stories he expresses his desire to "realize" life, which means his wish for experiences that will reaffirm closeness and belongingness.

He also senses the need on the part of a man or woman for a father. In B-8 in one of his philosophical ruminations he sees that a man fulfills two needs for a woman—as a sexual object and as a father figure. So the subject in this story marries an older man who serves also as a father. But later in this story the woman rejects him as a father because he refuses to be authoritative in any way with her and he tries to let her have as free a hand as possible (B-8). In B-3 one man serves as a "spiritual father" to his close buddy in the Army. The officer in B-1 has to order his men about.

This need for the closeness of a mother and the strength of a father creates in Jimmy his greatest conflict—the conflict between adherence to discipline and his great need for freedom and independence. He sees a boy as dominated by his mother (A-5) even though his mother has just put the light on and has left an apple for him (A-6). In A-7 there is a childless woman who satisfies her need for children by befriending a young man. He tells of a man who is attracted to a girl because she demanded nothing of him (B-4). The conflict for him is whether to live under the rules (B-3) or to revolt against discipline

(B-1). He has a great horror of confinement—the confinement of the city, of religious doctrine, of the rules of society (B-9). He has the urge to roam and would like to "chuck the whole thing" (B-1). Society, religion, Christianity do not give a man room to grow (A-1). He has a fear of developing dependence on anyone else (B-4) and wishes to be uninhibited, free, untrammeled (B-10). A woman seeks divorce (B-9). The soldier dreads returning home where he will have once again to submit to the influence of his family (B-11).

In 1940 there was longing and despair on the part of the male figure. But in story A-7 in 1953 a man deserts an older woman for a younger, which causes the older to become insanely jealous.

The boy of course grows and this goes on for years without discovery, and then it comes to the time when he meets a younger girl, a girl his own age, one whom he wants to marry . . . he does meet this other girl and has good intentions of marrying her and he of course drops this first woman like a hot potato, explaining to her that she of course is married. . . . When he does drop her the former woman has jealous rages and she goes down to this young man's office and does everything she can to see him. He wants nothing to do with her, tries to make it a final act but she as a woman could not realize that any such thing she took all this into herself and made of it a love affair, a love I should say, whilst to him it was just an affair in growing process and finally one night he is visiting in the town and she shoots at him through the window, and the case goes to court. She kills him. (Jimmy, subject 37, story A-7, 1953)

This more mature attitude on his part is reflected in story B-1 (1953). This is the picture which in 1940 led to the story of the strong young man falling in love with a farmer's sister, but in 1953 this same picture yields a story of a man in officers' training, revolting at the discipline and restriction of freedom. The story tells of his own inner struggle for independence.

. . . Well to take him beyond this point, beyond the picture, well, he's about to leave, to chuck the whole thing, he's got his back to the building and he sees others going to class, drilling, and so forth. It presents a challenge to him. If others can take this, he can take it too, and come through it and still be himself. . . . Just carrying a burden that he thinks is inflicted upon him and determined to carry it and to let it have no effect on him. So he goes back and because he has breached the rules, he is for a period subjected to more stringent discipline, punishment of a sort and he bears it very independently, not a chip on his shoulder but just an iron-front to him, going in and letting no one come near. . . . And as a result of this, the whole thing becoming a challenge to him on a personal basis, the whole code of discipline, etc., and he is determined that he will live by those rules of discipline and still be bigger than them. He does a very good job and he comes out very well, becomes an officer and gets sent out to sea again on a ship. . . . Well, this slowly came upon him and he again without realizing it passed on to them the same discipline that he had learned. And he still found that by getting more control of himself he was disciplining himself again, he was gaining more and more freedom, and not only [sighs] was he gaining freedom, but he was growing, as a person. He had less and less of himself to bother about. His—self had become— well, disciplined, and so having less of himself to bother about he could relate better to people, because he was interested more and more in them, because his interest in people did not come necessarily out of a need for himself, only for himself, he wasn't going to people to satisfy his own needs, but was going to them a great deal more out of interest to them and so, if you're interested in others, they naturally become interested in you. . . . And the roving urge is the first step, to seek the Navy, to leave the farm, etc. He realized this was a necessary thing. He didn't have to go far, he didn't have to fight as he did in this picture, walk with the clenched fist out of the institution to be himself. He realized that the battle was within yourself, and you could be the self you wanted to be, not the self that was thrust upon you by other men. From then on, his work begins. He found a way and all he has to do is to grow and be what he can manage. (Jimmy, subject 37, story B-1, 1953)

Jimmy's stories present a number of conflicts or difficult decisions. In the Army there is the conflict between a sort of animal existence where one yields to primitive animal impulses and the personal and responsible existence in civilian life where one is judged by social values (B-11). There is the conflict between knowing and having, and being (A-3). There is the conflict between knowledge about life and living (B-2). The girl in B-2 with the book in her lap may understand a lot about life, but this is no substitute for "living that thing, having that thing, being that thing." There is the conflict between marriage and a career (B-2). A woman has to decide whether she marries for love (pleasure from husband) or children (B-8). And he sees himself to blame for these conflicts (B-4).

The stories in 1953 have more open sexual references. These references were perhaps present in 1940, but more by implication; whereas in 1953 he does not feel the same restraint and comes to the point more directly.

Jimmy is concerned about sex and its place in life. He seems to be aware of sexual fear which is based on lack of knowledge of the sexual world which means that attitudes toward sex are based on fantasy (B-7). There is doubt but that his sex urges places him in conflict. He tells of a sexually impotent man who has never known his wife (A-7) and how the wife seeks satisfaction elsewhere. In another story (B-8) the same theme occurs and a woman who has married a studious but impotent man (a man who lives mildly by his inhibitions) "starts to find—and finds—another man, which is not hard." In B-7 the husband is gentle with his wife on their wedding night. He refers to the animal in man (B-10) and one of the characters in a story (A-8) is horrified by the grossness of sex. But he says that man is more than an animal (A-1) and that sexual activity by itself is not completely satisfying (A-7). Sex becomes a symbol of warmth (B-7).

What Jimmy dreads in his relationship with his mother is that she will completely dominate him, swallow him up and prevent him from being himself—an independent person. He puts great stress on self-determination (A-10), of mapping one's own course, of making one's own decisions. He ridicules the person who will go to a fortuneteller to find out what will happen to him, rather than making decisions concerning his own goals and having the stamina to carry them out (A-10). Life in the Army is depersonalized (B-11). He speaks of growing to be a full, mature, self-realizing person (B-1, B-2), yet dreads the loss of protection that the Army provides.

Jimmy has an interesting concept of growth. The girl in B-5 who came to this country from Poland, went to school, married, and had children "has had experiences, has grown from her experiences because these experiences occurred within her and as a result she has become more of a person." This is essentially the principal finding of the present study.

Several times he contrasts in this way the inner with the outer. He speaks of the beauty of the soul to be contrasted with physical beauty (A-2), and he tells of two girls who mismarried because they judged by surface appearances (A-8)—"Never judge a book by its cover."

This becoming a person in his own right presents a formidable challenge to Jimmy. He has vague ambitions of building a fortune (A-1), but then he fears that he will crack up and will not be able to face making his own decisions and taking their consequences (B-1). Life presents a challenge to him—"if others can take it, I can too" (B-1).

Jimmy puts stress on self-awareness. The maid in the hotel does not know what she feels (A-9), and her awareness is limited to the immediate. Jimmy speaks of "complete awareness" (A-1), of learning about oneself (A-5), and he believes that by knowing oneself one gets to know all people (B-1). So Jimmy feels a need for being alone with one's emotions, of having a room of one's own in which he can think (B-6).

Yet this being alone should not estrange one from life (B-9), but should enable one to relate more effectively with others. Jimmy places great importance on being able to form friendships (B-1, B-2, B-3). The officer in B-1 seeks friends with the men below him in rank. The young man left the big impersonal city and returned to his home town where he would get the feeling of belonging (A-1). But he does not admire the person whose whole existence depends on the group. He speaks with evident admiration of the teacher who "one day finds a young girl who is in the group and is accepted by the group, yet stands out from it. She can leave it and take it as she chooses" (B-2). He would quit a relationship when its meaning and usefulness are gone (B-3). He despises the self-centered person (B-2) but admires anyone who is interested in persons (B-1). Throughout his stories Jimmy shows a high degree of sensitivity to human relations.

Jimmy has given thought to the meaning of love. Love is the giving of the whole person, "the emptying and giving out of the complete man" which would make it more than sexual love (A-7). Love involves a personal relationship. In love there is equality, for love that is worship tends to subjugate. "When you love you don't worship, you want to be part of it, you want to live it" (A-2). When a person loves, it "perambulates through him and affects those about him" (A-2). Those in love live happily after facing every struggle. True love is forgiving. The woman whose husband has an affair with her sister forgives him when he confesses (B-4) and she gains strength from the fact that her husband came back.

As is the case with so many who are struggling to master conflict in their own lives, Jimmy's solutions for himself overflow and he would become a teacher of others (B-2, B-3, B-6, B-9) "to help them to be themselves, how they can share themselves and share others." The man brooding in B-6 seeks to solve the conflicts of others by becoming a writer. By laughing at others he actually becomes a writer of tragedy.

Standing apart from these philosophical themes is the theme of envy and jealousy. The girl reading a book envies the girl who is walking by on a date (A-3); the older woman becomes jealous when the young boy who she has befriended meets a girl his own age whom he wants to marry (A-7). The girl in B-4 envies her sister and later suffers guilt because of it; and the girl who was left behind in Poland when the family became separated during the war is jealous of her sister who came to the United States and has many advantages. And this envy leads to jealous anger. The older woman shoots to kill the boy who left her for a girl his own age (A-7). The American girl who has an affair with a man in Mexico becomes angry when she feels she is just taken for granted (B-10). Some of this envy would seem to be rooted in sibling rivalry, but some of it is definitely Oedipal. And this jealousy also indicates paranoid tendencies.

Jimmy is sensitive to rejection, which appears in several of his stories. The boy gives up the older woman when he finds a more satisfying relation with a girl his own age (A-7). The studious girl rejects men because she believes she is not attractive to them (A-3). There is rejection in the Cinderella story (B-4), and the American girl finally is forced to reject her sister who was brought up in Poland after she finds that the Polish girl is consumed by jealousy. All this engenders guilt and generosity and sympathy which are used as compensations to neutralize the guilt (B-5).

Rivalry and the hostility that it arouses lead to depression. In story A-1 a character ruminates on death which "defeats all men's striving." The girl who feels that she is not attractive to boys becomes dejected (A-3). Picture B-6 suggests dejection, which leads the character in the story to become a writer. The soldier in B-11 responds to his depression by drinking. There is reason to believe that these last two stories are autobiographical. His search for a mother, which is powerful and deep, again is symbolized by drinking, but against this need he rebels and tries to find a way out by writing, teaching others, and philosophizing.

Jimmy's stories are much more interpretive and full of philosophizing than those of any other subject. In many respects his point of view is admirable. We must remember, however, that Jimmy is himself still struggling to resolve these conflicts in his own life so that one must not be misled by his teachings to assume that he has conquered his own difficulties. Now that Jimmy is married so much depends on his wife and whether through his relationship with her he will be able to achieve the independence and self-determination that part of himself craves.

EXCERPT FROM THE RORSCHACH REPORT

Rich, productive, interesting, dilated personality. Artistically talented. His energies are not disciplined and not well channeled. He is acutely sensitive in his perceptions of the world. There is much drive, physical energy, and ambition. He has a capacity to enter and leave emotional situations easily. He becomes carried away by his imagination. Excellent social adaptation. Popular and genuinely likable. Optimistic and tends to reach higher than he can attain but his aspirations have a schizoid quality.

Aggressive impulses sublimated through a spiritual or aesthetic attitude. He has deep feelings of inadequacy as a man and ambivalence toward women. He cannot combine tender and aggressive feelings for the same woman. His Oedipal ties have never been adequately resolved. He alternates between passive feminine identification and aggressive masculine self-assertion. Oppositional ties to mother deeply repressed. Strong sensual ties pronounced. Feelings of guilt about aggressive aspects of sex.

Strong fear of father and deep feelings of the father's disapproval of sex. He denies to himself that he is disappointed in sex.

Always able to inhibit impulses of rage even when they are appropriate. Helpless and passive with authority figures. He has a strong sense of dependence on parents and the need to free himself of it.

Much spontaneity, liveliness, and empathic rapport. He is afraid of deep emotional contact. He has secret rejecting attitudes toward people. Tension and anxiety mount, making close contacts unpleasurable. He feels ill-at-ease with people.

Depressive moods and a feeling of self-rejection but these feelings are not pronounced. He can easily withdraw into a highly schizoid personal world. Schizophrenic features seem to be well controlled.

John, Subject 39

JOHN AS AN ADOLESCENT

As a seventeen-year-old boy from a family of low cultural level, John was a good student—clean-cut, cooperative, interested in automobiles and automechanics. He did odd jobs and earned much money. His mother characterized him as headstrong.

SYNOPSIS OF ADOLESCENT FANTASY

His adolescent stories showed very strong aggressive and destructive tendencies against which he defended himself by reaction formations and projection as a reformer, protecting others from aggression. There was a psychopathic flavor to his stories in which characters were crafty, contemptuous of authority and the law. There was a callousness and sadism toward the opposite sex. Having a good time was followed by punishment, and morality was equated with church attendance and religious belief.

There were wild joy rides in automobiles and fear of cars and trucks. Driving a car was pictured as dangerous.

He viewed females cynically, with suspicion, disillusionment, and distrust. Dangerous, injurious things happened to the person who dealt with the opposite sex. Marriage led to difficulties and unhappiness and the woman who did not properly take care of her husband and neglected to feed him was always to blame.

The subjects were basically dependent. Home atmosphere was pictured as uncongenial and there was a desire to leave home, but deprivation and anxiety forced him back to a dependent position.

Father was depicted as stingy, mother as generous. Success depended on hard work and his characters were enterprising. But to get ahead you must cooperate with those in authority. There was a desire for money and what it will buy.

JOHN AS AN ADULT

As a man John speaks forcefully and dynamically, with loud laughter and table-thumping. He is an easy talker and not nervous or self-conscious.

He graduated from high school, went on to study automobile mechanics, and later took night courses in chemical engineering at New York University. He is foreman in an auto plant, and is a hustler and a driver of his men.

He has a dim view of marriage. He boasts of going out with chorus girls and models, spending heavily on them, and says many girls want to marry him, but he is afraid of marriage.

He still lives at home with his mother and unmarried sister in the poorer part of town, but he has given his mother an expensive Cadillac.

CORRESPONDENCE BETWEEN ADOLESCENT FANTASY
AND ADULT PERSONALITY

The stories John told as an adolescent foreshadowed his adjustments as a man. Story A-2 showed clearly his need to work and strive as a way of fending off anxiety.

Young fellow. Nothing to do. Standing on corner. Canvassed by passing magazine salesman to be distributor of national magazine. Young man sees chance to make spending money. Consents. He starts canvassing neighbors. In due time establishes nice route. He secures spending money, bicycle, sport equipment, and all other premiums salesman offers for good work. In due time promoted to salesman with all boy distributors. Succeeds to climb 'til manager of men. To all fellows who call on him for advice he tells them, "If you want to succeed you have to work hard." (John, subject 39, story A-2, 1940)

Actually John today is a hard worker and is resourceful. He is much interested in money and places considerable value on it.

His mother's influence is illustrated in story A-7.

Here's fellow, pretty well along in school and it is graduation. Mother is proud of son and day before graduation tells him to keep up his character and keep things she taught him as a guide in life. After graduation his mother passes on. He comes on under her principles and makes a success of self. (John, subject 39, story A-7, 1940)

But his mother, in spite of having given him ambition, has also made him insecure. In his adolescent fantasies he was constantly beset by fear of failure, of not having enough to eat. Story B-6 illustrates this well.

Young man graduates from school. Looks for job. He has gone to different city and is boarding with people. Fails to get any work and funds are decreasing quickly. After few weeks of not finding a job finds he's broke.

Doesn't know what to do. Told if he doesn't pay rent he'll have to leave boarding house. He decides no employment available. Best thing to do is commit suicide. Opens gas jet. Sits in room. Someone outside smells gas, saves him in time. When some passer by sees condition of him, passer by offers him employment. After he recuperates he goes to work and then sees there is always hope for anything. (John, subject 39, story B-6, 1940)

One must remember that John is still unmarried and lives at home with his mother, toward whom he is generous. John has distorted ideas of sex. Two stories which illustrate this are given here in full, in spite of the fact that they are long and rambling (A-8 and A-5).

Here's a class of boys and girls, sophomores listening to Weekly Bulletin. Announcement of dance sponsored by junior class, open only to junior classmen. Fellows disappointed. Can't attend. Girls have a chance to get in. Following week all soph girls make sure they are noticed by juniors. Juniors noted them but none want to ask sophs to dance. Girls disappointed, try to scheme. Two sisters here. Decided to get one of Junior girls attending dance, and injure her so she couldn't attend. [Confusion—hesitation.] Following day girls go bicycle riding. See junior. Purposely injure her. Nothing happens to her. Falls. But none the worse off. Two sisters disappointed. Try another idea. Try tripping junior in gym. Also fails. Day of dance comes. Hasn't been asked to go. So they decide to go stag. Try to get past doors. Two other fellows in junior class who had been refused by all the girls as escorts. They decided to go stag also. In front of school both meet. Girls are more than willing to go to dance and go in. In middle of dance fellows suggest to go out for ride. Girls go. Going around corner when door opens. One of girls falls out. Face all cut up. Other girl none the worse off, for accident. Goes out with these fellows after other girl taken out. (Oh!) On way back to dance fellow applies brakes quickly. Girl's head goes through windshield. Also all cut up. Fellows are not sorry for what happened. Give her horse laugh. Take her home. Two girls stay home for few weeks trying to get faces back to where they were. Lose out on schoolwork. This was all that was needed to keep them back as sophs. Following year hear same announcement as last year. Just ignore it this time. Hope that next they'll be juniors and attend prom. (John, subject 39, story A-8, 1940)

Here's girl leaving home in morning. On way to school meets couple of fellows. Nice day and fellows persuade her to play truant. She decides to go with them and they go for a ride. Ride for quite some time and fellows decide to do bad things. She objects to goings on and is put out of car. She starts walking for home and in due time gets tired and weary. Nightfall approaches. Still miles from home and no money. She sits down by side of road and passing police officer sees her. Asks her what's the matter. She tells she wants to go home and no money. She goes with officer. He provides funds to get home. She arrives home and following day sees

Appendix A. Resumé of the Subjects 331

fellows again. They nag her and she decides not to associate with boys any more. (John, subject 39, story A-5, 1940)

It is rather clear that John equates automobile driving with sexual activity in fantasy and this may help to explain his life-long interest in automobiles. Somehow his interest in sex has been redirected into a passion for automobiles, but automobile driving (sex) is dangerous and almost sure to result in accident and injury. There are definite castration fantasies ("face all cut up"). He takes a very cynical if not sadistic attitude toward girls. ("Girls go out with those fellows. On way back from dance fellow applies brakes quickly. Girl's head goes through windshield. She is also cut up. Fellows are not sorry for what happens. They gave her the horse laugh.") His attitude toward women seems to be that they are heartless, disinterested and fickle. Story B-1 illustrates this.

Fellow and girl on wedding day, happy and full of joy with the world. After honeymoon return back. Man returns to employment and wife tends to home. He comes home every day and has to prepare own meals and is disgusted. After a while he does not appear home for meals but eats out. His wife doesn't care and decides he doesn't love her any more. One evening he doesn't feel hungry and comes home and has argument with wife and leaves house permanently. Wife files petition for divorce and it is granted. Man is contented living as previously and in few months former wife married again. He sees her ruin her second husband's life and decides to put man wise to it. Other man refuses to take former's advice and in short time is getting divorced also. (John, subject 39, story B-1, 1940)

These attitudes toward sex and women are reflected in his present attitudes toward women. He boasts of his ability to make conquests of attractive women but he shuns marriage.

CHANGE IN FANTASY: JOHN, SUBJECT 39

Fantasy theme	Amount of change
Success	−5
Pleasure	−4
Eroticism	+5
Morality	+3

CHANGE IN FANTASY

The stories John tells in 1953 show great hostility, fear and distrust of women, and cynicism toward marriage. These themes run through all of his stories.

This year a fellow, Freddie, was going out with four sisters in one family that were about a year apart each one of them, and he got real interested in one of them and she was the best daughter of the family and she was a real believer in horoscopes, crystal balls, and what have you. And he goes for the same malarky and junk so she finally convinces him, they were down on the Jersey shore somewhere at a Gypsy Swami's. They go in there and both of them go in together and they start asking this Swami what does he see in their future. They were going steady and the Swami figured "Well, I might as well make this good because maybe I can give them a tip about getting married as both of them look right for each other." So he gives them this story that they are the ideal couple for each other and they are going to settle down and make a perfect pair. Well Freddie believes it one tenth of the way and yet he doesn't believe it and Freddie finally in one of his weak moments decides to marry her. He was a Catholic and she was a Protestant and she converted to a Catholic and they were married and they got an apartment for themselves. Well then it got to the point where he just wanted to go around, they had no children at the time, he wanted to go around doing the town and she didn't want to. She just wanted to stay at home. Everytime he went out and done the town his wife would think that he was out with me and she would say who did you go out with Joe and he would stutter and would not say yes or no. Before I knew it I was in more hot water than I have ever been in. So one day he comes up to me and says to me don't ever get married. The time I went to the Swami he gave me a song and dance and I figured it was just a lot of malarky. I married in the church and the religion says I can't get a divorce and I can't live with the woman so what shall I do so I said that is your problem and he came to the conclusion that he was going to stick it out. They have been miserable for the past seven years. (John, subject 39, story A-10, 1953)

Apparently the same attitude was present in 1940 in symbolic form—that is, in his fantasies about automobiles and in the danger of reckless driving. Over the years, as he matured, he faced his reality situations which were present only in symbolic form in adolescence. The same fear and distrust are still present, but now they are unabashedly projected onto women. It is probably of some significance that reference to automobiles is less prominent in his 1953 stories—their place is taken by his more direct discussion of sex and marriage.

Along with this greater directness about sex there is a projection that women are immoral, impossible to live with, and that marriage ends in misery.

I'll make this one a little better than the others. I'll call the lady Virginia Hill. This girl is from Minnesota and very emotionally unstable. She met this fellow while he was in the Army and she married him about six years ago. The fellow's a normal individual about thirty years old and she's about twenty-five or -six. She's always looking no matter where she's at for some young, dashing individual. He's practically of the same opinion. He'd like to go to all the floor shows, side shows, and whatever have you, where they have burlesque. So, Thursday night he goes to the burlesque where he wants to go and she goes out. They have no children. So, he goes out and gets a couple of beers in him and comes home about twelve o'clock and looks around and the wife ain't home. So, he says, "I guess I'll go to bed." So, he tosses around in the bed and at three o'clock he gets up and finds that Virginia ain't home yet. So, he gets up and starts reading the paper. About 3:25 she decides to come in from where she's at. She was out with an Air Force lieutenant. The guy figured it was an easy date so he took her for all it was worth. He wouldn't even let her get out of the hotel there so finally she comes in and tells him that her husband wants to see her so she goes home. They get into an argument. The husband says, "Where have you been?" She says, "Well, I was out with the girls." He says, "Where did you get mauled up as much as you did?" "Oh, I ain't mauled up." He accuses her of adultery and she says, "No." Right then and there he walks out of the house and says to hell with her. He just moves out of the house completely. She's there and she comes crying back to him that she didn't do anything wrong and all that. He wouldn't believe her, but after her pleas he takes her back but never trusts her again. She didn't go out for about a year after that but she still got this desire to have more men than her husband. She runs across this girl friend and says, "My husband doesn't satisfy me—what do you think I should do?" So, the girl, real inquisitive, says, "Why doesn't he satisfy you?" She says, "I don't know—just doesn't know the right acts or what." So she says, "Well, if he doesn't satisfy you, why don't you just divorce him?" "If I divorce him I won't have anything and I'll be worse off than now." After the girl friend talks to her for about six months, she asks that a divorce be granted. The guy goes on his way and she goes on her way. (John, subject 39, story B-7, 1953)

One distinct change in the stories is the loss of pleasure in 1953 that is found in the 1940 stories. For instance, in story B-8 (1940, given above), it is said that "a fellow decided to go out for a ride before going home. Young girl consents to go off for joy ride." In early adolescence sex is seen as something joyous but in 1953 only the hopeless, disappointing aspects of sex are emphasized. This parallels the shift from aggression to depression seen in the stories of some of the younger subjects.

Another shift from the 1940 to the 1953 stories is in the theme of success. In 1940 success depends on hard work and the characters are enterprising but in 1953 themes of loafing, being shiftless and indolent appear. There is no doubt but that the earlier drive for success which he has worked out in his own life was a defense against anxiety. In part this is an omnipotent striving against a feeling of inferiority and dependence but in part it is a defense against his femininity which he must disguise by an overpowering masculinity. Story B-6 in 1953 illustrates this new tendency.

This must be a guy without a trouble in the world. Down in the North Carolina hills sitting in his house. It's getting kind of cold sitting outside. Here's a guy who came up here and looked around New York City and seen how crazy people live here, how they rushed around, and he decided that his grandparents and his great-grandparents lived down in the hills of Kentucky on moonshine and he might as well go down, too. So, he went back down here and bought him a thirty-acres of land for about $1,000. He sold his car and bought this thirty acres of land, about two hogs, six or eight chickens. Just enough to keep himself going and just enough food to keep himself alive. He had no wife. He was just shiftless and independent. He just sits there and rocks his life away. He's going to be about one hundred and twenty years old and not a worry in the world. I got a buddy of mine who's out there. He was down there during the war. [Do you envy him?] The guy's got more brains than any of us. He just sits down there and watches the cars go by. The guy's got more brains than 90 percent of the people around here. (John, subject 39, story B-6, 1953)

Apparently, having demonstrated his competence in his work (and with women—at a price), he is able to admit the underlying indolence. When one has achieved success in life there is less need to fantasy it.

EXCERPT FROM THE RORSCHACH REPORT

Over-ambitious, energetic, driving person with highly labile emotional excitability. Strong desire to impress people—generally exhibitionistic. No limit to his need to control natural forces and people.

Driving energy comes from pervasive and intense destructive aggression and hatred which he has channeled into the goal to do something big.

Diganosis lies between a psychopathic personality and a schizoaffective disorder.

His identification is feminine although his concept of role is an aggressive, active, masculine one. The poorly controlled exhibitionism betrays his effeminacy (like a hysterical woman).

His role toward both parents negative. Toward the father he feels small, helpless, forced into passivity which thinly veils his outrage and hatred at such coercion. There is an acute chronic tension and anxiety against which his only defense is to keep constantly active—anxiety has resulted in serious ego damage and a blunting of affect.

Sadomasochistic elements are strong. His relationship to his world alternates between rebellion and compliance.

He is impulsive, rash in judgment. He has an explosive temper. He is afraid of betraying his sense of inferiority.

Albert, Subject 40

ALBERT AS AN ADOLESCENT

Albert's mother died when he was four and a half years old. He and his sister were taken by their maternal grandparents; later he was taken by his paternal grandparents, who were sickly people, and he was cared for largely by an unmarried aunt. The grandparents could not tolerate noise so Albert had to walk softly. The household was depressing—unaffectionate and undemonstrative, although his own mother had been demonstrative and affectionate. However, Albert was described as cheerful and enthusiastic. He wanted to be wanted and to have affection, but could not believe that others liked him. His father remarried when Albert was thirteen. He worked in his father's garage after school hours but his father was impatient and yelled at him. His aunt said of him: "He doesn't make friends easily, but gets along well with friends he has. Critical of people. Expects them to come up to certain standards. Doesn't dance—feels uncomfortable. He doesn't go out with girls." Of himself, he said: "I never go out with girls, because I'm too critical. I find people's faults too easily, perhaps when I recognize them as some of my own. I have a sort of inferiority complex because of all the kidding at my expense."

SYNOPSIS OF ADOLESCENT FANTASY

When he was seventeen his fantasies largely revolved around father figures. Subjects were angry and depreciating toward father figures, whom they saw as rejecting and indifferent and helping to ruin their sons. Yet at the same time they were dependent on the father figures and hence could not openly defy them. The aggressive impulses led to anxiety and guilt. There were themes of disillusionment, dejection, defeat, futility, hopeless resignation, and a desire to get things without effort—to receive passively, like an infant.

ALBERT AS AN ADULT

As a thirty-year-old man Albert was reserved but friendly. He was nervous during the interview yet exhibited strong assertiveness on points made. After high school he studied at the University of Rochester, Indiana University, and the University of Maryland, where he graduated, but he did poorly in college as he had no goal. Since graduating he has had ten jobs, but in each case he got angry at the boss, grew discouraged, and left. He was very critical of his next-to-last boss, but is now back working for him again.

He has had many girl friends but goes after women unobtainable either because of religion or because they are married. He speaks of girls as a distraction. He is now engaged and hopes to marry in a few months.

He is being psychoanalyzed and claims he is always fighting with his analyst.

He did quite a lot of drinking in the Army but is not a heavy drinker now. He says he is not aggressive enough to sell anything or to persuade or convince people. He does not admire his relatives. He has high but vague ideals.

CORRESPONDENCE BETWEEN ADOLESCENT FANTASY
AND ADULT PERSONALITY

Albert's 1940 stories reflect some of his later attitudes in a remarkably faithful way. His main problem has been his relations with authority figures, and this difficulty was clearly portrayed in his 1940 stories. Story B-1 (given on p. 34) is most revealing. The significance of this story in the light of his subsequent job history is so apparent that it needs no comment.

Story B-7 shows how he feels that a father is indifferent and rejecting.

Girl just home from date and mother waiting up for her. Mother has warned her against staying out late. Girl liked good time. Lately keeping late hours. This time her mother decided she'd have to forbid daughter from going out altogether. Caused argument. Daughter deliberately disobeyed mother. Went out. Father never wanted to take interest in her. Didn't do anything to discipline her. This condition caused continual quarrels between mother and father. When girl finally got in trouble father didn't want to have anything to do with her. (Albert, subject 40, story B-7, 1940)

Story A-7 shows Albert's rebellious attitude toward authority.

(Had that—so familiar.) Boy just sent home from school. He really didn't mean harm but with group of boys got into trouble and indefinitely expelled. Mother had worked very hard to secure education for son and she realized what lack of education had done for her. Son had always wanted to quit school but because mother so determined to keep him there he made best of it. When mother saw he kept getting in trouble with authorities she finally gave in and let him quit. That's all. (Albert, subject 40, story A-7, 1940)

In his 1953 interview he said that he believed Eisenhower was a wet blanket and a complete phony but he liked him better than MacArthur, whom he could not stand at all.

Story A-2, told in 1940, reveals something of his attitude toward girls at that time.

This boy met girl at party and he's rather—he rather likes her. Knows her for quite a while but never has spoken to her for more than a few minutes at a time. She acted friendly at party and he was excited at prospect of seeing her. He feels he knows her well enough to call on her and he goes to her house. She treats him friendly enough but he feels she's merely being hospitable and her attitude at party was the same. Though he likes her he doesn't want to take advantage of her good nature by coming often as he feels she doesn't enjoy his company and he never bothers her again. (Albert, subject 40, story A-2, 1940)

This is to be contrasted with the attitude expressed in story 40 (original series) in which erotic interests were clearly evident although they were repressed in reality when he was an adolescent.

Young lady just married. Spending honeymoon at Florida winter resort. Very happy. Ideal couple. Both had same interests. Enjoyed doing same things. They are, however—they do have bitter quarrels but relationship so close it really overcomes that. Married life turns out as happy as any and neither ever regrets the step they had taken. (Albert, subject 40, story 40, 1940)

He is unable to follow through on his interest in a girl because he feels that "she doesn't enjoy his company," and so he "doesn't want to take advantage of her good nature." Here he projects his own feelings of unworthiness and attributes them to another person. It is possible

In 1940 he says "through no effort on the man's part he is the recipient of good fortune." But in 1953 he is more hopeful. He speaks of "the hope that people have of something that will bring riches, wealth, or power." But he ends the story "they will never rise out of the social position that they are in at the present time or the background that they came from."

There is a noticeable omission of themes of marriage and eroticism in the 1953 stories as opposed to the 1940 stories, four of which were centered around the theme of romance and marriage. From the interview one surmises that Albert has had sexual problems—he has normal sexual impulses but "there was always some barrier that would prevent the relationship from leading to marriage." He himself credits his psychoanalysis with helping him to change his attitude with regard to heterosexual relationships. He claims "that before he got his analysis his relations with girls was more unsatisfactory and that he had always been afraid of the idea of marriage . . . he has always been afraid of making a mistake in this area. He does not believe that his relationship with this girl [to whom he is now engaged] is a case of romantic love. He simply likes her, respects her, and feels good with her."

So this change in his attitude toward women is reflected in his stories by the failure to introduce erotic themes, indicating that his conflict and pressures in this area have subsided.

Another change that is discernible is less passivity, especially being the object of aggression from someone else. Story B-1 illustrates this. The 1953 story given on page 34 should be carefully compared with the 1940 story given on the same page.

In 1940 he says "it would never occur to him to defend himself against his father." But in 1953 he says "he must have had a fight with someone at home and the expression is one of intense anger." Here is a change, but one would say that he has only begun to find a more mature way of adjusting to his frustration with authority figures. One may surmise that this change, too, is the result of his psychoanalysis. In his interview he says that he "is always fighting with his analyst and is always trying to make the analyst come down to the level of himself." It should be noted that he says of himself that he is never aggressive enough to make a good salesman or to persuade or convince people and that the two persons he admires most are Gandhi and Schweitzer. And it should be noted that both times in story B-1 the solution is to run away from the conflict. So Albert still has some way to go in working out a better adjustment.

EXCERPT FROM THE RORSCHACH REPORT

An obsessive-compulsive disorder in a very intellectual person. Compulsive pattern has resulted in a restriction of imaginative forces and self-assertive energy. His desire for achievement is slight and he seems to be frustrated in his capacity to structure his environment according to his own needs. Self-esteem is low and self-confidence is damaged.

He has confused sexual identification with underlying homosexual conflicts and feelings of inadequacy as a man. Perhaps there have been some overt homosexual experiences. Pervasive sexual anxiety. Sexualization of any situations that are objectively nonsexual. Castration anxiety. He is afraid of sexual contacts with women in spite of preoccupation with sex. Deeper feelings fixated on an oral level. A wish to take a feminine, passive role.

He has a need to please people based on his fear of rejection. There are mild ideas of reference. He is suspicious and feels that others are hostile to him. Voyeuristic impulses toward women.

His affect is overintellectualized. He expresses social relations as strained and uncomfortable. He is eager for support and nurturance.

He might become dependent on alcohol for reassurance and anxiety reduction.

His relationship with authority figures is one of defense and dependency.

Appendix B. The Case of Jack

There was more than usual desire to include Jack as one of the subjects in this follow-up study. Jack's case was presented in detail in *Adolescent Fantasy*, and was used by the author in his courses in Projective Techniques for many years to illustrate the Thematic Apperception Test method. Considerable curiosity has been expressed by students and others as to Jack's subsequent career. It was felt that he could have continued the delinquent trends which he exhibited in earlier childhood, or his ambitions and higher ideals might have prevailed to enable him to find a respectable station in life.

Dr. Jensen traced Jack to an address in an eastern city, but found that the family had moved without leaving a forwarding address with the post office and none of the neighbors knew where they had gone. All clues were fruitless and he was not included among the subjects in the main study. Some years later a search was made in telephone books in all communities in the eastern part of the country that were in the collection of the library of the Columbia University School of Business. Hope that his name would be found was about given up when it appeared in the very last book on the shelves. Jack responded to a letter and telephone call by signifying his willingness to serve as a subject in the follow-up study and an appointment was made to see him in the YMCA where most of the other subjects in the study had been seen.

Jack as an Adolescent

As a fifteen-year-old boy, Jack was a state ward and lived with a guardian. His father died of an accident and subsequent illness when he was eight, and his mother had a hard time providing for the family.

Appendix B. The Case of Jack

An older brother was a ne'er-do-well, while an older sister was wild and had been in a reformatory at one time on a morals charge. Two younger sisters, for whom Jack felt a special affection, lived with an aunt. Jack had a sympathetic guardian toward whom he expressed much loyalty. Jack expressed fondness for his guardian's son. He had a poor reputation in school and was in constant trouble with his teachers. He had a hot temper, but after an aggressive episode he would calm down and apologize. He was suspended from school on one occasion for making trouble in the cafeteria. He was a member of the Sea Scouts and hoped to join the Navy.

Jack as an Adult

Jack, a thirty-two-year-old man, is heavy-set and sturdy, but he also gives the impression of softness and of not having hard muscles. He is easy to meet, pleasant, agreeable, friendly and not at all ill-at-ease. He has an ingenuous expression and his complexion is a little on the pink side. He speaks fairly well, but when he becomes fully spontaneous there are traces of an uncultured background. After getting into the Picture-Story Test he became hot, took off his lumber jacket and smoked three or four cigarettes. At this task he tried very hard, like a school boy who is attempting to make a good impression on the teacher.

He entered into the Rorschach with much gusto and took delight in seeing things in the plates. He worked at each card for a long time, turning it into every position, and attempting to find objects in the small details.

He had three years of naval service on a destroyer in the Pacific, was at Guadalcanal and saw a ship explode nearby. He is married and has two little girls age five and six, of whom he is very fond. When he comes home at night they want him to tell stories to them. His wife was somewhat suspicious of his coming to see the examiner.

The transcript of the interview held with Jack is reported here in full rather than in abbreviated form because of its interest. Jack told his life story ingenuously and candidly, and one has the impression that he made every effort to state his case frankly and without reserve, as he thought was expected of him in the situation. There is little doubt that he tried to make a favorable impression.

All twenty stories of the Picture-Story Test are given in full, followed by an analysis of them. The Rorschach protocol is also given, together with the complete interpretation prepared by Mrs. Dudek.

Interview with Jack in 1957

Jack: Well, you see I was living with foster people at the time. I didn't live with my own family. My father died when I was a little boy. So in the first place I didn't like school. I didn't see why they put you through it. I figured you didn't need it. So I just figured, well, I just don't like school, there's no sense in me going to school. That was my attitude all the time and when I passed in the ninth I decided that—well even before I passed I decided—as soon as I could I'd get out of school because I wanted to go to work. Then I always felt that the people that were raising me had a son of their own and, er, the man I called Dad—I called the people I lived with Mr. and Mrs. Holland. I called her Mom—Mother—so I asked her if it was all right if I quit school and naturally they tried to talk me out of it. And I always felt that I should try to earn my way a little myself, you know. So when the term ended there I quit and I went to work.

Interviewer: What kind of work did you do?

Jack: Well, first I went to work in a cafeteria. Then they went on strike up there. It was in Lewisburg. Well, so when they went on strike I decided they can't do that to me, so I just quit and I found me another job. Some old man in Ellenville, he had a landscaping service. So he ran an advertisement in the paper—young healthy man, you know, young man wanted—healthy and everything—willing to learn, so I went to work for him.

Interviewer: How old were you when you went to work for him?

Jack: I was sixteen. So when I went to work for him I liked the work and everything. It was hard work. But I always had that idea in the back of my mind that I'd love to go in the Navy. Then I couldn't wait to become seventeen. I even tried to get in when I was sixteen, when I was working for him. This was Mr. —— in Ellenville. He was a nice fellow, treated me good and easy there. I worked for him quite a while there, until I decided to go in the Navy. I went down and enlisted and off I went. That's all the work I did before I went in.

Interviewer: How old were you when you enlisted?

Appendix B. The Case of Jack

Jack: Seventeen. It was after we were in the war. I went in in 1942.

Interviewer: Did you get a ship?

Jack: Yes, right away. I went to boot camp for six weeks training and then I went on a ship. Went on a destroyer. Yes, a little newer than that type (pointing to a picture on the wall). That was the type before mine (cough).

Interviewer: Where did you go?

Jack: First we went up to Maine, then down to Cuba to break the ship in—what they call a break-in period. This was a brand new ship so we broke the ship in—came back and took trial runs and everything. We went through the canal, the Panama Canal. Then we went right out to Hawaii and Guadalcanal, because at that time they were desperate you know. They needed ships so bad out there. Actually we didn't have too much training at all. We went out green practically, you know. We stayed out there for eighteen months in the islands. Then we took a five-day trip to Australia. Then we came back up for a few more months here, back in the islands again, then we came back to the States. When we come back to the States it was for a refitting, what they call a refitting, just before Saipan. I guess you remember that. It was just before that landing and everything. So they give us a fourteen-day leave to come home. Then we went back out again for the Philippine campaign and all to the end of the war.

Interviewer: Did you go through any bombings?

Jack: Oh, yes, quite a few of them—bombardments and landings. Well we went right up I guess for three years of it. Sometimes once or twice a month we would have a landing—take the Marines in.

Interviewer: Did you separate before the Japan surrender?

Jack: I was in until I was 21—see, so the war ended while I was still in there. Right after the war we went over to China—I put in a few months over there and then we came back to the States—We decommissioned the ship and then I went on another one and we decommissioned that one. My time was up and I come out.

Interviewer: What was your rank when you came out?

Jack: Oh, don't ask me that. I was Seaman First when I come out. . . . I just couldn't take that baloney they hand out, you know. I don't know. I can't stand anybody walking on me. Personally I got along. If the boss and I get along, I'm all right. Soon as they try to push me a little then I get hot under the collar and I push back and that's no good in the Navy. You've got to learn to take your orders. Some of that stuff I couldn't see because it was silly to me. Naturally I was in trouble all the time. I'd say it was one of the best things ever happened to me.

Interviewer: Did you get any special training, special skills?

Jack: Well, seamanship I learned pretty good. That's about all I'd say. The main thing I learned in there was, well, it would be hard to explain to anyone who wasn't on a ship. It was what you call leading seaman. In other words it was a man knew what he was doing all the time yet he couldn't hold the rate, but they make you a leading seaman. Well, like some of the fellows that come aboard new on a ship. I used to show them all the works, what to do, and help 'em. They would come in and get rates. You see they were smart enough to get their rates and keep 'em and hold 'em. Whereas me, I'd go ahead and get my rate and then give some officer a lot of guff and I would lose it again. Many a time, quite a while there, I was master of arms—master sergeant and that's senior policeman on the whole ship. You see I used to handle all of the duties of the master of arms and seaman and boatsmates. In other words any job they had to do there, I knew how to do it. Sometimes I'd be in charge of 20 or 30 men and that's one thing I'd say I did in the Navy, was learn how to handle men, how to give orders without being—you know, some guys if you gave them an order they'll want to know who you're trying to talk to, you know. More or less you learn a lot of diplomacy in there, that's what I think.

Interviewer: What did you do next?

Jack: Well, when I come out, come home to these people that raised me, you know.

Interviewer: Do they live now in Ellenville?

Jack: No, they moved to Raratan at that time and now they're down at Redstone. So naturally I always figured they are my mother and father, you know. They're my people.

Interviewer: Is —— their name or is it your name?

Jack: No, that's my own name. See my father died when I was about eight years old. My mother had five children altogether, so I actually don't know the true story there because I was too young to realize what was going on. It seems like my mother couldn't provide for all of us so the state took us. So they were going to put us either in a home or in a foster home. It was the state board of children's guardians and when I went to live with these people they had a boy of their own, a little younger than I am and they just wanted a boy to be company for him, you know. So they didn't figure that I would stay there that long and neither did I. I figured it was just a temporary stop. As I lived there, they took a liking to me and I liked them, naturally. They treated me like a son and I treated them just like my parents. So when I come out of the Navy, naturally that was the only home I knew, so I went back. So when I got home—

Interviewer: Glad to see you, were they?

Jack: Oh, yes. Terrific. In fact my mother she wrote to me every day I was out there and she always said that she was glad that was one thing she was glad that I did. I wrote her every day that I could, you know. Sometimes we were in an air raid or something where we couldn't get mail out I didn't write. When I come home Mr. Holland he asked me, he says, "What are you going to do now?" "I don't know. I'll get a job someplace." So I figured that I'd maybe get a job on a tug—tugboat, maybe, in New York, maybe painting bridges or something like that. I learned a lot of rigging in the Navy. Then I heard that rigging paid good. So then he said, "You actually don't know what you're going to do then?" I said "No." He says "Well," he says. See he is a foreman down there where I work now. "Well," he says, "look we got an apprenticeship program down in one place in the factory there." And he says "We got an apprenticeship open for a tool and die worker. Why don't you come down and try that—learn yourself a trade?" He said "After you get your trade you can do anything—that you always have, like an education. You're not going to college or anything, so you might as well learn a trade." He told me "You can be a tool and die maker if you're handy and you use your head and your common sense." So naturally in my head I always figured a tool and die maker had to know a lot, which they do. And I told him, I says "I'd be willing to go but I don't think I could make it, to tell you the truth, because with figures I'm just absolutely about on—the third-grade level. I mean I can't—mathematics or trigonometry and all that I don't know, which I always figured a tool and die maker has to know." So he talked to me and he says "Look, you can always drop out if it's too hard for you." He says "Come and try it."

Interviewer: He was very sympathetic, wasn't he?

Jack: He was trying to look out for me, you know. So I went down there and I went crazy for the first few weeks there. Gee, everything was too complicated to suit me, you know.

Interviewer: Was it a kind of school they put you in?

Jack: No. You know, it was a regular factory and they put you to work but they actually train you on the job.

Interviewer: But you have somebody close by you all the time?

Jack: Yes. We have—we, like now we have eight or nine tool and die makers there, been there in the business for years and they take an apprentice, they put him on a job. Maybe today I'll work with you. Whatever job you're working on you'll explain it all to me and let me do some of the work. Maybe the next day I'll work with somebody else and that's the way I'm supposed to learn. So as far as the work went I held my own—I was pretty good at it—not pretty good, I mean I wasn't *too* bad.

Interviewer: That was about ten years ago, was it?

Jack: Yeah. So I went ahead and I took the apprenticeship term there they had. But I always—when it come to the figure part of it, figuring out the angles and mathematics and things, I just can't hold my own at it. Luckily for me they had what they call a tool designer. See, they make up a print—you follow that print. You just do the hand work. You machine it, file it, you do all the hand work on it. With that part of it I'm all right. I can build it and read the print, file it down and make it smooth and whatever has to be done with it. So very seldom do we ever get a job where it really takes sitting down and figuring it out. And when I do get a job like that I take it to one of the designers and ask him to help me out with it.

Interviewer: You never did learn the mathematics side of it, did you?

Jack: Naw. I tried three or four times. I even went and bought books on mathematics, but I just can't get it through my head for some reason.

Interviewer: Still working at that same place?

Jack: Yeah, for ten years. Well, after four years I finished my apprenticeship. Now I'm a full-fledged die maker for the past six years. I do all right except when it comes to them parts where it comes to figuring, you know.

Interviewer: Do you have a family?

Jack: Yes. I've got two little girls—another one on the way. I don't know whether it's going to be a boy or girl this time.

Appendix B. The Case of Jack

Interviewer: Back in school times you didn't notice the girls much did you?

Jack: Well I'd say average. About—say, when I was in the ninth grade I was just about to notice 'em.

Interviewer: Where did you meet your wife?

Jack: I met her where I worked. Right after I went to work there I seen her working around the place and liked her, nice girl. Then a lot of the girls had bad names, you know, because you didn't know whether they were running around with different guys that were married. I figured she looked good and I would find out. Everyone around the place had a good word for her and she always looked like a decent girl to me. Then I got to know her pretty good and found out she was decent. So I guess we just fell in love and that was it.

Interviewer: You had known other girls before, hadn't you?

Jack: Oh, yeah. She really hit the spot, that's it. I wanted a clean-living girl that would stay home and cook.

Interviewer: How long have you been married?

Jack: Oh, eight years, next July it will be nine years.

Interviewer: What kind of person is she?

Jack: Well, I'm not bragging because she's my wife, but I think she's about the best. At times I can be the hardest person in the world to get along with and other times I can be the easiest because I'm more or less a little on the stubborn side. You know if I decide that I'm not going to do something I just don't want to do it. And sometimes I even hurt myself to hurt somebody else, I don't know. If a person gets me mad enough if I want to do a certain thing I won't deliberately do it, maybe just to hurt them. So my wife she's just like if everything is o.k. with me it's o.k. with her. In fact I feel sorry for her sometimes because I feel like I pick on her, you know. She might make supper sometime and she'll burn something on the table or something and I'll say "Well, gee, why didn't you watch the thing, you know?" She'll say "Well, I was busy with the kids," you know, and then I'll say "Well, why didn't you watch it?" Then I'll start lighting into her about it. Then maybe about ten minutes after—I'm spieling off at her —I start to realize, it could have happened to me just as easy as it happened to her, you know. And I've found out that sometimes I'm pretty hard to live with that way I think.

Interviewer: Is she good with the children?

Jack: Very good.

Interviewer: Two little girls, you say, five and six, what are their names?

Jack: Dolly's the oldest and she's six and a half and Emma, she's five and a half—about a year apart. Yes, they like me and I like them too. In fact every night we have a little ceremony there. Soon as I finish eating my supper and they're finished, I have to put my one daughter on one knee and the other on the other knee then they got to smooch me up a little bit, you know. They hug me and then they call my wife over and say "Come on, mother, you get on too," and they all try to pile on my lap, you know. Just the other night I says "What am I going to do when the other baby comes?" I says "There won't be any room any more." So we have a good time now.

Interviewer: Now your father died when you were eight years old from an accident, didn't he?

Jack: Well, he, er—as I remember it now—I could be wrong—first he had an accident. He was a lineman on one of these service trucks, you know. He used to put up these trolley wires and things. It seems that, I remember that he fell off the, er, truck and hurt his spine somehow. He used to wear a big brace. I remember that. And then when these big snowstorms would come along he used to drive the truck with the snow plow on it and as I remember it, he came down with this here cold—had the grippe. A big snowstorm come up, you know, and they pulled him out on it. Naturally he wanted to earn that little extra money because he had five kids there. And he wasn't supposed to go out yet. So he went out anyway to get the money and got pneumonia. So he was in the hospital for a while. As I remember it, it was pleurisy and pneumonia that he died from.

Interviewer: And your brother, you had an older brother didn't you?

Jack: Yeah.

Interviewer: What's become of him?

Jack: Well, he got married and—he wasn't married too long—and, er, he was married a couple of years there, see. I haven't kept in too close a contact with him.

Interviewer: You didn't?

Jack: No.

Interviewer: Wasn't he a little wild there for a time?

Jack: Oh, he was all the time—he still is, I imagine, from stories I hear now and then. You know, like once in a while one of my sisters will write me a letter. In fact my youngest sister she had a baby not too long ago. She had it christened so she asked me if I would come over. So I went over. I mean, I don't hate my family or anything like that, but I always figured when I get with them they're a different class of people from me now. I don't know, they just can't talk the same language with me. And I go over there to this christening the other week and they were all telling me about Dick—Dick is and Dick was. He still borrows money off my mother. I guess he's pretty wild yet. He runs around, don't have any job too long.

Interviewer: You had an older sister too, didn't you?

Jack: Yeah, an older sister Emma.

Interviewer: What happened to her?

Jack: Well, she got married and went to Connecticut or Massachusetts. I think its Massachusetts she went to live with her husband. She works up there.

Interviewer: Was she a little wild for a while?

Jack: I can't remember. I think she was—she had a little trouble there and in fact I think they put her away for a while.

Interviewer: What do you mean, put her away?

Jack: In a reformatory.

Interviewer: Is she all right now?

Jack: Oh, yes. She's got two little boys and two girls and as I remember this here one boy I met here a couple of weeks ago, everybody including my wife said, boy I've never seen such a kid in all my life. He was as pleasant as you ever want to see a kid and polite and, er, like at the christening there he took care of the baby and made sure she had her bottle and everything and I said my God, if my kids ever were to turn out to be as nice as him, I'd be happy, you know. He's a perfect gentleman.

Interviewer: You had two younger sisters, didn't you?

Jack: Yeah. Virginia and Ellen.

Interviewer: You were fond of them weren't you?

Jack: Well, that's part of my own family like that but I always felt sorry for them too because they were younger than I, you know.

Interviewer: They went in a foster home too, didn't they?

Jack: My aunt took them. I think she took them under the foster-parent arrangement. I'm not sure though. But when they were younger, you know, I tried, I don't know, be like a big brother to them. When I got work I'd go up there and my young sister she always wanted a bicycle and I never could buy it for her so I saved some money up and I bought her a bicycle. And I used to try to get to see them more because I knew they were two little innocents, you know.

Interviewer: And your mother, is she still alive?

Jack: Yes, she's alive. She lives in New City now and she remarried.

Interviewer: You told Mr. Wexler you were kind of bashful about visiting your mother. Do you remember that?

Jack: Well, Mrs. Holland used to tell me I should go to see my mother. You know, she says "After all, she's still your mother." I don't know whether you'd call it too busy. I just didn't bother to go to see her all the time, you know.

Interviewer: How do you feel about her now?

Jack: About the same. I went to see her a few times now since I've been married. But to tell you the truth, it's more like just paying my respects. The funny part of it, my sister called me up just about a month ago. She says "I'm going to bring somebody up to the house that wants to see you." So I'm waiting there and she comes up to the house and its my own father's stepfather, in other words my grandfather. He said, "Well I'm proud of you. You have at least got your own home, you have a nice family, turned out good and your brother's still the same." He says "Your mother still lends him money when he wants it. He wouldn't talk to anybody if he fell over them." He says "I've wondered many times if you had the opportunities he had whether you would have turned out like him," you know. He has no feelings for anyone. You see he's the type of fellow that would do things that I wouldn't even think of, you know. Like one time right after I got married I hadn't seen him for maybe three or four years. He calls me up on the telephone. He says "Hey, Jack, do me a favor." I says "What can I do for you?" Because I mean if its reasonable I'll help anybody out. So I says "What can I do for you?" He says "A couple of fellows and I are going up to Pennsylvania hunting." He says "How about lending me your car?" I says "Dick, I can't lend you my car. I need my car for work." He says "That's a helluva way," you know. He says "You're my brother and all." He says "I'll only be out for a couple of days." He says "Can't you get a ride to work no more?" So naturally I refused him so when he hung up I told my wife. I says "Boy that's really what you call nerve." I says "I couldn't do something like that." I said I wouldn't even think of asking anybody for something like that. But, er, that's the way he thinks. He just figures that everybody'll bend over for him and do whatever he wants them to do.

Interviewer: Was there a man that was living in your home with your mother when you as children had to break up?

Jack: Yes. I think there was a—that fellow was a kind fellow—I think he was a boarder.

Interviewer: He didn't mean anything did he?

Jack: You mean to the children?

Interviewer: I mean to your mother.

Jack: Yes. I think that he did. I think that—let's say they were living together. That's mainly I think why the state took us children. Because she wasn't working or anything. I think he was just living there and supporting us and everything else.

Interviewer: Now your foster parents had a boy too, didn't they?

Jack: Yeah. Robert.

Interviewer: What happened to him?

Jack: Oh, he just got married last May. In fact we moved him to his house, down to his house in August. Married a nice girl.

Interviewer: You liked him then, did you?

Jack: Oh, yes. I don't think there's anybody could dislike him because he's quiet and he'll do anything for you and he won't go out of his way to make any trouble. He goes out of his way to avoid it.

Interviewer: Your foster parents—did they treat you the same as they treated him? They didn't favor him over you?

Jack: No. As long as I ever lived there I could truthfully say that them people—if they went out at Christmas time they bought their son a sled and it was, let's say, worth ten dollars. They used to turn around to me and say, "Well, Jack, do you want a sled or what do you want with ten dollars?" I mean we got treated just as equal as could be. In fact, I think they went out of their way to make it equal. I don't even think if I was in the same position I wouldn't have favored my own a little bit more, I don't know but, er, anything he got, I got it if I wanted it.

Interviewer: What kind of house do you live in?

Jack: I live in, well I call it a four-and-a-half room bungalow. It's got two bedrooms and a living room, a kitchen and dinette combined.

Interviewer: When you were a little boy they said you were running with gangs.

Jack: Well, that was the kids in the neighborhood, you know the boys there, you know. I don't say today it would be exactly a gang. Well, it would be all the boys in the neighborhood, you know.

Interviewer: I got the impression you were out of the house more than the other children.

Jack: I was because I guess there were times when my mother would be out. I wouldn't even know where she would be. Off I'd go. Like a carnival had drove into town or something—I'd be up at the carnival—be walking around that place maybe 'til 10 or 11 at night.

Interviewer: When you were in school did you have any trouble with teachers and so on, what was the trouble there?

Jack: Well, I'll go back to what I said before. Mainly I couldn't go for anybody trying to put something in me that I didn't want. That's all there was to it. If I said something was black and the teacher said it was red, I would still say it was black, that way, you know. I used to have—maybe you'd call it a temper or whatever you wanted to call it—but I was sure evereybody was against me. Not everybody, but at times you know, I'd get that feeling—maybe I'd look at the teacher when she was balling me out for something and I'd say "What are you picking on me for?" You know, that's the attitude I'd take and, er, I used to have a pretty good temper. But like that day when I got in the Navy. I got with them fellows—I found out you have to live with people, more or less. I got over a lot of that.

Interviewer: Well, did you feel that there were times when you might want to go on the bad side?

Jack: No. I don't think that I—the only thing I will say though was when I was a young kid, when I was little—with my own family, that is, I used to travel with these kids in the neighborhood and they were all older than me and naturally when my older brother would do something I'd want to do it and I more or less looked up to him as a leader and that I should follow, you know. What he was doing I figured was good. I'd do it too.

Interviewer: So there's where you had to make a choice didn't you?

Jack: Yeah. Well, like I said, when I went to live with these people, the Hollands, I found out how differently other people live. It was just ignorance, I guess, on my part before. Then I found out when you do go to a table you have to say please, you're supposed to, and if there's candy on the table, you shouldn't try to grab all you can get. You should leave some for the rest of the people. I hadn't learned all that before. Well, I'd say if I didn't go with them I would have wound up probably in jail maybe at times. At least I wouldn't have wound up the way I have. I know that much.

Interviewer: You feel it was a different kind of life than you knew.

Jack: Well, it was a word we used to have for it—common, you know. Like Mrs. Holland used to say to me "That's no way to do" (a certain thing, you know). She'd say "That's the common way of doing it." You know she'd—like, maybe, if I went out—we went out —to someone's house or something. We'd have a supper or something and I'd ask for more, or something. She'd say "Don't act common like that," you know. "Act a little more grown-up and polite."

Interviewer: Where you're working now, do you still feel the same way about people as you did in the Navy?

Jack: No, I don't because in the Navy it seems, er—it always seems to me like a lot of baloney in there, you know. To tell you the truth, things that were so unnecessary. Like you'd just get through painting a bulkhead and an officer would come up the next day and say "Let's get that bulkhead painted up." I'd say, "Well, sir, I just painted it yesterday." "Well, paint it again." And as soon as he got through painting that one, he'd have me scraping off this one and things like that got me burning up. I mean, I couldn't see it.

Interviewer: Made work for you, did they, to keep you busy?

Jack: Well, the work I didn't mind because I don't mind work but, er, a lot of little things, like, er, well, like one officer come up to me and that's one time when I got broke, you know, I lost my rate. This fellow got me mad, you see. I was a Coxswain that time, I had one stripe. Well, the fellows were painting the side of the ship and I'm standing there. I'm not supposed to work, you see. I'm a rated man. I'm supposed to instruct them while they do it. So, these fellows, they knew how to paint the side of a ship. I didn't have to show them nothing. So I'm standing there and the guys are painting away. They wanted to get done so they can go on liberty. I figured, well, I'm wasting my time here, you know. I don't like to stand round doing nothing. So I took off over the side and I started swinging a paint brush too, painting the ship. So, helping them out. This officer comes up to me and says "What are you doing there, mate?" I says "I'm painting, sir." He says "What are you painting for?" I say "I want to help the guys out. They're in a hurry to get done so they can go on liberty." He says "Well, you're a rated man. You're not supposed to work like that." I says "Well I figured it wouldn't hurt nothing." Next day we were working on a bulkhead there. Same group of fellows. I got a *Life* magazine in my hand that somebody gave me. At least I have a lot of books and things. You know, old books. I'm glancing through this book. The fellows are over there working. Same old sir comes up to me and says "What are you doing?" I say "I'm looking at a *Life* magazine." He says "Why aren't you up there working?" "Just because you told me not to yesterday, sir." He says "Well, you get up there and go to work." I said no. Well, that's the mistake I made. I should never have refused an officer. So naturally he put me on report. I went to the captain's mast. The captain asked me what happened. I told him. He said "Well, you disobeyed an order." He says "I got to take your rating away from you." So right or wrong, you're wrong. Don't care what you do. And I couldn't see that in the Navy. And a lot of little things like that they got me burning up over them. I just got disgusted with it and that was it. I mean I wouldn't mind if a fellow gave you an order that's half-way decent, you know, a little sense to it. Things like that used to get me mad and I'd blow my top over them. Now I've calmed down quite a bit. I still get mad once in a while but I try to ease off, you know.

Interviewer: What broke you?

Jack: Well, my wife broke me. Ha. Ha. I'll tell you a story about that. Yeah, she calmed me down. I was ranting off for something one night. I was mad over something, I don't know. She wanted to go some place and I blowed my top over it, you know. So my sister-in-law was sitting there at the table with us. I'm yapping away there a mile a minute. A good five minutes, I guess, blowing my top. So they're both just sitting there looking at me. When I'm all finished the house is quiet, you know, and I come to a stop like, you know. I was busy blowing my top. So when it was all over with they're just sitting there, looking at me. So my wife turns around. She says "You all finished?" I said "Yeah." She says "Well, what'd you get so mad about?" She says. "I didn't argue with you. My sister didn't argue with you." She says "There you are ranting away for five minutes." She says "Make you feel better?" She says "Boy, I don't know what I'm going to do with a guy like you." You know I think that changed me more than anything. Because I started to think boy, I must have been some sight, ha. ha. Every time now and then, once in a while, I get going on a tantrum like that I stop and think well, it isn't doing me any good. I ease off.

Interviewer: Well you met some nice people and they helped you.

Jack: Oh, yeah. I met the best of them. Well, that's one thing I can truthfully say, that most of the people, my schoolteachers and—I think they all tried to help me more than I realized it, you know. Because I can remember when I was even going to school there some of the things I did—I was definitely wrong in them. I think the teachers had a lot of patience with me.

Interviewer: Do you have any friends, buddies or cronies?

Jack: Oh, yeah. I have a few—quite a few friends.

Interviewer: Did you ever go in for the, uh, lodges?

Jack: No, I always steered clear of that stuff because, er, I don't know—some guys they like to go in for all that rigamarole. I don't know what do you call it. They go for these meetings and politics and things. I don't go for that.

Interviewer: Do you belong to any clubs?

Jack: No.

Interviewer: How about church?

Jack: Well, I still don't go to church which I should, I know.

Interviewer: Not very religious are you?

Jack: Well, I wouldn't say that. I think I feel very deeply about religion, perhaps, but I just don't attend the church.

Interviewer: What is your religion?

Jack: Well, I was brought up as a Presbyterian, I think. I don't have a church for years.

Interviewer: So you get along without one very well.

Jack: I hope I do. I don't know.

Interviewer: You're very religious?

Jack: Yes, I think I am because, well, I can give you an example. When I was in the Navy there, we used to have what they called holiday routine. That was—actually we were supposed to stand on watches seven days a week and everything. We had to man the guns all times we could and in the Navy you always have a watch to stand. So on Sundays they used to tell us, you know, if you're going to church—sometimes they used to have church on a different ship—a bigger ship, you know—they'd hold a big mass. The Catholics and Jews they had their services. They used to tell the fellows well, er, anyone going to church don't have to stand their watch. Well, I noticed a lot of these fellows they would go to church just so they wouldn't have to stand the watch and work. Well, off they'd go and I'd stand the watch. I never went to church. There were other days like when we come back to the States where the fellows didn't have to stand watches. They could have went to church on Sunday. They didn't go. I used to figure well, and I still feel that way, if I had to go to church just to get out of work I'm not going. I can't see being— to me that's being a hypocrite. The same way with a friend of mine. We were out drinking and having a good time and he was what I call a religious fellow. So he says, er, this happened to be a weekend we were out boozing up and we were pretty well bopped up couple of times there. We were walking around the town, having a good time and he finally realized it was Sunday and there he is—he's half drunk. He says "I gotta go to church." I say well, go ahead. He says "Well I want you to come with me." I says "Well I don't usually go to church." I says "I don't even understand the routine about it." He says "Well, you come along with me or I won't go." I says "Well, you go ahead and I'll go with you."

Interviewer: He was Catholic, was he?

Jack: Yeah. So he says well, "First we got to get a bottle of whiskey." I says "What are you going to church for?" He says "Well, I gotta go to church Sundays." I says "With a bottle of whiskey?" He says "Oh, we'll leave that outside." I says "Oh, I'm not going to church with you." I says "I can't see it." I had a big argument with him. I mean I believe in God I think as strong as the next guy and I respect Him more than a lot of people because I'd never knock a nun, which isn't my religion. I'd never knock a rabbi or say anything against him, which I know a lot of people that go to church would do.

Interviewer: In other words you want your religion to be inward?

Jack: That's right. I think it's in your heart more than it is anywhere.

Interviewer: Of course the fellows did some boozing in the Navy, didn't they?

Appendix B. The Case of Jack

Jack: Well, I'd say of 300 men on our ship 299 did, anyway (loud laughter) just about everyone, I guess.

Interviewer: How about girls now. Do you have any now?

Jack: No. I, er, when I was in the Navy, to tell you the truth, I was pretty well wild. I mean I'd go with any woman, it wouldn't matter to me who she was, and I'd drink anything and I used to be drunk I'd say 50 percent of the time that I could get it, you know. Just trying to be a smart guy, I guess. Then after a while I got to like it pretty much so when I left the ship the guys used to kid me. They'd say "Boy, I'd like to see you in civilian life. You'll never sober up," you know. Because I was always drinking in the Navy. So I says when the time comes for me to settle down I'm going to settle down and that's going to be it. So I didn't even believe it myself to tell you the truth. When I got home Mrs. Holland she knew just what I was because I never lied to her. I told her. I says I was wild. I wasn't innocent. I was with women. I drank a lot and I still liked to drink then. So when I got married—I mean I didn't like it to the extent that I would drink it during the daytime but I liked to go out at night and go to a tavern and have a few with my wife or whoever. And she didn't like it. She would have two highballs and that would be it, for her. So this one night Holland—see I happened to be living there at that time after I was married. We lived in the attic room. We went out to the tavern to play shuffleboard and have a few beers. I come home and I got sick. Boy, I was sick. I was throwing up all over the place. I couldn't figure out what it was. So then a couple of times after that I drank beer I got sick. I says "I'm not drinking it any more." So after that every time we went out any place I wouldn't drink any beer. Maybe I'd have a little sip of a highball and that would be it. And that's just the way it's got.

Interviewer: When things go wrong, say at work or things like that, do you take a drink sometime?

Jack: No, I don't drink at all now. Fact if, er, I had company come to the house or something, I ask them what they care for and then I have a glass of soda. Because if, er, I drink now I get sick over it.

Interviewer: Are you a fellow that—would you call yourself a nervous person?

Jack: I'd say I'm a worrier.

Interviewer: You are a worrier.

Jack: Yeah. Like when my daughter gets sick or something, I worry over it and I feel well it should have been me instead of her, you know.

Interviewer: Do you get butterflies in your stomach over it?

Jack: I don't get sick over it, no. But it's on my mind, like. Like if right about now my car gets a, say, a hole in the radiator or something and I know I don't have the money to get it fixed I'll be riding home, thinking about it and then when I do get home, I'll go to bed and then go to sleep with it on my mind and then when I get up tomorrow morning it will still be there. And I know that's bad for me, you know. I know that's no good but I can't prevent it. I try not to worry about things like that. Actually they're little incidentals but I just worry over things like that.

Interviewer: Do you ever get depressed or down in the dumps?

Jack: Yeah, when I see bills coming up or something and I know I don't have the money for 'em, you know. Or if I know my wife feels like a new dress or something and I know I don't have the money to pay for it, I start feeling bad, you know, that maybe I should be doing better toward her or something, I don't know.

Interviewer: What do you plan to do the next five or ten years?

Jack: Well, right now I'm looking forward to my new addition to the family mainly. And, er, trying maybe to get a garage on my house which I know I need that bad, and mainly what I look forward to is make sure I got a job there to pay for everything I need, you know. I don't want to live too big but I like to hold my own.

Interviewer: You look forward to staying with the same company, do you?

Jack: Yeah. I do, if they're there yet and I'm there yet, I don't know. Well, I don't think I could do much better. Of course I am as high as I can go in my field right now.

Interviewer: But the children call for a lot, don't they?

Jack: Yeah. Well, like I did before, I'll probably do again. I used to—when I first bought my house I used to go out and work part time nights. I used to work in this shop during the daytime and then some of these smaller shops they'd hire a man for two or three hours a night—what they call part-time work. I used to do quite a bit of that. I'll do that mainly for the money and the experience. Because in these small shops they don't have the equipment a bigger shop has and you got to use your common sense a little bit more—do with what you have.

Interviewer: And how do you vote?

Appendix B. The Case of Jack

Jack: Republican and Democrat? Neither one. I try to look at the records more or less and I go according to that.

Interviewer: How did you vote last time?

Jack: Last time I voted for Eisenhower.

Interviewer: You think he's o.k.?

Jack: No. This time I don't because first of all, I don't think he's doing right for the—one of my biggest worries is education for my kids and especially in the town where I live, they only go half a day—school—see and I don't feel that any kid can get anything out of a half a day in school. By the time they get in and get their cloaks off and the teachers get settled down and they've had their rest period, it's time to go home again. So I can't see where they can get an education and things the way they are. And that's one of the main reasons I wouldn't vote for him because—when he gave away that Tidelands oil deal down there in Texas and all, I mean, the way I could see it, he's giving these big companies and the millionaires more every month that goes by and he's taking from the little people. Now I don't blame the man personally, naturally, but I think he could put his foot down a little more on this thing.

Interviewer: What did you think of Stevenson?

Jack: I didn't think he was good enough man to vote for because to tell you the truth, I, er, I think to have a man in there that's president, you gotta have a man's that's, well, more what they call dynamic, you know? More like a leader. I don't think Stevenson was that type.

Interviewer: How about Nixon?

Jack: Nixon I think is too much of a politician. He'd be a good man if he really wanted to, I think, but right now he's worried about the guys behind him, the guys that are pushing him and he's gonna do for them. That's the way I feel. In other words, he's gonna wash the hand that feeds him.

Interviewer: Well, who do you think is a strong man in this country?

Jack: A strong man in this country? Well, I couldn't say. That one would be a hard one to pick. Quite a few of your labor people.

Interviewer: Well, how do you feel toward people of other races? Negroes?

Jack: Well the Negro situation, I feel sorry for 'em but then again—

Interviewer: Do you work with them?

Jack: No. We have 'em in our shop but not in our department. Very few Negroes are machinists. I feel sorry for 'em but I still say that—maybe I'm wrong in saying it—I don't mind working with them. I don't mind eating in the same restaurant with them—too much. But I don't want to sleep near them and I don't want to live too close with them or anything like that. Because the things I see I can't stand because I've seen—now in New City here. I've seen beautiful neighborhoods—I mean some of the best in the whole state as far as I'm concerned—beautiful homes, doctors lived in 'em and everything where these people moved in and today they're just wrecks. They're not responsible enough I don't think and I know like the school situation—well that's been going on now for a few weeks down in our shop—we've been talking it over, you know. Naturally I feel sorry for the Negro. If he wants an education he should be able to get it, I feel, but then again I start to think, if I send my daughter to school—like one of my father's nieces—she had to go to a school and they were holding dance lessons. So there was mixed pupils there, part of them white. So the teacher made her, told her, she had to dance with this colored boy. Now I stop and think, now if my daughter was going to school I wouldn't want her to dance with one of them and I wouldn't want her to be eating at the same table or I wouldn't want, er, when I see anybody, er, look for mixed marriages I, er, can't see that. That disgusts me. But as far as them getting educated or having the same as me—I feel sorry that they can't have it, they should have it. But in their own, I say. They should have their own schools and I'll have mine as far as I'm concerned that way. But I still think they should have it equal, not, er, unequal. That's my feeling toward it.

Interviewer: Well, I guess we've talked about everything. Is there anything you want to ask me?

Jack: Well, I just want to know if I'm normal, that's about all. Like I know many a time like Mrs. Holland she used to say to me "Jack—" my teachers used to say the same thing and fellows that I knew, they used to say "You can be the nicest guy and you can be the most miserable just depending on your mood and, er, you can be quiet a lot of times and other times you're just as wild as they come." And to me, er, I mean that strikes me funny because as I see other people they just about the same all the time.

Interviewer: So you can be quite different at times?

Jack: Jekyll and Hyde they call it, that's all.

Interviewer: Well things have really turned out for you quite differently, haven't they?

Jack: Definitely. I think I learned right from wrong from them people whereas I didn't know it before.

Interviewer: You're doing pretty well.

Jack: I'm doing pretty good and—

Interviewer: I think you really are. So, like I say, you have a lot to be thankful for.

Jack: Yeah. That's the way I look at it. I feel maybe another kid in the same position I was in wouldn't a got the breaks I got maybe.

Interviewer: Yes, and the Hollands. You could have gone with a family that wouldn't have steered you in the right direction.

Jack: Oh, yeah.

Interviewer: And wouldn't you say you had a very nice girl for a wife? She helped you but you picked her out too, didn't you?

Jack: Well, I think I did, I don't know. Maybe she picked me. Ha. Ha.

Interviewer: Well, mutual maybe, but you knew what you wanted?

Jack: Oh, definitely. When I first seen her I figured that's the girl for me. I mean I knew girls that were more beautiful, I'd say, nicer shapes, but I knew above all they wouldn't make me the wife that she would—more or less glamor girls, you know.

Interviewer: Well I don't think we need to meet again. I thought when I came here I might have you come back next week but since you got here half an hour early I think we won't need to come together again.

Picture-Story Test, 1957: Series A

PICTURE ONE

Well, this would tell me that this fellow's been away for a long time. Maybe he left when he was a little younger. Maybe he's been away for a few years—come back, maybe, to his old neighborhood. Looking around just to see how it's changed. He's on his way home probably. He's probably wondering how his family's going to greet him, whether they'll be happy to see him. I imagine that he's traveled quite a bit—maybe took a trip around the country or something like that—maybe he worked a little. Now he's coming home and kind of just standing there, taking in the scenery, probably doing more wondering than anything else. [Wondering how they are going to greet him?] Yes.

PICTURE TWO

Well, you know, I look at this picture. The first thing I'm wondering now—is this a girl or a boy because today they have the different hair cuts. The girls have hair cuts in that style. She has—it looks like feminine features except for the hands. Well I choose it as a boy by the looks of the hands and it looks like a neck tie there. I'd say that this person's just knocking on a door, maybe waiting to meet someone he's looking for in the neighborhood. Or he could be knocking on the door because he came to this house to do some work for the people. Seems he's resting in the style more of the person that's going to work and I'd say that this fellow is just knocking on the door there to get greeted by the people that's in the house, thinking that he's going to do some work for them. I believe he's expected in the house and maybe he was told to come like for instance, on a Saturday, maybe to clean the cellar out or something like that. People have just hired him, maybe. That's about all I can get out of it.

PICTURE THREE

Well it seems to me that—not trying to make a story out of this. It seems that once there was a girl that lived in a small town and this town wasn't a big city—it was just more or less a suburb town—maybe we'll just call it Plainview, or something like that. In this town of Plainview there was boys and girls—ordinary people—but there wasn't too much recreational facilities here. The children in the town, most of the people in the town, on account of its size, most everybody knew one another and had grown up together. It seems like this one girl, we'll call her Judy, she wasn't as popular with boys of her own age, which was around fifteen or sixteen years old, because she didn't particularly have good looks and she was a little more snooty than the rest and declined to go out, let's say polish up the town a little bit. Then Judy got a little older. She started thinking maybe when she was around seventeen and she wondered why she didn't have the fun the other children had because she used to sit in the house reading books, a very studious girl, she used to see the other children out there—the other kids her own age having a lot of fun and going on dates. Judy just sat home and figured "Why wasn't I born good looking like the rest of them?" "Why do I have to be a wallflower?" in other words. That's the story, I guess, in this picture.

PICTURE FOUR

It seems that there was a fellow—we'll call him John—John had a boat for sale and he advertised it in the paper. He ran the advertisement a few days, advertising a sixteen-foot outboard boat, very good condition, with the motor and everything on it, fully equipped. The reason he wanted to get rid of this boat was because he wanted to get something a little bigger. So he had this boat up for sale and various people came to see it. Some were interested and some weren't. Some didn't have the money. This one fellow he comes up to the house, looks at the boat. He's interested in it, like to buy it. So he sells the boat to this other fellow that's come up to the house—call him Joe, maybe—decides well, he'll get together with Joe because Joe didn't have quite enough money to pay for the boat right immediately—the cash. So he got together with Joe and Joe decided he'd pay him the balance in a week or two. So a week or two went by and Joe comes up to the house and talks to John and maybe tries to get him to come down on the price a little bit. John told him, he says, "Well, I advertised the boat at a certain price. You agreed to pay it. You didn't have the cash and I was a good enough fellow to hold it for you for a week." He says, "now why do you try to get it cheaper?" The guy starts knocking the boat, this guy Joe. He says "Well it ain't worth the money that you asked for it," and things like that. Then he says, "I'll pay you the money," he says, "but I don't really think the boat's worth it." Then he gets kind of keyed off about it. He buys the boat anyway but tries to act as though he's pretty mad over the deal.

PICTURE FIVE

They don't give you much to go on in these pictures. Well, we'll say this girl's name was Marlene. She lives out in the country. Could be the present day or maybe twenty, thirty years ago. She lives out on a say a ranch, out in Nevada someplace and it seems that all her life she's been happy. She had cattle around—all types of animals. She never had any worries or cares—always a happy child. She went through school. Now she's become a little older, she's gone to high school. She's starting to read in her books about these different countries, maybe different cities and one day on her way home from school, she don't have any work to do or anything when she gets home, she's pretty well caught up with the work, so she just decides to sit down and take in the scenery, daydream a little bit. While she's sitting there daydreaming she's thinking about these other countries, how the people live and maybe about these bigger cities, and let's say she's daydreaming maybe that someday she'll be able to go to a large city and see just what it looks like.

PICTURE SIX

Now this one's a little easier. Let's see, this fellow's name is Danny. He comes from, well, a good clean home. Could be an only child or maybe he has brothers and sisters. Well, it seems that Danny was out now and then with the fellows in the neighborhood. He's a clean-living boy, he always comes home on time. One night he asked his mother that the fellows were going down to the seashore, down to the amusement park and if he could go with them. His mother says, go ahead. Couple of older fellows were going to drive down in their car. So Danny goes for the ride. Tells his mother he won't be home 'til later and everything's all right. So naturally his mother's worried a little bit. She waits up for him. She gets a little tired so she decides well she'll go up in her room and go to sleep. It appears that she loves the son so much, just like most mothers do, she can't get any sleep. So she's just lying on the bed, taking it easy, trying to go to sleep. But she's worried about her son anyway. She knows her son will be home late. She knows where he is. So it's not really a fear that she doesn't know where he's at or anything like that but still the mother's worried. So she decides she'll just have to stay awake and wait for him. So it gets to be pretty late in the morning, maybe two o'clock or so, according to the clock here, and she hears the door open, the key opening the door. Danny walks in the hallway. She had already put a little food out for him, and left a light burning for him and the mother comes to the head of the stairs. She greets him and she's glad that he got home safe anyway.

PICTURE SEVEN

Well, this picture to me looks like—I'll start off by saying the boy's name is Billy. Maybe his sister's name is Elsie. It seems that Billy's been maybe wanting to buy a gun or maybe something for himself, so I'll just say a gun for himself. It seems that Billy wanted this gun to go hunting and he was a good, clean boy, worked hard, loved his family. So Billy decided he'd ask his mother and father if he could have this gun, maybe for his birthday. So his mother and father promised him that if he got good marks in school, did his chores around the house and everything, he could have this gun for his birthday. So Billy worked hard and studied hard. He tries to do the best he can to get this gun because it was important to him. Well, after three or four months went by and he was doing very good, there came a little bit of tragedy in the family. His mother and father had a little trouble with their car and it cost a lot of money to fix the old car up so they wanted to get this new car. Well, if they went and got the new car then Billy couldn't very well have his gun. So his mother and father were going to give up the car because they had already made the promise to Billy and they didn't want to go back on a promise. It seems that Elsie, his sister, a little older than Billy, had a little more knowledge of the ways of people's feelings and everything, so she decided she'd talk to Billy and maybe try to make Billy give up wanting this gun so badly. So she tried to explain to Billy how badly her father and mother needed the car. The father needed the car for work. She said to Billy, well, the gun is important to you but the car is important to Mom and Dad and they're going to have to do something but they don't want to go back on their promise to you. So she told Billy all about it. Billy decided that he'd talk to Mom and Dad and say, well, let's forget the gun for another year and you get your car.

PICTURE EIGHT

I remember one, the one with the fellow and the girl in bed or on the edge of the bed, or something. That was embarrassing to me. That one I never forgot—I don't know why.

Well, I'll say this is a story about two girls—Broadway dancers. One was Helen and the other one was Margie. Margie was a girl that got around a little bit more than the average home-town girl. She kicked around quite a bit. She went to this Broadway show to apply for a job. The other girl, Helen, she was a small-town girl. Had a little talent so she came to town to see if she could get a job too. They meet up in this stage company or movie where there's dancing and singing to produce a show. They both go before the producer of the show and the director. There's fifty or sixty girls there, trying out for the parts. It seems that at one point there they had just about every girl that they needed except maybe one or two more. So it seems that to me Margie was thinking that maybe Helen might get this part. She needs the part. She's thinking to herself, now why should this girl get a part in the show when I've kicked around quite a bit and I've danced more than she's ever danced and everything. But Helen had dance teachers teaching her. She's been taught the right way. In other words, she had talent where the other girl has it just from experience. So Margie's thinking to herself that she just better not get this job more or less over her dead body, because she figures she has more talent than Helen has.

PICTURE NINE

It seems that this woman lives in a neighborhood where there's one or two friendly neighbors. Usually after the husbands go to work in the morning they get up, get the children off to school, and go about their housework. So, Mrs. Brown, we'll call this lady, she's doing her housework and it's getting a little later in the morning, it's not time for the children to come home from school yet so due to maybe more or less habit, she goes to the back door looking for her next-door neighbor, maybe Mrs. Jones. She calls over to Mrs. Jones. They don't go over to the fence or anything because they're right in the middle of their housework but they want to get the news of the day about the neighborhood. It seems that the township committee passed the ordinance which would maybe provide them with better streets. They're talking it over.

PICTURE TEN

Well, there were two young people. Could have lived in any town. Happened to meet one another during their school days. Not out of school yet. We'll call the girl Sarah and the boy Johnny. Seems that Sarah and Johnny happened to fall in love. Naturally it's just a puppy love affair but they believe in it with all their hearts and they figure

Appendix B. The Case of Jack

that neither one of them will ever want to be separated. So Sarah and Johnny go to their parents and tell them that they'd like to get married. Their parents say that they should not get married because Johnny doesn't have a job. Things are getting pretty tough all over, maybe on account of the war. On account of the draft, Johnny might be called back—called into the service, rather. So Sarah and Johnny decide, well, they're a little young yet so they don't realize what their mother and father are trying to tell them. They don't believe it. So Sarah and Johnny, a little superstitious, like all children, happen to see this here—I don't know what we will call this fellow here—well, he's supposed to be a mindreader, a mentalist, call him Whami, or something like that. They see him advertised in the paper and they decide that if their parents are right this fellow should be able to tell them one way or another. So they decide they'll go see him. They don't want to disregard their parents and yet they don't truly believe them because it don't seem possible that a picture that's so rosy in their eyes could be maybe so bad. So they go to this Whami and they ask him whether Johnny'll be called into the service, whether there'll be a war, whether they'd be happy if they got married against their parents' advice. It seems that Whami is thinking well, what should I tell these two kids now. Should I tell them the truth—maybe they won't believe in me and if I do pour it on a little thick, tell them there's going to be no draft, no war, maybe have them try to believe me, they'll be going against their parents. So even though he's kicked around quite a bit, probably pulled a little cheating in his life, he figures well, they're only kids and I'm not going to try to lead them astray. So he tells them the truth, that actually he can't read the future, that Johnny could be drafted and there could be a war.

Picture-Story Test, 1957: Series B

PICTURE ONE

Jack: These look pretty hard. [Coughs, clears throat. Pause.]
Examiner: Something doesn't come, right off, is that it?
Jack: That's right. [Long pause.] We'll call this man—eh—Mr. John or something like that. Mr. John seems like he had a few cows and lived on a small farm. It seems like in the past his cows seemed to break down the fence and roam [pause] roam the country, so Mr. Brown

was getting a little tired of it. So it seems that this one day [pause] the cows get out again and he was notified. So he has to go out and scour the country and look them up and as he's going through the door he—he's kind of a little mad over it and wondering why that cows always seem to get through his fence. [Pause.] Finally he just has to go out and dig them up some place. They're hidden all over the shrub and brush I guess. [Pause.]

Examiner: How does it turn out?

Jack: Well, I guess he gets his cows back and finds out that he has to just put up with it till he can get a newer fence.

Examiner: Then he feels better, does he?

Jack: Well, he feels bad at the time and he feels bad—eh [clears throat]—eh, maybe in the months to come. Until he can get a little money together and go out and get a new fence and then they'd be happy over it of course.

Examiner: You ever live on a farm?

Jack: No, not really. [Laughs.] I haven't lived on one—oh, we had a small chicken farm when I was a boy.

PICTURE TWO

Jack: [Coughs.] This looks a little easier—this one. [Pause.] Do you want me to give names to the characters?

Examiner: If you feel like it, yes.

Jack: It's easier not to. You can forget the name of the character in the middle of the story. [Pause.] Well, let's call this girl Belle and her mother—eh [long pause]—eh, I guess I'd properly call her mother by her last name, Mrs. Jones—Mrs. Belle Jones's daughter in the picture. It seems that Belle Jones was starting to go around with the boys and the fellows her own age and getting a little above the school age and figuring that she's a grown woman now. And every day she comes home from school she wants to ditch her homework and just take off and have a good time. Her mother just wants to try to talk her into straightening out and realizing that she's not as old as she feels. It seems that every day that Belle comes home and gets all dolled up and goes down to the corner and meets the rest of the girls and goes gallivanting around town and have a good time. Meanwhile her mother keeps trying to talk her down a little bit and keep her from going off the wrong path maybe. [Clears throat.] Well, Belle naturally she don't believe her mother because after all grownups—eh—they just don't have the same outlook as children her own age. They're more or less old-fashioned. So Belle keeps listening to her mother. Her mother's telling her—trying to tell her not to dress up like a gypsy and try not to act too smart. And, she's—eh—naturally she's not paying much heed to her mother what she's talking about. And it seems to be a struggle for a couple of years between her mother and her. They just can't get together and understand each other. Finally, as she does get a little older she—eh [pause] Belle's met a nice fellow. She's finished school. She's—eh—pretty well settled down now. She didn't go bad or anything like that, so her mother's pretty well satisfied with her. Meanwhile, she's standing here in front of the mirror expecting her best beau to call. They've just been engaged. Not through anything in the picture but it's a feeling I have. And her mother's standing back and thinking—well, for a while I thought she was going off the deep end but she turned out pretty good after all.

PICTURE THREE

It seems that this one youngster—call him—eh—Johnny. He's about seventeen years old. Just got his first car. And then, saved all the money he could get hold of and went out and bought this car. Naturally he couldn't afford a new car and he had to pick one up at the used-car lot. So he went out and bought this car and [pause] he didn't pay too much for it. He paid more than the thing was worth. So—uh—when he bought the car, Johnny knew there'd be a lot of work on it. So he was trying to figure out a good way to save expense. Maybe he'd do some of the work himself. [Clears throat.] He didn't know too much about cars. So he—uh—so the fellow in the picture is—eh—not even—uh—not quite a friend—just a person he's met and he's heard about that is a good mechanic. So he decides to pay him a visit to see if he can get this car fixed up, what it would cost him. Goes over to see this fellow, Joe. So—uh—he's asking Joe—uh—a few thousand questions about this automobile of his—how to do this and how to do that. This Joe he's standing there thinking—well, what's this kid doing here? He's trying to get free advice. And besides, well, I'll listen to him and give him a bum steer now and then and see what happens. So he tells Johnny just how to go about fixing things—how he should go about fixing them but in between he's telling Johnny he's going to need a special tool for that, a special tool for this—he's going to take a line-up on this where you need a special tool. So Johnny's starting to think— My goodness! If I have to buy all these tools I'll never get the job done. So he asks Joe, how about you fixing it and I'll pay you. Maybe I could work along with you on it. Then Joe tells him— Now you're being a smart kid, he says. He says, I don't mind instructing you and letting you help me out, he says, as long as I get the job. But I'm not going to give you free advice. Whereas you go home and do the work yourself and I'm not getting anything from it. So that was the deal they made that Johnny would work along with Joe on his car. And they strike up a pretty good friendship. Johnny becomes a pretty good mechanic himself.

PICTURE FOUR

Jack: Boy, I love these. [Pause.] One represents a [clears throat] what you call a mother's pet and one that doesn't, say the black sheep of the family. These two girls were sisters. One was little Miss Innocent. That's what I thought. She's her mother's favorite.

Examiner: She's the one with the flower in her hand?

Jack: Yeah—flower of the family, I'd say. The other girl—eh—she just doesn't stand out. Maybe she isn't as good-looking, maybe not as bright. Maybe she just seems to do everything wrong. And—uh [pause] it seems that—eh [clears throat] the girl that was the flower of the family, as I call her, she was having a little trouble with her sister. She was trying to figure out how she could get her in a little more trouble. Her sister was usually in trouble anyway. So she would lie against her sister and her mother would just take her part all the time. So the girl that didn't rate with the mother as much as the flower here she just had a pretty rough life all the way around. Because the mother always took the other girl's part. It seems that one day they were going at it pretty good and—eh [pause] they were having a battle of some sort. Well anyway, she goes up to her mother and she tells her mother about her sister. And that she—eh—took her new dress and she did this and she did that. And the mother takes the flower's part, naturally. The other poor girl—she's just standing in the background, wondering why her sister does this to her—she don't stand a chance. She tries to be nice to her. But the other girl is just spoiled all the time and the mother takes her part. She's standing in the background wondering why her mother keeps taking the flower's part and why the girl we call the flower would just keep picking on her all the time.

Examiner: And how does she feel?

Jack: She feels pretty—eh—low over it and she more or less feels a little sorry for both of them that they don't have the understanding that they should have.

PICTURE FIVE

It seems that this girl was married. She had a little child—child named Billy. [Pause.] This woman was called Martha. She has a little boy and she keeps telling the boy to stay away from that river. It seems that the boy keeps running back to this river, as if it has a natural attraction for him. So, as many times as he's been to this river and had his fanny slapped for it he still goes back there. Most of the time he plays around the house, but every once in a while he winds up back at his river which isn't far from the house. One day this girl, Martha, she's missing her son. She can't find him. She looks all over the neighborhood and she asking different passers-by if they seen him, different neighbors. Nobody's seen hide nor hair of him. So she gets worried. After she gets worried a little bit she gets a little desperate. She's running around all over the neighborhood asking people and naturally people are helping her look, but she's actually starting to get frightened and wondering now what happened to her son. Because actually she's starting to figure the river right away. So she runs to her next door neighbor. She tells her maybe she should call the police. She don't know. She don't want to cause the police too much trouble. She don't want them maybe running down to the neighborhood and maybe her son is safe and sound. She just don't know what to do. So she runs to a neighbor and asks advice. Meanwhile she's practically frightened out of her wits. So the neighbor woman tells her to call the police and tries to steer her straight on what to do. Of course they're both excited, so she calls the police up. They come down and they start searching the neighborhood and dragging the river, and the fire department and the whole town is practically out looking for her son. Finally she finds him. He's playing under the bed some place, in the house. Nothing really to be frightened of.

Examiner: Did you ever hear a story like that before?

Jack: I read them every day in the newspaper. I guess that's what gave me the idea. Pretty frightening, I imagine.

PICTURE SIX

So call this fellow Slim. Slim—eh—he's an average sort of fellow. He—eh—goes and comes, goes to work, goes to church, fairly decent looking fellow, average. Seems that Slim [pause] Slim is invited to go fishing with the fellows and he turns down the invitation because— eh [pause] he is waiting for his brother to come in from out of town. He tells the boys that he can't go fishing with them and starts sitting around waiting for his brother. So he don't want to leave the house because he knows that if his brother comes and there's no one home he'd be awful put out about it. So he decides to stay home and wait instead of going and having a good time with the boys. [Clears throat.] So he sits around and waits and waits and waits and still his brother don't come. So after a few hours of sitting around and it's getting dark out—damn it [pause] he's starting to sit there and starting to think that brother of mine should have come. That's a heck of a way to do a thing like this. He said I could have went and had a good time with the fellows and I'm sitting home and waiting and he ain't shown up at all. He's getting pretty miserable over it. He's getting a little mad now, sitting there. He's figuring, well, his brother spoiled his whole day of enjoyment. He didn't mind it to begin with but now that he isn't coming it's burning him up a little bit. So he comes to find out that his brother don't even call up on the phone or nothing. So he's getting madder and madder and sitting there and—and blue. He decides, well, that's life, that's all there is to it. You can't do nothing with a fellow like my brother, you know. So a little later the telephone rings and this fellow says he's sorry he couldn't come, he couldn't come earlier because he had a little trouble on the road and couldn't get to a telephone early enough. Now he's had his car fixed he's coming into town. He'll see him a little late, that's all. Slim [pause] buckles up and he feels pretty good now. His brother's going to come after all. The day wasn't really wasted.

Examiner: Is he still mad with his brother?

Jack: Not after he gets the telephone call, everything was pretty well straightened out.

Examiner: So he forgets things quickly, does he?
Jack: Yes [laughs].

PICTURE SEVEN

Well, this number seven reminds me of the other picture. The other case was a boy. Well, I'd say this picture told a story just the opposite from the boy's picture. As I remember in that picture there's a—the story I told that his parents were pretty happy that he got home. On this one they seem to be pretty mad. It seems when this girl Doris went out on a date she was supposed to be home early. Her mother told her to be home by twelve. She didn't mind her going to the dance. Doris promised that she'd be home in time and her mother said, all right she could go with the children and dance her head off if she wanted to as long as she'd be home by twelve. So naturally Doris goes out with the gang and—eh—the few older ones in the crowd they don't have to be home so early. The ones that weren't older, they—their parents didn't worry about it so much as what her parents worried. [Clears throat.] So they decided they'd take a ride and get some hamburgers after the dance. Naturally all the kids have cars [pause]. This fellow that Doris is with [clears throat] decides he'd go and get hamburgers with them, so they all pile in the cars after the dance and Doris and her boy go. She told him she had to be home early and he just gives a little laugh and he says, I'll get you there early. And he meant early in the morning. So off they go. So Doris is getting worried. She's trying to be a good kid. Of course the fellow he's got the car and she can't drive it and she don't feel like getting out and walking in the middle of the night. So she decides to stick with him. She has to. So they wind up going to the hamburger place and having a hamburger and having a good time—singing—kidding around. Finally her fellow decides to take her home. Well, twenty-five after three in the morning Doris walks in the house. Her father's waiting up for her. Her mother's waiting up demanding to know what's going on here. She promised she'd be home by twelve. They told her she couldn't come in after twelve so they're pretty well put out over it. Naturally Doris is scared to death that her parents are going to [pause] maybe discipline her—er [pause] so she walks in the house and she's pretty well scared and her father's raising the roof, and her mother. Then when she tells them the story of what happened, well, the father realizes, well, maybe the poor kid did try but after all they would rather have her stay with the fellow that had the car than trying to walk home in the middle of the night on the roads all alone. So she gets in the house and she explains it all to her family and they decide [laughs] better luck next time, that's all.

PICTURE EIGHT

This little girl we'll call Jane. She—eh [pause] let's say she's just a newlywed married to a G.I. She—eh—she gets married to this fellow. He's in the Army. She thinks life's going to be all peaches and cream. So right after they're married the fellow is transferred to camp someplace in the United States and she follows him. So they get a couple of rooms together and when he's off duty he stays home with her, naturally, living off base. When he's on duty he has to stay on the base. So finally—eh—his time comes to be transferred. He has to be transferred overseas. His wife can't understand what's going on. She don't have the outlook like most girls that what's inevitable has to come. She has to take it. She can't see why *her* husband has to be transferred overseas and she figures maybe she can get him out of it somehow. So she comes up to his commanding officer and tries to tell him that there's plenty of single fellows that can go overseas. Why does my husband have to go? In fact, there's plenty of men right in town here that have been in the Army, and they're single and they'd like to go overseas. And here is her husband. He just married. He don't want to leave his wife. Newlyweds. And he'd rather not go overseas and she can't understand why the Army don't leave these younger fellows go that want to go and keep the men that want to stay. So she goes up to his commanding officer and trying to explain this to him. Trying to maybe to get him out of it to stay with her. She says—she tells the commanding officer she's willing to travel any place where he can go but she's not allowed to go overseas with him. So why not keep him here in the States and send some other fellow. So the commanding officer has to explain to her how come her husband has to go. It's not his duty to tell him to go. His orders come in the same as anybody else's. It's not his fault that he has to go. He has a pretty rough time convincing her. Finally he talks to her like a father and gets it all straightened out. Naturally her husband goes overseas because he has to follow orders. The commanding officer feels bad over it and so does she. But in the end that's the way it turns out that he goes and she stays. Naturally he'll come back and take up where they left off.

PICTURE NINE

This one's a little easier. It has more detail. [Clears throat.] It seems that this fellow called Jim has figured that anybody works and becomes a normal person just wastes their energy and their time, see. He decided to go in for a little crime. He finds out that—eh [pause] he can get away with quite a bit. He feels that he's a little above intelligence as far as the average person is concerned—he's a little above them. He goes out and he has a good time—uh—shooting dice, running books, numbers rackets, different things, plus a few [pause] quite a few little things that are not legal anyway. So he winds up in jail. It seems that all his life people tried to tell him that the road to take—and he wouldn't listen to them, just figuring—always figured that he was a pretty smart boy. So now that he's behind bars he's sitting there pondering what happened to him. He couldn't understand this. He thought he was pretty shrewd. So then he decides that—uh—especially after he looks across the street and sees the church in the background there every Sunday people are out there all dressed up, walking to church with their children. He decides he could have been doing that himself instead of sitting up here behind bars. He's trying to figure out whether he made them think that he was so smart that he can get away with everything. Now he's finally after all these years coming to his senses that he wasn't so smart—that anybody could be a crook until they are caught. And as he sits his time away in the cell here he's naturally sorry that he didn't follow the average person's outlook on crime. And he's more or less become sorry that he ever figured he was so smart that he could get away with everything. So it winds up that in his time in jail he decides he'd go straight, in other words.

Examiner: How does he turn out?

Jack: He turns out to be a pretty good man. He finds out that he wasn't as smart as he thought he was.

PICTURE TEN

It seems that this girl [pause] let's call her Dolly, happens to go to the library one night to pick up some books. She's a girl around nineteen, twenty years old. She goes to the library to get her books, picks them up. She's the same—she usually goes once or twice a month to pick up these books. She's a pretty decent little kid. She reads a lot; she winds up in the library this one night. Gets her books and she's on her way home [clears throat] she has about ten or fifteen blocks to walk. Usually in the summertime, in the fall, she decides not to take a bus. She walks. So this one night she's walking home from the library; it's starting to get dark. Fact is, it's getting pretty dark already. She sees somebody walking behind her [clears throat] in a suspicious way. So she decides, well, maybe this person is following her. So the more she thinks about it the more she's convinced the man in the back is following her. So naturally she takes different turns and crosses different streets and everything to find out. It seems that every street that she takes this fellow behind her keeps following. She's getting pretty well scared now. She's wondering what's going to happen—this fellow maybe jump her, maybe try to take her purse [pause]. She didn't want to run up to anybody and accuse the person behind her because she don't really know if he's following her or not. Yet every indication shows that he is. So naturally she's scared half to death as she's walking home. So finally she gets inside of her own home. She feels a little better. But she still don't think she's safe yet so she walks a little faster naturally. As she starts to walk faster she sees this fellow dropping back. So she runs up to her house, gets in her house and looks out the window and the fellow walks right on by. She sees it was a neighbor of hers who wouldn't have harmed her anyway. She was just suspicious. Then she decided, well, sometimes it pays to be scared and suspicious and sometimes it don't, that's all, but she's glad that she was anyway.

PICTURE ELEVEN

Well, I could see a picture here as plain as day—something I'd like to happen. Of course it concerns me. Well, it shows me getting up in the morning. [Pause.] Two little daughters are in the house. Naturally they have just got up. I just got up and they're practically jumping all over me, fooling around with me and kidding me and asking me where we're going today. So I tell them that maybe we'll just take a ride. [Clears throat.] So we get in the car and off we go, the wife and two kids. So it seems that this road that I'm taking just has a natural

Appendix B. The Case of Jack

attraction for the shore. The two children are wondering where we're going and keep asking me all the time, Daddy where are we going? I say, I don't know. In the first place by this time I know where I'm going. So down to the shore we go. When we get to the shore they find out we're at the ocean and I didn't bring their bathing suits. So they ask why I didn't bring their bathing suits. So I tell them, well, I'm going to take them fishing today. So I go in back of the car and get out two little fishing rods for the children and get my own out and one for my wife. We walk out in the surf and we start fishing. Naturally, each child catches a fish and I catch mine and my wife catches hers. We're all pretty well happy over it. The surprising thing about this, though, is that I always told the children that I'd get little fishing rods that they could go fishing with which they'd never done. Well, this day I'd taken them down there and really given them a terrific surprise. Because that's something they never expected in the first place. And then when I got the two little fishing rods out of the trunk of the car, that was a new toy to them. That was a big thing. So we all catch our fish and we go home and I think the kids like me just about twice as much as they ever did before.

Analysis of Jack's 1957 Stories

As one reviews the stories of Jack told in 1957, there is evidence of considerable growth. In 1940 there was conflict between positive and negative forces, and it was not possible to tell which would get the upper hand. But in 1957 the positive forces are definitely ascendant. As in 1940, there is still a strong wish to be loved, wanted, and accepted. In 1957 he started his stories by telling of the fellow who had been away from home a long time and he wonders how his family will accept him when he returns (A-1). A boy knocking on a door wonders how he will be greeted by the person who answers (A-2). A mother loves her son so much "just like most mothers do," that she worried about him and sits up for him when he is out late (A-6). A father does not want to disappoint his children (B-11).

Here one finds that Jack is able to see the situation not only from the point of view of the child who does not want to be neglected, but also of the father who does not want to disappoint his children. This is definite growth in identification with the good parent.

In 1940 there was much concern over rejection. This is still present in 1957 (the man in A-1 wonders how his family is going to greet him), but is much reduced in intensity. A girl feels that she is not good-looking and is not popular with boys her own age (A-3). A girl "doesn't rate" with her mother (because she is not as good looking or is not as bright) as much as her sister (B-4). A man is disappointed by his brother who fails to meet an appointment (A-6). But on the whole the emphasis in the 1957 stories is more on the pleasure of parental acceptance than in the fear of rejection.

The theme of the good parent recurs several times in the 1957 stories. Jack has learned the pleasures of parental generosity, sacrifice, and devotion to children. The mother who waits up for her son leaves food for him (A-6). Parents of a girl who is out late "soften" when they know her story (B-7). A father gets fishing rods for his two small daughters and they like him twice as much (B-11). Parents are satisfied with a daughter who does not go bad (B-2). Parents plan to postpone the purchase of a new car so that their son can have a gun (A-7). A man gives up a fishing trip so he can be with his brother (A-6). But children, too, learn to be generous. The boy who wanted the gun is persuaded by his sister that he should yield to his parents (A-7).

Having become a father, Jack views relations between parents and children with an entirely new perspective. In 1940 there were themes of parental domination and cruelty of fathers and husbands who "are no good, drink heavily, are cruel to their wives, and desert their families." There were also threatening mother figures and there were several stories of accidents and injuries that happen to the head of the family. Apparently these fantasies have been worked through, as they do not appear in 1957. Now there are themes of parental responsibility. A mother keeps trying to "talk down" her wild adolescent daughter "to keep her from going off the wrong path" (B-2). Another mother tells her little boy to stay away from the river and the boy has his fanny slapped for going there (B-5). Parents feel that they must discipline their adolescent daughter who stays out too late (B-7). The commanding officer talks to the wife of one of the men under him "like a father" (B-8).

And now he is able to observe with a little perspective the resistance of children, especially adolescents, to their parents (A-10, B-2, B-5). But he also sees that in spite of the desire for experiences and pleasure Doris (B-7) is "trying to be a good kid."

Appendix B. The Case of Jack

In 1940 Jack emphasized his loneliness and his feeling that others were unfriendly. In 1957 this has changed and he feels much more accepted by others. The man who gets another to repair his car "strikes up a pretty good friendship" (B-2). In a small town "most everyone knew one another and had grown up together" (A-3). He tells of "friendly neighbors" who discuss community improvements (A-9). This is an entirely new attitude, one which was not present in 1940.

In story A-5 Jack tells of a girl who never had any worries or cares —always a happy child. This story marks the change that has occurred since 1940, when Jack told many stories about being isolated, alone, and cruelly treated.

Death, which figured so prominently in the 1940 stories, is not mentioned once in 1957.

The themes of aggression have practically disappeared in 1957. Hunting (A-7) is accepted today as a sublimation of aggressive impulses; giving bad advice is only a mild form of aggression. There is only one reference to crime (B-9) and this is invited by the picture of the man in jail. His reaction to crime is that it is stupid and that the criminal is not very smart. "Anyone can be a crook until he is caught." The guilt that was apparent in 1940 seems practically to have vanished. One story tells of a girl whose mother tries to keep her "from going off the wrong path" (B-2). When she finally meets a nice fellow and "settles down" and doesn't "go bad or anything like that" her mother is pretty well satisfied with her. Hovering parental concern for children is a recurring theme in 1957.

The conflict between good and bad seems on the way to being resolved in favor of the good. There is reference to a clean-living boy from a good clean home who always comes home on time (A-6), a good clean boy who worked hard and loved his family (A-7), a decent fellow (B-6), a decent kid who reads a lot (B-10), and a man who goes to work, goes to church, and is fairly decent looking fellow (B-6). A girl who would lie against her sister is definitely discredited in a story (B-4). There is merit in keeping a promise (A-7). This emphasis on decency, goodness, and cleanliness is so blatant as to make one suspect hypocrisy and insincerity. But everything points to Jack's attitude as being naïvely genuine, sincere, and ingenuous. From his interview we learn that Jack dislikes the other members of his own family and believes that the life that he has learned from his foster parents has definitely set him apart from his brother, sisters, and his mother. This resolution of the moral conflict is a definite act of learning for Jack and one that he is still in the process of assimilating. Jack was sensitive to the moral conflict in 1940, but it was more of a conflict then. In 1940 there was reference to themes of reform. In 1957 it is not so much a matter of reform as an accepted pattern of life. The themes of reparation are no longer present.

As in 1940, romantic love is still prominent in Jack's fantasies. An engaged girl expects her beau to call (B-2). A girl is going to a dance (B-7). There is a puppy love affair in which "neither of them will ever want to be separated" (A-10). Married life is going to be all peaches and cream (B-8). This theme, present also in 1940, impresses one as being still adolescent, as though Jack had failed to mature in his concept of marriage.

There is still an emphasis on having pleasure (B-7). Reading books is contrasted with having fun and going on dates (A-3), and to repress pleasure is interpreted as being snooty. An adolescent girl who figures that she is a grown woman now "gallivants around town and has a good time" (B-2). That this "having a good time" means sex is evident because in this story the girl doesn't "go bad."

Jealousy, which was prominent in the 1940 stories, appears once in 1957 (B-4). The reaction to this situation is depressive (she feels low over it). Depression which was not noted in 1940 makes its appearance in 1957, but it still is not a prominent theme. The man who stays at home to meet his brother grieves over his loss of the pleasure of fishing, and gets blue (B-6). But there are only two times that depression enters as a theme.

Anxiety, too, makes an appearance in 1957. The mother who lives near the river is "practically frightened out of her wits" that her son may have been drowned (B-5). Both the parents of the boy (A-6) and the girl (B-7) worry when their adolescent offspring are out too late, and the girl in B-7 is afraid of the parent's anger.

In 1940 it is reported that Jack has "high ideals and aspirations of a not-too-realistic sort." But by 1957 these aspirations are modest indeed. A girl fantasies traveling to see places and daydreams that some day she will be able to go to a large city (A-5). In another story a man wanted to get a bigger boat for himself (A-4). But a persistent theme in 1957 is his mediocrity. There is a story of a girl who lived in a small town with ordinary people (A-3). The criminal finally comes

Appendix B. The Case of Jack

to his senses with the realization that he is not so smart (B-9). The girl in B-4 is neither good-looking nor bright. In reality Jack feels humble and insignificant because of his lack of education, and he apparently is struggling to reconcile himself to his position in life. But one girl in A-8 competes with another girl who is better educated and who "has been taught in the right way."

Jack continues the same attitude toward work that he showed in 1940. It is more than a coincidence that in A-2 the boy knocking on the door, willing to work—even such menial work as cleaning the cellar—was also seeking work such as cleaning yards and cellars in 1940. The boy in B-3 who bought a used car on which a lot of work needed to be done decided he would do some of the work himself to save expenses.

Having enough money to meet the demands of modern living is certainly a problem with Jack, since he introduces the theme in four of his stories. A man does not have enough money to buy the boat that he wants (A-7). A farmer has to wait until he can get enough money to buy a new fence (B-1). A man tries to save expense in getting his car repaired (B-3). The father whose son wants to buy a gun is pinched for money (A-7).

Jack's feminine identification, which was noted in 1940—and is also a feature of his Rorschach—is again clearly indicated in his 1957 stories. Jack identifies convincingly with the female characters in his stories. In A-2 he wonders whether the figure in the picture is a girl or a boy. He senses vividly the yearnings of the adolescent girl in A-3, B-2, and B-7. Sibling rivalry is between sisters (B-4). Two mothers are concerned over their children (B-5 and A-6). A woman tries to prevent her soldier husband from going overseas (B-8). And the story from the picture with two young people who went to the fortune-teller (A-10) is still told from the point of view of the girl.

The stories also display much passivity. Characters want things to happen rather than assert themselves to bring about what is desired. The man who tries to get a man to come down on the price of a boat is taken advantage of, and finally yields to the other's importunity (A-4). The girl on her way home from school daydreams (A-5). The mother in B-5 asks her neighbors for advice. The two young people are undecided about getting married (A-10). A man waits the whole day long for his brother (B-6). In two stories there is the theme of being imposed on and taken advantage of (A-4, B-3). But, on the other hand, the mother in B-5 does not want to cause trouble to the police and the girl who is taken advantage of by her sister resorts to propitiation (B-4). In B-3 a character makes a weak attempt to take an active role by pumping the other fellow for information, but is unable to hold this position. In fact, the "deal" which results in "striking up a pretty good friendship" suggests a passive homosexual attitude. Typically, police in fantasy represent the external prohibiting and punishing authority, and the inner superego. But in B-5 the mother calls on the police for help in finding her son.

The really aggressive characters in the stories are women. In A-7 a sister persuades her brother to give up his wish for a gun. Margie decides that Helen can get the job only over her dead body (A-8). The wife tries to persuade the commanding officer to excuse her husband from having to go overseas (B-8).

However, anger as a reaction to his own passivity in 1957 is new, and was not present in 1940. He now resents being taken advantage of. The man in story A-4 "buys the boat anyway, but tries to act as though he's pretty mad over the deal." One may suspect that this is a projection and that he is angry at his own weakness on yielding—a defense against his femininity. He criticizes the boat when he does not have enough money to buy it. The man who waits for his brother gets "madder and madder" (B-6). Parents of the adolescent daughter are "pretty well put out" over her staying out late (B-7). The farmer whose cows get into the neighbors' property is "getting a little tired of it," but "he has to put up with it until he can get a new fence" (B-4).

One definite sign of growth on Jack's part is his greater discrimination between fantasy and reality. Call it disillusionment, or fatalism, or another illustration of his passivity, if you will, but it means that Jack has learned the necessity of submitting to the order of things. Assuming that he identifies with the Swami in A-10, he makes the decision to tell the truth—"that Johnny would be drafted and there could be a war." The criminal in B-9 learns that he cannot follow his own whims, and finds that he is not as smart as he thought he was. Even the commanding officer in B-8 cannot go against the rules. In this story he shows how he learned to accept his place as a cog in the machinery of modern living, even though he still feels like protesting as the young wife did in this story. He exhibits pity for those who do not have un-

Appendix B. The Case of Jack

derstanding of human relations (which he thinks he has?) (B-4). And he probably identifies with Elsie in A-7, who "has a little more knowledge of the ways of people's feelings and everything."

Even so, Jack's stories have a Pollyannish tinge. The tendency to brush off tragedy and evil by a happy ending was present in 1940, but this tendency is more pronounced in 1957. The boy who might have been drowned was home playing under the bed (B-5). After his brother telephones that he is on the way "Slim bucks up and feels pretty good—the day wasn't really wasted" (B-6). The girl who incurred her parents' anger because she stayed out late was not disciplined after all (B-7).

Suspicion and mistrust, not present in 1940, appear in one of the 1957 stories (B-10).

On the whole there is greater change in the stories of Jack than in many of the other subjects in the study. When we first knew Jack in 1940 he was still adjusting to the break-up of his parental home and to the new foster home in which he had been assigned by the state. In discussing Jack in *Adolescent Fantasy*, his need for strong figures with which he could identify was pointed out, and it was thought that he would have to look for such a person in a teacher. At that time the positive influence of the foster parents was not realized. But his foster home satisfied some of Jack's yearnings and with the passage of time he identified more closely with his foster parents and grew away from the members of his natural family. The world has become a more friendly place and the theme of friendlessness has disappeared. Aggression practically disappears from fantasy and death is not mentioned. There is no reference to punishment, repentance, or reform. Oedipal themes are no longer present.

To take the place of these a passive, feminine attitude, discernible in 1940, becomes much more pronounced. The conflict between good and bad has weakened and Jack shows clearly that he gives assent to conventional moral standards. To be wanted and to belong, present in 1940, is still a strong need in 1957, and there are themes of winning love. Romantic views of love and marriage and the craving for pleasure are also still powerful in 1957. In fact, many of Jack's current stories have a decided adolescent flavor, as though Jack was belatedly enjoying some of the fantasies normally to be found in adolescents. Jack is still struggling with his acceptance of his position in the world. He expresses humble attitudes and there is absence of high aspiration, but nevertheless he feels competitive with another person of higher station, wealth, or education. He is willing to work, and feels keenly that he does not have money for all the things that he would like to have. Instead of seeing parental domination as an oppressive force, as he did when he was an adolescent, now as a father he sees the necessity for firmness and control in dealing with children. There are traces of anxiety, depression, and suspiciousness in 1957, which were not present in 1940. On the whole, Jack has profited by his experiences as he has grown out of adolescence so that he is now able to meet the problems of early adulthood with realism and a positive sense of social responsibility.

RORSCHACH PROTOCOL *1957*

Key: L = location   D = determinant   C = content   O-P = original-popular

Initial response	*Inquiry* [1]	L	D	C	O-P
Card I	*Card I*				
1. Butterfly landing under a tree and on some oak leaves. It is just sitting.	1. Just a shape, and the butterfly is just resting. It is on the leaf and the point of the leaf is sticking out on each side.	W	FM	A	
	Additional: 1a. Two cats looking out of the dark. This makes me think of Hallowe'en. Actually the two cats are the two sets of white spots which represent the eyes and the outlines of the cats' faces are distinct, or rather they merge, one with the other.	[WS	FM, Fc′	A	]

---

[1] In the Rorschach, after the subject has responded to each card the examiner conducts an "inquiry" in which he asks the subject where and how he sees each response that he has made.

Appendix B. The Case of Jack

RORSCHACH PROTOCOL *1957* (*Continued*)

Initial response	Inquiry	L	D	C	O-P
Card II	Card II				
1. Two dogs, nose to nose, dancing.	1. Standing up to one another.	D	FM	A	P
2. A party hat.	2. A dinner hat such as people might wear at a fancy party.	D	F	Obj	
	Additional: 2a. Two people leaning back to back, wearing the hats.	[D	M	H	]
3. Butterfly.	3. A dressed up butterfly—red butterfly.	D	FC	A	P
4. Two moths.	4. Two moths coming up to a landing with a light shining from behind. The little black lines represent the streamers of light. The light is intercepted by the moths who are in front of the light.	D	FM,m	A	
5. Three dark spots. (This was changed later to two spots.)	5. These are the three spots, slightly tinted, reddish, on the inside of the black figures. (He did not name them, but simply pointed them out.)				
6. Worms, crawling over dogs.	6. These are the little red patches attached to the large black near the top. (He speaks of a general worminess and the red color is part of them. They seem to be crawling over the dogs.)	dd	FM,C	A	o
7. A Chinese pagoda.	7. The roof of it. There is a little faint line near the top. It has the shape of a pagoda.	D	F	Arch	

RORSCHACH PROTOCOL *1957* (*Continued*)

Initial response	Inquiry	L	D	C	O-P
Card III	Card III				
1. I see two, looks like men dancing. Looks like they got—what you call these things that the women wear over their hands—muffs, I believe they look like. Looks like they each have them in their hands. High heeled shoes they have on, tight pants maybe, maybe some sort of a mask on that resembles something out of this world—I don't know what it would be.		W	M	H	P
2. The red marks look like, let's say, part of the X ray maybe, with two sections of the chest. That's what I think it would be, maybe.	2. A picture of the lungs. The color helped me to think of it.		D	FC	X ray
3. I turn this card upside down and when I look on the left here, it looks like a parrot, maybe, sitting up on a perch, hollering down or something.			D	FM	A
4. The one on the right has a face more like a little monkey. [You mean the parrot?] No, this one looks like a parrot to me, the one on the left, the face, the head, the other one looks like a monkey's face.	4. The monkey's tail is hanging down. He is chattering or scolding. He is looking down on an antelope.		D	FM	A
5. Actually that's maybe a vase or something between the two men there, maybe some sort of a fancy vase sitting on the floor.	5. The vase is sitting on the floor. The black threads are the design on it. It flares out at the top like a vase.		DS	F	Obj

Appendix B. The Case of Jack

RORSCHACH PROTOCOL *1957* (*Continued*)

Initial response	Inquiry	L	D	C	O-P
Card IV	**Card IV**				
1. That looks to me like an X ray picture, the texture of it. Lines mean an X ray picture.	1. (A whole response.) The midline is the spine. The texture helps me to think of an X ray as there are lighter and darker portions of it.	W	kF	X ray	
2. This part up in the center here—I don't know which is top or bottom—but it reminds me of a snail's head that I've seen in pictures.		d	F	Ad	
3. This section right in here could be a—what do you call them?—jesters, you know those court jesters? Looks like a funny hat like they'd wear and the chin's sticking out like a court jester.	3. The jester has a ruff around his neck, a tall hat, and his chin is sticking out.	D	F	Hd	
4. I turn them back this way. I don't know if I can keep track of it but that looks like part of a flower, an exotic flower, maybe a leaf on an orchid. That's what it is, I guess. I could probably pick some more out of it.	4. The center is the top of the orchid. The texture on the side makes me think of the texture of an orchid streaked with color.	D	Fc	Pl	
Card V	**Card V**				
1. Oh, I keep getting that butterfly.	1. A cut-off whole leaving out the two side extensions.	W	F	A	P
2. And right in here, I don't know if you've ever seen a dog lay down and stretch both legs out toward the back, but that's what it reminds me of.		D	FM	A	

RORSCHACH PROTOCOL *1957* (*Continued*)

Initial response	Inquiry	L	D	C	O-P

Card V

Card V

3. The very top in here reminds me of a Punch and Judy head, little puppets. Of course I'm only working more or less on the center.

3. Punch is on the left; Judy is on the right. (By looking closely he seemed to be able to differentiate and the left looked more like a male figure, the right more like a female figure—that portion of the two top horns where they come close together so that the noses almost touch. He also refers to the tall hats that they are wearing.)

D M H

4. I didn't look toward the outer edge. I think if I look toward the outer edge I see thunder clouds. That's all I can see on here.

4. A black mass.

D KC' Cl

Additional: 4a. I see legs sticking out on each side.

[D F Hd]

Card VI

Card VI

1. This section right in here, those two little light spots remind me of an owl—two owls—just the shape of them, you know and right above them.

1. Two owls, sitting on a branch in the distance, side by side.

d FM, FK A

2. If I look at the forms I can see like two chipmunks sitting up there facing one another. Boy, I get a lot of animals here, don't I?

2. Now instead of looking like chipmunks, they look like prairie dogs with the little paws held up and they are back to back.

d FM A

3. The other thing that could be is a maybe some sort of animal skin stretched out to dry like

3. A muskrat skin. The belly is cut out. Also I can see the paws and legs. This is

D Fk Aobj

Appendix B. The Case of Jack

RORSCHACH PROTOCOL *1957* (*Continued*)

Initial response	Inquiry	L	D	C	O-P
Card VI	Card VI				
you see pinned on a board in some of these Western pictures and things.	the inside. The skin has been scraped and this is just a shape. It has been scraped in such a way that the blood vessels show, which is represented by the texture.				
4. I see two little hooks up at the top here that could be—they remind me of something—maybe waves from an ocean. Not like the actual waves, like drawn ones—like somebody put in a drawing.	4. One on both sides. (This card is now held upside down. These are the two little curved hooks at the very bottom of the figure.)	d	F	N	
5. If I look at one side of it, it will look like a map of a lake or something—if I just split it in half and look at the one side.		D	F	Map	
6. The top here looks like it could be two like ceramic book-end statues with little figures on the side.	6. (This is at the very top of the card. He speaks of the split down the middle and the dark outline at the very top looks like two figurines that make ceramic book-ends.)	d	F	Obj	
7. It seems to be like an image of a man standing up in there with his hands down on his sides—that real dark spot at the top and that is just about it, I guess. I see other light and dark spots but I can't make anything out of them.	7. A man, standing at attention with arms held stiffly down at his sides.	D	M	H	

Appendix B. The Case of Jack

RORSCHACH PROTOCOL *1957* (*Continued*)

Initial response	Inquiry	L	D	C	O-P
Card VII	**Card VII**				
1. (Long pause.) This looks like a bear standing here. (Longer pause.)	1. Two ears, a nose, mouth and an eye.	D	F	Ad	
2. You want something what it is just reminding me of? Like this figure here would remind me of like a, well, what would you say, a little kid making a face, going to school, like I'd be, you know. That's what this reminds me of. Two of them, face to face. The other side seems to have a bear, well, both sides are practically the same. So what I see here, I see here also.	2. An impish face. One on the right has chocolate on his mouth, smeared.	D	M,c'	H	P
3. I'm trying to see if I can make something out of the white sheet more. I just can't seem to make anything out of that. That could remind me here of an atomic bomb explosion going off there.	3. The white space. The general space. The shock wave is coming out. The shock wave is forcing itself out from the center.	S	Fm	Explosion	
4. If it had a little flatter base, here, this white spot in here could represent a, let's say a fancy jar, or vase or something, made of delicate glass.	4. It would look more like a fancy jar if it had a flatter bottom.	S	F	Obj	
5. That reminds me like you'd see on a map, lakes on a map, maybe.	5. A chain of lakes on a map.	W	F	Geo	
6. Down in here—it don't look anything like it—but it reminds me of a kid's Fourth of July sparkler, looks like one's sticking up	6. A child's Fourth of July sparkler. The dark part is the handle and the light part above is the sparkler.	d	Fc'	Obj	

Appendix B. The Case of Jack

RORSCHACH PROTOCOL *1957* (*Continued*)

Initial response	Inquiry	L	D	C	O-P

Card VII

there and it reminds me of a little sparkler.

7. This bear's head, if you turn it upside down it reminds me of an elephant as far as the nose goes, an elephant with a bump on its head. That's what that reminds me of.

Card VII

7. I see an elephant mainly by the trunk.

    Additional: 7a. When turned over it looks like a bear's head. This is not to be confused with the bear's head on response 1.

    D   F   Ad

    [D   F   Ad]

Card VIII

1. Yes, this is pretty technical. The first thing I think about this is a medical chart, maybe, like I've seen in these medical books with the heart out of line and the lungs and things. That's the first thing that would remind me of and of course it looks just the spine down in there, all the membranes going off, or something.

2. These two red pieces on the side remind me of a rodent, say of the rat family. Yet it don't remind me of a rat, maybe something like a muskrat—a bigger rat, stalking. It's not running or sitting, it seems like it's just creeping to something.

3. This part here reminds me of a—er, petals on a rose. Because I happen to like that color of rose, I guess. I don't know why.

Card VIII

1. The whole thing. The spine is in the center. The colors on the chart make me think of the charts in medical books that I have seen.

    W   C/F   At

2. The head of a rodent. Now as I look at it again, it looks more like a wolf, the back and the legs. The colors don't associate.

    D   FM   A   P

3. Mainly the color and not so much the shape of a rose.

    D   CF   N

RORSCHACH PROTOCOL *1957* (*Continued*)

Initial response	Inquiry	L	D	C	O-P
Card VIII	**Card VIII**				
4. Looks like somebody dropped some nice strawberry ice cream.	4. The dark flecks are the kinds of spots that you see in strawberry ice cream.	D	CF	Ice cream	
5. The darker colors—like the center between the darker colors reminds me of, what do you call that thing? Out on the desert they had these cows drop dead and they always withered up, yes, the head part of the carcass.	5. The skull of a cow in the desert.	D	F	At	
6. This reminds me of a fishing plug in here. The only reason it reminds me of one is because I guess I go fishing, not that it looks like it.	(Additional: 6a. This same center part which he originally saw as a fishing plug now looks to him like a rocket with fins on the side.)	dd [dd	F F	Obj Obj]	
7. This looks like a little whistle in here. A whistle a kid would hold in his mouth, you know. This little long piece.	7. This same center dark portion now looks like a child's whistle.	dd	F	Obj	
8. These two parts right up in here would make me think of maybe two masks on a Mardi Gras clown or something. That's about all I can make out of that one.	8. The two masks have hair as is worn by Harpo Marx.	D	F	Obj Mask	
Card IX	**Card IX**				
1. Would it represent blobs of ink (laughs).	1. The whole thing but mainly the greener areas.	W	CF	Ink	
2. This up at the top reminds me of a jelly fish, like a Portuguese Man-of-War, at least. This has almost got the shape on the top. Of course the Portu-	2. With long streamer tentacles.	D	FM	A	

Appendix B. The Case of Jack 395

RORSCHACH PROTOCOL *1957 (Continued)*

Initial response	Inquiry	L	D	C	O-P
Card IX	Card IX				
guese Man-of-War has a lot of tentacles, I guess you'd call it, hanging down. I never got hit by one.					
3. I see a little figure like. It looks like an eye and the snout on a camel. I'm sure he's been stabbed.	3. On the side looks like an elk or a moose.		D	F	Ad
4. This reminds me of water here, the ocean water, more or less— green, salty water.	4. It's the color of sea water as one might see in an oil painting.		D	C	Water
5. In this little scene, you can see a vase in there. Because it's folded it always turns up that way. If you always looked at one side of it, you wouldn't get that effect.	5. This looks like a heavy glass vase, rolled in a semi- circular fashion.		DS	Fc	Obj
6. It reminds me of, if I look at it this way, like— like clouds more or less like a hurricane, this bluish-green one here.	6. The green, dark clouds, the orange, the wind-blown part.		D	CF,m	Cl
7. Looks to me like a little sea horse in here.	7. Mainly the belly, the shape of the belly of a sea horse as it curves out.		D	F	A
	Additional: 7a. I also see the map of Italy shaped like a boot.		[D	F	Map]
8. An appendix inside of a medical drawing in here.	8. The inner dark object looks like an appendix as one sees in a medical chart.		dd	F	At
Card X	Card X				
1. I see more bugs! (laughs.)		W		F	A
2. Up in here it looks to me like a, I don't know			D	(M)	A

Appendix B. The Case of Jack

RORSCHACH PROTOCOL *1957* (Continued)

Initial response Card X	Inquiry Card X	L	D	C	O-P
what kind of bird it would be but there are some exotic birds that have a tassle on their head. It looks like two of them sassing each other face to face, like we'd call a toe-to-toe argument. Mouth and eyes.					
3. This thing here looks like a rabbit's head.	3. A rabbit's ears are sticking up. I see a nose, two ears, the darker spots are the eyes. The green is not part of it.	D	F	Ad	P
4. Like you have in Guadalcanal or in 90 percent of them Pacific Islands look like this. I guess from the air. I haven't seen them from land. On the maps they look like that.		W	FK	Geo	
5. This looks like a bunch of seaweed here.	5. Blue. Makes me think of deeper water where the seaweed would be.	D	CF	Seaweed	
6. Like a yellow canary here.	6. The yellow on the side. The color makes me think of a canary. I see the wings, the tail and also a beak.	D	FC	A	
7. Let's see what I can make out of this white part here. Some sort of a passage between two islands, maybe. That's what it looks like it could be. Water there.		S	F	Geo	
8. This reminds me of maybe a flaming torch that the Marathon runners	8. The torch that Marathon runners carry, one ball out at	D	F	Obj	

Appendix B. The Case of Jack 397

RORSCHACH PROTOCOL *1957* (*Continued*)

Initial response	Inquiry	L	D	C	O-P
Card X	Card X				

used to carry back before my time.

the top of the flame.

9. This part right in here reminds me of a picture I saw when I was a kid. You know they have a face like that—like the March calendars—all windblown. Looks like it's all puffed up, ready to blow the wind.

9. I see a head and nose, and the cheek puffed out.

    D   M   Hd

10. If I look at the white part here, if I didn't have all this other stuff in here it could be the head of Abraham Lincoln with a beard on the bottom here.

10. The head of Abraham Lincoln.

    S   F   Hd

11. The little orange spot in the middle reminds me of a sugar maple tree—has a little leaf on it, you know the butterflies that fall to the ground. That is what that reminds me of—falling sugar maple seeds.

    D   Fm   N

12. These two spots here remind me of one of my favorite breakfasts—sunny-side-up eggs, it could be. The only thing is the center is orange like the eggs but the outside's yellow, it isn't white.

12. A fried egg with a slightly darker round spot in the middle.

    D   CF   Egg

13. This little part right in here looks like a, like sometimes you see snow on a house hanging over the leaders and gutters, melting down. In other words after a snowstorm the sun

    d   Fm   Snow

RORSCHACH PROTOCOL *1957* (*Continued*)

Initial response	Inquiry	L	D	C	O-P
Card X	Card X				
gets hitting it, kind of melts down a little.					
14. This part in here would remind me of a, let's say a comical character, the man in a diving suit right in here.	14. This is a comical character in a diving suit.	D	F	H	
15. These red things look like seahorses at the top here or the bottom, I don't know which one it is.	15. Just the shape. The green is not part of it.	D	F	A	
16. The little orange thing over here reminds me of a guinea pig sitting down on its belly.	16. Mainly the shape of the head and back. Also an eye.	D	FM	A	
17. These two things bother me. Some of them look like they remind me of something but I don't know what. They remind me of something in the ocean, I know that. They remind me of coral. You can see a lot of it in beautiful colors—all blue.	17. Coral. Just the shape, not the color. It made me think of coral because under the ocean they are all beautiful colors.	W	CF	Coral	

Interpretation of the Rorschach

The Rorschach presents the picture of an obsessive-compulsive ego organization in an intelligent, self-conscious, feminine passive man. He appears to have a good deal of intellectual and emotional drive, but he is handicapped from asserting himself by a strong general passivity, by feelings of inadequacy as a man, and by a compulsive cautiousness. There is also a tendency to be distracted by inconsequential activity, as a way of channeling anxiety.

His reality contact, his logic, and his reasoning are good. He is able to see the world as other people do, and able to make the necessary conventional adjustments. He shows a well-developed imagination or fantasy, and he has a strong tendency to oppositionalism which in combination tend to set him apart from the mass as an individual. His judgment is generally reliable. However, he has a tendency to lose sight of the goal, and his oppositionalism is often self-destructive. There is a caution and timidity which prevents him from making better use of his excellent intellect. His social adjustment seems to be fairly adequate, though the initial impression he makes is by no means his best.

The main areas of disturbance center around a confusion in sexual identity, a phobic reaction to close sensual and erotic contact, and a repression of aggressive energy. The identification seems to be predominantly feminine. There was probably a confusion of parental sexual roles. He has assumed a passive and probably submissive relationship with men. This is, however, tempered by his oppositionalism. He seems to feel inadequate with male authority figures, perhaps especially intellectually inferior. He finds it very difficult to compete with men, although he has more than the necessary equipment both intellectually and in terms of complexity of personality. His attitude toward his mother and women in general seems to be one of rejection. There is also a good deal of repressed but deep rage and hostility. He is unable to assume an adult masculine loving role with them, and can be described as a very ungiving male. He seems to function best with them when he can assume an unconscious oral, dependent, little-boy role, where his needs for nurturance and support are subtly satisfied. However, since he has difficulty in accepting as well as giving, he is never free of a sense of guilt in such relationships. He feels and places a great deal of distance between himself and women, as a result of his unconscious hostility toward them.

The relationship to the father seems to have been superficially good, but unconsciously, in some way, seductive. In any case, the patient reacted by submitting to him emotionally. It is possible that the father was actually a warmer person than the mother, and the passive feminine identity was the patient's way of avoiding a fear of castration. He seems to have projected a wisdom and omniscience onto his father which necessitated a rigid caution on his part. In any case, he was never fully able to identify with his father, and has always looked for a strong and powerful and wise male with whom he could make an identification. He tends to look up to authority figures, while he unconsciously defies them.

There is likely to have been some emotional traumatization in the sexual area, and this is probably what accounts for his phobic reaction to closeness. He is afraid of being hurt, and is probably oversensitive to criticism and rejection. Feeling so inadequate as a male, he is likely to magnify small failures. He shows very little spontaneity and freedom as a sexual male. Although he is unable to give in emotionally to women, he is likely to feel coerced and pushed around by them even when no basis for such feelings exists. He may appear compliant but the sexual act is to him an aggressive and destructive experience. There is a good deal of castration anxiety, but he rationalizes it away very effectively. He has a strong tendency to denial, and there is also a strong tendency to rationalization where aggression is concerned. He is not likely to recognize his own hostility or his own fears. His insight into himself is quite poor, although he tends to be introspective.

He is interested in people and dependent on them for the gratification of his emotional needs. He is basically a dependent man, although his self-consciousness and his restraint may cover this up. His affect may be described as more feminine than masculine, as it generally is in the feminine passive-obsessive types. He is not, however, effeminate. The oral needs further give his affect a gentle and dependent quality. In spite of his compulsive control he seems to be fairly spontaneous in the expression of his feelings and makes a friendly impression. However, the repressed hostility often gives his feelings a sharp edge. He also often feels self-conscious with people and at such times the impression he gives is of forced and empty intellectualized contact. He has a tendency to have short intermittent moods of depression, but this is not pronounced.

The repressed aggression is not likely to be experienced as a problem by the patient, since the feminine passive identification is ego syntonic. He feels a keen sense of inadequacy, however, although for the wrong reason—i.e., he projects it to the intellectual level.

The neurotic structure on the whole has a good deal of stability, although there is much unconscious tension, and a frequent feeling of distance between himself and people. He has a wish for a more goal-directed and "nobler" life, but he does not have the courage and the necessary aggressive self-assertion to try to achieve it.

Appendix B. The Case of Jack

Summary

The case of Jack, presented in detail, is instructive because it shows the persistence of personality as well as certain modifications that have taken place as a result of experience.

From a psychological point of view the outstanding quality of Jack's personality is his passivity and feminine identification. This was noted in adolescence (see *Adolescent Fantasy*, p. 270), and is still more apparent in 1957. He is not effeminate, but the feminine identification shows in his passivity, dependency, and tendency to permit himself to be imposed upon. He is inadequate with male authority figures, as shown both by his relations with teachers in school and officers in the Navy, and he lacks aggressive self-assertion. Instead, he resents being imposed upon and becomes angry, probably as much from his own yielding as from the injustice of superior male figures. In such situations he becomes angry, "blows his top," becomes suspicious and mistrustful, and is sure that everyone is against him or is forgetful of him. The Rorschach report speaks of repressed rage and hostility. These make him cautious and timid, as, for instance, in his mistrust of his own powers when he entered apprenticeship as a tool and die worker. He has a keen sense of inadequacy, projected to the intellectual level, and he adopts attitudes of humility. This makes him adopt modest goals and think of himself as incompetent and insignificant. In reacting to his passivity and dependency he also becomes stubborn and oppositional and this often forces him to defeat his own purposes, as illustrated when he became defiant toward a superior officer in the Navy. In such instances he may hurt himself in order to hurt someone else. As a result he lacks pride and will demean himself to do the humblest tasks.

As when adolescent, Jack has a strong need to be loved, wanted, and accepted. As an adult he does not feel so lonely and friendless as he did when younger, but he still has strong needs for the support of a family. But he is oversensitive to rejection and criticism. Because of his passivity he has found it difficult to accept as well as to give, and being placed in a dependent, receiving position makes him feel guilty. Jack left school early to go to work in part because of the obligation which he felt toward his foster parents.

As an adolescent, conflicting forces were struggling for supremacy in Jack—his anger and hatred which would have made him antisocial and more constructive forces of striving toward better things. The latter have clearly gained ascendancy now that Jack is an adult. As an adult he subscribes to ideals of decency, goodness, and cleanliness as an accepted pattern of life, not of reform. This he ascribes to the influence of his foster parents, who counseled him not to be "common." The influence of his foster parents was present in 1940, but the potency of this influence was not recognized at that time. The forces which are influential in determining the direction of personality development are present and observable at all times in every individual, but our knowledge does not yet permit us to discriminate between the important and less important factors with assurance.

One of the outcomes of his allegiance to the values of his foster parents is his rejection of his own family, particularly his brother, toward whom he feels definitely superior, and also toward his mother. He says that going to see his mother is like "paying his respects."

Now that Jack is a father, he shows his identification with the good parent. He feels an obligation to provide for his family and he is generous toward them, although he now sees the need for exercising restrictive control as well. His ability adequately to provide for his family seems to be a source of anxiety and worry for him.

As one surveys Jack's growth out of adolescence into adulthood, in spite of his passivity, sporadic episodes of losing his temper and stubbornness, it is apparent that he is making a satisfactory adjustment. He has acquired a trade, is a steady worker, has married well, has two children, and has a house of his own. He is more than fulfilling his adolescent aspirations.

Index

Accident, as theme, 28(*tab.*), 29, 32(*tab.*)
Achievement, *see* Education; Success; Vocation
Adjustment, of subjects, 173, 201-6; and age, 15; social, 148(*tab.*)-152; Rorschach ratings of, correlated with interview, 151; and aggression, 152; and psychosexual adjustment, 152; rankings of, 176-87; correlations, 176-78; ranking procedure and criteria, 178-84; composite rankings, accuracy, 184; discrepancies between ratings from Symonds Picture-Story Test, Rorschach Test, and interview, 184-87; and personality, 192; sexual, 211; *see also* Psychosexual adjustment; Sexual adjustment; Social relationships; Vocational adjustment
Adolescence: themes of, 31; early, themes of, 41; and heterosexual interests, 103-5; intensity of feelings, 198-99
Adolescent fantasy, *see* Fantasy, adolescent
Adolescent Fantasy (Symonds), 1, 2-4, 27, 33, 57, 135, 176, 189, 214, 221, 222, 272, 277, 294, 385, 401
Adorno, Theodor W., 12*n*
Affect, 152(*tab.*)-155, 171, 173, 174, 212
Age of subjects, 16(*tab.*)-17; at marriage, 22(*tab.*); effect on fantasy and personality, *see* Adolescence; Fantasy; Personality
Aggression, 171-72, 174-75; as characteristic of adolescent fantasy, 31, 41, 42, 189; and depression, 33, 88-90; and adult fantasy, 48; in adolescent fantasy and adult behavior, 51, 57-61, 71-73, 189-90, 209-10; and experience, 75-76, 79, 81, 86, 88-90, 91; in adolescent and adult personality, 99(*tab.*)-100; Rorschach description of, 120, 143(*tab.*)-148, 163, 212; and social adjustment, 152, 201
Albert (subject 40), 7, 20, 180, 181; adolescent and adult fantasy compared, 34-36, 43(*tab.*); adolescent fantasy compared to later experience and personality, 50, 53, 59-60, 72; change in fantasy, 77, 82, 83; adolescent and adult personality compared, 97(*tab.*), 99(*tab.*), 102(*tab.*), 104(*tab.*), 105, 106(*tab.*), 107, 110(*tab.*), 113(*tab.*), 115(*tab.*), 116(*tab.*); Rorschach analysis, 126(*tab.*), 126, 127, 127(*tab.*), 129, 132, 138(*tab.*), 140, 143(*tab.*), 148(*tab.*), 152(*tab.*), 155(*tab.*), 156, 157(*tab.*), 160(*tab.*), 163(*tab.*), 164, 166; from adolescent to adult, 196, 202, 203, 205; resumé, 335-41
Altruism: as theme, 28(*tab.*), 29-30, 31(*tab.*); as defense mechanism, 60, 86-87, 90, 91
Altus, William David, 17*n*
Ambition, *see* Self-striving
Anger, as theme, 28(*tab.*), 31(*tab.*), 35, 48, 161
Anxiety, 46; change in, 28(*tab.*), 31(*tab.*); in adolescence, 33-34; in adolescent fantasy and later personality and experience, 51, 66-71, 72, 189-90, 209-10; and depression, 66-68; defenses against, 68-71, 86-88, 160(*tab.*)-162; change of, related to experience, 86-94; Rorschach description of, 160(*tab.*)-162; correlation of Rorschach and interview ratings, 162; as meas-

Index

Anxiety (*Continued*)
ured by Rorschach and interview, 171-72, 212
Artistic interests of subjects, 67-68
Atkinson, John W., 48*n*
Authoritarian personality, 215
Authoritarian Personality Study, 12-13
Authority, subjects' attitude toward, 23-24

Barbara (subject 20), 43(*tab*.), 179, 184-85, 185-86; adolescent fantasy compared to later experience and personality, 55, 56, 64, 65, 73; change in fantasy, 78, 85, 90, 93; adolescent and adult personality compared, 97(*tab*.), 99(*tab*.), 104(*tab*.), 105, 109(*tab*.), 112(*tab*.), 114(*tab*.); Rorschach analysis, 126(*tab*.), 127(*tab*.), 129, 131, 135, 138(*tab*.), 140, 141, 142, 143(*tab*.), 147, 148(*tab*.), 151, 152(*tab*.), 155(*tab*.), 157(*tab*.), 158, 160, 160(*tab*.), 163(*tab*.), 164, 165(*tab*.), 166; from adolescent to adult, 195, 198; resumé, 264-71
Beck, Samuel J., 122*n*, 123, 124, 125
Behavior, relation to thematic apperception test, 4; and erotic adolescent fantasy, 54-57, 189-90; and fantasy, 193, 200-201; adult, and adolescent fantasy, 209-10; and the Rorschach, 212
Bellak, Leopold, 48*n*
Binder, Hans, 124, 125
Blank card, see Picture B-11
Brady, Gertrude G., 121*n*

Card, see Picture
Cass, William A., 122*n*, 123, 124, 125
Castration, 65-66, 75, 81
Catherine (subject 12), 43(*tab*.), 180, 182-83, 186, 197; adolescent fantasy compared to later experience and personality, 51-52, 54, 55-56, 57-58, 64, 72; change in fantasy, 80, 82, 89-90, 91, 94; adolescent and adult personality compared, 96(*tab*.), 100(*tab*.), 101, 101(*tab*.), 103(*tab*.), 104, 106(*tab*.), 109(*tab*.), 112(*tab*.), 113; Rorschach analysis, 126(*tab*.), 126, 127, 127(*tab*.), 132, 138(*tab*.), 143(*tab*.), 148(*tab*.), 152-53(*tab*.), 155(*tab*.), 157(*tab*.), 158, 159, 160(*tab*.), 161, 163(*tab*.), 163, 164, 168; resumé, 233-40

Celia (subject 28), 37-38, 43(*tab*.), 179, 182, 184-85, 185-86; adolescent fantasy compared to later experience and personality, 51, 52-53, 55, 59, 60-61, 64, 65, 67, 72; change in fantasy, 74, 85, 87, 90, 92; adolescent and adult personality compared, 98(*tab*.), 99(*tab*.), 100, 104(*tab*.), 105, 110(*tab*.), 112(*tab*.), 115(*tab*.), 116(*tab*.), 117; Rorschach analysis, 126(*tab*.), 126, 127(*tab*.), 129, 131, 135, 138(*tab*.), 141, 143(*tab*.), 145, 148(*tab*.), 152(*tab*.), 154, 155(*tab*.), 156, 157(*tab*.), 160(*tab*.), 163(*tab*.), 164, 164(*tab*.), 166(*tab*.); from adolescent to adult, 195, 198, 201, 203; resumé, 287-93
Chamoulaud, Muriel I., 176, 177
Character: relation to fantasy, 3-4; relation to thematic apperception method, 4
Children, at interview, 9; of subjects, 23(*tab*.); number related to sexual adjustment, 130
Clark, Rodney A., 48*n*
Comparison: of data, 1940 with 1953 study, 2; of Rorschach Test and Symonds Picture-Story Test, see Rorschach Test; Symonds Picture-Story Test
Competitiveness, see Aggression
Concealment, as theme, 28(*tab*.), 31(*tab*.)
Concept of self, see Self, subjects' concept of
Conflict, 15
Confusion as to sex, see Sex role
Control, 165(*tab*.)-166, 171, 173, 174, 212; Rorschach Test and interview measurements of, correlated, 171
Crime: against person, 28(*tab*.), 31(*tab*.), 33; against property, 28(*tab*.), 29, 31, 31(*tab*.)
Criminal death, as theme, 28(*tab*.), 29, 31, 31(*tab*.)
Cross-sexual identification, 57

Death, 36, 46; accidental or natural, 28(*tab*.), 29, 31, 31(*tab*.); criminal, 28(*tab*.), 29, 31, 31(*tab*.)
Death wishes, 72
Defense mechanisms, appearance in fantasy, 190
Dejection, see Depression
Dependency, 51-54, 189-90, 209-10

Index

Depression, 126, 173, 181, 212; increase of, in fantasy, 28(*tab.*), 29, 30(*tab.*), 31, 31(*tab.*), 32, 33, 39, 42, 83, 189, 200, 209; stories of, 37, 40, 41, 46, 159; and anxiety, 66-68; and aggression, 88-90; and negative endings, 91; as measured by the Rorschach, 166-67, 211; correlation of, in Rorschach and Symonds Picture-Story Test, 167; relation of, in Rorschach and interview observations, 172

Disappointment, *see* Depression

Discouragement, *see* Depression

Disobedience: disobedience-rebellion, 28(*tab.*), 31(*tab.*); disobedience-coercion, 28(*tab.*), 31(*tab.*)

Dorothy (subject 30), 8, 179, 180, 184-85, 185-86; adolescent and adult fantasy compared, 38, 43(*tab.*); adolescent fantasy compared to later experience and personality, 54, 54-55, 69, 72; change in fantasy, 83, 89, 91, 93; adolescent and adult personality compared, 98(*tab.*)-99, 103(*tab.*), 108(*tab.*), 110(*tab.*), 112(*tab.*), 116(*tab.*), 117, 117(*tab.*); Rorschach analysis, 126(*tab.*), 127(*tab.*), 133, 137, 138(*tab.*), 139, 142, 143(*tab.*), 148(*tab.*), 149, 150, 152(*tab.*), 155(*tab.*), 157(*tab.*), 160(*tab.*), 161, 163(*tab.*), 164, 164(*tab.*), 165(*tab.*); from adolescent to adult, 196, 198; resumé, 299-305

Drive, 163(*tab.*)-164, 171, 173, 174

Drummond, Robert, vi, 43*n*, 45

Dudek, Stephanie (analyst of Rorschach reports), vi-vii, 43*n*, 119, 120, 121, 129, 149, 161, 165, 167, 176, 177, 209

Dullness, 67

Edgar (subject 10), 126-27

Edith (subject 17), 43(*tab.*), 45, 46, 199, 200, 203; adolescent fantasy compared to later experience and personality, 60, 63, 66-67, 69, 72; change in fantasy, 83, 91; adolescent and adult personality compared, 96(*tab.*), 98(*tab.*), 100(*tab.*), 103(*tab.*), 109(*tab.*), 112(*tab.*), 113; Rorschach analysis, 126(*tab.*), 126, 127(*tab.*), 133, 138(*tab.*), 143(*tab.*), 144-45, 148(*tab.*), 152(*tab.*), 157(*tab.*), 160(*tab.*), 163(*tab.*), 163, 166(*tab.*), 166; resumé, 252-57

Education, 191, 210; of subjects, 18(*tab.*), 19; identified with success, 62-63; of subjects, aspirations and achievements, 109(*tab.*)-111; and adjustment, 202-3; and vocation, 204; for adulthood, 206-7

Edwin (subject 33), 43(*tab.*), 181, 182, 204, 205, 213; adolescent fantasy compared to later experience and personality, 63, 64, 72; change in fantasy, 84, 90, 92; adolescent and adult personality compared, 97(*tab.*), 98(*tab.*), 104(*tab.*), 110(*tab.*), 112(*tab.*), 115(*tab.*); Rorschach analysis, 126(*tab.*), 127(*tab.*), 134, 138(*tab.*), 142, 143(*tab.*), 146, 148(*tab.*), 152-53(*tab.*), 154, 155(*tab.*), 156, 157(*tab.*), 158, 159, 160(*tab.*), 162, 163(*tab.*), 164, 164(*tab.*), 165(*tab.*), 167; resumé, 310-11

Effort, 29(*tab.*), 32(*tab.*)

Ego strength, 178, 180-81

Eisenhower, Dwight D., 25, 60, 337, 361

Elizur, Abraham, 172*n*

Empathy, 149

Ending, of story, *see* Stories

Energy level, 163(*tab.*)-164, 171, 174

Environment, effect on fantasy, 75-94, 189

Eroticism, 51, 77, 93; as theme, 28(*tab.*), 31(*tab.*); in adolescent fantasy leading to later behavior, 54-57, 189-90, 209-10; *see also* Sex; Marriage

Erotic themes, 46

Escape: as theme, 28(*tab.*), 29, 31(*tab.*), 32, 209; from parental home, 76, 94, 189

Excitement, as theme, 28(*tab.*), 31(*tab.*)

Experience, adult, and change in fantasy, 50-73, 213

Failure, 61

Family, and adolescent adjustment, 196-98

Fantasy: relation to character, 3-4; sexual, 32; change and stability, 34-49, 74-75, 188; correspondence to experience, 50-73; and personality, 50-73, 189-93; change and experience, 74-94; and environment, 75, 189; indicating unresolved problems, 75, 82-85, 191-92; disappearance of passive themes, 79, 80; change to active themes, 81-82; realism in, 90-94; change in, 188-89, 213; significance of, 188-93; and reality, 192; and behavior, 193, 200-201

Fantasy, adolescent: characteristic themes of, 31, 32, 41; characteristics of, 189; relation to adult personality, 189-93, 213; modified by adult experience, 199-200; and adjustment, 201; and adult behavior, 209-10
Father figure, 59-60, 72, 73, 80, 81; see also Parents
Feminine identification, 46, 56, 211; as theme, 28(tab.), 31(tab.), 32-33; increase in, 78, 79; measured by Rorschach, 138(tab.)-142
Fine, Rubin, 27
Frenkl-Brunswik, Else, 12-13
Freud, Anna, 194, 195
Friends of subjects, 108(tab.)
Fromm, Erich, 1

Gill, Merton, 123n
Gillman, Robert D., 122n, 124n
Giving-receiving, 28(tab.), 31(tab.), 32, 76, 209
Guilt, 42, 46, 56, 72; as theme, 28(tab.), 29, 31(tab.); in adolescence, 33-34, 41; produced by hostility, 52, 60, 161; level of, 86-94; defense against, 86-88; shift of defense against, 88-94

Happiness, 179-80
Herz, Marguerite R., 121n
Heterosexual interests of subjects, 103(tab.)-105; see also Sex; Homosexuality
Hobbies, subjects', 114(tab.)-116, 118
Homosexuality, 129-30
Hopelessness, 42
Hostility, 46, 72; as fantasy theme, 28(tab.), 29, 31, 31(tab.); in adolescent fantasy and later behavior, 51, 57-61, 86; in adult fantasy, 75, 81; and guilt, 161

Ideas, in stories, 29
Identification, see Cross-sexual identification; Feminine identification; Masculine identification; Sex role
Identity, personal and sexual, subjects' sense of, 138(tab.)-142, 167-68, 170, 211
Illness, as theme, 28(tab.), 29, 32(tab.); psychosomatic, 70
Imagination, 155
Inadequacy, personal, 158, 211
Inferiority, 33, 61, 63-64, 171, 173
Inhibition, 165, 166; of subjects, due to recording, 8; see also Repression; Control
Insight, 155
Intellectualization, 67-68, 161
Intelligence, 155; and I.Q. of subjects, 16(tab.)-17; correlation between Rorschach and I.Q. ratings of, 157
Intermarriage, 24
Interpersonal relationships of subjects, see Social relationships
Interview, 3, 5, 95-96, 208; procedure, 5-12; purpose, 6-7; scope, 10-12; compared with Authoritarian Personality Study, 12-13; transcription, 13; description of salient aspects of personality, 97-118; subjects' responses to, 101-2(tab.), 118; correlated with the Rorschach, 120, 151, 162, 166; personality ratings, error in, 121; findings in, related to the Rorschach, 131-38, 140-41, 144-48, 150-51, 153, 156, 158, 161-62, 163-64, 165-66, 167-69; compared with the Rorschach and fantasy, 170-75, 184-87
I.Q., see Intelligence
Isabel (subject 18), 43(tab.), 87, 179, 185-86, 195, 198, 213; adolescent fantasy compared to later experience and personality, 50, 51, 53, 55, 72; adolescent and adult personality compared, 101(tab.), 104(tab.), 105, 109(tab.), 112(tab.); Rorschach analysis, 126(tab.), 126, 127(tab.), 129, 131, 135, 138(tab.), 143(tab.), 147, 148(tab.), 149, 150, 152(tab.), 153, 155(tab.), 157(tab.), 160(tab.), 163(tab.), 164(tab.), 166(tab.); resumé, 257-58

Jack (subject 4), 5, 195, 197, 208, 214; as an adolescent, 1-2, 342-43; case of, 342-402; as an adult, 343-44; interview, 344-63; stories of, Symonds Picture-Story Test, 363-79; stories of, analysis, 379-86; Rorschach protocol, 386-98(tab.); Rorschach interpretation, 398-400; summary, 401-2
Jealousy, 28(tab.), 32(tab.)
Jensen, Arthur R., 5, 102; as interviewer, vi, 7-9, 144, 150, 153-54, 160, 167, 208, 243; and authoritarian personality, 24; as analyst of stories, vi, 70, 74, 136, 141, 316; and the Rorschach, 119; and interview ratings, vi, 120, 121, 151, 162, 166; and adjust-

Index

ment rankings, 176, 177, 178, 181, 209
Jerome (subject 7), 179, 213; adolescent and adult fantasy compared, 40-41, 43(tab.); adolescent fantasy compared to later experience and personality, 52, 62, 72; change in fantasy, 83, 83-84; adolescent and adult personality compared, 96(tab.), 99(tab.), 100, 103(tab.), 109(tab.), 112(tab.), 113, 117(tab.); Rorschach analysis, 126(tab.), 127(tab.), 132, 138(tab.), 140, 143(tab.), 148(tab.), 152-53(tab.), 155(tab.), 157(tab.), 159, 161, 164(tab.); from adolescent to adult, 196, 201, 204, 205; resumé, 221-22
Jimmy (subject 37), 1, 43(tab.), 80, 82, 181, 214; adolescent fantasy compared to later experience and personality, 53, 54, 69-70, 72-73; adolescent and adult personality compared, 97(tab.), 104(tab.), 106(tab.), 107(tab.), 108, 110(tab.), 113(tab.); Rorschach analysis, 126(tab.), 126, 127(tab.), 129, 134, 135, 137, 138(tab.), 143(tab.), 148(tab.), 152-53(tab.), 155(tab.), 156, 157(tab.), 160(tab.), 163(tab.), 164(tab.), 166(tab.), 169; from adolescent to adult, 195, 198, 202, 203, 205; resumé, 317-27
John (subject 39), 78, 80, 83, 179, 185; adolescent and adult fantasy compared, 43(tab.), 45, 46; adolescent fantasy compared to later experience and personality, 55, 62, 65-66, 68-69, 73; adolescent and adult personality compared, 97(tab.), 98(tab.), 99(tab.), 100(tab.), 104(tab.), 105, 110(tab.), 113(tab.), 115(tab.), 117(tab.); Rorschach analysis, 126(tab.), 126, 127(tab.), 129, 131-32, 135, 136, 138(tab.), 139, 140, 142, 143(tab.), 144, 148(tab.), 152(tab.), 154, 155(tab.), 157(tab.), 159, 160(tab.), 163(tab.), 165, 167; from adolescent to adult, 196, 202, 203, 205; resumé, 328-35
Joke, *see* Trick
Julia (subject 25), 43(tab.), 127(tab.), 213; adolescent fantasy compared to later experience and personality, 54, 62, 63, 72; change in fantasy, 91-92, 93; adolescent and adult personality compared, 102(tab.), 103, 103(tab.), 108(tab.), 110(tab.), 112(tab.), 115(tab.); from adolescent to adult, 195, 206; resumé, 281-82

Karl (subject 11), 8, 43(tab.), 83, 84, 180, 181; adolescent fantasy compared to later experience and personality, 51, 53, 55, 57, 69, 70, 71; adolescent and adult personality compared, 96(tab.), 99(tab.), 100(tab.), 109(tab.), 112(tab.), 113; Rorschach analysis, 126(tab.), 126, 127(tab.), 129, 131, 138(tab.), 143(tab.), 144, 148(tab.), 152-53(tab.), 156, 157(tab.), 160(tab.), 163(tab.), 164, 164(tab.), 165(tab.), 166, 167; from adolescent to adult, 195, 197-98, 204; resumé, 227-33
Kinsey, Alfred C., 128
Klausner, Samuel Z., 17
Klebanoff, Seymour G., 48n
Klein, Melanie, 87
Klopfer, Bruno, 123, 124, 125
Klopfer-Kelly-Davidson System, Rorschach scoring, 124
Kruskel-Wallis One-way Analysis of Variance by Ranks, 54n

Laura (subject 13), 43(tab.), 180; adolescent fantasy compared to later experience and personality, 54, 56, 57-58, 72, 73; change in fantasy, 76, 77, 91, 93; adolescent and adult personality compared, 96(tab.), 98(tab.), 99, (tab.), 100(tab.), 101, 101(tab.), 106(tab.), 109(tab.), 112(tab.), 114(tab.), 116(tab.); Rorschach analysis, 126(tab.), 126, 127(tab.), 132-33, 138(tab.), 143(tab.), 148(tab.), 152(tab.), 154, 155(tab.), 157(tab.), 160(tab.), 164(tab.), 165, 165(tab.), 166; from adolescent to adult, 195, 197, 199; resumé, 240-44
Lewin, Kurt, 191
Lindzey, Gardner, 48n
Logic, 155
Love, 46, 81

Mabel (subject 22), 179, 185, 186, 199, 201; adolescent and adult fantasy compared, 43(tab.), 45, 46-48; adolescent fantasy compared to later experience and personality, 53, 59, 62, 72; change in fantasy, 76, 86-87, 91, 94; adolescent and adult personality compared, 106(tab.), 107, 109(tab.), 112(tab.), 114(tab.), 115(tab.), 116; Rorschach analysis, 126(tab.), 126, 127(tab.), 129, 138(tab.), 143(tab.), 145, 148(tab.), 152-53(tab.), 153, 155(tab.),

Index

Mabel (*Continued*)
156, 157(*tab.*), 158, 160(*tab.*), 163 (*tab.*), 164, 164(*tab.*), 165(*tab.*), 166 (*tab.*); resumé, 276-80
McClelland, David C., 48*n*
McReynolds, Paul, 122*n*, 123, 124, 125
Magic, 189, 209
Margaret (subject 24), 43(*tab.*), 181, 213; adolescent fantasy compared to later experience and personality, 50-51, 54, 57-59, 72; change in fantasy, 77-78, 89, 92; adolescent and adult personality compared, 97(*tab.*), 103 (*tab.*), 110(*tab.*), 112(*tab.*), 114(*tab.*); Rorschach analysis, 126(*tab.*), 126, 127(*tab.*), 129, 143(*tab.*), 145, 148 (*tab.*), 152(*tab.*), 154, 155(*tab.*), 157 (*tab.*), 160(*tab.*), 163(*tab.*), 164, 164 (*tab.*), 165, 166(*tab.*); resumé, 280-81
Marital status of subjects, 21-22(*tab.*)
Marriage, 46, 77, 85, 129-38; and adjustment, 202, 204-6
Masculine identification, 46, 65, 85, 211; as theme, 28(*tab.*), 31(*tab.*), 32-33, 209; and Symonds Picture-Story Test, 56; as measured by the Rorschach, 138-42
Masochism, 56, 58, 68, 90
Meili-Dworetzki, Gertrude, 123, 125
Mental functioning, 155(*tab.*)-157, 171, 173, 174, 212
Military service, of subjects, 20-21
Molish, Herman, 122*n*, 123
Morality, 46; as theme, 28(*tab.*), 32 (*tab.*)
Mother figure, 73, 80, 81; hostility toward, 57-59, 72; emancipation from, 197; *see also* Parents
Murray, Henry A., 48*n*
Mystery, 28(*tab.*), 32(*tab.*); as theme in adolescence, 29, 41, 209; and sexual fantasy, 32, 77, 189

Nancy (subject 31), 9, 179, 181, 195, 199; adolescent and adult fantasy compared, 43(*tab.*), 45, 46; adolescent fantasy compared to later experience and personality, 53, 54, 70, 73; change in fantasy, 76, 78, 84; adolescent and adult personality compared, 97(*tab.*), 100(*tab.*), 102(*tab.*), 103(*tab.*), 110 (*tab.*), 112(*tab.*), 115(*tab.*), 117(*tab.*); Rorschach analysis, 126(*tab.*), 126, 127(*tab.*), 134, 137, 138(*tab.*), 143 (*tab.*), 147, 148(*tab.*), 150-51, 152 (*tab.*), 155(*tab.*), 157(*tab.*), 160(*tab.*), 165(*tab.*), 166(*tab.*), 166, 168-69; resumé, 305-10
Natalie (subject 21), 43(*tab.*), 81, 88, 179, 186; adolescent fantasy compared to later experience and personality, 52, 54, 57-59, 68, 72; adolescent and adult personality compared, 97(*tab.*), 99(*tab.*), 101(*tab.*), 106(*tab.*), 107, 109(*tab.*), 112(*tab.*); Rorschach analysis, 126(*tab.*), 126, 127(*tab.*), 129, 133, 138(*tab.*), 139, 143(*tab.*), 148 (*tab.*), 152-53(*tab.*), 157(*tab.*), 158, 159, 162, 163(*tab.*), 164, 165(*tab.*), 166(*tab.*); from adolescent to adult, 196, 199, 203; resumé, 271-76
Nervous signs, 116(*tab.*)-117, 118
Neurotic tendencies, freedom from, 178, 180-81
Nixon, Richard, 361
Norton, C. E., 128

Oedipal relationships of subjects, 78, 167-69, 173, 212
Oedipal themes: in stories, 1, 38, 51, 61; in adolescence, 54-55, 56, 57, 58, 59, 60, 61, 72
Olive (subject 27), 36-37, 43(*tab.*), 81, 92, 182; adolescent fantasy compared to later experience and personality, 64, 67, 67-68, 72; adolescent and adult personality compared, 97(*tab.*), 98 (*tab.*), 102(*tab.*), 110(*tab.*), 112(*tab.*), 115(*tab.*); Rorschach analysis, 120, 126(*tab.*), 126, 127(*tab.*), 136-37, 138 (*tab.*), 143(*tab.*), 145, 148(*tab.*), 150, 152-53(*tab.*), 155(*tab.*), 156, 157(*tab.*), 160(*tab.*), 162, 163(*tab.*), 165(*tab.*), 166; from adolescent to adult, 195, 196, 205; resumé, 282-87
Orality, 28(*tab.*), 32, 32(*tab.*), 51, 53, 209
Outcomes, *see* Stories

Pansy (subject 29), 43(*tab.*), 179, 197, 202; adolescent fantasy compared to later experience and personality, 50, 52, 53, 56, 57-58, 68, 72, 73; change in fantasy, 74, 85, 89; adolescent and adult personality compared, 97(*tab.*), 98(*tab.*), 100(*tab.*), 102(*tab.*), 106(*tab.*), 107(*tab.*), 108, 110(*tab.*), 112(*tab.*); Rorschach analysis, 126(*tab.*), 126, 127(*tab.*), 130, 138(*tab.*), 142, 143(*tab.*), 146, 148

Index

(*tab.*), 149, 150, 152-53 (*tab.*), 154, 155 (*tab.*), 157 (*tab.*), 160 (*tab.*), 164 (*tab.*), 165, 166; resumé, 294-99
Paranoia, 126
Parents: subjects' relations with, 105 (*tab.*)-107, 118, 191; and adolescent adjustment, 196-98
Passivity, 28 (*tab.*), 29, 31, 32 (*tab.*)
Pathology, 125-27
Personality: relation to thematic apperception method, 4; relation to interview, 6-7, 95-118; stability of, 42-43 (*tab.*), 43-49, 195-96; and fantasy, 50-73, 188-93; correspondence to experience, 50-73; adolescent related to adult, 95-118, 190-91; described by the Rorschach, 170-72; relation to anxiety, 172; described by Picture-Story Test, 172-73; as resolution of fantasy, 192, 212; adolescent, 194-95; adjustment of, from adolescent to adult, 195-99; overt, relation to Rorschach and to Symonds Picture-Story Test, 212; adult, and adolescent fantasy, 213
Personality characteristics, general, 96-99 (*tab.*), 118
Physical characteristics of subjects, persistence of, 100 (*tab.*)-101, 118
Picture-Story Test, *see* Symonds Picture-Story Test
Picture A-1, stories to: mentioned, 50, 51-52, 53, 135, 321, 322, 324, 325, 326, 379, 380; quoted, 69-70, 215-16, 224, 237-38, 241, 284, 301, 363-64
Picture A-2, stories to: mentioned, 52, 53, 135, 141, 159, 291, 320, 324, 325, 329, 379, 383; quoted, 142, 218-19, 255-56, 292, 302, 308-9, 318-19, 337, 364
Picture A-3, stories to: mentioned, 54, 55, 70, 135, 137, 159, 267, 323, 326, 380, 381, 382; quoted, 216-17, 250, 255, 262, 263, 284, 364-65
Picture A-4, stories to: mentioned, 50, 51, 68, 76, 382, 383, 384; quoted, 37-38, 229, 259-60, 266, 296, 365
Picture A-5, stories to: mentioned, 55, 60, 62, 67, 69, 135, 136, 137, 159, 321, 325, 381, 382, 383; quoted, 254, 269, 273, 289, 292, 301, 303, 313-14, 330-31, 365-66
Picture A-6, stories to: mentioned, 52, 53, 55, 136, 137, 159, 321, 379, 380, 381, 382, 383; quoted, 35, 42, 207, 230, 275, 290, 295, 308-9, 313, 314-15, 366
Picture A-7, stories to: mentioned, 52, 62, 63, 137, 266, 319, 321, 324, 325, 326, 380, 381, 383, 384, 385; quoted, 64, 235, 239, 295, 315, 322, 329, 337, 367
Picture A-8, stories to: mentioned, 55, 60, 62, 137, 324, 383, 384; quoted, 141, 242-43, 254, 260, 330, 367-68
Picture A-9, stories to: mentioned, 53, 60, 135, 137, 159, 160, 292, 325, 381; quoted, 238, 289-90, 368
Picture A-10, stories to: mentioned, 58, 65, 85, 135, 137, 142, 217, 266, 324, 380, 382, 383, 384; quoted, 230-31, 232, 248-49, 283, 291, 296, 298, 301-2, 332, 339, 368-69
Picture B-1, stories to: mentioned, 50, 59, 64, 321, 324, 325, 336, 338, 340, 383; quoted, 34-35, 40-41, 46-48, 237, 246-47, 285-86, 289, 297-98, 302-3, 318, 322-23, 331, 369-70
Picture B-2, stories to: mentioned, 55-56, 323, 324, 325, 380, 381, 382; quoted, 235, 246, 263, 266-67, 275, 295-96, 370-71
Picture B-3, stories to: mentioned, 135, 137, 321, 325, 383, 384; quoted, 219, 259, 270, 273, 371-72
Picture B-4, stories to: mentioned, 57, 59, 159, 321, 322, 323, 325, 326, 380, 381, 382, 383, 384, 385; quoted, 223, 261, 273, 284-85, 286, 372-73
Picture B-5, stories to: mentioned, 46, 53, 56, 60, 136, 142, 241, 324, 326, 380, 382, 383, 384, 385; quoted, 35-36, 217-18, 243, 250-51, 254, 296-97, 312-13, 373-74
Picture B-6, stories to: mentioned, 51, 57, 60, 62, 67, 321, 325, 326, 381, 382, 383, 384, 385; quoted, 39-40, 159, 223, 225, 229, 232, 247, 248-50, 253, 255, 268, 277-78, 289, 298, 303, 307, 308, 314, 329-30, 334, 338-39, 374-75
Picture B-7, stories to: mentioned, 53, 136, 249, 277, 302, 321, 324, 380, 382, 383, 384, 385; quoted, 38, 220, 231, 241-42, 246, 248, 262-63, 332-33, 336-37, 375-76
Picture B-8, stories to: mentioned, 51, 52-53, 55, 63, 70, 137, 300, 302, 307, 321, 323, 324, 333, 380, 382, 383, 384; quoted, 38, 231, 242, 256, 261, 273-74, 278, 290, 309-10, 319, 376-77
Picture B-9, stories to: mentioned, 69, 135, 136, 142, 218, 221, 231, 265, 322, 325, 381, 383, 384; quoted, 41-42, 230, 235-36, 254, 291-92, 377

Picture B-10, stories to: mentioned, 51, 135, 137, 142, 160, 221, 270, 322, 324, 326, 381, 385; quoted, 230, 235-36, 267, 268-69, 274, 279, 288, 303-4, 308, 315-16, 338, 377-78
Picture B-11 (blank card), stories to: mentioned, 86, 159, 321, 322, 323, 324, 326, 380; quoted, 225-26, 261, 269, 279, 378-79
Picture 7 (1940 series), story to: mentioned, 265
Picture 15 (1940 series), story to: mentioned, 265
Picture 16 (1940 series), stories to: quoted, 236; mentioned, 265
Picture 30 (1940 series), story to: quoted, 306
Picture 37 (1940 series), story to: quoted, 306
Picture 40 (1940 series), stories to: mentioned, 265, 294; quoted, 337
Piotrowski, Zygmunt, vi
Planning, as theme, 29(tab.), 32(tab.)
Pleasure, as theme, 28(tab.), 32(tab.)
Plot, see Trick
Political affiliation of subjects, 24-25
Pomeroy, Wardell B., 128n
Popularity, subjects' concern about, 46
Population, in 1940 study, 2, 4-5; description of, 14; age of, 16(tab.)-17; I.Q. of, 16(tab.)-17; residence of, 17
—— in 1953 study, 5; description of, 16-26; age of, 16(tab.)-17; I.Q. of, 16(tab.)-17; residence of, 17(tab.), 21(tab.); education, 18(tab.), 19; vocation, 19-20; and military service, 20-21; and marriage, 21-22(tab.); and children, 23(tab.); religion, 23-24 (tab.); and political affiliation, 24-25; nosological diagnosis of, by Rorschach test, 125-27; general Rorschach description of, 211; as adolescents, 213; as adults, 213
Poverty, 48
Prediction, from 1940 study, 1-2, 170-75; see also Fantasy; Personality; Behavior
PST, see Symonds Picture-Story Test
Psychogram Scoring Sheet for Verbal Projective Techniques, 27
Psychosexual adjustment of subjects, 127(tab.)-138, 152, 170, 212
Punishment, as theme, 28(tab.), 31, 32(tab.), 189, 209

Rabin, Albert I., 122n, 123
Racial backgrounds of subjects, 25
Ralph (subject 2), 179, 180; adolescent and adult fantasy compared, 39, 40, 41-42, 43(tab.); adolescent fantasy compared to later experience and fantasy, 57, 63-64, 65, 70, 71, 73; change in fantasy, 75, 76, 80, 86, 88-89; adolescent and adult personality compared, 96(tab.), 100(tab.), 105(tab.), 107, 109(tab.), 112(tab.), 114(tab.), 115(tab.), 116(tab.); Rorschach analysis, 126(tab.), 127(tab.), 129, 131, 138(tab.), 140, 143(tab.), 148(tab.), 152-53(tab.), 154, 155(tab.), 156, 157 (tab.), 160(tab.), 161, 164(tab.), 166, 167; from adolescent to adult, 195, 196, 197, 203, 204; resumé, 215-20
Rankings, see Adjustment; Interview; Rorschach Test; Symonds Picture-Story Test
Rapaport, David, 123, 124, 125
Reaction formation, 72, 89, 93, 277; against anxiety, 68-70; and aggression, 146
Realism, in fantasy, 92-94
Reality, 156, 192
Receiving, see Giving-receiving
Reform, as theme, 28(tab.), 29, 32(tab.), 189, 209
Rejection, as theme, 28(tab.), 32(tab.), 46
Religion, of subjects, 23-24(tab.)
Reparation, 86-87, 90
Repentance, as theme, 28(tab.), 32(tab.)
Repression, 165, 277; and fantasy, 81, 90, 93; and sex, 130; and aggression, 144; as defense against anxiety, 161; and feeling, 174
Residence of subjects: socio-economic areas, 17(tab.); change of, 21(tab.)
Responsibility, 42
Restlessness, 15
Riviere, Joan, 87
Roby, Thornton B., 48n
Rodnick, Eliot H., 48n
Roger (subject 8), 9, 43(tab.), 179, 182; adolescent fantasy compared to later experience and personality, 54, 57, 64, 71, 73; change in fantasy, 76, 86, 89, 90-91; adolescent and adult personality compared, 96(tab.), 103 (tab.), 109(tab.), 112(tab.), 114(tab.); Rorschach analysis, 126(tab.), 126,

Index

127(*tab.*), 138(*tab.*), 141-42, 143(*tab.*), 148(*tab.*), 152(*tab.*), 154, 155(*tab.*), 157(*tab.*), 158, 159, 160(*tab.*), 163(*tab.*), 164, 165(*tab.*), 166(*tab.*), 166, 168; from adolescent to adult, 196, 203; resumé, 222-26

Rorschach, Hermann, 124

Rorschach signs, frequency, 122(*tab.*)-125

Rorschach Test, 6, 208, 211, 213; procedure, 8; transcription, 10, 119; description and analysis of subjects, 119-69; scoring, 119-20; scoring error, 120-21; correlated with Symonds Picture-Story Test, 120; correlated with interview, 120; statistical analysis of, 121-25; ratings of adjustment correlated with interview, 151; intelligence ratings correlated with I.Q., 157; anxiety ratings correlated with interview, 162; ratings of control correlated with interview, 166; evaluation of depression correlated with Symonds Picture-Story Test, 167; comparison with interview and fantasy, 170-75, 185-87; and personality, 170; control ratings correlated with interview, 171; agreement with fantasy, 174-75; adjustment rankings, 176; adjustment rankings correlated with Symonds Picture-Story Test, 178; and psychological adjustment, 185-87; and behavior, 212

Rotter, Julian L., 122*n*, 124*n*

Roy (subject 6), 42, 43(*tab.*), 66, 72, 180, 213; change in fantasy, 76, 77, 79, 89, 91, 93, 94; adolescent and adult personality compared, 99(*tab.*), 101(*tab.*), 103(*tab.*), 109(*tab.*), 112(*tab.*), 113, 116(*tab.*); Rorschach analysis, 126-27, 132, 138(*tab.*), 143(*tab.*), 146, 148(*tab.*), 150, 152(*tab.*), 155(*tab.*), 156, 157(*tab.*), 159, 160(*tab.*), 161, 163(*tab.*), 164(*tab.*), 165(*tab.*), 167; from adolescent to adult, 199, 204; resumé, 220-21

Sam (subject 9), 180, 203, 204, 213; adolescent and adult fantasy compared, 39-40, 43(*tab.*), 45, 46; adolescent fantasy compared to later experience and personality, 52, 54, 56, 57, 59, 61, 71, 72; change in fantasy, 83, 89, 91; adolescent and adult personality compared, 96(*tab.*), 103(*tab.*), 109(*tab.*), 112(*tab.*), 114(*tab.*), 116(*tab.*); Rorschach analysis, 126(*tab.*), 126, 127(*tab.*), 129, 138(*tab.*), 139, 143(*tab.*), 146, 148(*tab.*), 152-53(*tab.*), 155(*tab.*), 156, 157(*tab.*), 158, 159-60, 160(*tab.*), 161, 163(*tab.*), 165(*tab.*), 166(*tab.*); resumé, 226-27

Sanford, Robert N., 48*n*

Schafer, Roy, 123*n*

Schizophrenia, 126

Self, subjects' concept of, 157(*tab.*)-160, 171-72, 212; attitudes, 173, 174

Self-confidence, 42, 61; presence of, 28(*tab.*), 32(*tab.*); lack of, 29(*tab.*), 32(*tab.*)

Self-control, 87

Self-esteem, 158, 171, 211

Self-striving, 51, 61-66, 189-90, 209-10

Separation, 29(*tab.*), 32(*tab.*), 46; see also Escape

Sex, 54-55, 56, 57, 77, 128-38, 189; definitions of, 128; aspects revealed by the Rorschach, 128-29

Sex identification, see Masculine identification; Feminine identification

Sex role, 174; confusion of, 28(*tab.*), 31(*tab.*), 129-31, 139, 167-68; identity, 212

Sexual adjustment, 130, 211; disturbance of, in adolescence, 104-5; relation to aggression, 144

Sexuality, 29(*tab.*), 32(*tab.*)

Sex wish-life, 173, 212

Seymour (subject 36), 43(*tab.*), 179, 180, 181, 182; adolescent fantasy compared to later experience and personality, 52, 54, 63, 72; change in fantasy, 74, 76-77; adolescence and adult personality compared, 97(*tab.*), 100(*tab.*), 104(*tab.*), 106(*tab.*), 107, 108(*tab.*), 110(*tab.*), 113(*tab.*), 115(*tab.*), 116(*tab.*); Rorschach analysis, 126(*tab.*), 126, 127(*tab.*), 129, 134, 138(*tab.*), 148(*tab.*), 153(*tab.*), 155(*tab.*), 157(*tab.*), 161, 163(*tab.*), 164, 165(*tab.*), 169; from adolescent to adult, 197, 199-200, 205; resumé, 311-17

Sheviakov-Friedberg Questionnaire, 3

Sibling: rivalry, 60-61, 67, 69, 72, 73, 80, 81; subjects' relations with, 107(*tab.*)-108, 191

Silverman, Sylvia, v, 7, 102, 176, 177

Slavson, S. R., 206

Index

Social relationships of subjects, 148 (*tab.*)-152, 170, 191, 210, 212; Rorschach ratings of, correlated with interview ratings, 151
Socio-economic areas of subjects' community, 17(*tab.*)
Stella (subject 19), 43(*tab.*), 180, 181, 186; adolescent fantasy compared to later experience and personality, 54, 60, 62-63, 67, 72; change in fantasy, 80, 81, 87, 89; adolescent and adult personality compared, 103(*tab.*), 107 (*tab.*), 108, 109(*tab.*), 112(*tab.*); Rorschach analysis, 126(*tab.*), 126, 127 (*tab.*), 133, 138(*tab.*), 143(*tab.*), 148 (*tab.*), 150, 152-53(*tab.*), 155(*tab.*), 156, 157(*tab.*), 159, 160(*tab.*), 161, 163(*tab.*), 164(*tab.*), 165, 166(*tab.*), 166; from adolescent to adult, 203, 204; resumé, 258-64
Stevenson, Adlai E., 361
Stories: transcription of, 6, 10, 29; analysis of, 27-49; positive endings, 28 (*tab.*), 32(*tab.*), 33, 39, 40-41, 189; negative endings, 28(*tab.*), 32(*tab.*); computation of length, 29; similarities in formal factors, 45; shift of endings, 90-92
Strangeness, *see* Mystery
Striving, *see* Effort
Subject 1, *see* Wallace
Subject 2, *see* Ralph
Subject 4, *see* Jack
Subject 6, *see* Roy
Subject 7, *see* Jerome
Subject 8, *see* Roger
Subject 9, *see* Sam
Subject 10, *see* Edgar
Subject 11, *see* Karl
Subject 12, *see* Catherine
Subject 13, *see* Laura
Subject 14, *see* Viola
Subject 17, *see* Edith
Subject 18, *see* Isabel
Subject 19, *see* Stella
Subject 20, *see* Barbara
Subject 21, *see* Natalie
Subject 22, *see* Mabel
Subject 24, *see* Margaret
Subject 25, *see* Julia
Subject 27, *see* Olive
Subject 28, *see* Celia
Subject 29, *see* Pansy
Subject 30, *see* Dorothy
Subject 31, *see* Nancy

Subject 33, *see* Edwin
Subject 36, *see* Seymour
Subject 37, *see* Jimmy
Subject 39, *see* John
Subject 40, *see* Albert
Subjects, general description, *see* Population
Success, 29(*tab.*), 32(*tab.*), 46, 61, 178-79
Superego, high standards, influence of, 259
Symonds, Percival M.: as interviewer, 7; cited, 119*n*; rankings of adjustment, 176, 177, 209; criteria of adjustment rankings, 178-81; adjustment rankings correlated with Jensen rankings, 178; see also *Adolescent Fantasy*
Symonds Picture-Story Test, v-viii, 3, 5, 119-21, 208, 212, 213; administration procedure, 6-8; transcription of stories, 10; and sexual identification, 56; correlation with the Rorschach, 120; scoring of, 120; sampling error in, 121; related to Rorschach findings, 135-38, 141-42, 144-48, 151-52, 153-54, 157, 158-60, 162, 164, 166, 174-75; correlation with interview, 162; compared to Rorschach and interview, 170-75; and adjustment, 176, 178; adjustment ratings compared to interview, 184-85

Thematic apperception method, 2, 4, 27; *see also* Symonds Picture-Story Test
Themes, inventory of, 3, 27-29(*tab.*); count of, 27-29(*tab.*), 208, 213; stability of occurrence, 27-29, 34-49; change of, 30-43; of early adolescence, 31, 41; symbolic of sex, 135
Thetford, William Newton, 122*n*, 123
Thiesen, Warren G., 122*n*, 123
Thinking, as theme, 29(*tab.*), 32(*tab.*)
Thompson, G. M., 171*n*
Transcription of stories, 6, 10
Trick, as theme, 29(*tab.*), 32(*tab.*), 32, 41, 209

Vernon, Philip E., 171*n*
Viola (subject 14), 43(*tab.*), 180, 181-82; adolescent fantasy compared to later experience and personality, 54, 57-58, 64-65, 67, 72, 73; change in fantasy, 81, 86, 90; adolescent and adult personality compared, 96(*tab.*), 101(*tab.*), 106(*tab.*), 109(*tab.*), 112

Index

(tab.), 116(tab.), 117(tab.); Rorschach analysis, 126(tab.), 126, 127 (tab.), 133, 136, 138(tab.), 143(tab.), 146-47, 148(tab.), 151, 152-53(tab.), 154, 157(tab.), 160(tab.), 161, 163 (tab.), 164, 164(tab.), 166(tab.); from adolescent to adult, 197, 201-2, 203, 204; resumé, 244-52

Vocational adjustment, 83-84, 85, 202, 203-4

Vocations of subjects, 19-20; adolescent aspirations and adult achievements, 112(tab.)-114, 191, 210; and hobbies, 116

Wallace (subject 1), 181, 213; adolescent and adult fantasy compared, 43(tab.), 45, 46; adolescent fantasy compared to later experience and personality, 54, 63, 73; change in fantasy, 75, 76, 77, 78, 91; adolescent and adult personality compared, 96(tab.),
101(tab.), 105(tab.), 106, 107, 109 (tab.), 112(tab.), 114(tab.); Rorschach analysis, 126(tab.), 126, 127 (tab.), 129, 132, 138(tab.), 143(tab.), 144, 148(tab.), 152-53(tab.), 154, 155 (tab.), 157(tab.), 160(tab.), 163(tab.), 164(tab.), 166(tab.), 167; from adolescent to adult, 194-95, 202; resumé, 214-15

Wallis, W. Allen, 54n
Ward, Lynd, 3
Wexler, Milton, v, 7, 15, 102, 176, 177, 352
Wischner, George J., 122n, 124, 125
Wish, see Death wishes; Sex wish-life
Wishful thinking, 79; as theme, 29(tab.), 31, 32(tab.), 209; and realism in fantasy, 90, 92-93
Wong, Kit Lee, vii, 43

Zeigarnik, Bluma, 191
Zeigarnik effect, 191
Zubin, Joseph, 121n